Summary of Contents

W9-BNT-337

BUILD YOUR OWN DATABASE DRIVEN WEB SITE USING PHP & MYSQL

BY **KEVIN YANK**
4TH EDITION

Build Your Own Database Driven Web Site Using PHP & MySQL

by Kevin Yank

Copyright © 2009 SitePoint Pty. Ltd.

Managing Editor: Chris Wyness   **Editor:** Kelly Steele

Technical Editor: Andrew Tetlaw   **Cover Design:** Alex Walker

Indexer: Russell Brooks

Printing History: **Latest Update:** December 2009

    1st Ed. Aug. 2001, 2nd Ed. Feb. 2003,

    3rd Ed. Oct. 2004

    Fourth Edition: July 2009

Published by SitePoint Pty. Ltd.

48 Cambridge Street Collingwood
VIC Australia 3066.
Web: www.sitepoint.com
Email: business@sitepoint.com

ISBN 978-0-9805768-1-8
Printed and bound in the United States of America

About the Author

As Technical Director for SitePoint, Kevin Yank keeps abreast of all that is new and exciting in web technology. Best known for the book you are reading right now, he also co-authored *Simply JavaScript* (http://www.sitepoint.com/books/javascript1/) with Cameron Adams and *Everything You Know About CSS Is Wrong!* (http://www.sitepoint.com/books/csswrong1/) with Rachel Andrew. In addition, Kevin hosts the *SitePoint Podcast* (http://www.sitepoint.com/podcast/) and writes the *SitePoint Tech Times*, a free email newsletter that goes out to over 240,000 subscribers worldwide.

Kevin lives in Melbourne, Australia and enjoys speaking at conferences, as well as visiting friends and family in Canada. He's also passionate about performing improvised comedy theater with Impro Melbourne (http://www.impromelbourne.com.au/) and flying light aircraft. Kevin's personal blog is *Yes, I'm Canadian* (http://yesimcanadian.com/).

About the Technical Editor

Andrew Tetlaw has been tinkering with web sites as a web developer since 1997. At SitePoint he is dedicated to making the world a better place through the technical editing of SitePoint books, kits, articles, and newsletters. He is also a busy father of five, enjoys coffee, and often neglects his blog at http://tetlaw.id.au/.

About SitePoint

SitePoint specializes in publishing fun, practical, and easy-to-understand content for Web professionals. Visit http://www.sitepoint.com/ to access our blogs, books, newsletters, articles, and community forums.

To my parents, Cheryl and Richard, for making all this possible.

Table of Contents

Chapter 8   Content Formatting with Regular Expressions 241

Chapter 9   Cookies, Sessions, and Access Control 261

Appendix A MySQL Syntax Reference 389

Preface

PHP and MySQL have changed.

Back in 2001, when I wrote the first edition of this book, readers were astonished to discover that you could create a site full of web pages without having to write a separate HTML file for each page. **PHP** stood out from the crowd of programming languages, mainly because it was easy enough for almost anyone to learn and free to download and install. The **MySQL** database, likewise, provided a simple and free solution to a problem that, up until that point, had been solvable only by expert programmers with corporate budgets.

Back then, PHP and MySQL were special—heck, they were downright miraculous! But over the years, they have gained plenty of fast-moving competition. In an age when anyone with a free WordPress[1] account can set up a full-featured blog in 30 seconds flat, it's no longer enough for a programming language like PHP to be easy to learn; nor is it enough for a database like MySQL to be free.

Indeed, as you sit down to read this book, you probably have ambitions that extend beyond what you can throw together using the free point-and-click tools of the Web. You might even be thinking of building an exciting, new point-and-click tool of your own. WordPress, after all, is built using PHP and MySQL, so why limit your vision to anything less?

To keep up with the competition, and with the needs of more demanding projects, PHP and MySQL have had to evolve. PHP is now a far more intricate and powerful language than it was back in 2001, and MySQL is a vastly more complex and capable database. Learning PHP and MySQL today opens up a lot of doors that would have remained closed to the PHP and MySQL experts of 2001.

That's the good news. The bad news is that, in the same way that a butter knife is easier to figure out than a Swiss Army knife (and less likely to cause self-injury!), all these dazzling new features and improvements have indisputably made PHP and MySQL more difficult for beginners to learn.

---

[1] http://wordpress.com/

Worse yet, PHP has completely abandoned several of the beginner-friendly features that gave it a competitive advantage in 2001, because they turned out to be oversimplifications, or could lead inexperienced programmers into building web sites with gaping security holes. This is a problem if you're the author of a beginner's book about PHP and MySQL.

PHP and MySQL have changed, and those changes have made writing this book a lot more difficult. But they have also made this book a lot more important. The more twisty the path, the more valuable the map, right?

In this book, I'll provide you with a hands-on look at what's involved in building a database driven web site using PHP and MySQL. If your web host provides PHP and MySQL support, you're in great shape. If not, I'll show you how to install them on Windows, Mac OS X, and Linux computers, so don't sweat it.

This book is your map to the twisty path that every beginner must navigate to learn PHP and MySQL today. Grab your favorite walking stick; let's go hiking!

Who Should Read This Book

This book is aimed at intermediate and advanced web designers looking to make the leap into server-side programming. You'll be expected to be comfortable with simple HTML, as I'll make use of it without much in the way of explanation. No knowledge of Cascading Style Sheets (CSS) or JavaScript is assumed or required, but if you *do* know JavaScript, you'll find it will make learning PHP a breeze, since these languages are quite similar.

By the end of this book, you can expect to have a grasp of what's involved in building a database driven web site. If you follow the examples, you'll also learn the basics of PHP (a server-side scripting language that gives you easy access to a database, and a lot more) and **Structured Query Language** (**SQL**—the standard language for interacting with relational databases) as supported by MySQL, the most popular free database engine available today. Most importantly, you'll come away with everything you need to start on your very own database driven site!

What's in This Book

This book comprises the following 12 chapters. Read them in order from beginning to end to gain a complete understanding of the subject, or skip around if you only need a refresher on a particular topic.

Chapter 1: *Installation*

Before you can start building your database driven web site, you must first ensure that you have the right tools for the job. In this first chapter, I'll tell you where to obtain the two essential components you'll need: the PHP scripting language and the MySQL database management system. I'll step you through the setup procedures on Windows, Linux, and Mac OS X, and show you how to test that PHP is operational on your web server.

Chapter 2: *Introducing MySQL*

Although I'm sure you'll be anxious to start building dynamic web pages, I'll begin with an introduction to databases in general, and the MySQL relational database management system in particular. If you have never worked with a relational database before, this should definitely be an enlightening chapter that will whet your appetite for what's to come! In the process, you'll build up a simple database to be used in later chapters.

Chapter 3: *Introducing PHP*

Here's where the fun really starts. In this chapter, I'll introduce you to the PHP scripting language, which you can use to build dynamic web pages that present up-to-the-moment information to your visitors. Readers with previous programming experience will probably only need a quick skim of this chapter, as I explain the essentials of the language from the ground up. This is a must-read chapter for beginners, however, as the rest of this book relies heavily on the basic concepts presented here.

Chapter 4: *Publishing MySQL Data on the Web*

In this chapter you'll bring together PHP and MySQL, which you'll have seen separately in the previous chapters, to create some of your first database driven web pages. You'll explore the basic techniques of using PHP to retrieve information from a database and display it on the Web in real time. I'll also show you how to use PHP to create web-based forms for adding new entries to, and modifying existing information in, a MySQL database on the fly.

xxii

Chapter 5: *Relational Database Design*

Although you'll have worked with a very simple sample database in the previous chapters, most database driven web sites require the storage of more complex forms of data than you'll have dealt with to this point. Far too many database driven web site designs are abandoned midstream or are forced to start again from the beginning, because of mistakes made early on during the design of the database structure. In this critical chapter you'll learn the essential principles of good database design, emphasizing the importance of data normalization. If you're unsure what that means, then this is definitely an important chapter for you to read!

Chapter 6: *Structured PHP Programming*

Techniques to better structure your code are useful in all but the simplest of PHP projects. The PHP language offers many facilities to help you do this, and in this chapter, I'll cover some of the simple techniques that exist to keep your code manageable and maintainable. You'll learn to use include files to avoid having to write the same code more than once when it's needed by many pages of your site, and I'll show you how to write your own functions to extend the built-in capabilities of PHP and to streamline the code that appears within your scripts.

Chapter 7: *A Content Management System*

In many ways the climax of the book, this chapter is the big payoff for all you frustrated site builders who are tired of updating hundreds of pages whenever you need to make a change to a site's design. I'll walk you through the code for a basic content management system that allows you to manage a database of jokes, their categories, and their authors. A system like this can be used to manage simple content on your web site; just a few modifications, and you'll have a site administration system that will have your content providers submitting content for publication on your site in no time—all without having to know a shred of HTML!

Chapter 8: *Content Formatting with Regular Expressions*

Just because you're implementing a nice, easy tool to allow site administrators to add content to your site without their knowing HTML, that content can still be jazzed up, instead of settling for just plain, unformatted text. In this chapter, I'll show you some neat tweaks you can make to the page that displays the contents of your database—tweaks that allow it to incorporate simple formatting such as bold or italicized text, among other options.

Chapter 9: *Cookies, Sessions, and Access Control*

What are sessions, and how are they related to cookies, a long-suffering technology for preserving stored data on the Web? What makes persistent data so important in current ecommerce systems and other web applications? This chapter answers all those questions by explaining how PHP supports both cookies and sessions, and explores the link between the two. You'll then put these pieces together to build a simple shopping cart system, as well as an access control system for your web site.

Chapter 10: *MySQL Administration*

While MySQL is a good, simple database solution for those without the need for many frills, it does have some complexities of its own that you'll need to understand if you're going to rely on a MySQL database to store your content. In this section, I'll teach you how to perform backups of, and manage access to, your MySQL database. In addition to a couple of inside tricks (like what to do if you forget your MySQL password), I'll explain how to repair a MySQL database that has become damaged in a server crash.

Chapter 11: *Advanced SQL Queries*

In Chapter 5 we saw what was involved in modeling complex relationships between pieces of information in a relational database like MySQL. Although the theory was quite sound, putting these concepts into practice requires that you learn a few more tricks of Structured Query Language. In this chapter, I'll cover some of the more advanced features of this language to help you juggle complex data like a pro.

Chapter 12: *Binary Data*

Some of the most interesting applications of database driven web design include some juggling of binary files. Online file storage services are prime examples, but even a system as simple as a personal photo gallery can benefit from storing binary files (that is, pictures) in a database for retrieval and management on the fly. In this chapter, I'll demonstrate how to speed up your web site by creating static copies of dynamic pages at regular intervals—using PHP, of course! With these basic file-juggling skills in hand, you'll go on to develop a simple online file storage and viewing system, and learn the ins and outs of working with binary data in MySQL.

Where to Find Help

PHP and MySQL are moving targets, so chances are good that, by the time you read this, some minor detail or other of these technologies has changed from what's described in this book. Thankfully, SitePoint has a thriving community of PHP developers ready and waiting to help you out if you run into trouble, and we also maintain a list of known errata for this book you can consult for the latest updates.

The SitePoint Forums

The SitePoint Forums[2] are discussion forums where you can ask questions about anything related to web development. You may, of course, answer questions, too. That's how a discussion forum site works—some people ask, some people answer and most people do a bit of both. Sharing your knowledge benefits others and strengthens the community. A lot of fun and experienced web designers and developers hang out there. It's a good way to learn new stuff, have questions answered in a hurry, and just have fun.

The SitePoint Forums include separate forums for PHP and MySQL, as well as a separate forum covering advanced PHP Application Design:

- PHP: http://www.sitepoint.com/forums/forumdisplay.php?f=34
- PHP Application Design:
  http://www.sitepoint.com/forums/forumdisplay.php?f=147
- MySQL: http://www.sitepoint.com/forums/forumdisplay.php?f=182

The Book's Web Site

Located at http://www.sitepoint.com/books/phpmysql1/, the web site that supports this book will give you access to the following facilities:

The Code Archive

As you progress through this book, you'll note a number of references to the code archive. This is a downloadable ZIP archive that contains each and every line of

---

[2] http://www.sitepoint.com/forums/

example source code that's printed in this book. If you want to cheat (or save yourself from carpal tunnel syndrome), go ahead and download the archive.[3]

Updates and Errata

No book is perfect, and we expect that watchful readers will be able to spot at least one or two mistakes before the end of this one. The Errata page on the book's web site will always have the latest information about known typographical and code errors.

The SitePoint Newsletters

In addition to books like this one, SitePoint publishes free email newsletters, such as *SitePoint Tech Times*, *SitePoint Tribune*, and *SitePoint Design View*, to name a few. In them, you'll read about the latest news, product releases, trends, tips, and techniques for all aspects of web development. Sign up to one or more SitePoint newsletters at http://www.sitepoint.com/newsletter/.

Your Feedback

If you're unable to find an answer through the forums, or if you wish to contact us for any other reason, the best place to write is books@sitepoint.com. We have a well-staffed email support system set up to track your inquiries, and if our support team members are unable to answer your question, they'll send it straight to us. Suggestions for improvements, as well as notices of any mistakes you may find, are especially welcome.

---

[3] http://www.sitepoint.com/books/phpmysql1/code.php

Conventions Used in This Book

You'll notice that we've used certain typographic and layout styles throughout this book to signify different types of information. Look out for the following items.

Code Samples

Code in this book will be displayed using a fixed-width font, like so:

```
<h1>A Perfect Summer's Day</h1>
<p>It was a lovely day for a walk in the park. The birds
were singing and the kids were all back at school.</p>
```

If the code is to be found in the book's code archive, the name of the file will appear at the top of the program listing, like this:

```
example.css
.footer {
  background-color: #CCC;
  border-top: 1px solid #333;
}
```

If only part of the file is displayed, this is indicated by the word *excerpt*:

```
example.css (excerpt)
  border-top: 1px solid #333;
```

If additional code is to be inserted into an existing example, the new code will be displayed in bold:

```
function animate() {
  new_variable = "Hello";
}
```

Also, where existing code is required for context, rather than repeat all the code, a
⋮ will be displayed:

```
function animate() {
    ⋮
    return new_variable;
}
```

Some lines of code are intended to be entered on one line, but we've had to wrap
them because of page constraints. A ➥ indicates a line break that exists for formatting
purposes only, and should be ignored.

```
URI .open("http://www.sitepoint.com/blogs/2007/05/28/user-style-she
➥ets-come-of-age/");
```

Tips, Notes, and Warnings

Hey, You!

Tips will give you helpful little pointers.

Ahem, Excuse Me ...

Notes are useful asides that are related—but not critical—to the topic at hand.
Think of them as extra tidbits of information.

Make Sure You Always ...

... pay attention to these important points.

Watch Out!

Warnings will highlight any gotchas that are likely to trip you up along the way.

Installation

In this book, I'll guide you as you take your first steps beyond the static world of building web pages with pure HTML. Together, we'll explore the world of database driven web sites and discover the dizzying array of dynamic tools, concepts, and possibilities that they open up. Whatever you do, don't look down!

Okay, maybe you *should* look down. After all, that's where the rest of this book is. But remember, you were warned!

Before you build your first dynamic web site, you must gather together the tools you'll need for the job. In this chapter, I'll show you how to download and set up the two software packages you'll need. Can you guess what they are? I'll give you a hint: their names feature prominently on the cover of this book! They are, of course, PHP and MySQL.

If you're used to building web sites with HTML, CSS, and perhaps even a smattering of JavaScript, you're probably used to uploading to another location the files that make up your site. Maybe this is a web hosting service that you've paid for; maybe it's a free service provided by your Internet Service Provider (ISP); or maybe it's a web server set up by the IT department of the company that you work for. In any case, once you copy your files to their destination, a software program called a **web server** is able to find and serve up copies of those files whenever they are requested by a web browser like Internet Explorer or Firefox. Common web server software programs you may have heard of include Apache and Internet Information Services (IIS).

PHP is a **server-side scripting language**. You can think of it as a plugin for your web server that enables it to do more than just send exact copies of the files that web browsers ask for. With PHP installed, your web server will be able to run little programs (called **PHP scripts**) that can do tasks like retrieve up-to-the-minute information from a database and use it to generate a web page on the fly before sending it to the browser that requested it. Much of this book will focus on writing PHP scripts to do exactly that. PHP is completely free to download and use.

For your PHP scripts to retrieve information from a database, you must first *have* a database. That's where **MySQL** comes in. MySQL is a **relational database management system**, or **RDBMS**. We'll discuss the exact role it plays and how it works later, but briefly it's a software program that's able to organize and manage many pieces of information efficiently while keeping track of how all of those pieces of information are related to each other. MySQL also makes that information really easy to access with server-side scripting languages like PHP. MySQL, like PHP, is completely free for most uses.

The goal of this first chapter is to set you up with a web server equipped with PHP and MySQL. I'll provide step-by-step instructions that work on recent Windows, Mac OS X, and Linux computers, so no matter what flavor of computer you're using, the instructions you need should be right here.

Your Own Web Server

If you're lucky, your current web host's web server already has PHP and MySQL installed. Most do—that's one of the reasons why PHP and MySQL are so popular. If your web host is so equipped, the good news is that you'll be able to publish your first database driven web site without having to shop for a web host that supports the right technologies.

The bad news is that you're still going to need to install PHP and MySQL yourself. That's because you need your own PHP-and-MySQL-equipped web server to test your database driven web site on before you publish it for all the world to see.

When developing static web sites, you can often load your HTML files directly from your hard disk into your browser to see how they look. There's no web server software involved when you do this, which is fine, because web browsers can understand HTML code all by themselves.

When it comes to dynamic web sites built using PHP and MySQL, however, your web browser needs some help! Web browsers are unable to understand PHP scripts; rather, PHP scripts contain instructions for a PHP-savvy web server to execute in order to *generate* the HTML code that browsers can understand. So in addition to the web server that will host your site publicly, you also need your own private web server to use in the development of your site.

If you work for a company that has an especially helpful IT department, you may find that there's already a development web server provided for you. The typical setup is that you must work on your site's files on a network drive that's hosted by an internal web server that can be safely used for development. When you're ready to deploy the site to the public, your files are copied from that network drive to the public web server.

If you're lucky enough to work in this kind of environment, you can skip most of this chapter. However, you'll want to ask the IT boffins responsible for the development server the same questions I've covered in the section called "What to Ask Your Web Host". That's because you'll need to have that critical information handy when you start using the PHP and MySQL support they've so helpfully provided.

Windows Installation

In this section, I'll show you how to start running a PHP-and-MySQL-equipped web server on a Windows XP, Windows Vista, or Windows 7 computer. If you're using an operating system other than Windows, you can safely skip this section.

All-in-one Installation

I normally recommend that you install and set up your web server, PHP, and MySQL individually, using the official installation packages for each. This is especially useful for beginners, because it gives you a strong sense of how these pieces all fit together. If you're in a rush, however, or if you need to set up a temporary development environment to use just for a day or two, the following quick-and-dirty solution may be preferable.

You can skip ahead to the section called "Installing Individual Packages" if you want to take the time to install each piece of the puzzle separately.

WampServer (where *Wamp* stands for Windows, Apache, MySQL, and PHP) is a free, all-in-one program that includes built-in copies of recent versions of the Apache web server, PHP, and MySQL. Let me take you through the process of installing it:

1. Download the latest version from the WampServer web site.[1] After downloading the file (as of this writing, WampServer 2.0g is about 16MB in size), double-click it to launch the installer, as shown in Figure 1.1.

Figure 1.1. The WampServer installer

2. The installer will prompt you for a location to install WampServer. The default of **c:\wamp** shown in Figure 1.2 is an ideal choice for most purposes, but if you have strong feelings about where it's installed, feel free to specify your preferred location.

---

[1] http://www.wampserver.com/en/

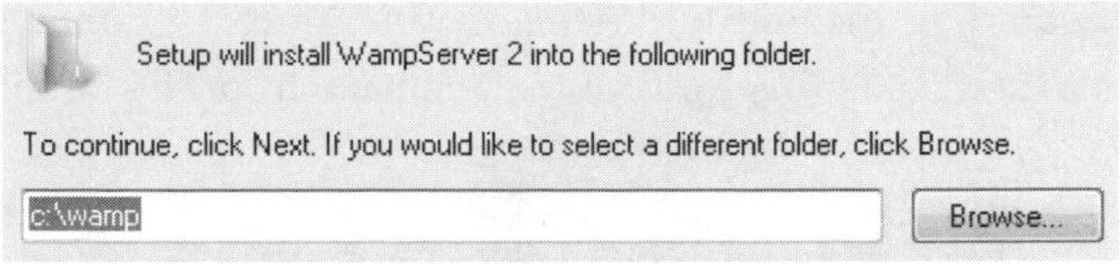

> Setup will install WampServer 2 into the following folder.
>
> To continue, click Next. If you would like to select a different folder, click Browse.
>
> c:\wamp   Browse...

Figure 1.2. The default installation directory is a good choice

3. At the end of the installation, WampServer will ask you to choose your default browser. This is the web browser it will launch when you use the included system tray icon tool to launch your browser. If you have Firefox installed it will ask if you'd like to use it as your default browser. If you answer **No**, or have a different browser installed, it will ask you to select the executable file for the browser you want to use. As shown in Figure 1.3, it selects Internet Explorer (**explorer.exe**) for you, which is fine. If you're using an alternative browser such as Safari or Opera, you can browse to find the **.exe** file for your browser if you want to.

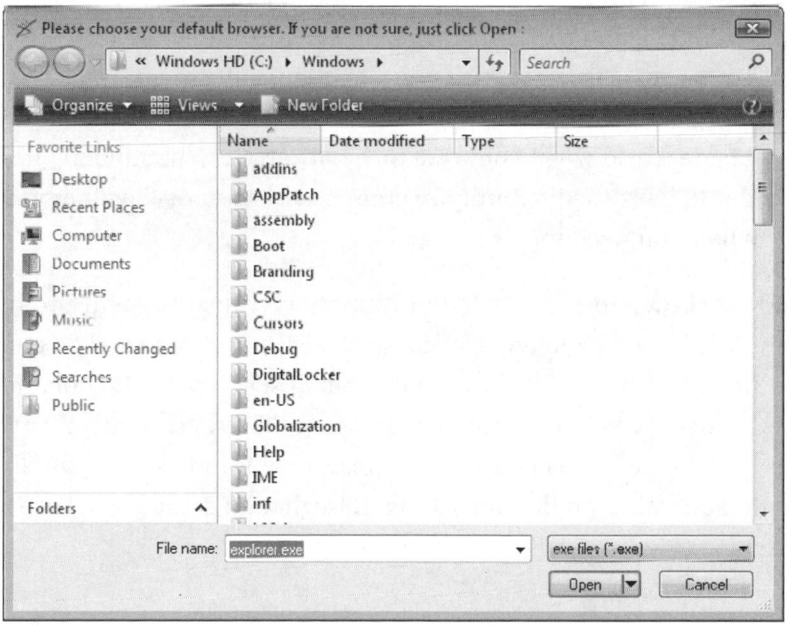

Figure 1.3. The default choice of Internet Explorer is fine

4. As WampServer is installed, it fires up its built-in copy of the Apache HTTP Server, a popular web server for PHP development. Windows will likely display

a security alert at this point, like the one in Figure 1.4, since the web server attempts to start listening for browser requests from the outside world.

Figure 1.4. This security alert tells you Apache is doing its job

If you want to make absolutely sure that Apache rejects connections from the outside world, and that only a web browser running on your own computer can view web pages hosted on your development server, feel free to click **Keep blocking**. WampServer has its own built-in option to block connections from the outside world when you want to, however, so I recommend clicking **Unblock** in order to have the flexibility to grant access to your development server if and when you need to.

5. Next, as shown in Figure 1.5, the WampServer installer will prompt you for your SMTP server and email address. A PHP script can send an email message, and these settings tell it the outgoing email server, and the default "from" address to use. Type in your email address, and if you can remember your Internet Service Provider's SMTP server address, type it in too. You can always leave the default value for the time being, though, and set it manually if and when you need to send email using a PHP script.

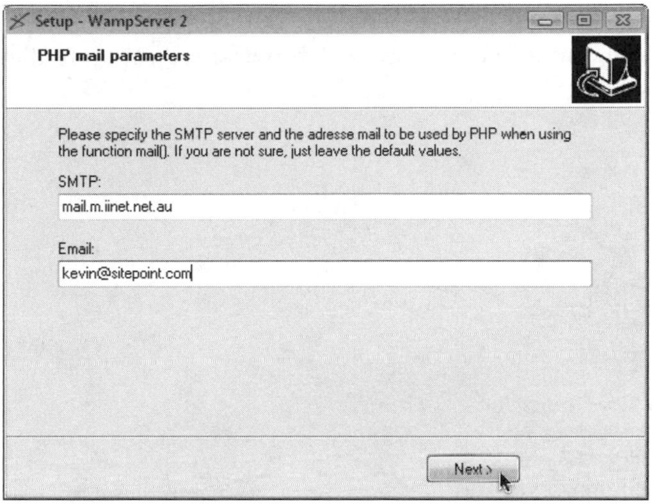

Figure 1.5. Fill in your Internet Service Provider's SMTP server address if you know it

Once the installation is complete, you can fire up WampServer. An icon will appear in your Windows System Tray. Click on it to see the WampServer menu shown in Figure 1.6.

Figure 1.6. The WampServer menu

By default, your server can only be accessed by web browsers running on your own computer. If you click the **Put Online** menu item, your server will become accessible to the outside world.

To test that WampServer is working properly, click the **Localhost** menu item at the top of the WampServer menu. Your web browser will open to display your server's home page, shown in Figure 1.7.

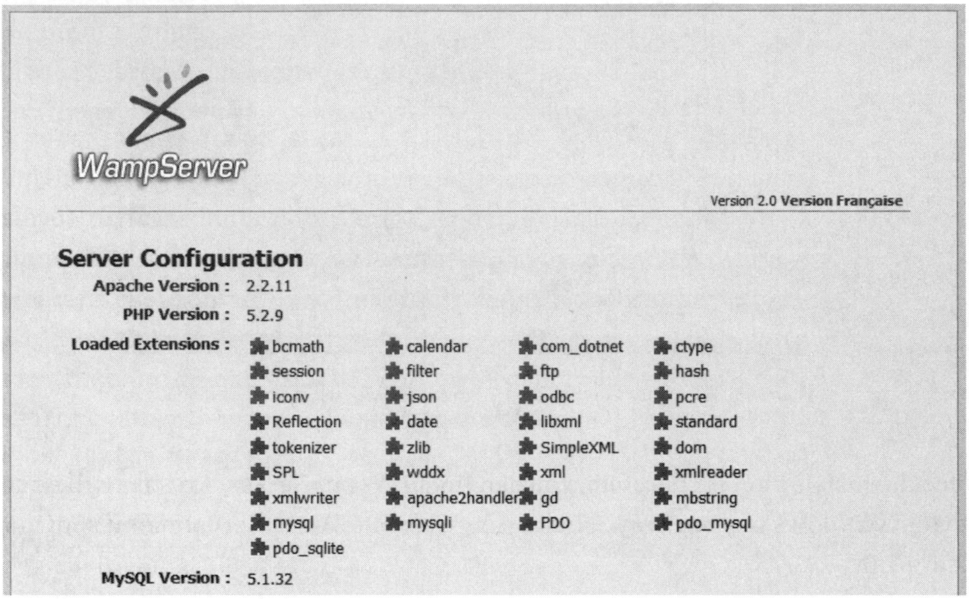

Figure 1.7. The home page provided by WampServer confirms Apache, PHP, and MySQL are installed

When you're done working with WampServer, you can shut it down (along with its built-in servers) by *right-clicking* the System Tray icon and choosing **Exit**. When you're next ready to do some work on a database driven web site, just fire it up again!

Later in this book, you'll need to use some of the programs that come with the MySQL server built into WampServer. To work properly, these programs must be added to your Windows system path.

To add the MySQL command prompt programs that come with WampServer to your Windows system path, follow these instructions:

1.   Open the Windows Control Panel. Locate and double-click the **System** icon.

2.   Take the appropriate step for your version of Windows:

   • In Windows XP, switch to the **Advanced** tab of the **System Properties** window.

   • In Windows Vista or Windows 7, click the **Advanced system settings** link in the sidebar.

3.   Click the **Environment Variables...** button.

4.   In the list labeled **User variables for** *user*, look for a variable named **PATH**.

   • If it exists, select it and click the **Edit...** button.

   • If there's no variable, click the **New...** button and fill in the **Variable name** by typing **PATH**.

5.   Add the path to WampServer's MySQL **bin** directory[2] as the **Variable value**:

   • If the **Variable value** is empty, just type in the path.

   • If there is already text in the **Variable value** field, add a semicolon (**;**) to the end of the value, then type the path after that.

6.   Click the **OK** button in each of the open windows to apply your changes.

Installing Individual Packages

Installing each individual package separately is really the way to go if you can afford to take the time. That way you learn how all the pieces fit together, but have the freedom to update each of the packages independently of the others. Ultimately, it's always worthwhile becoming familiar with the inner workings of any software with which you'll be spending a lot of time.

Installing MySQL

As I mentioned above, you can download MySQL free of charge. Simply proceed to the MySQL Downloads page[3] and click the **Download** link for the free MySQL

---

[2] The exact path will depend on where you've installed WampServer and which version of MySQL it contains. On my system, the path is **C:\wamp\bin\mysql\mysql5.1.34\bin**. Use Explorer to take a look inside your WampServer installation's files to figure out the exact path on your system.

[3] http://dev.mysql.com/downloads/

Community Server. This will take you to a page with a long list of download links for the current recommended version of MySQL (as of this writing, it's MySQL 5.1).

At the top of the list you'll see links for Windows and Windows x64. If you're positive you're running a 64-bit version of Windows, go ahead and follow the **Windows x64** link to download the **Windows Essentials (AMD64 / Intel EM64T)** package (about 28MB in size). If you know you're running a 32-bit version of Windows, or if you're at all unsure, follow the **Windows** link and download the **Windows Essentials (x86)** package (about 35MB)—it'll work even if it turns out you're running a 64-bit version of Windows. Click the **Download** button to grab the file.

Once you've downloaded the file, double-click it and go through the installation as you would for any other program. Choose the **Typical** option when prompted for the setup type, unless you have a particular preference for the directory in which MySQL is installed. When you reach the end, you'll be prompted to choose whether you want to **Configure the MySQL Server now**. Select this to launch the configuration wizard,[4] and choose **Detailed Configuration**, which we'll use to specify a number of options that are vital to ensuring compatibility with PHP. For each step in the wizard, select the options indicated here:

1. **Server Type**

   Assuming you're setting up MySQL for development purposes on your desktop computer, choose **Developer Machine**.

2. **Database Usage**

   Unless you know for a fact that you will need support for transactions (as such support is usually superfluous for most PHP applications), choose **Non-Transactional Database Only**.

3. **Connection Limit**

   Select **Decision Support (DSS)/OLAP** to optimize MySQL for a relatively modest number of connections.

---

[4] In my testing, I found that the configuration wizard failed to actually launch automatically, even with this option checked. If you run into the same problem, just launch the MySQL Server Instance Config Wizard from the Start Menu after the installation has completed.

4. **Networking Options**

    Uncheck the **Enable Strict Mode** option to ensure MySQL's compatibility with older PHP code that you might need to use in your own work.

5. **Default Character Set**

    Select **Best Support For Multilingualism** to tell MySQL to assume you want to use UTF-8 encoded text, which supports the full range of characters that are in use on the Web today.

6. **Windows Options**

    Allow MySQL to be installed as a Windows Service that's launched automatically; also select **Include Bin Directory in Windows PATH** to make it easier to run MySQL's administration tools from the command prompt.

7. **Security Options**

    Uncheck the **Modify Security Settings** option. It's best to learn how to set the root password mentioned at this juncture without the assistance of the wizard, so I'll show you how to do this yourself in the section called "Post-Installation Set-up Tasks".

Once the wizard has completed, your system should now be fully equipped with a running MySQL server!

To verify that the MySQL server is running properly, type **Ctrl+Alt+Del** and choose the option to open the Task Manager. Click the **Show processes from all users** button unless it's already selected. If all is well, the server program (**mysqld.exe**) should be listed on the **Processes** tab. It will also start up automatically whenever you restart your system.

Installing PHP

The next step is to install PHP. Head over to the PHP Downloads page[5]. There are four different versions of PHP 5.3.x for Windows: VC6 Non Thread Safe, VC6 Thread Safe, VC9 Non Thread Safe, and VC9 Thread Safe. Talk about confusing!

---

[5] http://windows.php.net/download/

First of all, you definitely want a Thread Safe version of PHP. The Non Thread Safe versions are not suitable for use as a plugin for Apache.

Secondly, assuming you will install (or have already installed) a version of the Apache HTTP Server from httpd.apache.org (we'll be doing this shortly), you will need the VC6 version of PHP. In short, to follow the instructions in this book, you need the **VC6 Thread Safe** version of PHP 5.3 for Windows. Choose the zip package; avoid the **installer** version, which is easier to install, but lacks the same flexibility attained by installing PHP manually.

What about PHP 4?

At the time of writing, PHP 5 is firmly entrenched as the preferred version of PHP. For several years after PHP 5's initial release, many developers chose to stick with PHP 4 due to its track record of stability and performance, and indeed today many bargain-basement web hosts have yet to upgrade to PHP 5. There's no longer any excuse for this, however; PHP 5 is by far the better choice, and development of PHP 4 has been completely discontinued. If your web host is still living in the PHP 4 past, you're better off finding a new web host!

PHP was designed to run as a plugin for existing web server software such as Apache or Internet Information Services, so before you can install PHP, you must first set up a web server.

Many versions of Windows come with Microsoft's powerful Internet Information Services (IIS) web server, but not all do. Windows XP Home, Windows Vista Home, and Windows 7 Home Basic (among others) are without IIS, so you need to install your own web server on these versions of Windows if you want to develop database driven web sites. On top of that, assorted versions of Windows come with different versions of IIS, some of which vary dramatically in how you configure them to work with PHP.

With that in mind, if you're still considering IIS, you should know it's also relatively uncommon to host web sites built using PHP with IIS in the real world. It's generally less expensive and more reliable to host PHP-powered sites on servers running some flavor of the Linux operating system, with the free Apache web server installed. About the only reason for hosting a PHP site on IIS is if your company has already invested in Windows servers to run applications built using ASP.NET (a Microsoft technology built into IIS), and you want to reuse that existing infrastructure to host a PHP application as well.

Although it's by no means a requirement, it's generally easiest to set up your development server to match the environment in which your web site will be deployed publicly as closely as possible. For this reason, I recommend using the Apache web server—even for development on a Windows computer. If you insist (or your boss insists) on hosting your PHP-based site using IIS, you will find the necessary installation instructions in the **install.txt** file contained in the PHP zip package you downloaded from the PHP web site.

If you need to install Apache on your computer, surf on over to The Apache HTTP Server Project[6] and look for the version of Apache described as the best available (as of writing it's version 2.2.16, as shown in Figure 1.8).

Apache HTTP Server 2.2.16 Released	2010-07-25

The Apache HTTP Server Project is proud to announce the release of version 2.2.16 of the Apache HTTP Server ("httpd"). This version is principally a security and bugfix release.

Notably, this release addresses CVE-2010-1452 (cve.mitre.org), a remote denial of service bug in mod_cache and mod_dav. This release further addresses the issue CVE-2010-2068 within mod_proxy_ajp, mod_proxy_http, mod_reqtimeout.

This version of httpd is a major release and the start of a new stable branch, and represents the best available version of Apache HTTP Server. New features include Smart Filtering, Improved Caching, AJP Proxy, Proxy Load Balancing, Graceful Shutdown support, Large File Support, the Event MPM, and refactored Authentication/Authorization.

Download | New Features in httpd 2.2 | ChangeLog for 2.2.16 | Complete ChangeLog for 2.2

click this

Figure 1.8. The best available version—accept no substitutes!

Once you get to the Download page, scroll down to find the links to the various versions available. The one you'll want is **Win32 Binary without crypto**, shown in Figure 1.9.

- Unix Source: httpd-2.2.16.tar.gz [PGP] [MD5] [SHA1]
- Unix Source: httpd-2.2.16.tar.bz2 [PGP] [MD5] [SHA1]
- Win32 Source: httpd-2.2.16-win32-src.zip [PGP] [MD5] [SHA1]
- Win32 Binary without crypto (no mod_ssl) (MSI Installer): httpd-2.2.16-win32-x86-no_ssl.msi [PGP] [MD5] [SHA1] this one
- Win32 Binary including OpenSSL 0.9.8o (MSI Installer): httpd-2.2.16-win32-x86-openssl-0.9.8o.msi [PGP] [MD5] [SHA1]
- Other files

Figure 1.9. This is the one you need

---

[6] http://httpd.apache.org/

Once the file has downloaded, double-click on it as usual to start the installation wizard. After a few steps, you'll arrive at the **Server Information** screen.

If you were setting up a web server to be accessed publicly on the Web, the options on this screen would be important. For the purposes of setting up a development server, you can type whatever you like. If you know your computer's network name, type that in for the Server Name. Feel free to put in your correct email address if, like me, you're a stickler for the details. If you already have a web server running on your computer (for example, if you have also set up IIS to do some ASP.NET development on the same computer), you may need to select the **only for the Current User, on Port 8080, when started Manually** option on this screen, so as to avoid a conflict with the existing web server running on port 80.

On the next screen, choose the **Typical** option for the **Setup Type**, and follow the wizard from there to complete the installation. When it's done, you should see a new icon for the Apache Service Monitor running in your System Tray. If you chose the default option to have Apache start up automatically, the status indicator should be green, as shown in Figure 1.10; otherwise, you'll need to start Apache manually as shown in Figure 1.11 before you can use it.

Figure 1.10. The green light means Apache is up and running

Figure 1.11. Choose **Start** to fire up Apache manually

You can also use the Apache Service Monitor icon to stop Apache running, once you've finished your web development work for the day.

When you have Apache up and running, open your web browser of choice and type http://localhost into the location bar. If you chose the option to run Apache on port

8080, you will need to type http://localhost:8080 instead. Hit **Enter**, and you should see a page like that shown in Figure 1.12 that confirms Apache is working correctly.

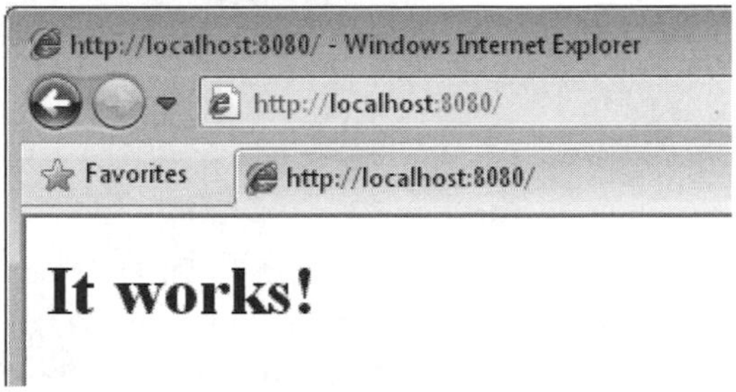

Figure 1.12. You can take my word for it!

With Apache standing on its own two feet, you can now install PHP. Follow these steps:

1. Unzip the file you downloaded from the PHP web site into a directory of your choice. I recommend **C:\PHP** and will refer to this directory from this point forward, but feel free to choose another directory if you like.

2. Find the file called **php.ini-development** in the PHP folder and make a duplicate copy of it. The easiest way to do it is to right-click and drag the file's icon a short distance, drop it in the same Explorer window, and choose **Copy Here** from the pop-up menu. This will leave you with a new file named along the lines of **php - Copy.ini-development** (depending on the version of Windows you're using). Find this new file and rename it to **php.ini**. Windows will ask if you're sure about changing the filename extension (from **.ini-dist** to **.ini**); click **Yes**.

Windows Hides Known Filename Extensions by Default

When you rename the file to **php.ini**, you might notice that the new filename that appears next to the icon is actually just **php**. If this happens, it's because your copy of Windows is set up to hide the filename extension if it recognizes it. Since Windows knows that **.ini** files are Configuration Settings files, it hides this filename extension.

As you can imagine, this feature can cause a certain amount of confusion. When you return to edit the **php.ini** file in the future, it would help to be able to see its full filename so you could tell it apart from the **php.gif** and **php.exe** files in the same folder.

To switch off filename extension hiding, open the Windows Control Panel and search for Folder Options. Open the Folder Options window and switch to the **View** tab. Under **Files and Folders**, uncheck the **Hide extensions for known file types** checkbox, as shown in Figure 1.13.

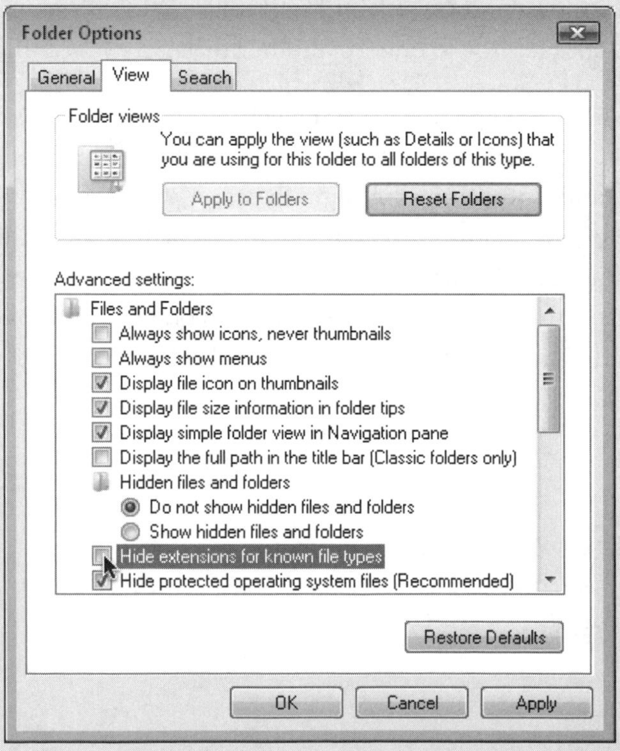

Figure 1.13. Make filename extensions visible for all files

3. Open the **php.ini** file in your favorite text editor. If you have no particular pref-
    erence, just double-click the file to open it in Notepad. It's a large file with a
    lot of confusing options, but look for the line that begins with `doc_root` (Note-
    pad's **Edit > Find...** feature will help). Out of the box, this line looks like this:

```
doc_root =
```

To the end of this line, add the path to your web server's document root directory. For the Apache server, this is the **htdocs** folder in the main Apache web
server directory. If you installed Apache in the default location, the path should
be "**C:\Program Files\Apache Software Foundation\Apache2.2\htdocs**". If you installed it elsewhere, find the **htdocs** folder and type its path:

```
doc_root = "C:\Program Files\Apache Software Foundation\Apache2.
➥2\htdocs"
```

Just a little further down in the file, look for the line that begins with `;exten-
sion_dir`, remove the semi-colon from the start of the line, and set it so that it
points to the **ext** subfolder of your PHP folder:

```
extension_dir = "C:\PHP\ext"
```

Scroll further down in the file, and you'll see a bunch of lines beginning with
`;extension=`. These are optional extensions to PHP, disabled by default. We
want to enable the MySQL extension so that PHP can communicate with MySQL.
To do this, remove the semicolon from the start of the **php_mysqli.dll** line:

```
extension=php_mysqli.dll
```

php_mysqli, not php_mysql

Just above the line for `php_mysqli.dll` there is a line for `php_mysql.dll`.
The *i* in `php_mysqli` stands for *improved*. You want to enable the new improved MySQL extension. The one without the *i* is obsolete, and some of its
features are incompatible with current versions of MySQL.

Keep scrolling even further down in the file, and look for a line that starts with ;session.save_path. Once again, remove the semicolon to enable this line, and set it to your Windows **Temp** folder:

```
session.save_path = "C:\Windows\Temp"
```

Save the changes you made and close your text editor.

That takes care of setting up PHP. Now you can set up your Apache server to use it as a plugin:

1. Run Notepad as Administrator. This is necessary because the Apache configuration file, by default, can only be edited by an administrator. To do this, find the **Notepad** icon in your Start Menu (under **All Programs** > **Accessories**) and right-click on it. Click the **Run as administrator** menu item.

2. Choose **File** > **Open…** in Notepad. Browse to the **conf** subfolder in your Apache installation folder (by default, **C:\Program Files\Apache Software Foundation\Apache2.2\conf**), and select the **httpd.conf** file located there. In order to make this file visible for selection, you'll need to select **All Files (*.*)** from the file type drop-down menu at the bottom of the **Open** window.

3. Look for the existing line in this file that begins with DirectoryIndex, shown here:

```
<IfModule dir_module>
    DirectoryIndex index.html
</IfModule>
```

This line tells Apache which filenames to use when it looks for the default page for a given directory. Add **index.php** to the end of this line:

```
<IfModule dir_module>
    DirectoryIndex index.html index.php
</IfModule>
```

4. All of the remaining options in this long and intimidating configuration file should have been set up correctly by the Apache install program. All you need to do is add the following lines to the very end of the file:

```
LoadModule php5_module "C:/PHP/php5apache2_2.dll"
AddType application/x-httpd-php .php
PHPIniDir "C:/PHP"
```

Make sure the `LoadModule` and `PHPIniDir` lines point to your PHP installation directory, and note the use of forward slashes (/) instead of backslashes (\) in the paths.

PHP and Future Apache Versions

Historically, major new versions of the Apache server have required new versions of the .dll file you see referenced in the `LoadModule` line above. If you take another look in your PHP installation directory, for example, you'll see there are also **php5apachc.dll** and **php5apache2.dll** files there. These files were provided for use with Apache 1.3 and Apache 2.0, respectively.

By the time you read this, it's possible that Apache has undergone another major release (for instance, Apache 2.3), which might need yet another new .dll file. For example, Apache 2.3 might require you to use a new file named **php5apache2_3.dll**.

If you *are* using a subsequent version of Apache, and if you *do* see a .dll file that looks like it might correspond to your Apache version, try adjusting the `LoadModule` line accordingly. You can always return and edit this file again later if Apache fails to load PHP correctly.

5.   Save your changes and close Notepad.

6.   Restart Apache using the Apache Service Monitor system tray icon. If all is well, Apache will start up again without complaint.

7.   Double-click the Apache Service Monitor icon to open the Apache Service Monitor window. If PHP is installed correctly, the status bar of this window should indicate the version of PHP you have installed, as shown in Figure 1.14.

8.   Click OK to close the Apache Service Monitor window.

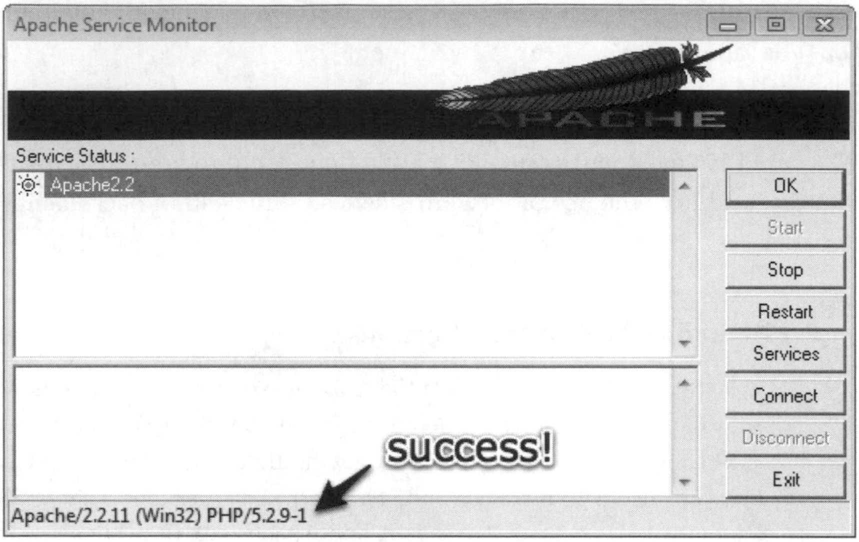

Figure 1.14. The PHP version number indicates Apache is configured to support PHP

With MySQL, Apache, and PHP installed, you're ready to proceed to the section called "Post-Installation Set-up Tasks".

Mac OS X Installation

Mac OS X distinguishes itself by being the only consumer OS to install both Apache and PHP as components of every standard installation. That said, these take a few tweaks to switch on, and you'll need to install the MySQL database as well.

In this section, I'll show you how to start running a PHP-and-MySQL-equipped web server on a Mac computer running Mac OS X version 10.5 (Leopard). If you're using an alternative to a Mac, you can safely skip this section.

All-in-one Installation

I normally recommend that you install and set up your web server, PHP, and MySQL individually, using the official installation packages for each. This process is especially useful for beginners, because it gives you a strong sense of how these pieces all fit together. If you're in a rush, however, or if you need to set up a temporary development environment to use just for a day or two, a quick-and-dirty solution may be preferable.

You can skip ahead to the section called "Installing Individual Packages" if you want to take the time to install each piece of the puzzle separately.

MAMP (which stands for Mac, Apache, MySQL, and PHP) is a free, all-in-one program that includes built-in copies of recent versions of the Apache web server, PHP, and MySQL. Let me take you through the process of installing it:

1. Download the latest version from the MAMP web site.[7] After downloading the file (as of this writing, MAMP 1.9.1 is about 170MB in size), double-click it to unzip the disk image (**MAMP_MAMP_PRO_1.9.1.dmg**), then double-click the disk image to mount it, as shown in Figure 1.15.

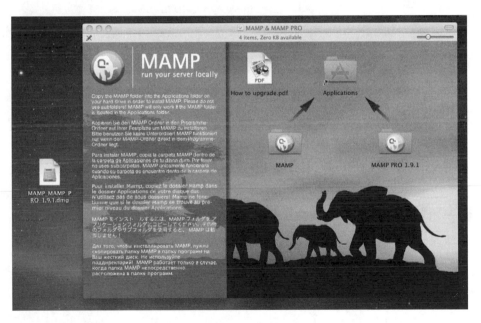

Figure 1.15. The MAMP package

2. As instructed in the disk image window, drag the **MAMP** folder icon over to the **Applications** folder icon to install MAMP on your system (you can ignore the **MAMP PRO** folder). After the copy operation has completed, you can drag the **MAMP** icon on your desktop to the **Trash** icon on your dock to eject it (it will turn into an **Eject** icon), then delete the disk image, as well as the original **.zip** file you downloaded.

---

[7] http://www.mamp.info

Browse to your **Applications** folder and find the new **MAMP** folder there. Open it, and double-click the **MAMP** icon inside to launch MAMP. As MAMP starts up, the following will happen. First, the MAMP window shown in Figure 1.16 will appear. The two status indicators will switch from red to green as the built-in Apache and MySQL servers start up. Next, MAMP will open your default web browser and load the MAMP welcome page, shown in Figure 1.17.

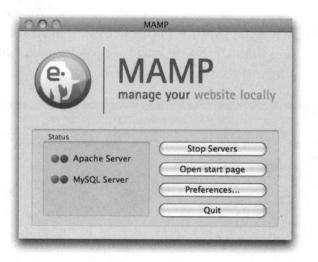

Figure 1.16. The MAMP window

Figure 1.17. The MAMP welcome page confirms Apache, PHP, and MySQL are up and running

When you're done working with MAMP, you can shut it down (along with its built-in servers) by clicking the **Quit** button in the MAMP window. When you're next ready to do some work on a database driven web site, just fire it up again!

Later in this book, you'll need to use some of the programs that come with the MySQL server built into MAMP. To work properly, these programs must be added to your Mac OS X system path.

To add the MySQL command prompt programs that come with MAMP to your Mac OS X system path, follow these instructions:

1. Open a Terminal window.[8]

    *   If you're running Mac OS X 10.5 (Leopard) or later, type these commands:

```
Machine:~ user$ sudo su
Password: (type your password)
sh-3.2# echo '/Applications/MAMP/Library/bin' >> /etc/paths.d
➥/MAMP
sh-3.2# exit
```

 What to Type

The *Machine:~ user*$ portion (where *Machine* is your computer's name) represents the prompt that's already displayed. You only need to type the command, which is shown in bold.

    *   If you're running Mac OS X 10.4 (Tiger) or earlier, type these commands:

```
Machine:~ user$ touch .profile
Machine:~ user$ open .profile
```

This should open the hidden **.profile** file in TextEdit. This file contains a list of Terminal commands that are executed automatically whenever you open a new Terminal window. If you've never installed command prompt programs on your system before, this file will be completely empty. In any case, add this line to the end of the file:

```
export PATH=$PATH:/Applications/MAMP/Library/bin
```

Save your changes, and quit TextEdit.

2. Close the Terminal window to allow this change to take effect.

---

[8] To open a Terminal window, launch the **Terminal** application, which you can find in the **Utilities** folder in the **Applications** folder.

Installing Individual Packages

Installing each individual package separately is really the way to go if you can afford to take the time. You gain the opportunity to learn how all the pieces fit together, and you have the freedom to update each of the packages independently of the others. Besides, it's always worthwhile being familiar with the inner workings of any software with which you'll be spending a lot of time.

The following instructions assume you're running Mac OS X 10.5 (Leopard) or later. If you're running an earlier version of Mac OS OX, you should stick with the all-in-one option.

Installing MySQL

Apple maintains a fairly comprehensive guide to installing MySQL on Mac OS X on its Mac OS X Internet Developer site[9] if you want to compile MySQL yourself. It's much easier, however, to obtain the precompiled binary version directly from the MySQL web site.

Start by visiting the The MySQL Downloads page.[10] Click the **Download** link for the free MySQL Community Server. This will take you to a page with a long list of download links for the current recommended version of MySQL (as of this writing, it's MySQL 5.1).

Click the **Mac OS X (package format)** link. You will be presented with the list of downloads shown in Figure 1.18. Which one you need to choose depends on your operating system version and platform architecture. If your system is running Mac OS X version 10.6 (Snow Leopard), you can ignore the Mac OS X 10.5 and 10.4 links. If you know your Mac has a 64-bit processor, you can safely pick the **Mac OS X ver. 10.6 (x86, 64-bit), DMG Archive** version. If you're at all unsure, your best bet is the **Mac OS X ver. 10.5 (x86, 32-bit), DMG Archive** version—all it requires is that you have an Intel-based Mac (to be sure, check the processor information in the **About This Mac** window, which you can access from the Apple menu). If you have an older, PowerPC-based Mac, you'll need one of the PowerPC versions. The 32-bit version is the safe bet, since it will run on 64-bit systems too.

---

[9] http://developer.apple.com/internet/macosx/osdb.html
[10] http://dev.mysql.com/downloads/

Generally Available (GA) Releases   Development Releases

MySQL Community Server 5.1.50

Select Platform:

Mac OS X ▼   Select

Mac OS X ver. 10.6 (x86, 64-bit), Compressed TAR Archive	5.1.50	78.0M	Download
(mysql-5.1.50-osx10.6-x86_64.tar.gz)		MD5: bef52515449ac82a2870da05c1414bba	
Mac OS X ver. 10.6 (x86, 32-bit), Compressed TAR Archive	5.1.50	76.3M	Download
(mysql-5.1.50-osx10.6-x86.tar.gz)		MD5: 379b255726074f6fb3e4eda299ef9341	
Mac OS X ver. 10.6 (x86, 64-bit), DMG Archive	5.1.50	77.8M	Download
(mysql-5.1.50-osx10.6-x86_64.dmg)		MD5: 452fdb8ec7988d6b6d4de64c3fb69305	
Mac OS X ver. 10.6 (x86, 32-bit), DMG Archive	5.1.50	76.2M	Download
(mysql-5.1.50-osx10.6-x86.dmg)		MD5: 5a24a9bf71b80d4b8140c1af08dffb1b	
Mac OS X 10.5 (x86, 64-bit), Compressed TAR Archive	5.1.50	68.8M	Download
(mysql-5.1.50-osx10.5-x86_64.tar.gz)		MD5: a07faad6777d30f0fc315ddd9f4194eb	
Mac OS X 10.5 (x86, 32-bit), Compressed TAR Archive	5.1.50	66.1M	Download
(mysql-5.1.50-osx10.5-x86.tar.gz)		MD5: d800cdb99020420f7a27941012ce53a2	
Mac OS X 10.5 (x86, 64-bit), DMG Archive	5.1.50	68.7M	Download
(mysql-5.1.50-osx10.5-x86_64.dmg)		MD5: eb87ea30e07f63c759b7d3502f157d4d	
Mac OS X 10.5 (x86, 32-bit), DMG Archive	5.1.50	66.0M	Download
(mysql-5.1.50-osx10.5-x86.dmg)		MD5: 519f82ba2b4a17a5578a2b4a9c828c44	
Mac OS X 10.4 (x86, 32-bit), Compressed TAR Archive	5.1.50	128.6M	Download
(mysql-5.1.50-osx10.4-i686.tar.gz)		MD5: ec04db5c6ef79eb839eee6ee17a72c3a	

Figure 1.18. The 32-bit version of MySQL for Intel processors will work on most current Macs

Once you've downloaded the **mysql-*version*-osx*version*-*platform*.dmg** file, double-click it to mount the disk image. As shown in Figure 1.19, it contains the installer in **.pkg** format, as well as a **MySQLStartupItem.pkg** file. Double-click the installer, which will guide you through the installation of MySQL.

Figure 1.19. The MySQL Mac OS X package contains lots of goodies

Once MySQL is installed, you can launch the MySQL server. Open a Terminal window[11] and type this command:

```
Machine:~ user$ sudo /usr/local/mysql/bin/mysqld_safe
```

What to Type

The `Machine:~ user$` portion (where *Machine* is your computer's name) represents the prompt that's already displayed. You only need to type the command, which is shown in bold.

Once you have typed the command, hit **Enter**.

This command runs the **mysqld_safe** script with administrator privileges. You'll be prompted to input your password to do this, then a status message will confirm that MySQL is running.

Once MySQL is running, you can switch it to background execution by typing **Ctrl+Z** to stop the process, and then typing this command to let it continue running in the background:

```
Machine:~ user$ bg
```

You can then quit the Terminal application and MySQL will continue to run as a server on your system. When you want to shut down the MySQL server, open a new Terminal window and type this command:

```
Machine:~ user$ sudo /usr/local/mysql/bin/mysqladmin shutdown
```

Though you'll gain plenty of geek cred for memorizing these commands, there's a much less tedious way to control your MySQL server. Back in the installation disk image shown in Figure 1.19, you'll notice a file named **MySQL.prefPane**. Double-click this to install a new pane in Mac OS X's System Preferences, and the window shown in Figure 1.20 will open.

---

[11] To open a Terminal window, launch the **Terminal** application, which you can find in the **Utilities** folder in the **Applications** folder.

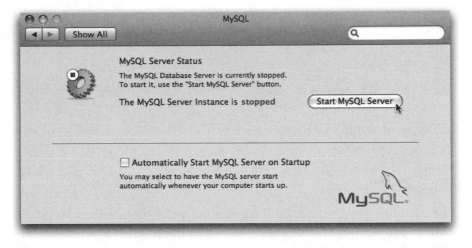

Figure 1.20. The MySQL System Preferences pane

This window will tell you if your MySQL server is running or not, and lets you start it up and shut it down with the click of a button!

Presumably, you'll want your system to launch the MySQL server at startup automatically so that you can avoid having to repeat the above process whenever you restart your system. The system preferences pane has a checkbox that does this, but for this checkbox to do anything you must first install the **MySQLStartupItem.pkg** from the installation disk image.

When you have everything set up the way you want it, you can safely drag the MySQL installation disk icon on your desktop to the trash, then delete the **.dmg** file you downloaded.

One last task you'll want to do is add the **/usr/local/mysql/bin** directory to your system path. Doing this enables you to run programs like **mysqladmin** and **mysql** (for which we'll have plenty of use later in this book) in the Terminal without typing out their full paths. Pop open a new Terminal window and type these commands:

```
Machine:~ user$ sudo su
Password: (type your password)
sh-3.2# echo '/usr/local/mysql/bin' >> /etc/paths.d/mysql
sh-3.2# exit
```

Close the Terminal window and open a new one to allow this change to take effect. Then, with your MySQL server running, try running the **mysqladmin** program from your home directory:

```
Machine:~ user$ mysqladmin status
```

If everything worked the way it's supposed to, you should see a brief list of statistics about your MySQL server.

Installing PHP

Mac OS X 10.5 (Leopard) comes with Apache 2.2 and PHP 5 built right in! All you need to do to use them for development is switch them on:

1. Open System Preferences (**System Preferences...** on the Apple menu).

2. In the main System Preferences menu, click **Sharing** under **Internet & Wireless**.

3. Make sure that **Web Sharing** is checked, as shown in Figure 1.21.

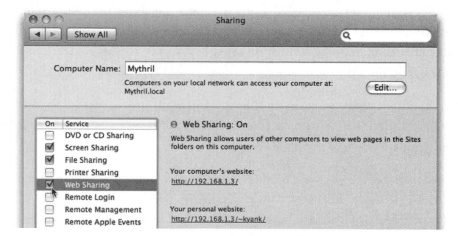

Figure 1.21. Enable Web Sharing in Mac OS X

4. Quit System Preferences.

5. Open your browser, type http://localhost into the address bar, and hit **Enter**. Your browser should display the standard Apache welcome message shown in Figure 1.22.

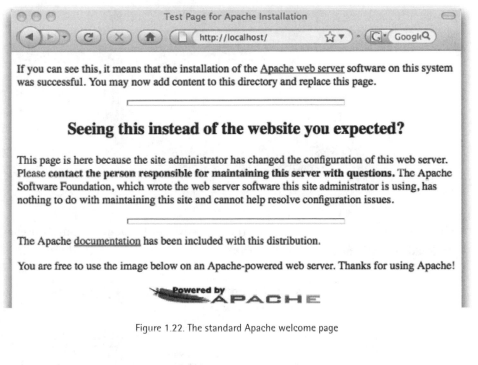

Figure 1.22. The standard Apache welcome page

With this procedure complete, Apache will be run at startup automatically on your system. You're now ready to enhance this server by enabling PHP support:

1. In the Finder menu bar, choose **Go** > **Go to folder** (⇧+⌘+**G**), and type **/private/etc/apache2/** before clicking **Go**.

2. In the Finder window that opens, there should be a file named **httpd.conf**. This is the Apache configuration file. By default, it's read-only. Right-click the file and choose **Get Info** (⌘+**I**) to open the file's properties. Scroll down to the bottom of the **httpd.conf Info** window to find the **Sharing & Permissions** setting.

    By default, the settings in this section are disabled. Click the little lock icon shown in Figure 1.23 to enable them. Enter your password when prompted.

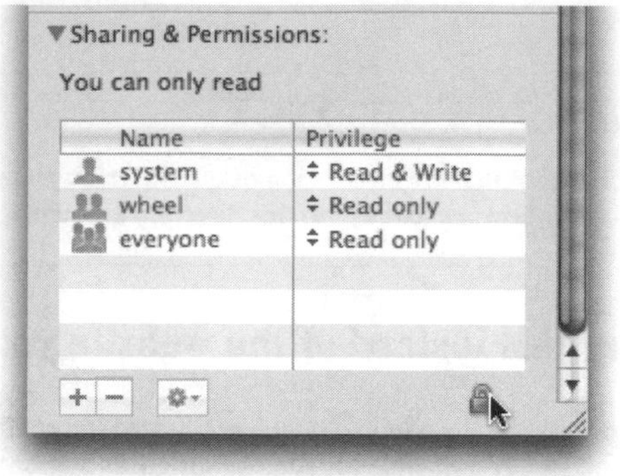

Figure 1.23. Click the lock to make changes to these settings

To make this file editable, change the value in the **Privilege** column for **everyone** to **Read & Write**, as shown in Figure 1.24.

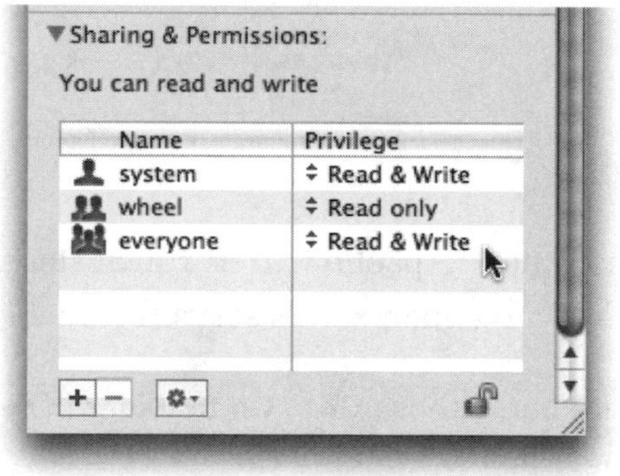

Figure 1.24. Set the permissions for **everyone** to **Read & Write**

3. Back in the Finder window for the **apache2** folder, right-click in the background of the folder window and choose **Get Info** to open the folder's properties. As in the previous step, set the **Sharing & Permissions** settings from **everyone** to **Read & Write**.

4. Finally, double-click the `httpd.conf` file to open it in TextEdit.

5. In the **httpd.conf** file, search for this line:

```
#LoadModule php5_module          libexec/apache2/libphp5.so
```

Enable this command by deleting the hash (#) character at the start of the line.

6.   Save your changes, and quit TextEdit.

7.   If you like to tidy up after yourself, you can go back and reset the privileges on the **httpd.conf** file and the **apache2** folder. This will keep other users of your computer from making changes to the Apache configuration.

8.   Open a Terminal window and type this command to restart Apache:

```
Machine:~ user$ sudo /usr/sbin/apachectl restart
```

Type your password when prompted.

9.   Load http://localhost in your browser again to make sure that Apache is still running.

Your computer is now equipped with an Apache web server with PHP support. If you need to make changes to Apache's configuration, you know how to edit its **httpd.conf** file using the instructions above. The PHP plugin, however, has its own configuration file, named **php.ini**, and you need to edit that file to tell PHP how to connect to your MySQL server.

With the version of PHP built into Mac OS X, there is no **php.ini** file by default—PHP just runs with the default settings. In order to modify those settings, you'll need to open Terminal and copy the **/private/etc/php.ini.default** file to **/private/etc/php.ini**:

```
Machine:~ user$ cd /private/etc
Machine:etc user$ sudo cp php.ini.default php.ini
Password: (type your password)
```

To make this new **php.ini** file editable by users like yourself, use the same procedure described above for editing **httpd.conf**: in Finder use **Go** > **Go to folder** to open **/private/etc**, modify the permissions of both the **php.ini** file and the folder that contains it, then open the file with TextEdit.

Scroll down through the file or use **Edit** > **Find** > **Find...** (⌘+**F**) to locate the `mysql.default_socket` option. Edit this line of the **php.ini** file so that it looks like this:

```
mysql.default_socket = /tmp/mysql.sock
```

You should only have to add the portion in bold.

Scroll down further to locate the `mysqli.default_socket` option (`mysqli`, not `mysql`), and make the same change:

```
mysqli.default_socket = /tmp/mysql.sock
```

Save your changes, quit TextEdit, and restore the file and directory permissions if you want to. Finally, open a Terminal window and type this command to restart Apache once more:

```
Machine:~ user$ sudo /usr/sbin/apachectl restart
```

Type your password when prompted. Once Apache is up and running again, load http://localhost in your browser once more to make sure that all is well.

That's it! With MySQL, Apache, and PHP installed, you're ready to proceed to the section called "Post-Installation Set-up Tasks".

Linux Installation

This section will show you the procedure for manually installing Apache, PHP, and MySQL under most current distributions of Linux. These instructions were tested under Ubuntu 8.10;[12] however, they should work on other distributions such as Fedora,[13] Debian,[14] openSUSE,[15] and Gentoo[16] without much trouble. The steps involved will be very similar, almost identical.

Most Linux distributions come with a **package manager** of one kind or another. Ubuntu's Synaptic Package Manager[17] is a graphical front end to APT,[18] the Debian package manager. Other distributions use the older RPM package manager. Regardless of which distribution you use, prepackaged versions of Apache, PHP, and MySQL should be readily available. These prepackaged versions of software are really easy

---

[12] http://www.ubuntu.com
[13] http://fedoraproject.org
[14] http://www.debian.org
[15] http://www.opensuse.org
[16] http://www.gentoo.org
[17] https://help.ubuntu.com/community/SynapticHowto
[18] http://www.debian.org/doc/user-manuals#apt-howto

to install; unfortunately, they also limit the software configuration options available to you. For this reason—and because any attempt to document the procedures for installing the packaged versions across all popular Linux distributions would be doomed to failure—I will instead show you how to install them manually.

If you already have Apache, PHP, and MySQL installed in packaged form, feel free to use those versions, and skip forward to the section called "Post-Installation Setup Tasks". If you encounter any problems, you can always uninstall the packaged versions and return here to install them by by hand.

Installing MySQL

Start by downloading MySQL. Simply proceed to the MySQL Downloads page[19] and click the **Download** link for the free MySQL Community Server. This will take you to a page with a long list of download links for the current recommended version of MySQL (as of this writing, it's MySQL 5.1).

Click the link near the top of the list to go to the **Linux (non RPM packages)**. Now you need to choose the package that corresponds to your system architecture. If you're positive you're running a 64-bit version of Linux, go ahead and download the **Linux (AMD64/Intel EM64T)** package (about 120MB in size). If you're running a 32-bit version of Linux, download the **Linux (x86)** package (about 115MB)—it'll work even if it turns out you're running a 64-bit version of Linux. It may be a little unclear, but the **Pick a mirror** link shown in Figure 1.25 is the one you need to click to download the file.

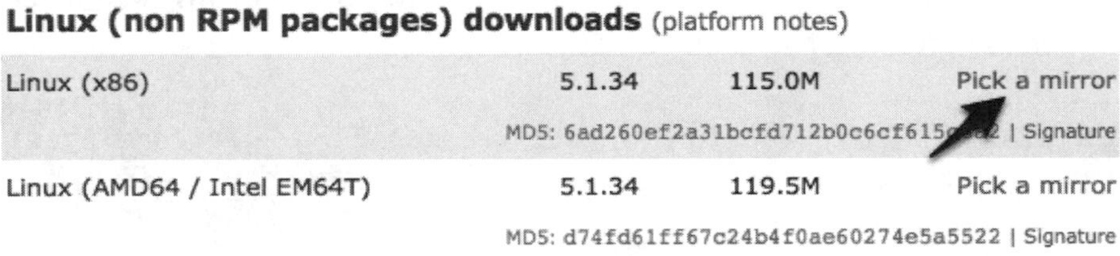

Linux (non RPM packages) downloads (platform notes)

Linux (x86)	5.1.34	115.0M	Pick a mirror
	MD5: 6ad260ef2a31bcfd712b0c6cf615c...		Signature
Linux (AMD64 / Intel EM64T)	5.1.34	119.5M	Pick a mirror
	MD5: d74fd61ff67c24b4f0ae60274e5a5522		Signature

Figure 1.25. Finding the right link can be tricky—here it is!

Once you've downloaded the file, open a Terminal and log in as the root user:

```
user@machine:~$ sudo su
```

---

[19] http://dev.mysql.com/downloads/

You will, of course, be prompted for your password.

Change directories to **/usr/local** and unpack the downloaded file:

```
root@machine:/home/user# cd /usr/local
root@machine:/usr/local# tar xfz ~user/Desktop/mysql-version-linux-
➥platform.tar.gz
```

The second command assumes you left the downloaded file on your desktop, which is the **Desktop** directory in your home directory. You'll need to replace *user* with your username, *version* with the MySQL version you downloaded, and *platform* with the architecture and compiler version of the release you downloaded; this is so that the command exactly matches the path and filename of the file you downloaded. On my computer, for example, the exact command looks like this:

```
root@mythril:/usr/local# tar xfz ~kyank/Desktop/mysql-5.1.34-linux-x
➥86_64-glibc23.tar.gz
```

After a minute or two, you'll be returned to the command prompt. A quick `ls` will confirm that you now have a directory named **mysql-*version*-linux-*platform***. This is what it looks like on my computer:

```
root@mythril:/usr/local# ls
bin  games    lib  mysql-5.1.34-linux-x86_64-glibc23  share
etc  include  man  sbin                               src
```

Next, create a symbolic link to the new directory with the name **mysql** to make accessing the directory easier. Then enter the directory:

```
root@machine:/usr/local# ln -s mysql-version-linux-platform mysql
root@machine:/usr/local# cd mysql
```

While you can run the server as the root user, or even as yourself (if, for example, you were to install the server in your home directory), you should normally set up on the system a special user whose sole purpose is to run the MySQL server. This will remove any possibility of an attacker using the MySQL server as a way to break into the rest of your system. To create a special MySQL user, type the following commands (still logged in as root):

```
root@machine:/usr/local/mysql# groupadd mysql
root@machine:/usr/local/mysql# useradd -g mysql mysql
```

Now give ownership of your MySQL directory to this new user:

```
root@machine:/usr/local/mysql# chown -R mysql .
root@machine:/usr/local/mysql# chgrp -R mysql .
```

MySQL is now installed, but before it can do anything useful, its database files need to be installed, too. Still in the new **mysql** directory, type the following command:

```
root@machine:/usr/local/mysql# scripts/mysql_install_db --user=mysql
```

Now everything's prepared for you to launch the MySQL server for the first time. From the same directory, type the following command:

```
root@machine:/usr/local/mysql# bin/mysqld_safe --user=mysql &
```

If you see the message mysql daemon ended, then the MySQL server was prevented from starting. The error message should have been written to a file called *hostname*.**err** (where *hostname* is your machine's host name) in MySQL's **data** directory. You'll usually find that this happens because another MySQL server is already running on your computer.

If the MySQL server was launched without complaint, the server will run (just like your web or FTP server) until your computer is shut down. To test that the server is running properly, type the following command:

```
root@machine:/usr/local/mysql# bin/mysqladmin -u root status
```

A little blurb with some statistics about the MySQL server should be displayed. If you receive an error message, check the *hostname*.**err** file to see if the fault lies with the MySQL server upon starting up. If you retrace your steps to make sure you followed the process described above, and this fails to solve the problem, a post to the SitePoint Forums[20] will help you pin it down in little time.

---

[20] http://www.sitepoint.com/forums/

If you want your MySQL server to run automatically whenever the system is running, you'll have to set it up to do so. In the **support-files** subdirectory of the **mysql** directory, you'll find a script called **mysql.server** that can be added to your system startup routines to do this. For most versions of Linux, you can do this by creating a link to the **mysql.server** script in the **/etc/init.d** directory, then create two links to that: **/etc/rc2.d/S99mysql** and **/etc/rc0.d/K01mysql**. Here are the commands to type:

```
root@machine:/usr/local/mysql# cd /etc
root@machine:/etc# ln -s /usr/local/mysql/support-files/mysql.server
➥ init.d/
root@machine:/etc# ln -s /etc/init.d/mysql.server rc2.d/S99mysql
root@machine:/etc# ln -s /etc/init.d/mysql.server rc0.d/K01mysql
```

That's it! To test that this works, reboot your system, and request the status of the server with mysqladmin as you did above.

One final thing you might like to do for the sake of convenience is to place the MySQL client programs—which you'll use to administer your MySQL server later on—in the system path. To this end, you can place symbolic links to **mysql**, **mysqladmin**, and **mysqldump** in your **/usr/local/bin** directory:

```
root@machine:/etc# cd /usr/local/bin
root@machine:/usr/local/bin# ln -s /usr/local/mysql/bin/mysql .
root@machine:/usr/local/bin# ln -s /usr/local/mysql/bin/mysqladmin .
root@machine:/usr/local/bin# ln -s /usr/local/mysql/bin/mysqldump .
```

Once you've done this, you can log out of the root account. From this point on, you can administer MySQL from any directory on your system:

```
root@machine:/usr/local/bin# exit
user@machine:~$ mysqladmin -u root status
```

Installing PHP

As mentioned above, PHP is more a web server plugin module than a program. There are actually three ways to install the PHP plugin for Apache:

- as a CGI program that Apache runs every time it needs to process a PHP-enhanced web page
- as an Apache module compiled right into the Apache program
- as an Apache module loaded by Apache each time it starts up

The first option is the easiest to install and set up, but it requires Apache to launch PHP as a program on your computer every time a PHP page is requested. This activity can really slow down the response time of your web server, especially if more than one request needs to be processed at a time.

The second and third options are almost identical in terms of performance, but the third option is the most flexible, since you can add and remove Apache modules without having to recompile it each time. For this reason, we'll use the third option.

Assuming you don't already have Apache running on your computer, surf on over to the Apache HTTP Server Project[21] and look for the version of Apache described as "the best available version" (as of this writing it's version 2.2.11, as shown in Figure 1.26).

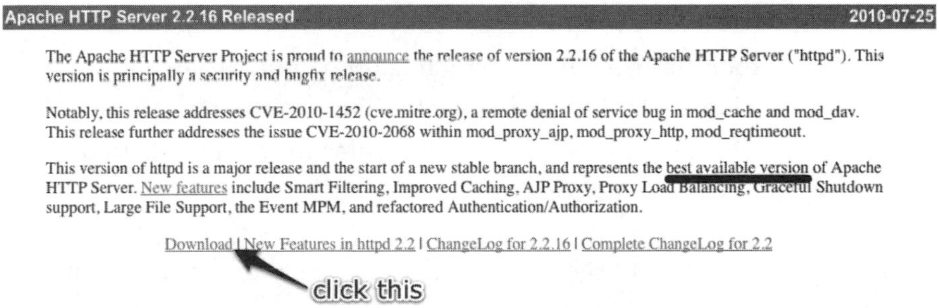

Figure 1.26. The best available version—accept no substitutes!

---

[21] http://httpd.apache.org/

Once you get to the Download page, scroll down to find the links to the various versions available. The one you want is **Unix Source**, shown in Figure 1.27. Both the **.tar.gz** or the **.tar.bz2** are the same; just grab whichever archive format you're used to extracting.

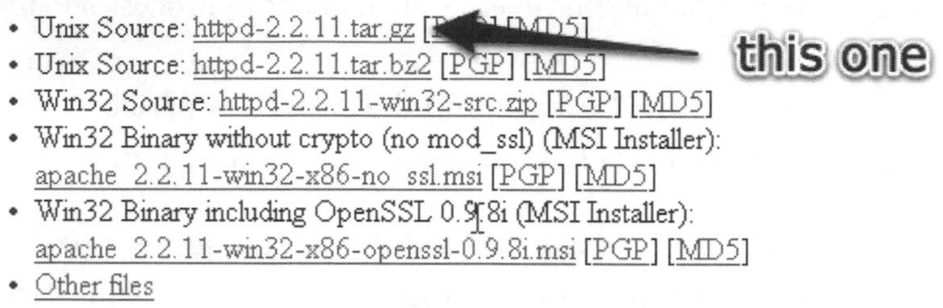

- Unix Source: httpd-2.2.11.tar.gz [PGP] [MD5]   this one
- Unix Source: httpd-2.2.11.tar.bz2 [PGP] [MD5]
- Win32 Source: httpd-2.2.11-win32-src.zip [PGP] [MD5]
- Win32 Binary without crypto (no mod_ssl) (MSI Installer): apache_2.2.11-win32-x86-no_ssl.msi [PGP] [MD5]
- Win32 Binary including OpenSSL 0.9.8i (MSI Installer): apache_2.2.11-win32-x86-openssl-0.9.8i.msi [PGP] [MD5]
- Other files

Figure 1.27. This is the one you need

What you've just downloaded is actually the source code for the Apache server. The first step, then, is to compile it into an executable binary installation. Pop open a Terminal, navigate to the directory where the downloaded file is located, then extract it, and navigate into the resulting directory:

```
user@machine:~$ cd Desktop
user@machine:~/Desktop$ tar xfz httpd-version.tar.gz
user@machine:~/Desktop$ cd httpd-version
```

The first step in compiling Apache is to configure it to your requirements. Most of the defaults will be fine for your purposes, but you'll need to enable dynamic loading of Apache modules (like PHP), which is off by default. Additionally, you should probably enable the URL rewriting feature, upon which many PHP applications rely (although it's unnecessary for the examples in this book). To make these configuration changes, type this command:

```
user@machine:~/Desktop/httpd-version$ ./configure --enable-so --enab
➥le-rewrite
```

A long stream of status messages will parade up your screen. If the process stops with an error message, your system may be missing some critical piece of software that's required to compile Apache. Some Linux distributions lack the essential development libraries or even a C compiler installed by default. Installing these should enable you to return and run this command successfully. Current versions of Ubuntu, however, should come with everything that's needed.

After several minutes, the stream of messages should come to an end:

```
⋮
config.status: creating build/rules.mk
config.status: creating build/pkg/pkginfo
config.status: creating build/config_vars.sh
config.status: creating include/ap_config_auto.h
config.status: executing default commands
user@machine:~/Desktop/httpd-version$
```

You're now ready to compile Apache. The one-word command make is all it takes:

```
user@machine:~/Desktop/httpd-version$ make
```

Again, this process will take several minutes to complete, and should end with the following message:

```
⋮
make[1]: Leaving directory `/home/user/Desktop/httpd-version'
user@machine:~/Desktop/httpd-version$
```

To install your newly-compiled copy of Apache, type sudo make install (the sudo is required, since you need root access to write to the installation directory).

```
user@machine:~/Desktop/httpd-version$ sudo make install
```

Enter your password when prompted.

As soon as this command has finished copying files, your installation of Apache is complete. Navigate to the installation directory and launch Apache using the apachectl script:

```
user@machine:~/Desktop/httpd-version$ cd /usr/local/apache2
user@machine:/usr/local/apache2$ sudo bin/apachectl -k start
```

You'll likely see a warning message from Apache complaining that it was unable to determine the server's fully qualified domain name. That's because most personal computers are without one. Don't sweat it.

Fire up your browser and type http://localhost into the address bar. If Apache is up and running, you should see a welcome message like the one in Figure 1.28.

Figure 1.28. You can take my word for it!

As with your MySQL server, you'll probably want to configure Apache to start automatically when your system boots. The procedure to do this is similar; just copy and link the **apachectl** script from your Apache installation:

```
user@machine:/usr/local/apache2$ sudo su
root@machine:/usr/local/apache2# cd /etc
root@machine:/etc# ln -s /usr/local/apache2/bin/apachectl init.d/
root@machine:/etc# ln -s /etc/init.d/apachectl rc2.d/S99httpd
root@machine:/etc# ln -s /etc/init.d/apachectl rc0.d/K01httpd
```

To test that this works, restart your computer and then hit the http://localhost page in your browser again.

With a shiny new Apache installation up and running, you're now ready to add PHP support to it. To start, download the PHP Complete Source Code package from the PHP Downloads page.[22] Again, the **.tar.gz** and **.tar.bz2** versions are identical; just download whichever you're used to extracting.

The file you downloaded should be called **php-*version*.tar.gz** (or **.bz2**). Pop open a new Terminal window, navigate to the directory containing the downloaded file, extract it, and move into the resulting directory:

---

[22] http://www.php.net/downloads.php

```
user@machine:~$ cd Desktop
user@machine:~/Desktop$ tar xfz php-version.tar.gz
user@machine:~/Desktop$ cd php-version
```

To install PHP as an Apache module, you'll need to use the Apache **apxs** program. This will have been installed along with the Apache server if you followed the instructions above to compile it yourself; but if you're using the copy that was installed with your distribution of Linux, you may need to install the Apache development package to access Apache **apxs**. You should be able to install this package by using the package manager included with your Linux distribution. For example, on Debian Linux, you can use apt-get to install it as follows:

```
user@machine:~$ sudo apt-get install apache-dev
```

Now, to install PHP, you must be logged in as root:

```
user@machine:~/Desktop/php-version$ sudo su
[sudo] password for user: (type your password)
root@machine:/home/user/Desktop/php-version#
```

The first step is to configure the PHP installation program by telling it which options you want to enable, and where it should find the programs it needs to know about (such as Apache **apxs** and MySQL). The command should look like this (all on one line):

```
root@machine:/home/user/Desktop/php-version# ./configure
➡ --prefix=/usr/local/php --with-apxs2=/usr/local/apache2/bin/apxs
➡ --with-mysqli=/usr/local/mysql/bin/mysql_config
```

The --prefix option tells the installer where you want PHP to be installed (**/usr/local/php** is a good choice).

The --with-apxs2 option tells the installer where to find the Apache **apxs** program mentioned above. When installed using your Linux distribution's package manager, the program is usually found at **/usr/sbin/apxs**. If you compiled and installed Apache yourself as described above, however, it will be in the Apache binary directory, at **/usr/local/apache2/bin/apxs**.

The --with-mysqli option tells the installer where to find your MySQL installation. More specifically, it must point to the **mysql_config** program in your MySQL installation's **bin** directory (**/usr/local/mysql/bin/mysql_config**).

Again, a parade of status messages will appear on your screen. When it stops, check for any error messages and install any files it identifies as missing. On a default Ubuntu 8.10 installation, for example, you're likely to see an error complaining about an incomplete libxml2 installation. To correct this particular error, open Synaptic Package Manager, then locate and install the **libxml2-dev** package (**libxml2** should already be installed). Once it's installed, try the configure command again.

After you watch several screens of tests scroll by, you'll be returned to the command prompt with the comforting message "Thank you for using PHP." The following two commands will compile and then install PHP:

```
root@machine:/home/user/Desktop/php-version# make
root@machine:/home/user/Desktop/php-version# make install
```

Take a coffee break: this will take some time.

Upon completion of the make install command, PHP will be installed in **/usr/local/php** (unless you specified a different directory with the --prefix option of the **configure** script above). Now you just need to configure it!

The PHP configuration file is called **php.ini**. PHP comes with two sample **php.ini** files called **php.ini-dist** and **php.ini-recommended**. Copy these files from your installation work directory to the **/usr/local/php/lib** directory, then make a copy of the **php.ini-dist** file and call it **php.ini**:

```
root@machine:/home/user/Desktop/php-version# cp php.ini* /usr/local/
➥php/lib/
root@machine:/home/user/Desktop/php-version# cd /usr/local/php/lib
root@machine:/usr/local/php/lib# cp php.ini-dist php.ini
```

You may now delete the directory from which you compiled PHP—it's no longer needed.

We'll worry about fine-tuning **php.ini** shortly. For now, we need to tweak Apache's configuration to make it more PHP-friendly. Locate your Apache **httpd.conf** configuration file. This file can usually be found in the **conf** subdirectory of your Apache installation (**/usr/local/apache2/conf/httpd.conf**).

To edit this file you must be logged in as root, so launch your text editor from the Terminal window where you're still logged in as root:

```
root@machine:/usr/local/php/lib# cd /usr/local/apache2/conf
root@machine:/usr/local/apache2/conf# gedit httpd.conf
```

In this file, look for the line that begins with DirectoryIndex. This line tells Apache which filenames to use when it looks for the default page for a given directory. You'll see the usual **index.html**, but you need to add **index.php** to the list:

```
<IfModule dir_module>
  DirectoryIndex index.html index.php
</IfModule>
```

Finally, go right to the bottom of the file and add these lines to tell Apache that files with names ending in **.php** should be treated as PHP scripts:

```
<FilesMatch \.php$>
  SetHandler application/x-httpd-php
</FilesMatch>
```

That should do it! Save your changes and restart your Apache server with this command:

```
root@machine:/usr/local/apache2/conf# /usr/local/apache2/bin/
➥apachectl -k restart
```

If it all goes according to plan, Apache should start up without any error messages. If you run into any trouble, the helpful individuals in the SitePoint Forums[23] (myself included) will be happy to help.

---

[23] http://www.sitepoint.com/forums/

Post-Installation Set-up Tasks

Regardless of which operating system you're running, or how you set up your web server—once PHP is installed and the MySQL server is functioning, the very first action you need to perform is assign a **root password** for MySQL.

MySQL only allows authorized users to view and manipulate the information stored in its databases, so you'll need to tell MySQL who's authorized and who's unauthorized. When MySQL is first installed, it's configured with a user named `root` that has access to do most tasks without even entering a password. Your first task should be to assign a password to the `root` user so that unauthorized users are prohibited from tampering with your databases.

Why Bother?

It's important to realize that MySQL, just like a web server, can be accessed from any computer on the same network. If you're working on a computer connected to the Internet, then, depending on the security measures you've taken, anyone in the world could connect to your MySQL server. The need to pick a difficult-to-guess password should be immediately obvious!

To set a root password for MySQL, you can use the **mysqladmin** program that comes with MySQL. If you followed the instructions to install MySQL separately (as explained earlier in this chapter), the **mysqladmin** program should be on your system path. This means you can pop open a Terminal window (or in Windows, a Command Prompt) and type the name of the program without having to remember where it's installed on your computer.

Go ahead and try this now, if you've yet to already. Open a Terminal or Command Prompt and type this command:[24]

```
mysqladmin -u root status
```

When you hit **Enter** you should see a line or two of basic statistics about your MySQL server, like this:

---

[24] If you're using Windows and are unfamiliar with the Command Prompt, check out my article *Kev's Command Prompt Cheat Sheet* [http://www.sitepoint.com/article/command-prompt-cheat-sheet/] for a quick crash course.

```
Uptime: 102261  Threads: 1  Questions: 1  Slow queries: 0  Opens: 15
 Flush tables: 1  Open tables: 0  Queries per second avg: 0.0
```

If you're seeing a different message entirely, it's probably one of two options. First, you might see an error message telling you that the **mysqladmin** program was unable to connect to your MySQL server:

```
mysqladmin: connect to server at 'localhost' failed
error: 'Can't connect to MySQL server on 'localhost' (10061)'
Check that mysqld is running on localhost and that the port is 3306.
You can check this by doing 'telnet localhost 3306'
```

This message normally means that your MySQL server simply isn't running. If you have it set up to run automatically when your system boots, double-check that the setup is working. If you normally launch your MySQL server manually, go ahead and do that before trying the command again.

Second, if you're using MAMP on the Mac, you'll probably see this error message instead:

```
mysqladmin: connect to server at 'localhost' failed
error: 'Access denied for user 'root'@'localhost' (using password: N
➥0)'
```

This error message means that the root user on your MySQL server already has a password set. It turns out that, with your security in mind, MAMP comes with a root password already set on its built-in MySQL server. That password, however, is *root*—so you're probably still going to want to change it using the instructions below.

One way or the other, you should now be able to run the **mysqladmin** program. Now you can use it to set the root password for your MySQL server:

```
mysqladmin -u root -p password "newpassword"
```

Replace *newpassword* with whatever password you'd like to use for your MySQL server. Make sure it's one you can remember, because if you forget your MySQL root password, you might need to erase your entire MySQL installation and start over from scratch! As we'll see in Chapter 10, it's usually possible to recover from such a mishap, but it's definitely a pain in the neck.

Here's a spot for you to record your MySQL root password in case you need to:

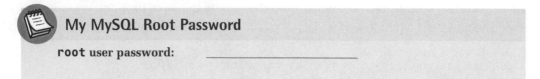

My MySQL Root Password

root user password: _____

When you hit **Enter**, you'll be prompted to enter the current password for the root MySQL user. Just hit **Enter** again, since the root user has no password at this point, unless you've used MAMP to set up MySQL on your Mac; in this case you should type **root**, the default root MySQL password on MAMP.

Let me break this command down for you, so you can understand what each part means:

mysqladmin

This, of course, is the name of the program you wish to run.

-u root

This specifies the MySQL user account you wish to use to connect to your MySQL server. On a brand new server, there is only one user account: root.

-p

This tells the program to prompt you for the current password of the user account. On a brand new MySQL server, the root account has no password, so you can just hit **Enter** when prompted. It's a good idea, however, to make a habit of including this option, since most of the time you *will* need to provide a password to connect to your MySQL server.

password "*newpassword*"

This instructs the mysqladmin program to change the password of the user account to *newpassword*. In this example, whatever password you specify will become the new password for the root MySQL user.

Now, to try out your new password, request once again that the MySQL server tell you its current status at the system command prompt, but this time include the -p option:

```
mysqladmin -u root -p status
```

Enter your new password when prompted. As before, you should see a line or two of statistics about your MySQL server.

Since the root account is now password-protected, attempting to run this command without the -p switch will give you an "Access Denied" error.

You're done! With everything set up and running, you're ready to write your first PHP script. Before we do that, however, you might want to write a short email to your web host.

What to Ask Your Web Host

While you tinker with PHP and MySQL on your own computer, it might be good to start collecting the information you'll need when it comes time to deploy your first database driven web site to the public. Here's a rundown of the details you should be asking your web host for.

First, you'll need to know how to transfer files to your web host. You'll upload PHP scripts to your host the same way you normally send the HTML files, CSS files, and images that make up a static web site, so if you already know how to do that, it's unnecessary to bother your host. If you're just starting with a new host, however, you'll need to be aware of what file transfer protocol it supports (FTP or SFTP), as well as knowing what username and password to use when connecting with your (S)FTP program. You also have to know what directory to put files into so they're accessible to web browsers.

In addition to these, you'll also need to find out a few details about the MySQL server your host has set up for you. It's important to know the host name to use to connect to it (possibly localhost), and your MySQL username and password, which may or may not be the same as your (S)FTP credentials. Your web host will probably also have provided an empty database for you to use, which prevents you from interfering with other users' databases who may share the same MySQL server with you. If they have provided this, you should establish the name of that database.

Have you taken in all that? Here's a spot to record the information you'll need about your web host:

My Hosting Details

File transfer protocol: ▪ FTP
                           ▪ SFTP

(S)FTP host name: _____

(S)FTP username: _____

(S)FTP password: _____

MySQL host name: _____

MySQL username: _____

MySQL password: _____

MySQL database name: _____

Your First PHP Script

It would be unfair of me to help you install everything—but stop short of giving you a taste of what a PHP script looks like until Chapter 3. So here's a little morsel to whet your appetite.

Open your favorite text or HTML editor and create a new file called **today.php**. Type this into the file:

```
<!DOCTYPE html PUBLIC "-//W3C//DTD XHTML 1.0 Strict//EN"
    "http://www.w3.org/TR/xhtml1/DTD/xhtml1-strict.dtd">
<html xmlns="http://www.w3.org/1999/xhtml" xml:lang="en" lang="en">
  <head>
    <title>Today&rsquo;s Date</title>
    <meta http-equiv="content-type"
        content="text/html; charset=utf-8"/>
  </head>
  <body>
    <p>Today&rsquo;s date (according to this web server) is
      <?php

      echo date('l, F dS Y.');

      ?>
    </p>
  </body>
</html>
```

Editing PHP Scripts in Windows with Notepad

Windows users should note that, to save a file with a `.php` extension in Notepad, you'll need to either select *All Files* as the file type, or surround the filename with quotes in the **Save As** dialog box; otherwise, Notepad will unhelpfully save the file as **today.php.txt**, which will fail to work.

Editing PHP Scripts in Mac OS X with TextEdit

Mac OS X users are advised to be careful when using TextEdit to edit **.php** files, as it saves them in Rich Text Format, with an invisible **.rtf** filename extension by default. To save a new **.php** file, you must first remember to convert the file to plain text by selecting **Format** > **Make Plain Text** (⇧+⌘+T) from the TextEdit menu.

TextEdit also has a nasty habit of mistaking existing **.php** files for HTML documents when opening them, and attempting to display them as formatted text. To avoid this, you must select the **Ignore rich text commands** checkbox in the **Open** dialog box.

Try a Free IDE!

As you can tell from the preceding warnings, the text editors provided with current operating systems are a little unsuitable for editing PHP scripts. There are a number of solid text editors and Integrated Development Environments (IDEs) with rich support for editing PHP scripts that you can download for free. Here are a few that work on Windows, Mac OS X, and Linux:

NetBeans   http://www.netbeans.org/features/php/
Aptana   http://www.aptana.com/php
Komodo Edit   http://www.activestate.com/komodo_edit/

If you'd prefer to avoid typing out all the code, you can download this file—along with the rest of the code in this book—from the code archive. See the Preface for details on how to download the code archive.

Save the file, and move it to the **web root** directory of your local web server.

Where's My Server's Web Root Directory?

If you're using an Apache server you installed manually, the web root directory is the **htdocs** directory within your Apache installation (that is, **C:\Program Files\Apache Software Foundation\Apache2.2\htdocs** on Windows, **/usr/local/apache2/htdocs** on Linux).

For Apache servers built into WampServer, the web root directory is the **www** directory within your WampServer directory. You can reach it quickly by selecting the **www directory** menu item from the WampServer menu in your Windows System Tray.

If the Apache server you're using is built into Mac OS X, the web root directory is **/Library/WebServer/Documents**.

The Apache server built into MAMP has a web root directory in the **htdocs** folder inside the MAMP folder (**/Applications/MAMP/htdocs**). If you prefer using a different folder as your web root, you can change it on the **Apache** tab of the MAMP application's Preferences.

Open your web browser of choice, and type http://localhost/today.php (or http://localhost:*port*/today.php if Apache is configured to run on a port other than the default of 80) into the address bar to view the file you just created.[25]

> ### You Must Type the URL
>
> You might be used to previewing your web pages by double-clicking on them, or by using the **File > Open...** feature of your browser. These methods tell your browser to load the file directly from your computer's hard drive, and so they'll fail to work with PHP files.
>
> As previously mentioned, PHP scripts require your web server to read and execute the PHP code they contain before sending the HTML code that's generated to the browser. Only if you type the URL (http://localhost/today.php) will your browser request the file from your web server so that this can happen.

Figure 1.29 shows what the web page generated by your first PHP script should look like.

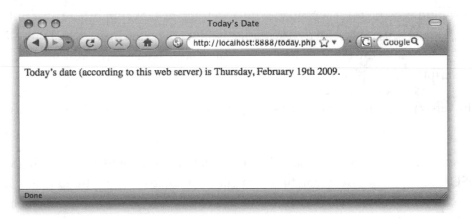

Figure 1.29. See your first PHP script in action!

Neat, huh? If you use the **View Source** feature in your browser, all you'll see is a regular HTML file with the date in it. The PHP code (everything between `<?php` and `?>` in the code above) was interpreted by the web server and converted to normal text before it was sent to your browser. The beauty of PHP, and other server-side

---

[25] If you installed Apache on Windows, you may have selected the option to run it on port 8080. If you're using MAMP, it's configured by default to run Apache on port 8888.

scripting languages, is that the web browser can remain ignorant—the web server does all the work!

Be reassured also that before too long you'll know code (like this example) as well as the back of your hand.

If the date is missing, or if your browser prompts you to download the PHP file instead of displaying it, then something is wrong with your web server's PHP support. If you can, use **View Source** in your browser to look at the code of the page. You'll probably see the PHP code right there in the page. Since the browser fails to understand PHP, it just sees <?php … ?> as one long, invalid HTML tag, which it ignores. Double-check that you have requested the file from your web server rather than your hard disk (that is, make sure the location bar in your browser shows a URL beginning with http://localhost), and make sure that PHP support has been properly installed on your web server using the instructions provided earlier in this chapter.

Full Toolbox, Dirty Hands

You should now be fully equipped with a web server that supports PHP scripts, a MySQL database server, and a basic understanding of how to use each of these. You should even have dirtied your hands by writing and successfully testing your first PHP script!

If the **today.php** script was unsuccessful for you, drop by the SitePoint Forums[26] and we'll be glad to help you figure out the problem.

In Chapter 2, you'll learn the basics of relational databases and start working with MySQL. I'll also introduce you to the language of database: Structured Query Language. If you've never worked with a database before, it'll be a real eye-opener!

---

[26] http://www.sitepoint.com/forums/

Introducing MySQL

In Chapter 1, we installed and set up two software programs: the Apache web server with PHP, and the MySQL database server.

As I explained in that chapter, PHP is a server-side scripting language that lets you insert into your web pages instructions that your web server software (in most cases, Apache) will execute before it sends those pages to browsers that request them. In a brief example, I showed how it was possible to insert the current date into a web page every time it was requested.

Now, that's all well and good, but things *really* become interesting when a database is added to the mix. In this chapter, we'll learn what a database is, and how to work with your own MySQL databases using Structured Query Language.

An Introduction to Databases

A database server (in our case, MySQL) is a program that can store large amounts of information in an organized format that's easily accessible through programming languages like PHP. For example, you could tell PHP to look in the database for a list of jokes that you'd like to appear on your web site.

In this example, the jokes would be stored entirely in the database. The advantages of this approach would be twofold: First, instead of having to write an HTML page for each of your jokes, you could write a single PHP script that was designed to fetch any joke from the database and display it by generating an HTML page for it on the fly. Second, adding a joke to your web site would be a simple matter of inserting the joke into the database. The PHP code would take care of the rest, automatically displaying the new joke along with the others when it fetched the list from the database.

Let's run with this example as we look at how data is stored in a database. A database is composed of one or more **tables**, each of which contains a list of **items**, or *things*. For our joke database, we'd probably start with a table called joke that would contain a list of jokes. Each table in a database has one or more **columns**, or **fields**. Each column holds a certain piece of information about each item in the table. In our example, our joke table might have one column for the text of the jokes, and another for the dates on which the jokes were added to the database. Each joke stored in this way would then be said to be a **row** or **entry** in the table. These rows and columns form a table that looks like Figure 2.1.

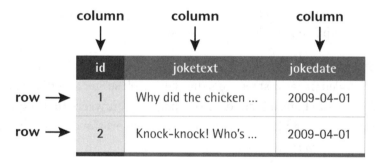

Figure 2.1. A typical database table containing a list of jokes

Notice that, in addition to columns for the joke text (joketext) and the date of the joke (jokedate), I've included a column named id. As a matter of good design, a database table should always provide a means by which we can identify each of its rows uniquely. Since it's possible that a single joke could be entered more than once on the same date, the joketext and jokedate columns can't be relied upon to tell all the jokes apart. The function of the id column, therefore, is to assign a unique number to each joke so that we have an easy way to refer to them and to keep track of which joke is which. We'll take a closer look at database design issues like this in Chapter 5.

So, to review, the table in Figure 2.1 is a three-column table with two rows, or entries. Each row in the table contains three fields, one for each column in the table: the joke's ID, its text, and the date of the joke. With this basic terminology under your belt, you're ready to dive into using MySQL.

Logging On to MySQL

Just as a web server is designed to respond to requests from a client (a web browser), the MySQL database server responds to requests from **client programs**. Later in this book, we'll write our own MySQL client programs in the form of PHP scripts, but for now we can use some of the client programs that come included with the MySQL server.

mysqladmin is an example of a MySQL client program. If you followed the instructions in Chapter 1, after setting up a MySQL server of your own, you used the **mysqladmin** client program to connect to the server, establish a password for the root user, and view basic statistics about the running server.

Another client program that comes with the MySQL server is called **mysql**. This program provides the most basic interface for working with a MySQL server, by establishing a connection to the server and then typing commands one at a time.

The **mysql** program can be found in the same place as **mysqladmin**, so if you followed the instructions in Chapter 1 to add this location to your system path, you should be able to open a Terminal window (or Command Prompt if you're using a Windows system) and type this command to run the **mysql** client program:

```
mysql --version
```

If everything is set up right, this command should output a one-line description of the version of the **mysql** client program that you've installed. Here's what this looks like on my Mac:

```
mysql  Ver 14.14 Distrib 5.1.31, for apple-darwin9.5.0 (i386) using
➡readline 5.1
```

If instead you receive an error message complaining that your computer is unable to recognize the mysql command, you should probably revisit the installation instructions provided in Chapter 1. Once you're able to run the mysqladmin commands in that chapter, the `mysql` command should work too. If you're still stuck, drop by the SitePoint Forums[1] and ask for some help.

Assuming the **mysql** program is running for you, you can now use it to connect to your MySQL server. First, make sure that server is running, then type this command and hit **Enter**:

```
mysql -u root -p
```

The *-u root* and *-p* parameters perform the same function for this program as they did for **mysqladmin** in Chapter 1. *-u root* tells the program you wish to connect to the server using the `root` user account, and *-p* tells it you're going to provide a password.

What you should see next is an `Enter password:` prompt. Enter the root password you chose for yourself in Chapter 1, and hit **Enter**.

If you typed everything correctly, the MySQL client program will introduce itself and dump you on the MySQL command prompt:

```
Welcome to the MySQL monitor.  Commands end with ; or \g.
Your MySQL connection id is 7
Server version: 5.1.31 MySQL Community Server (GPL)

Type 'help;' or '\h' for help. Type '\c' to clear the buffer.

mysql>
```

Let's use a few simple commands to take a look around your MySQL server.

The MySQL server can actually keep track of more than one database. This allows a web host to set up a single MySQL server for use by several of its subscribers, for example. So, your first step after connecting to the server should be to choose a database with which to work. First, let's retrieve a list of databases on the current server.

---

[1] http://www.sitepoint.com/forums/

Connecting to a Remote MySQL Server

The instructions in this chapter assume you're working with a MySQL server running on your own computer. Of course, when it comes time to publish your first PHP-and-MySQL-powered web site, you will need to know how to work with the MySQL server provided by your web host, or by your company's IT department.

Technically, the **mysql** program we're using in this chapter can connect to remote MySQL servers too. You just have to add an additional parameter when running it:

```
mysql -h hostname -u username -p
```

The *-h hostname* parameter (where *hostname* is the host name of the MySQL server to which you want to connect) tells the program to connect to a remote MySQL server instead of one running on the same computer. If you do this, you'll probably also need to specify a username other than `root`, since the administrator responsible for the MySQL server will probably want to keep the `root` password secret for security reasons.

In practice, most remote MySQL servers will block connections from client programs running on untrusted computers like yours. Disallowing this type of connection is a common security measure for MySQL servers used in production.

To work with a remote MySQL server, you might be able to connect to a trusted computer and run the **mysql** program from there, but a far more common approach is to use a program called phpMyAdmin to manage your remote databases. phpMyAdmin is a sophisticated PHP script that lets you work with your MySQL databases using a web-based interface in your browser. phpMyAdmin connects to the remote MySQL server in the same way as the PHP scripts we'll be writing later in this book.

I'll show you how to install and use phpMyAdmin in Chapter 10. For now, let's focus on learning to work with the MySQL server you've installed on your computer.

Type this command (including the semicolon!) and press **Enter**:[2]

```
mysql> SHOW DATABASES;
```

MySQL will show you a list of the databases on the server. If you're working on a brand new server, the list should look like this:

```
+--------------------+
| Database           |
+--------------------+
| information_schema |
| mysql              |
| test               |
+--------------------+
3 rows in set (0.00 sec)
```

The MySQL server uses the first database, named `information_schema`, to keep track of all the other databases on the server. Unless you're doing some very advanced stuff, you'll probably leave this database alone.

The second database, `mysql`, is special too. MySQL uses it to keep track of users, their passwords, and what they're allowed to do. We'll steer clear of this for now, though we'll revisit it in Chapter 10, when we discuss MySQL administration.

The third database, named `test`, is a sample database. You can actually delete this database because I'll show you how to create your own database in a moment.

No test on WampServer

As of this writing, WampServer's initial MySQL database has no `test` database in it. No need to be alarmed though; the developers of WampServer just thought it was as useless as I do, I guess!

Deleting stuff in MySQL is called "dropping" it, and the command for doing so is appropriately named:

```
mysql> DROP DATABASE test;
```

---

[2] As in Chapter 1, the `mysql>` prompt should already be visible on your screen; just type the command that comes after it.

If you type this command and press **Enter**, MySQL will obediently delete the database, displaying "`Query OK`" in confirmation. Notice that there's no confirmation prompt like "Are you sure?". You have to be very careful to type your commands correctly in the **mysql** client program because, as this example shows, you can obliterate your entire database—along with all the information it contains—with a single command!

Before we go any further, let's learn a couple of fundamentals about the MySQL command prompt. As you may have noticed, all commands in MySQL are terminated by a semicolon (`;`). If you forget the semicolon, MySQL will think you're still typing your command, and will let you continue on another line:

```
mysql> SHOW
    -> DATABASES;
```

MySQL shows that it's waiting for you to type more of your command by changing the prompt from `mysql>` to `->`. This handy feature allows you to spread long commands over several lines.

Case Sensitivity in SQL Queries

Most MySQL commands are not case-sensitive, which means you can type SHOW DATABASES, show databases, or ShOw DaTaBaSeS, and it will know what you mean. Database names and table names, however, are case-sensitive when the MySQL server is running on an operating system with a case-sensitive file system (like Linux or Mac OS X, depending on your system configuration).

Also, table, column, and other names must be spelled exactly the same when they're used more than once in the same command.

For consistency, this book will respect the accepted convention of typing database commands in all capitals, and database entities (databases, tables, columns, and so on) in all lowercase.

If you're halfway through a command and realize that you made a mistake early on, you may want to cancel the current command entirely and start over from scratch. To do this, type \c and press **Enter**:

```
mysql> DROP DATABASE\c
mysql>
```

MySQL will ignore the command you had begun to type and will return to the `mysql>` prompt to await another command.

Finally, if at any time you want to exit the MySQL client program, just type `quit` or `exit` (either will work). This is the only command where the semicolon is unnecessary, but you can use one if you want to.

```
mysql> quit
Bye
```

Structured Query Language

The set of commands we'll use to direct MySQL throughout the rest of this book is part of a standard called **Structured Query Language**, or **SQL** (pronounced as either "sequel" or "ess-cue-ell"—take your pick). Commands in SQL are also referred to as **queries**; I'll use these two terms interchangeably.

SQL is the standard language for interacting with most databases, so, even if you move from MySQL to a database like Microsoft SQL Server in the future, you'll find that most of the commands are identical. It's important that you understand the distinction between SQL and MySQL. MySQL is the database server software that you're using. SQL is the language that you use to interact with that database.

Learn SQL in Depth

In this book, I'll teach you the essentials of SQL that every PHP developer needs to know.

If you decide to make a career out of building database driven web sites, you'll find that it pays to know some of the more advanced details of SQL, especially when it comes to making your sites run as quickly and smoothly as possible.

If you'd like to dive deeper into SQL, I highly recommend the book *Simply SQL*[3] by Rudy Limeback (Melbourne: SitePoint, 2008).

---

[3] http://www.sitepoint.com/books/sql1/

Creating a Database

When the time comes to deploy your first database driven web site on the Web, you'll likely find that your web host or IT department has already created a MySQL database for you to use. Since you're in charge of your own MySQL server, however, you'll need to create your own database to use in developing your site.

It's just as easy to create a database as it is to delete one:

```
mysql> CREATE DATABASE ijdb;
```

I chose to name the database ijdb, for Internet Joke Database,[4] because that fits with the example I gave at the beginning of this chapter—a web site that displays a database of jokes. Feel free to give the database any name you like, though.

Now that you have a database, you need to tell MySQL that you want to use it. Again, the command is easy to remember:

```
mysql> USE ijdb;
```

You're now ready to use your database. Since a database is empty until you add some tables to it, our first order of business will be to create a table that will hold your jokes (now might be a good time to think of some!).

Creating a Table

The SQL commands we've encountered so far have been reasonably simple, but as tables are so flexible, it takes a more complicated command to create them. The basic form of the command is as follows:

```
mysql> CREATE TABLE table_name (
    ->    column1Name column1Type column1Details,
    ->    column2Name column2Type column2Details,
    ->    ⋮
    -> ) DEFAULT CHARACTER SET charset;
```

---

[4] With a tip of the hat to the Internet Movie Database. [http://www.imdb.com]

Let's continue with the joke table I showed you in Figure 2.1. You'll recall that it had three columns: id (a number), joketext (the text of the joke), and jokedate (the date on which the joke was entered). This is the command to create that table:

```
mysql> CREATE TABLE joke (
    ->    id INT NOT NULL AUTO_INCREMENT PRIMARY KEY,
    ->    joketext TEXT,
    ->    jokedate DATE NOT NULL
    -> ) DEFAULT CHARACTER SET utf8;
```

Looks scary, huh? Let's break it down:

CREATE TABLE joke (

This first line is fairly simple; it says that we want to create a new table named joke. The opening parenthesis (() marks the beginning of the list of columns in the table.

id INT NOT NULL AUTO_INCREMENT PRIMARY KEY,

This second line says that we want a column called id that will contain an integer (INT), that is, a whole number. The rest of this line deals with special details for the column:

1. First, when creating a row in this table, this column is not allowed to be left blank (NOT NULL).

2. Next, if we omit specifying a particular value for this column when we add a new entry to the table, we want MySQL to automatically pick a value that is one more than the highest value in the table so far (AUTO_INCREMENT).

3. Finally, this column is to act as a unique identifier for the entries in the table, so all values in this column must be unique (PRIMARY KEY).

joketext TEXT,

This third line is super simple; it says that we want a column called joketext, which will contain text (TEXT).

jokedate DATE NOT NULL

This fourth line defines our last column, called jokedate; this will contain a date (DATE), which cannot be left blank (NOT NULL).

```
) DEFAULT CHARACTER SET utf8;
```

The closing parenthesis ()) marks the end of the list of columns in the table.

`DEFAULT CHARACTER SET utf8` tells MySQL that you will be storing UTF-8 encoded text in this table. UTF-8 is the most common encoding used for web content, so you should use it in all your database tables that you intend to use on the Web.

Finally, the semicolon tells the **mysql** client program that you've finished typing your query.

Note that we assigned a specific data type to each column we created. `id` will contain integers, `joketext` will contain text, and `jokedate` will contain dates. MySQL requires you to specify in advance a data type for each column. This helps to keep your data organized, and allows you to compare the values within a column in powerful ways, as we'll see later. For a complete list of supported MySQL data types, see Appendix C.

Now, if you typed the above command correctly, MySQL will respond with "`Query OK`", and your first table will be created. If you made a typing mistake, MySQL will tell you there was a problem with the query you typed, and will try to indicate where it had trouble understanding what you meant.

For such a complicated command, "`Query OK`" is a fairly underwhelming response. Let's have a look at your new table to make sure it was created properly. Type the following command:

```
mysql> SHOW TABLES;
```

The response should look like this:

```
+----------------+
| Tables_in_ijdb |
+----------------+
| joke           |
+----------------+
1 row in set (0.02 sec)
```

This is a list of all the tables in your database (which we named `ijdb` above). The list contains only one table: the `joke` table you just created. So far, everything seems fine. Let's take a closer look at the `joke` table itself using a `DESCRIBE` query:

```
mysql> DESCRIBE joke;
+----------+----------+------+-----+---------+----------------+
| Field    | Type     | Null | Key | Default | Extra          |
+----------+----------+------+-----+---------+----------------+
| id       | int(11)  | NO   | PRI | NULL    | auto_increment |
| joketext | text     | YES  |     | NULL    |                |
| jokedate | date     | NO   |     | NULL    |                |
+----------+----------+------+-----+---------+----------------+
3 rows in set (0.10 sec)
```

As you can see, there are three columns (or fields) in this table, which appear as the three rows in this table of results. The details are a little cryptic, but if you look at them closely, you should be able to figure out what they mean. It's nothing to be too worried about, though. You have better things to do, like adding some jokes to your table!

We need to look at just one more task before you get to that, though: deleting a table. This task is as frighteningly easy as deleting a database. In fact, the command is almost identical. *Don't* run this command with your `joke` table, unless you actually do want to be rid of it!

```
mysql> DROP TABLE tableName;
```

Inserting Data into a Table

Your database is created and your table is built; all that's left is to put some actual jokes into the database. The command that inserts data into a database is called, appropriately enough, `INSERT`. This command can take two basic forms:

```
mysql> INSERT INTO tableName SET
    ->    column1Name = column1Value,
    ->    column2Name = column2Value,
    ->    ⋮
    -> ;
```

```
mysql> INSERT INTO tableName
    ->   (column1Name, column2Name, …)
    ->   VALUES (column1Value, column2Value, …);
```

So, to add a joke to our table, we can use either of these commands:

```
mysql> INSERT INTO joke SET
    -> joketext = "Why did the chicken cross the road? To get to
    ">  the other side!",
    -> jokedate = "2009-04-01";
```

```
mysql> INSERT INTO joke
    -> (joketext, jokedate) VALUES (
    -> "Why did the chicken cross the road? To get to the other
    ">  side!",
    -> "2009-04-01"
    -> );
```

Note that in both forms of the INSERT command, the order in which you list the columns must match the order in which you list the values. Otherwise, the order of the columns is unimportant.

As you typed this query, you'll have noticed that we used double quotes (") to mark where the text of the joke started and ended. A piece of text enclosed in quotes this way is called a **text string**, and this is how you represent most data values in SQL. You'll notice, for instance, that the dates are typed as text strings as well, in the form "YYYY-MM-DD".

If you prefer, you can type text strings surrounded with single quotes (') instead of double quotes:

```
mysql> INSERT INTO joke SET
    -> joketext = 'Why did the chicken cross the road? To get to
    '>  the other side!',
    -> jokedate = '2009-04-01';
```

You might be wondering what happens when the text of a joke itself contains quotes. Well, if the text contains single quotes, the easiest thing to do is surround it with double quotes. Conversely, if the text contains double quotes, surround it with single quotes.

If the text you want to include in your query contains both single *and* double quotes, you'll have to **escape** the conflicting characters within your text string. You escape a character in SQL by adding a backslash (\) immediately before it. This tells MySQL to ignore any "special meaning" this character might have. In the case of single or double quotes, it tells MySQL not to interpret the character as the end of the text string.

To make this as clear as possible, here's an INSERT command for a joke containing both single and double quotes:

```
mysql> INSERT INTO joke
    -> (joketext, jokedate) VALUES (
    -> 'Knock-knock! Who\'s there? Boo! "Boo" who?
    ->  Don\'t cry; it\'s only a joke!',
    -> "2009-04-01");
```

As you can see, I've marked the start and end of the text string for the joke text using single quotes. I've therefore had to escape the three single quotes within the string by putting backslashes before them. MySQL sees these backslashes and knows to treat the single quotes as characters within the string, rather than end-of-string markers.

If you're especially clever, you might now be wondering how to include actual backslashes in SQL text strings. The answer is to type a double-backslash (\\), which MySQL will see and treat as a single backslash in the string of text.

Now that you know how to add entries to a table, let's see how we can view those entries.

Viewing Stored Data

The command we use to view data stored in database tables, SELECT, is the most complicated command in the SQL language. The reason for this complexity is that the chief strength of a database is its flexibility in data retrieval. At this early point in our experience with databases we need only fairly simple lists of results, so we'll just consider the simpler forms of the SELECT command here.

This command will list everything that's stored in the joke table:

```
mysql> SELECT * FROM joke;
```

Read aloud, this command says "select everything from joke." If you try this command, your results will resemble the following:

```
+----+----------------------------------------------------------------
-+------------+
| id | joketext
| jokedate   |
+----+----------------------------------------------------------------
-+------------+
|  1 | Why did the chicken cross the road? To get to the other side!
| 2009-04-01 |
+----+----------------------------------------------------------------
-+------------+
1 row in set (0.00 sec)
```

The results look a little disorganized because the text in the joketext column is so long that the table is too wide to fit on the screen properly. For this reason, you might want to tell MySQL to leave out the joketext column. The command for doing this is as follows:

```
mysql> SELECT id, jokedate FROM joke;
```

This time, instead of telling it to "select everything," we told it precisely which columns we wanted to see. The results look like this:

```
+----+------------+
| id | jokedate   |
+----+------------+
|  1 | 2009-04-01 |
+----+------------+
1 row in set (0.00 sec)
```

That's okay, but we'd like to see at least *some* of the joke text? As well as being able to name specific columns that we want the SELECT command to show us, we can use functions to modify each column's display. One function, called LEFT, lets us tell MySQL to display a column's contents up to a specified maximum number of characters. For example, let's say we wanted to see only the first 20 characters of the joketext column. Here's the command we'd use:

```
mysql> SELECT id, LEFT(joketext, 20), jokedate FROM joke;
+----+----------------------+------------+
| id | LEFT(joketext, 20)   | jokedate   |
+----+----------------------+------------+
|  1 | Why did the chicken  | 2009-04-01 |
+----+----------------------+------------+
1 row in set (0.00 sec)
```

See how that worked? Another useful function is COUNT, which lets us count the number of results returned. If, for example, you wanted to find out how many jokes were stored in your table, you could use the following command:

```
mysql> SELECT COUNT(*) FROM joke;
+----------+
| COUNT(*) |
+----------+
|        1 |
+----------+
1 row in set (0.02 sec)
```

As you can see, you have just one joke in your table.

So far, all the examples have fetched all the entries in the table; however, you can limit your results to include only those database entries that have the specific attributes you want. You set these restrictions by adding what's called a **WHERE clause** to the SELECT command. Consider this example:

```
mysql> SELECT COUNT(*) FROM joke WHERE jokedate >= "2009-01-01";
```

This query will count the number of jokes that have dates greater than or equal to January 1, 2009. In the case of dates, "greater than or equal to" means "on or after." Another variation on this theme lets you search for entries that contain a certain piece of text. Check out this query:

```
mysql> SELECT joketext FROM joke WHERE joketext LIKE "%chicken%";
```

This query displays the full text of all jokes that contain the text "chicken" in their joketext column. The LIKE keyword tells MySQL that the named column must match the given pattern. In this case, the pattern we've used is "%chicken%". The

% signs indicate that the text "chicken" may be preceded and/or followed by any string of text.

Additional conditions may also be combined in the WHERE clause to further restrict results. For example, to display knock-knock jokes from April 2009 only, you could use the following query:

```
mysql> SELECT joketext FROM joke WHERE
    -> joketext LIKE "%knock%" AND
    -> jokedate >= "2009-04-01" AND
    -> jokedate < "2009-05-01";
```

Enter a few more jokes into the table and experiment with SELECT queries. A good familiarity with the SELECT command will come in handy later in this book.

You can do a lot with the SELECT command. We'll look at some of its more advanced features later, when we need them.

Modifying Stored Data

Having entered your data into a database table, you might like to change it. Whether you want to correct a spelling mistake, or change the date attached to a joke, such alterations are made using the UPDATE command. This command contains elements of the SELECT and INSERT commands, since the command both picks out entries for modification and sets column values. The general form of the UPDATE command is as follows:

```
mysql> UPDATE tableName SET
    ->   colName = newValue, …
    -> WHERE conditions;
```

So, for example, if we wanted to change the date on the joke we entered above, we'd use the following command:

```
mysql> UPDATE joke SET jokedate = "2010-04-01" WHERE id = "1";
```

Here's where that id column comes in handy: it enables you to single out a joke for changes easily. The WHERE clause used here works just as it did in the SELECT command. This next command, for example, changes the date of all entries that contain the word "chicken":

```
mysql> UPDATE joke SET jokedate = "2010-04-01"
    -> WHERE joketext LIKE "%chicken%";
```

Deleting Stored Data

Deleting entries in SQL is dangerously easy, which, if you've yet to notice, is a recurring theme. Here's the command syntax:

```
mysql> DELETE FROM tableName WHERE conditions;
```

To delete all chicken jokes from your table, you'd use the following query:

```
mysql> DELETE FROM joke WHERE joketext LIKE "%chicken%";
```

 ### Careful With That Enter Key!

Believe it or not, the WHERE clause in the DELETE command is actually optional.

Consequently, you should be very careful when typing this command! If you leave the WHERE clause out, the DELETE command will then apply to *all entries in the table*.

This command will empty the joke table in one fell swoop:

```
mysql> DELETE FROM joke;
```

Scary, huh?

Let PHP Do the Typing

There's a lot more to the MySQL database server software and SQL than the handful of basic commands I've presented here, but these commands are by far the most commonly used.

At this stage, you might be thinking that databases seem a little cumbersome. SQL can be fairly tricky to type—its commands tend to be rather long and verbose compared to other computer languages. You're probably already dreading the thought of typing in a complete library of jokes in the form of `INSERT` commands.

Don't sweat it! As we proceed through this book, you'll be surprised at how few SQL queries you actually type by hand. Generally, you'll be writing PHP scripts that type your SQL for you. If you want to be able to insert a bunch of jokes into your database, for example, you'll typically create a PHP script for adding jokes that includes the necessary `INSERT` query, with a placeholder for the joke text. You can then run that PHP script whenever you have jokes to add. The PHP script prompts you to enter your joke, then issues the appropriate `INSERT` query to your MySQL server.

For now, however, it's important for you to gain a good feel for typing SQL by hand. It will give you a strong sense of the inner workings of MySQL databases, and will make you appreciate the work that PHP will save you all the more!

To date, we've only worked with a single table, but to realize the true power of a relational database, you'll also need to learn how to use multiple tables together to represent potentially complex relationships between the items stored in your database. I'll cover all this and more in Chapter 5, in which I'll discuss database design principles and show off some more advanced examples.

For now, though, we've accomplished our objective, and you can comfortably interact with MySQL using the **mysql** client program. In Chapter 3, the fun continues as we delve into the PHP language, and use it to create several dynamically-generated web pages.

If you like, you can practice with MySQL a little before you move on by creating a decent-sized joke table. This knowledge will come in handy in Chapter 4.

Introducing PHP

PHP is a **server-side language**. This concept may be a little difficult to grasp, especially if you're used to designing pages using only client-side languages like HTML, CSS, and JavaScript.

A server-side language is similar to JavaScript in that it allows you to embed little programs (scripts) into the HTML code of a web page. When executed, these programs give you greater control over what appears in the browser window than HTML alone can provide. The key difference between JavaScript and PHP is the stage of loading the web page at which these embedded programs are executed.

Client-side languages like JavaScript are read and executed by the web browser, after downloading the web page (embedded programs and all) from the web server. In contrast, server-side languages like PHP are run by the web *server*, before sending the web page to the browser. Whereas client-side languages give you control over how a page behaves once it's displayed by the browser, server-side languages let you generate customized pages on the fly before they're even sent to the browser.

Once the web server has executed the PHP code embedded in a web page, the results of that code's execution take the place of the PHP code in the page. When the browser receives the page, all it sees is standard HTML code, hence the name: server-side language. Let's look back at the **today.php** example presented in Chapter 1:

```
chapter3/today.php
```
```
<!DOCTYPE html PUBLIC "-//W3C//DTD XHTML 1.0 Strict//EN"
    "http://www.w3.org/TR/xhtml1/DTD/xhtml1-strict.dtd">
<html xmlns="http://www.w3.org/1999/xhtml" xml:lang="en" lang="en">
  <head>
    <title>Today&rsquo;s Date</title>
    <meta http-equiv="content-type"
        content="text/html; charset=utf-8"/>
  </head>
  <body>
    <p>Today&rsquo;s date (according to this web server) is
    <?php

    echo date('l, F dS Y.');

    ?>
    </p>
  </body>
</html>
```

Most of this is plain HTML; however, the line between <?php and ?> is PHP code. <?php marks the start of an embedded PHP script and ?> marks the end of such a script. The web server is asked to interpret everything between these two delimiters, and to convert it to regular HTML code before it sends the web page to the requesting browser. The browser is presented with the following:

```
<!DOCTYPE html PUBLIC "-//W3C//DTD XHTML 1.0 Strict//EN"
    "http://www.w3.org/TR/xhtml1/DTD/xhtml1-strict.dtd">
<html xmlns="http://www.w3.org/1999/xhtml" xml:lang="en" lang="en">
  <head>
    <title>Today&rsquo;s Date</title>
    <meta http-equiv="content-type"
        content="text/html; charset=utf-8"/>
  </head>
  <body>
    <p>Today&rsquo;s Date (according to this web server) is
    Wednesday, April 1st 2009.    </p>
  </body>
</html>
```

Notice that all signs of the PHP code have disappeared. In its place, the output of the script has appeared, and it looks just like standard HTML. This example demonstrates several advantages of server-side scripting:

No browser compatibility issues

PHP scripts are interpreted by the web server alone, so there's no need to worry about whether the language you're using is supported by the visitor's browser.

Access to server-side resources

In the above example, we placed the date, according to the web server, into the web page. If we had inserted the date using JavaScript, we'd only be able to display the date according to the computer on which the web browser was running. Granted, there are more impressive examples of the exploitation of server-side resources; a better example might be inserting content pulled out of a MySQL database (*hint, hint* …).

Reduced load on the client

JavaScript can delay the display of a web page on slower computers significantly, as the browser must run the script before it can display the web page. With server-side code, this burden is passed to the web server machine, which you can make as beefy as your application requires.

Basic Syntax and Statements

PHP syntax will be very familiar to anyone with an understanding of C, C++, C#, Java, JavaScript, Perl, or any other C-derived language. If you're unfamiliar with any of these languages, or if you're new to programming in general, there's no need to worry about it!

A PHP script consists of a series of commands, or **statements**. Each statement is an instruction that must be followed by the web server before it can proceed to the next. PHP statements, like those in the above-mentioned languages, are always terminated by a semicolon (;).

This is a typical PHP statement:

```
echo 'This is a <strong>test</strong>!';
```

This is an echo statement, which is used to generate content (usually HTML code) to be sent to the browser. An echo statement simply takes the text it's given, and inserts it into the page's HTML code at the position of the PHP script that contains it.

In this case, we have supplied a string of text to be output: 'This is a <strong>test</strong>!'. Notice that the string of text contains HTML tags (<strong> and </strong>), which is perfectly acceptable. So, if we take this statement and put it into a complete web page, here's the resulting code:

chapter3/echo.php

```
<!DOCTYPE html PUBLIC "-//W3C//DTD XHTML 1.0 Strict//EN"
    "http://www.w3.org/TR/xhtml1/DTD/xhtml1-strict.dtd">
<html xmlns="http://www.w3.org/1999/xhtml" xml:lang="en" lang="en">
  <head>
    <title>Simple PHP Example</title>
    <meta http-equiv="content-type"
        content="text/html; charset=utf-8"/>
  </head>
  <body>
    <p><?php echo 'This is a <strong>test</strong>!'; ?></p>
  </body>
</html>
```

If you place this file on your web server, a browser that requests the page will receive this:

```
<!DOCTYPE html PUBLIC "-//W3C//DTD XHTML 1.0 Strict//EN"
    "http://www.w3.org/TR/xhtml1/DTD/xhtml1-strict.dtd">
<html xmlns="http://www.w3.org/1999/xhtml" xml:lang="en" lang="en">
  <head>
    <title>Simple PHP Example</title>
    <meta http-equiv="content-type"
        content="text/html; charset=utf-8"/>
  </head>
  <body>
    <p>This is a <strong>test</strong>!</p>
  </body>
</html>
```

The **today.php** example we looked at earlier contained a slightly more complex `echo` statement:

```
echo date('l, F dS Y.');
```

Instead of giving `echo` a simple string of text to output, this statement invokes a **built-in function** called `date` and passes *it* a string of text: `'l, F dS Y.'`. You can think of built-in functions as tasks that PHP knows how to do without your needing to spell out the details. PHP has many built-in functions that let you do everything from sending email to working with information stored in various types of databases.

When you invoke a function in PHP, you're said to be **calling** that function. Most functions **return** a value when they're called; PHP then replaces the function call with that value when it executes the statement. In this case, our `echo` statement contains a call to the `date` function, which returns the current date as a string of text (the format of which is specified by the text string in the function call). The `echo` statement therefore outputs the value returned by the function call.

You may wonder why we need to surround the string of text with both parentheses (`()`) and single quotes (`' '`). As in SQL, quotes are used in PHP to mark the beginning and end of strings of text, so it makes sense for them to be there. The parentheses serve two purposes. First, they indicate that `date` is a function that you want to call. Second, they mark the beginning and end of a list of **parameters** (or **arguments**) that you wish to provide, in order to tell the function what to do. In the case of the `date` function, you need to provide a string of text that describes the format in which you want the date to appear.[1] Later on, we'll look at functions that take more than one parameter, and we'll separate those parameters with commas. We'll also consider functions that take no parameters at all. These functions will still need the parentheses, though it's unnecessary to type anything between them.

---

[1] A full reference is available in the online documentation for the `date` function [http://www.php.net/date/].

Variables, Operators, and Comments

Variables in PHP are identical to variables in most other programming languages. For the uninitiated, a **variable** can be thought of as a name that's given to an imaginary box into which any **literal value** may be placed. The following statement creates a variable called $testvariable (all variable names in PHP begin with a dollar sign) and assigns it a literal value of 3:

```
$testvariable = 3;
```

PHP is a **loosely typed** language. This means that a single variable may contain any type of data, be it a number, a string of text, or some other kind of value, and may change types over its lifetime. So the following statement, if you were to type it after the statement above, assigns a new value to the existing $testvariable. In the process, the variable changes type: where it used to contain a number, it now contains a string of text:

```
$testvariable = 'Three';
```

The equals sign we used in the last two statements is called the **assignment operator**, as it's used to assign values to variables. Other operators may be used to perform various mathematical operations on values:

```
$testvariable = 1 + 1;  // Assigns a value of 2
$testvariable = 1 - 1;  // Assigns a value of 0
$testvariable = 2 * 2;  // Assigns a value of 4
$testvariable = 2 / 2;  // Assigns a value of 1
```

From the above examples, you can probably tell that + is the **addition operator**, - is the **subtraction operator**, * is the **multiplication operator**, and / is the **division operator**. These are all called **arithmetic operators**, because they perform arithmetic on numbers.

Each of the lines above ends with a **comment**. Comments are a way to describe what your code is doing. They insert explanatory text into your code—text that the PHP interpreter will ignore. Comments begin with // and they finish at the end of the same line. If you need a comment to span several lines, you can instead start your comment with /*, and end it with */. The PHP interpreter will ignore everything between these two delimiters. I'll use comments throughout the rest of this book to help explain some of the code I present.

Returning to the operators, there's another one that sticks strings of text together, called the **string concatenation operator**:

```
$testvariable = 'Hi ' . 'there!';   // Assigns a value of 'Hi there!'
```

Variables may be used almost anywhere that you use a literal value. Consider this series of statements:

```
$var1 = 'PHP';             // Assigns a value of 'PHP' to $var1
$var2 = 5;                 // Assigns a value of 5 to $var2
$var3 = $var2 + 1;         // Assigns a value of 6 to $var3
$var2 = $var1;             // Assigns a value of 'PHP' to $var2
echo $var1;                // Outputs 'PHP'
echo $var2;                // Outputs 'PHP'
echo $var3;                // Outputs '6'
echo $var1 . ' rules!';    // Outputs 'PHP rules!'
echo "$var1 rules!";       // Outputs 'PHP rules!'
echo '$var1 rules!';       // Outputs '$var1 rules!'
```

Notice the last two lines in particular. You can include the name of a variable right inside a text string, and have the value inserted in its place if you surround the string with double quotes instead of single quotes. This process of converting variable names to their values is known as **variable interpolation**. However, as the last line demonstrates, a string surrounded with single quotes will not interpolate the variable names it contains.

Arrays

An **array** is a special kind of variable that contains multiple values. If you think of a variable as a box that contains a value, then an array can be thought of as a box with compartments, where each compartment is able to store an individual value.

The simplest way to create an array in PHP is to use the built-in `array` function:

```
$myarray = array('one', 2, '3');
```

This code creates an array called $myarray that contains three values: 'one', 2, and '3'. Just like an ordinary variable, each space in an array can contain any type of value. In this case, the first and third spaces contain strings, while the second contains a number.

To access a value stored in an array, you need to know its **index**. Typically, arrays use numbers, starting with zero, as indices to point to the values they contain. That is, the first value (or element) of an array has index 0, the second has index 1, the third has index 2, and so on. In general, therefore, the index of the nth element of an array is $n-1$. Once you know the index of the value you're interested in, you can retrieve that value by placing that index in square brackets after the array variable name:

```
echo $myarray[0];       // Outputs 'one'
echo $myarray[1];       // Outputs '2'
echo $myarray[2];       // Outputs '3'
```

Each value stored in an array is called an **element** of that array. You can use an index in square brackets to add new elements, or assign new values to existing array elements:

```
$myarray[1] = 'two';    // Assign a new value
$myarray[3] = 'four';   // Create a new element
```

You can add elements to the end of an array using the assignment operator as usual, but leaving empty the square brackets that follow the variable name:

```
$myarray[] = 'the fifth element';
echo $myarray[4];       // Outputs 'the fifth element'
```

However, numbers are only the most common choice for array indices; there's another possibility. You can also use strings as indices to create what's called an **associative array**. This type of array is called associative because it associates values with meaningful indices. In this example, we associate a date (in the form of a string) with each of three names:

```
$birthdays['Kevin'] = '1978-04-12';
$birthdays['Stephanie'] = '1980-05-16';
$birthdays['David'] = '1983-09-09';
```

The `array` function also lets you create associative arrays, if you prefer that method. Here's how we'd use it to create the `$birthdays` array:

```
$birthdays = array('Kevin' => '1978-04-12',
    'Stephanie' => '1980-05-16', 'David' => '1983-09-09');
```

Now, if we want to know Kevin's birthday, we look it up using the name as the index:

```
echo 'My birthday is: ' . $birthdays['Kevin'];
```

This type of array is especially important when it comes to user interaction in PHP, as we'll see in the next section. I'll demonstrate other uses of arrays throughout this book.

User Interaction and Forms

For most database driven web sites these days, you need to do more that just dynamically generate pages based on database data; you must also provide some degree of interactivity, even if it's just a search box.

Veterans of JavaScript tend to think of interactivity in terms of event handlers, which let you react directly to the actions of the user—for example, the movement of the cursor over a link on the page. Server-side scripting languages such as PHP have a more limited scope when it comes to support for user interaction. As PHP code is only activated when a request is made to the server, user interaction can occur only in a back-and-forth fashion: the user sends requests to the server, and the server replies with dynamically generated pages.[2]

The key to creating interactivity with PHP is to understand the techniques we can use to send information about a user's interaction along with a request for a new web page. As it turns out, PHP makes this fairly easy.

---

[2] To some extent, the rise of Ajax techniques in the JavaScript world over the past few years has changed this. It's now possible for JavaScript code, responding to a user action such as mouse movement, to send a request to the web server, invoking a PHP script. For the purposes of this book, however, we'll stick to non-Ajax applications. If you'd like to learn how to use PHP with Ajax, check out *Build Your Own AJAX Web Applications* [http://www.sitepoint.com/books/ajax1/] by Matthew Eernisse (Melbourne: SitePoint, 2006).

The simplest method we can use to send information along with a page request is to use the **URL query string**. If you've ever seen a URL in which a question mark followed the file name, you've witnessed this technique in use. For example, if you search for "SitePoint" on Google, it will take you to the following URL to see the search results:

```
http://www.google.com/search?hl=en&q=SitePoint&btnG=Google+Search&
➥meta=
```

See the question mark in the URL? See how the text that follows the question mark contains things like your search query (`SitePoint`) and the name of the button you clicked (`Google+Search`)? That information is being sent along with the request for http://www.google.com/search.

Let's code up an easy example of our own. Create a regular HTML file called **welcome1.html** (no **.php** file name extension is required, since there will be no PHP code in this file) and insert this link:

chapter3/welcome1.html *(excerpt)*

```
<a href="welcome1.php?name=Kevin">Hi, I&rsquo;m Kevin!</a>
```

This is a link to a file called **welcome1.php**, but as well as linking to the file, you're also passing a variable along with the page request. The variable is passed as part of the query string, which is the portion of the URL that follows the question mark. The variable is called `name` and its value is `Kevin`. To restate, you have created a link that loads **welcome1.php**, and informs the PHP code contained in that file that `name` equals `Kevin`.

To really understand the effect of this link, we need to look at **welcome1.php**. Create it as a new HTML file, but, this time, note the **.php** file name extension—this tells the web server that it can expect to interpret some PHP code in the file. In the `<body>` of this new web page, type the following:

chapter3/welcome1.php *(excerpt)*

```php
<?php
$name = $_GET['name'];
echo 'Welcome to our web site, ' . $name . '!';
?>
```

Now, put these two files (**welcome1.html** and **welcome1.php**) onto your web server, and load the first file in your browser (the URL should be similar to http://localhost/welcome1.html, or http://localhost:8080/welcome1.html if your web server is running on a port other than 80). Click the link in that first page to request the PHP script. You should see that the resulting page says "Welcome to our web site, Kevin!", as shown in Figure 3.1.

Figure 3.1. Greet users with a personalized welcome message

Let's take a closer look at the code that made this possible. The most important line is this one:

```
chapter3/welcome1.php (excerpt)

$name = $_GET['name'];
```

If you were paying close attention in the section called "Arrays", you'll recognize what this line does. It assigns to a new variable called $name the value stored in the 'name' element of the array called $_GET. But where does the $_GET array come from?

It turns out that $_GET is one of a number of variables that PHP automatically creates when it receives a request from a browser. PHP creates $_GET as an array variable that contains any values passed in the query string. $_GET is an associative array, so the value of the name variable passed in the query string can be accessed as $_GET['name']. Your **welcome1.php** script assigns this value to an ordinary PHP variable ($name), then displays it as part of a text string using an echo statement:

chapter3/welcome1.php *(excerpt)*

```
echo 'Welcome to our web site, ' . $name . '!';
```

The value of the $name variable is inserted into the output string using the string concatenation operator (.) that we looked at in the section called "Variables, Operators, and Comments".

But look out! There is a **security hole** lurking in this code! Although PHP is an easy programming language to learn, it turns out it's also especially easy to introduce security issues into web sites using PHP if you're unaware of what precautions to take. Before we go any further with the language, I want to make sure you're able to spot and fix this particular security issue, since it's probably the most common kind of security issue on the Web today.

The security issue here stems from the fact that the **welcome1.php** script is generating a page containing content that is under the control of the user—in this case, the $name variable. Although the $name variable will normally receive its value from the URL query string in the link on the **welcome1.html** page, a malicious user could edit the URL to send a different value for the name variable.

To see how this would work, click the link in **welcome1.html** again. When you see the resulting page (with the welcome message containing the name "Kevin"), take a look at the URL in the address bar of your browser. It should look similar to this:

```
http://localhost/welcome1.php?name=Kevin
```

Edit the URL to insert a <b> tag before the name, and a </b> tag following the name, like this:

```
http://localhost/welcome1.php?name=<b>Kevin</b>
```

Hit **Enter** to load this new URL, and notice that the name in the page is now bold, as shown in Figure 3.2.

Figure 3.2. Easy exploitation will only embolden attackers!

See what's happening here? The user can type any HTML code into the URL, and your PHP script includes it in the code of the generated page without question. If the code is as innocuous as a <b> tag there's no problem, but a malicious user could include sophisticated JavaScript code that performed malicious actions like steal the user's password. All the attacker would have to do, then, would be to publish the modified link on some other site under the attacker's control, and then entice one of your users to click it. The attacker could even embed the link in an email and send it to your users. If one of your users clicked the link, the attacker's code would be included in your page and the trap would be sprung!

I hate to scare you with this talk of malicious hackers attacking your users by turning your own PHP code against you, particularly when you're only just learning the language. The fact is, however, that PHP's biggest weakness as a language is how easy it is to introduce security issues like this. Some might say that most of the energy you spend learning to write PHP to a professional standard is spent on avoiding security issues. The sooner you're exposed to these issues, however, the sooner you become accustomed to avoiding them, and the less of a stumbling block they'll be for you going forward.

So, how can we generate a page containing the user's name without opening it up to abuse by attackers? The solution is to treat the value supplied for the $name variable as plain text to be displayed on your page, rather than as HTML to be included in the page's code. This is a subtle distinction, so let me show you what I mean.

Copy your **welcome1.html** file and rename it to **welcome2.html**. Edit the link it contains so that it points to **welcome2.php** instead of **welcome1.php**:

chapter3/welcome2.html *(excerpt)*

```
<a href="welcome2.php?name=Kevin">Hi, I&rsquo;m Kevin!</a>
```

Copy your **welcome1.php** file and rename it to **welcome2.php**. Edit the PHP code it contains so that it looks like this:

chapter3/welcome2.php *(excerpt)*

```php
<?php
$name = $_GET['name'];
echo 'Welcome to our web site, ' .
    htmlspecialchars($name, ENT_QUOTES, 'UTF-8') . '!';
?>
```

There's a lot going on in this code, so let me break it down for you. The first line is the same as it was previously, assigning to $name the value of the 'name' element from the $_GET array. The echo statement that follows it is drastically different, though. Whereas previously, we simply dumped the $name variable, naked, into the echo statement, this version of the code uses the built-in PHP function htmlspecialchars to perform a critical conversion.

Remember, the security hole comes from the fact that, in **welcome1.php**, HTML code in the $name variable is dumped directly into the code of the generated page, and can therefore do anything that HTML code can do. What htmlspecialchars does is convert "special HTML characters" like "<" and ">" into HTML character entities like < and >, which prevents them from being interpreted as HTML code by the browser. I'll demonstrate this for you in a moment.

First, let's take a closer look at this new code. The call to the htmlspecialchars function is the first example in this book of a PHP function that takes more than one parameter. Here's the function call all by itself:

```php
htmlspecialchars($name, ENT_QUOTES, 'UTF-8')
```

The first parameter is the $name variable (the text to be converted). The second parameter is the PHP constant[3] ENT_QUOTES, which tells htmlspecialchars to convert single and double quotes in addition to other special characters. The third parameter is the string 'UTF-8', which tells PHP what character encoding to use to interpret the text you give it.

The Perks and Pitfalls of UTF-8 with PHP

You may have noticed that all of the example HTML pages in this book contain the following <meta> tag near the top:

```
<meta http-equiv="content-type"
    content="text/html; charset=utf-8"/>
```

This tag tells the browser that receives this page that the HTML code of the page is encoded as UTF-8 text.[4]

In a few pages, we'll reach the section on building HTML forms. By encoding your pages as UTF-8, your users can submit text containing thousands of foreign characters that your site would otherwise be unable to handle.

Unfortunately, many of PHP's built-in functions, such as htmlspecialchars, assume you're using the much simpler ISO-8859-1 character encoding by default. Therefore, you need to let them know you're using UTF-8 when you use these functions.

If you can, you should also tell your text editor to save your HTML and PHP files as UTF-8 encoded text, but this is only required if you want to type advanced characters (like curly quotes or dashes) or foreign characters (like "é") into your HTML or PHP code. The code in this book plays it safe and uses HTML character entities (for example, ’ for a curly right quote), which will work regardless.

---

[3] A PHP constant is like a variable whose value you're unable to change. Unlike variables, constants don't start with a dollar sign. PHP comes with a number of built-in constants like ENT_QUOTES that are used to control built-in functions like htmlspecialchars.

[4] UTF-8 is one of many standards for representing text as a series of ones and zeros in computer memory, called character encodings. If you're curious to learn all about character encodings, check out *The Definitive Guide to Web Character Encoding* [http://www.sitepoint.com/article/guide-web-character-encoding/].

Open up **welcome2.html** in your browser and click the link that now points to **welcome2.php**. Once again, you'll see the welcome message "Welcome to our web site, Kevin!". As you did before, modify the URL to include `<b>` and `</b>` tags surrounding the name:

```
http://localhost/welcome2.php?name=<b>Kevin</b>
```

This time, when you hit **Enter**, instead of the name turning bold in the page, you should see the actual text that you typed, as shown in Figure 3.3.

Figure 3.3. It sure is ugly, but it's secure!

If you view the source of the page, you can confirm that the `htmlspecialchars` function did its job and converted the "<" and ">" characters present in the provided name into the `&lt;` and `&gt;` HTML character entities, respectively. This prevents malicious users from injecting unwanted code into your site. If they try anything like that, the code is harmlessly displayed as plain text on the page.

We'll make extensive use of the `htmlspecialchars` function throughout this book to guard against this sort of security hole. No need to worry too much if you're having trouble grasping the details of how to use it for now. Before long, you'll find its use becomes second nature. For now, let's look at some more advanced ways of passing values to PHP scripts when we request them.

Passing a single variable in the query string was nice, but it turns out you can pass *more* than one value if you want to! Let's look at a slightly more complex version of the previous example. Save a copy of your **welcome2.html** file as **welcome3.html**, and change the link to point to **welcome3.php** with a query string as follows:

chapter3/welcome3.html *(excerpt)*

```html
<a href="welcome3.php?firstname=Kevin&amp;lastname=Yank">Hi,
  I&rsquo;m Kevin Yank!</a>
```

This time, our link passes two variables: `firstname` and `lastname`. The variables are separated in the query string by an ampersand (&, which must be written as & in HTML). You can pass even more variables by separating each *name=value* pair from the next with an ampersand.

As before, we can use the two variable values in our **welcome3.php** file:

chapter3/welcome3.php *(excerpt)*

```php
<?php
$firstname = $_GET['firstname'];
$lastname = $_GET['lastname'];
echo 'Welcome to our web site, ' .
    htmlspecialchars($firstname, ENT_QUOTES, 'UTF-8') . ' ' .
    htmlspecialchars($lastname, ENT_QUOTES, 'UTF-8') . '!';
?>
```

The `echo` statement is becoming quite sizable now, but it should still make sense to you. Using a series of string concatenations (`.`), it outputs "Welcome to our web site, " followed by the value of `$firstname` (made safe for display using `htmlspecialchars`), a space, the value of `$lastname` (again, treated with `htmlspecialchars`), and finally an exclamation mark.

The result is shown in Figure 3.4.

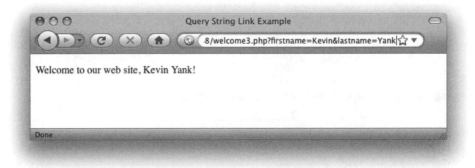

Figure 3.4. Create an even more personalized welcome message

This is all well and good, but we still have yet to achieve our goal of true user inter-action, where the user can enter arbitrary information and have it processed by PHP. To continue with our example of a personalized welcome message, we'd like to invite the user to type his or her name and have it appear in the resulting page. To enable the user to type in a value, we'll need to use a HTML form.

Create a new HTML file named **welcome4.html** and type in this HTML code to create the form:

chapter3/welcome4.html *(excerpt)*

```
<form action="welcome4.php" method="get">
  <div><label for="firstname">First name:
    <input type="text" name="firstname" id="firstname"/></label>
  </div>
  <div><label for="lastname">Last name:
    <input type="text" name="lastname" id="lastname"/></label></div>
  <div><input type="submit" value="GO"/></div>
</form>
```

 Self-closing Tags

The slashes that appear in some of these tags (such as `<input …/>`) are no cause for alarm. The XHTML standard for coding web pages calls for slashes to be used in any tag without a closing tag, which includes `<input/>` and `<meta/>` tags, among others.

Many developers prefer to code to the HTML standard instead of adopting XHTML and, in fact, this is a matter of some debate within web development circles. The upcoming HTML 5 standard leaves the choice up to the developer, so neither approach is strictly "more correct" than the other.

If you're curious about the factors to consider when making this decision for yourself, check out the relevant page of the SitePoint HTML Reference.[5]

The form this code produces is shown in Figure 3.5.[6]

---

[5] http://reference.sitepoint.com/html/html-vs-xhtml

[6] This form is quite plain-looking, I'll grant you. Some judicious application of CSS would make this—and all the other pages in this book—look more attractive. Since this is a book about PHP and MySQL, however, I've stuck with the plain look. Check out SitePoint books like *The Art & Science of CSS*

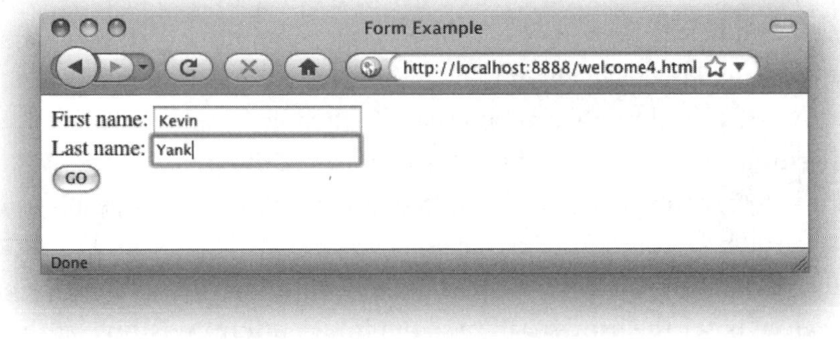

Figure 3.5. Make your own welcome message

Also make a copy of **welcome3.php** named **welcome4.php.** There's nothing that needs changing in this file.

This form has the exact same effect as the second link we looked at (with `first-name=Kevin&amp;lastname=Yank` in the query string), except that you can now enter whatever names you like. When you click the submit button (which is labeled **GO**), the browser will load **welcome4.php** and add the variables and their values to the query string for you automatically. It retrieves the names of the variables from the `name` attributes of the `<input type="text" />` tags, and obtains the values from the text the user types into the text fields.

Apostrophes in Form Fields

If you are burdened with the swollen ego of most programmers (myself included), you probably took this opportunity to type your *own* name into this form. Who can blame you?

If your last name happens to include an apostrophe (for example, Molly O'Reilly), the welcome message you saw may have included a stray backslash before the apostrophe (that is, "Welcome to our web site, Molly O\'Reilly!").

This bothersome backslash is due to a PHP security feature called **magic quotes**, which we'll learn about in Chapter 4. Until then, please bear with me.

[http://www.sitepoint.com/books/cssdesign1/] (Melbourne: SitePoint, 2007) for advice on styling your forms with CSS.

The `method` attribute of the `<form>` tag is used to tell the browser how to send the variables and their values along with the request. A value of `get` (as used in **welcome4.html** above) causes them to be passed in the query string (and appear in PHP's `$_GET` array), but there is an alternative. It can be undesirable—or even technically unfeasible—to have the values appear in the query string. What if we included a `<textarea>` tag in the form, to let the user enter a large amount of text? A URL whose query string contained several paragraphs of text would be ridiculously long, and would possibly exceed the maximum length for a URL in today's browsers. The alternative is for the browser to pass the information invisibly, behind the scenes.

Make a copy of **welcome4.html** and name it **welcome5.html**. The code for the form in this new page is exactly the same, but where we set the form `method` to `get` in the last example, here we set it to `post`. Of course, we've also set the `action` attribute to point at `welcome5.php`:

chapter3/welcome5.html *(excerpt)*

```
<form action="welcome5.php" method="post">
  <div><label for="firstname">First name:
    <input type="text" name="firstname" id="firstname"/></label>
  </div>
  <div><label for="lastname">Last name:
    <input type="text" name="lastname" id="lastname"/></label></div>
  <div><input type="submit" value="GO"/></div>
</form>
```

This new value for the `method` attribute instructs the browser to send the form variables invisibly, as part of the page request, rather than embedding them in the query string of the URL.

Again, make a copy of **welcome4.php** and name it **welcome5.php**.

As we're no longer sending the variables as part of the query string, they stop appearing in PHP's `$_GET` array. Instead, they're placed in another array reserved especially for "posted" form variables: `$_POST`. We must therefore modify **welcome5.php** to retrieve the values from this new array:

```
chapter3/welcome5.php (excerpt)
<?php
$firstname = $_POST['firstname'];
$lastname = $_POST['lastname'];
echo 'Welcome to our web site, ' .
    htmlspecialchars($firstname, ENT_QUOTES, 'UTF-8') . ' ' .
    htmlspecialchars($lastname, ENT_QUOTES, 'UTF-8') . '!';
?>
```

Figure 3.6 shows what the resulting page looks like once this new form is submitted.

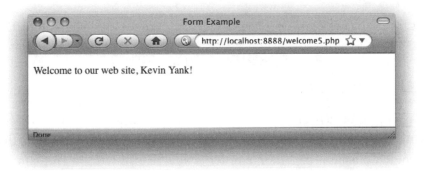

Figure 3.6. This personalized welcome is achieved without a query string

The form is functionally identical to the previous one; the only difference is that the URL of the page that's loaded when the user clicks the **GO** button will be without a query string. On the one hand, this lets you include large values, or sensitive values (like passwords), in the data that's submitted by the form, without their appearing in the query string. On the other hand, if the user bookmarks the page that results from the form's submission, that bookmark will be useless, as it lacks the submitted values. This, incidentally, is the main reason why search engines use the query string to submit search terms. If you bookmark a search results page on Google, you can use that bookmark to perform the same search again later, because the search terms are contained in the URL.

Sometimes, you want access to a variable without having to worry about whether it was sent as part of the query string or a form post. In cases like these, the special $_REQUEST array comes in handy. It contains all the variables that appear in both $_GET and $_POST. With this variable, we can modify our form processing script one more time so that it can receive the first and last names of the user from either source:

chapter3/welcome6.php *(excerpt)*

```php
<?php
$firstname = $_REQUEST['firstname'];
$lastname = $_REQUEST['lastname'];
echo 'Welcome to our web site, ' .
    htmlspecialchars($firstname, ENT_QUOTES, 'UTF-8') . ' ' .
    htmlspecialchars($lastname, ENT_QUOTES, 'UTF-8') . '!';
?>
```

That covers the basics of using forms to produce rudimentary user interaction with PHP. We'll look at more advanced issues and techniques in later examples.

Control Structures

All the examples of PHP code we've seen so far have been either one-statement scripts that output a string of text to the web page, or series of statements that were to be executed one after the other in order. If you've ever written programs in other languages (JavaScript, C, or BASIC) you already know that practical programs are rarely so simple.

PHP, just like any other programming language, provides facilities that enable you to affect the **flow of control**. That is, the language contains special statements that you can use to deviate from the one-after-another execution order that has dominated our examples so far. Such statements are called **control structures**. Don't understand? Don't worry! A few examples will illustrate perfectly.

The most basic, and most often used, control structure is the `if statement`. The flow of a program through an `if` statement can be visualized as in Figure 3.7.

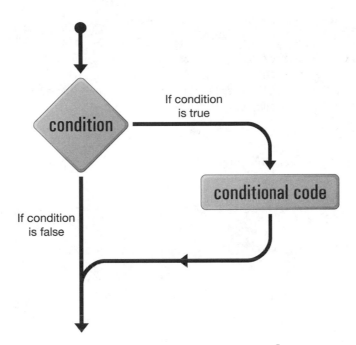

Figure 3.7. The logical flow of an if statement[7]

Here's what an if statement looks like in PHP code:

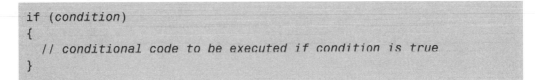

```
if (condition)
{
  // conditional code to be executed if condition is true
}
```

This control structure lets us tell PHP to execute a set of statements only if some condition is met.

If you'll indulge my vanity for a moment, here's an example that shows a twist on the personalized welcome page example we created earlier. Start by making a copy of **welcome6.html** called **welcome7.html**. For simplicity, let's alter the form it contains so that it submits a single name variable to **welcome7.php**:

---

[7] This diagram and several similar ones in this book were originally designed by Cameron Adams for the book, *Simply JavaScript* (Melbourne: SitePoint, 2006), which we wrote together. I have reused them here with his permission, and my thanks.

chapter3/welcome7.html *(excerpt)*

```
<form action="welcome7.php" method="post">
  <div><label for="name">Name:
    <input type="text" name="name" id="name"/></label></div>
  <div><input type="submit" value="GO"/></div>
</form>
```

Now make a copy of **welcome6.php** called **welcome7.php**. Replace the PHP code it contains with the following:

chapter3/welcome7.php *(excerpt)*

```
$name = $_REQUEST['name'];
if ($name == 'Kevin')
{
  echo 'Welcome, oh glorious leader!';
}
```

Now, if the name variable passed to the page has a value of 'Kevin', a special message will be displayed, as shown in Figure 3.8.

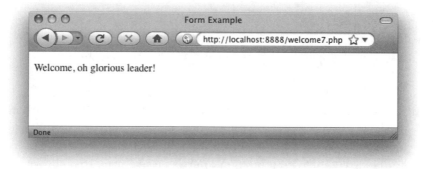

Figure 3.8. It's good to be the king

If a name other than Kevin is entered, this example becomes inhospitable—the conditional code within the if statement fails to execute, and the resulting page will be blank!

To offer an alternative to a blank page to all the plebs who have a different name to Kevin, we can use an **if-else statement** instead. The structure of an if-else statement is shown in Figure 3.9.

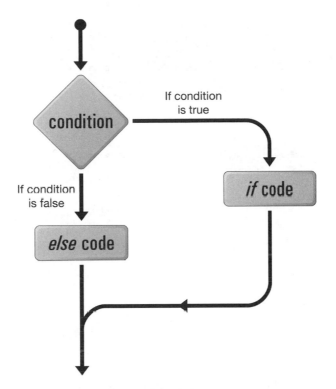

Figure 3.9. The logical flow of an if-else statement

The else portion of an if-else statement is tacked onto the end of the if portion, like this:

```
chapter3/welcome7.php (excerpt)

$name = $_REQUEST['name'];
if ($name == 'Kevin')
{
  echo 'Welcome, oh glorious leader!';
}
else
{
  echo 'Welcome to our web site, ' .
      htmlspecialchars($name, ENT_QUOTES, 'UTF-8') . '!';
}
```

Now if you submit a name other than Kevin, you should see the usual welcome message shown in Figure 3.10.

Figure 3.10. You gotta remember your peeps

The == used in the condition above is the **equal operator** that's used to compare two values to see whether they're equal.

 Double Trouble

Remember to type the double-equals (==). A common mistake among beginning PHP programmers is to type a condition like this with a single equals sign:

```
if ($name = 'Kevin')        // Missing equals sign!
```

This condition is using the assignment operator (=) that I introduced back in the section called "Variables, Operators, and Comments", instead of the equal operator (==). Consequently, instead of comparing the value of $name to the string 'Kevin', it will actually *set* the value of $name to 'Kevin'. Oops!

To make matters worse, the if statement will use this assignment operation as a condition, which it will consider to be true, so the conditional code within the if statement will always be executed, regardless of what the original value of $name happened to be.

Conditions can be more complex than a single check for equality. Recall that our form examples above would receive a first and last name. If we wanted to display a special message only for a particular person, we'd have to check the values of *both* names.

To do this, first make a copy of **welcome6.html** (which contains the two-field version of the form) called **welcome8.html**. Change the action attribute of the <form> tag to point to **welcome8.php**. Next, make a copy of **welcome7.php** called **welcome8.php**, and update the PHP code to match the following (I've highlighted the changes in bold):

chapter3/welcome8.php (excerpt)

```
$firstname = $_REQUEST['firstname'];
$lastname = $_REQUEST['lastname'];
if ($firstname == 'Kevin' and $lastname == 'Yank')
{
  echo 'Welcome, oh glorious leader!';
}
else
{
  echo 'Welcome to our web site, ' .
      htmlspecialchars($firstname, ENT_QUOTES, 'UTF-8') . ' ' .
      htmlspecialchars($lastname, ENT_QUOTES, 'UTF-8') . '!';
}
```

This updated condition will be true if and only if $firstname has a value of 'Kevin' and $lastname has a value of 'Yank'. The **and operator** in the condition makes the whole condition true only if both of the comparisons are true. A similar operator is the **or operator**, which makes the whole condition true if one or both of two simple conditions are true. If you're more familiar with the JavaScript or C forms of these operators (&& and || for and and or respectively), that's fine—they work in PHP as well.

Figure 3.11 shows that having only one of the names right in this example fails to cut the mustard.

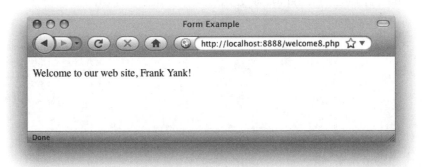

Figure 3.11. Frankly, my dear …

We'll look at more complicated conditions as the need arises. For the time being, a general familiarity with `if-else` statements is sufficient.

Another often-used PHP control structure is the **while loop**. Where the `if-else` statement allowed us to choose whether or not to execute a set of statements depending on some condition, the `while` loop allows us to use a condition to determine how many times we'll execute a set of statements repeatedly.

Figure 3.12 shows how a `while` loop operates.

Here's what a `while` loop looks like in code:

```
while (condition)
{
   // statement(s) to execute repeatedly as long as condition is true
}
```

The `while` loop works very similarly to an `if` statement. The difference arises when the condition is true and the statement(s) are executed. Instead of continuing the execution with the statement that follows the closing brace (}), the condition is checked again. If the condition is still true, then the statement(s) are executed a second time, and a third, and will continue to be executed as long as the condition remains true. The first time the condition evaluates false (whether it's the first time it's checked, or the 101st), the execution jumps immediately to the statement that follows the `while` loop, after the closing brace.

Loops like these come in handy whenever you're working with long lists of items (such as jokes stored in a database … *hint, hint*), but for now I'll illustrate with a trivial example, counting to ten:

```
                                        chapter3/count10.php (excerpt)
$count = 1;
while ($count <= 10)
{
   echo "$count ";
   ++$count;
}
```

This code may look a bit frightening, I know, but let me talk you through it line by line:

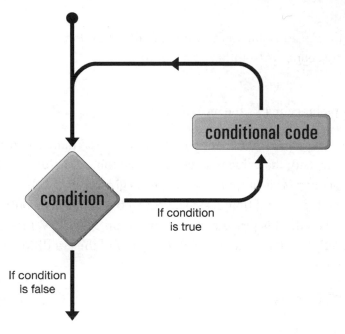

Figure 3.12. The logical flow of a while loop

```
$count = 1;
```

The first line creates a variable called $count and assigns it a value of 1.

```
while ($count <= 10)
```

The second line is the start of a while loop, the condition for which is that the value of $count is less than or equal (<=) to 10.

```
{
```

The opening brace marks the beginning of the block of conditional code for the while loop. This conditional code is often called the **body** of the loop, and is executed over and over again, as long as the condition holds true.

```
echo "$count ";
```

This line simply outputs the value of $count, followed by a space. To make the code as readable as possible, I've used a double-quoted string to take advantage of variable interpolation (as explained in the section called "Variables, Operators, and Comments"), rather than use the string concatenation operator.

```
++$count;
```

The fourth line adds one to the value of $count (++$count is a shortcut for $count = $count + 1—either one would work).

```
}
```

The closing brace marks the end of the `while` loop's body.

So here's what happens when this piece of code is executed. The first time the condition is checked, the value of $count is 1, so the condition is definitely true. The value of $count (1) is output, and $count is given a new value of 2. The condition is still true the second time it's checked, so the value (2) is output and a new value (3) is assigned. This process continues, outputting the values 3, 4, 5, 6, 7, 8, 9, and 10. Finally, $count is given a value of 11, and the condition is found to be false, which ends the loop.

The net result of the code is shown in Figure 3.13.

Figure 3.13. PHP demonstrates kindergarten-level math skills

The condition in this example used a new operator: <= (**less than or equal**). Other numerical comparison operators of this type include >= (**greater than or equal**), < (**less than**), > (**greater than**), and != (**not equal**). That last one also works when comparing text strings, by the way.

Another type of loop that's designed specifically to handle examples like that above, in which we're counting through a series of values until some condition is met, is called a **for loop**. Figure 3.14 shows the structure of a `for` loop.

Here's what it looks like in code:

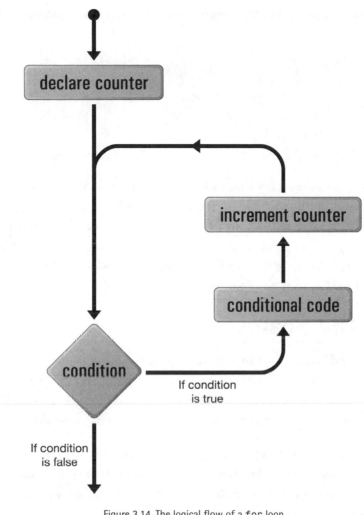

Figure 3.14. The logical flow of a for loop

```
for (declare counter; condition; increment counter)
{
  // statement(s) to execute repeatedly as long as condition is true
}
```

The *declare counter* statement is executed once at the start of the loop; the *condition* statement is checked each time through the loop, before the statements in the body are executed; the *increment counter* statement is executed each time through the loop, after the statements in the body.

Here's what the "counting to 10" example looks like when implemented with a `for` loop:

count10–for.php *(excerpt)*

```
for ($count = 1; $count <= 10; ++$count)
{
  echo "$count ";
}
```

As you can see, the statements that initialize and increment the `$count` variable join the condition on the first line of the `for` loop. Although, at first glance, the code seems a little more difficult to read, putting all the code that deals with controlling the loop in the same place actually makes it easier to understand once you're used to the syntax. Many of the examples in this book will use `for` loops, so you'll have plenty of opportunity to practice reading them.

Hiding the Seams

You're now armed with a working knowledge of the basic syntax of the PHP programming language. You understand that you can take any HTML web page, rename it with a **.php** file name extension, and inject PHP code into it to make it generate some or all of the page content on the fly. Not bad for a day's work!

Before we go any further, however, I want to stop and cast a critical eye over the examples we've discussed so far. Assuming your objective is to create database driven web sites that hold up to professional standards, there are a few unsightly blemishes we need to clean up.

The techniques in the rest of this chapter will add a coat of professional polish that can set your work apart from the crowd of amateur PHP developers out there. I'll rely on these techniques throughout the rest of this book to make sure that, no matter how simple the example, you can feel confident in the quality of the product you're delivering.

Avoid Advertising Your Technology Choices

The examples we've seen so far have contained a mixture of plain HTML files (with names ending in **.html**), and files that contain a mixture of HTML and PHP (with names ending in **.php**). Although this distinction between file types may be useful to you, the developer, there is no reason your users need to be aware of which pages of your site rely on PHP code to generate them.

Furthermore, although PHP is a very strong choice of technology to build almost any database driven web site, the day may come when you want to switch from PHP to some new technology. When that day comes, do you really want all the URLs for dynamic pages on your site to become invalid as you change the file names to reflect your new language of choice?

These days, professional developers place a lot of importance on the URLs they put out into the world. In general, URLs should be as permanent as possible, so it makes no sense to embrittle them with little "advertisements" for the programming language you used to build each individual page.

An easy way to do away with the file name extensions in your URLs is to take advantage of directory indexes. When a URL points at a directory on your web server, instead of a particular file, the web server will look for a file named **index.html** or **index.php** inside that directory, and display that file in response to the request.

For example, take the **today.php** page that I introduced at the end of Chapter 1. Rename it from **today.php** to **index.php**. Then, instead of dropping it in the root of your web server, create a subdirectory name **today**, and drop the **index.php** file in there. Now, load http://localhost/today/ in your browser (or http://localhost:8080/today/, or similar if you need to specify a port number for your server).

Figure 3.15 shows the example with its new URL. This URL omits the unnecessary **.php** extension, and is shorter and more memorable—both desirable qualities when it comes to URLs today.

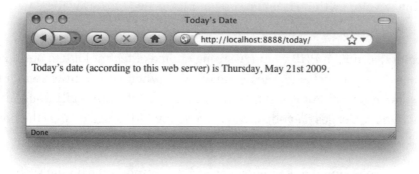

Figure 3.15. A more fashionable URL

Use PHP Templates

In the simple examples we've seen so far, inserting PHP code directly into your HTML pages has been a reasonable approach. As the amount of PHP code that goes into generating your average page grows, however, maintaining this mixture of HTML and PHP code can become unmanageable.

Particularly if you work in a team where the web designers are unsavvy, PHP-wise, having large blocks of cryptic PHP code intermingled with the HTML is a recipe for disaster. It's far too easy for designers to accidentally modify the PHP code, causing errors they'll be unable to fix.

A much more robust approach is to separate out the bulk of your PHP code, so that it resides in its own file, leaving the HTML largely unpolluted by PHP code.

The key to doing this is the PHP **include statement**. With an include statement, you can insert the contents of another file into your PHP code at the point of the statement. To show you how this works, let's rebuild the "count to ten" for loop example we looked at earlier.

Start by creating a new directory called **count10**, and create a file named **index.php** in this directory. Open the file for editing and type in this code:

```
                                          chapter3/count10/index.php
<?php
$output = ''; ❶
for ($count = 1; $count <= 10; ++$count)
{
   $output .= "$count "; ❷
}

include 'count.html.php'; ❸
?>
```

Yes, that's the *complete* code for this file. It contains no HTML code whatsoever. The for loop should be familiar to you by now, but let me point out the interesting parts of this code:

 Instead of echoing out the numbers 1 to 10, this script will add these numbers to a variable named $output. At the start of this script, therefore, we set this variable to contain an empty string.

❷ This line adds each number (followed by a space) to the end of the $output variable. The .= operator you see here is a shorthand way to add a value to the end of an existing string variable, by combining the assignment and string concatenation operators into one. The longhand version of this line is $output = $output . "$count ";, but the .= operator saves you some typing.

❸ This is an include statement, which instructs PHP to execute the contents of the **count.html.php** file at this location.[8]

---

[8] Outside of this book, you will often see includes coded with parentheses surrounding the filename, as if include were a function like date or htmlspecialchars, which is far from the case. These parentheses, when used, only serve to complicate the filename expression, and are therefore avoided in this book. The same goes for echo, another popular one-liner.

Since the final line of this file includes the **count.html.php** file, you should create this next:

```
<!DOCTYPE html PUBLIC "-//W3C//DTD XHTML 1.0 Strict//EN"
    "http://www.w3.org/TR/xhtml1/DTD/xhtml1-strict.dtd">
<html xmlns="http://www.w3.org/1999/xhtml" xml:lang="en" lang="en">
  <head>
    <title>Counting to Ten</title>
    <meta http-equiv="content-type"
        content="text/html; charset=utf-8"/>
  </head>
  <body>
    <p>
      <?php echo $output; ?>
    </p>
  </body>
</html>
```

This file is almost entirely plain HTML, except for the one line that outputs the value of the $output variable. This is the same $output variable that was created by the **index.php** file.

What we've created here is a **PHP template**—an HTML page with only very small snippets of PHP code that insert dynamically-generated values into an otherwise static HTML page. Rather than embedding the complex PHP code that generates those values in the page, we put the code to generate the values in a separate PHP script—**index.php** in this case.

Using PHP templates like this enables you to hand your templates over to HTML-savvy designers without worrying about what they might do to your PHP code. It also lets you focus on your PHP code without being distracted by the surrounding HTML code.

I like to name my PHP templates so that they end with **.html.php**. Although, as far as your web server is concerned, these are still **.php** files, the **.html.php** suffix serves as a useful reminder that these files contain both HTML and PHP code.

Many Templates, One Controller

What's nice about using `include` statements to load your PHP template files is that you can have *multiple* `include` statements in a single PHP script, and have it display different templates under different circumstances!

A PHP script that responds to a browser request by selecting one of several PHP templates to fill in and send back is commonly called a **controller**. A controller contains the logic that controls which template is sent to the browser.

Let's revisit one more example from earlier in this chapter: the welcome form that prompts a visitor for a first and last name.

We'll start with the PHP template for the form. For this, we can just reuse the **welcome8.html** file we created earlier. Create a directory named **welcome** and save a copy of **welcome8.html** called **form.html.php** into this directory. The only code you need to change in this file is the `action` attribute of the `<form>` tag:

chapter3/welcome/form.html.php

```
<!DOCTYPE html PUBLIC "-//W3C//DTD XHTML 1.0 Strict//EN"
    "http://www.w3.org/TR/xhtml1/DTD/xhtml1-strict.dtd">
<html xmlns="http://www.w3.org/1999/xhtml" xml:lang="en" lang="en">
  <head>
    <title>Form Example</title>
    <meta http-equiv="content-type"
        content="text/html; charset=utf-8"/>
  </head>
  <body>
    <form action="" method="post">
      <div><label for="firstname">First name:
        <input type="text" name="firstname" id="firstname"/></label>
      </div>
      <div><label for="lastname">Last name:
        <input type="text" name="lastname" id="lastname"/></label>
      </div>
      <div><input type="submit" value="GO"/></div>
    </form>
  </body>
</html>
```

As you can see, we're leaving the `action` attribute blank. This tells the browser to submit the form back to the same URL from which it received the form—in this case, the URL of the controller that included this template file.

Let's take a look at the controller for this example. Create an **index.php** script in the **welcome** directory alongside your form template. Type the following code into this file:

chapter3/welcome/index.php

```php
<?php
if (!isset($_REQUEST['firstname'])) ❶
{
  include 'form.html.php'; ❷
}
else ❸
{
  $firstname = $_REQUEST['firstname'];
  $lastname = $_REQUEST['lastname'];
  if ($firstname == 'Kevin' and $lastname == 'Yank')
  {
    $output = 'Welcome, oh glorious leader!'; ❹
  }
  else
  {
    $output = 'Welcome to our web site, ' .
        htmlspecialchars($firstname, ENT_QUOTES, 'UTF-8') . ' ' .
        htmlspecialchars($lastname, ENT_QUOTES, 'UTF-8') . '!';
  }

  include 'welcome.html.php'; ❺
}
?>
```

This code should look fairly familiar at first glance; it's a lot like the **welcome8.php** script we wrote earlier. Let me explain the differences:

❶   The first thing the controller needs to do is decide whether the current request is a submission of the form in **form.html.php** or not. You can do this by checking if the request contains a `firstname` variable. If it does, PHP will have stored the value in `$_REQUEST['firstname']`.

`isset` is a built-in PHP function that will tell you if a particular variable (or array element) has been assigned a value or not. If `$_REQUEST['firstname']` has a value, `isset($_REQUEST['firstname'])` will be true. If `$_REQUEST['firstname']` lacks a value, `isset($_REQUEST['firstname'])` will be false.

For the sake of readability, I like to put the code that sends the form first in my controller. What we need this `if` statement to check, therefore, is if `$_REQUEST['firstname']` is *not* set. To do this, we use the **not operator** (`!`). By putting this operator before the name of a function, you reverse the value that function returns from true to false, or from false to true.

Thus, if the request does *not* contain a `firstname` variable, then `!isset($_REQUEST['firstname'])` will return true, and the body of the `if` statement will be executed.

 If the request is not a form submission, the controller includes the **form.html.php** file to display the form.

 If the request *is* a form submission, the body of the `else` statement is executed instead.

This code pulls the `firstname` and `lastname` variables out of the `$_REQUEST` array, and then generates the appropriate welcome message for the name submitted.

❹ Instead of `echo`ing the welcome message, the controller stores the welcome message in a variable named `$output`.

❺ After generating the appropriate welcome message, the controller includes the **welcome.html.php** template, which will display that welcome message.

All that's left is to write the **welcome.html.php** template. Here it is:

```
                                              chapter3/welcome/welcome.html.php
<!DOCTYPE html PUBLIC "-//W3C//DTD XHTML 1.0 Strict//EN"
    "http://www.w3.org/TR/xhtml1/DTD/xhtml1-strict.dtd">
<html xmlns="http://www.w3.org/1999/xhtml" xml:lang="en" lang="en">
  <head>
    <title>Form Example</title>
    <meta http-equiv="content-type"
        content="text/html; charset=utf-8"/>
  </head>
  <body>
    <p>
      <?php echo $output; ?>
    </p>
  </body>
</html>
```

That's it! Fire up your browser and point it at http://localhost/welcome/ (or http://localhost:8080/welcome/ or similar if you need to specify a port number for your web server). You'll be prompted for your name, and when you submit the form, you'll see the appropriate welcome message. The URL should stay the same throughout this process.

One of the benefits of maintaining the same URL throughout the process of prompting the user for a name and displaying the welcome message is that the user can bookmark the page at any time during this process and gain a sensible result: when the user next returns, whether the form page or the welcome message was bookmarked, the form will be present itself once again. In the previous version of this example, where the welcome message had its own URL, returning to that URL without submitting the form would have generated a broken welcome message ("Welcome to our web site, !").

 Why So Forgetful?

In Chapter 9 I'll show you how to remember the user's name between visits.

Bring On the Database

In this chapter, we've seen the PHP server-side scripting language in action as we've explored all the basic language features: statements, variables, operators, comments, and control structures. The sample applications we've seen have been reasonably simple, but despite this we've taken the time to ensure they have attractive URLs, and that the HTML templates for the pages they generate are uncluttered by the PHP code that controls them.

As you may have begun to suspect, the real power of PHP is in its hundreds (even thousands) of built-in functions that let you access data in a MySQL database, send email, dynamically generate images, and even create Adobe Acrobat PDF files on the fly.

In Chapter 4, we'll delve into the MySQL functions built into PHP, and see how to publish the joke database we created in Chapter 2 to the Web. This chapter will set the scene for the ultimate goal of this book—creating a complete content management system for your web site in PHP and MySQL.

Publishing MySQL Data on the Web

This is it—the stuff you signed up for! In this chapter, you'll learn how to take information stored in a MySQL database and display it on a web page for all to see.

So far, you've installed and learned the basics of MySQL, a relational database engine, and PHP, a server-side scripting language. Now you're ready to learn how to use these new tools together to create a true database driven web site!

The Big Picture

Before we leap forward, it's worth taking a step back for a clear picture of our ultimate goal. We have two powerful tools at our disposal: the PHP scripting language and the MySQL database engine. It's important to understand how these will fit together.

The whole idea of a database driven web site is to allow the content of the site to reside in a database, and for that content to be pulled from the database dynamically to create web pages for people to view with a regular web browser. So, at one end of the system you have a visitor to your site who uses a web browser to request a page, and expects to receive a standard HTML document in return. At the other end you have the content of your site, which sits in one or more tables in a MySQL database that understands only how to respond to SQL queries (commands).

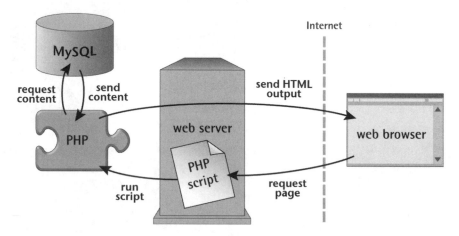

Figure 4.1. PHP retrieves MySQL data to produce web pages

As shown in Figure 4.1, the PHP scripting language is the go-between that speaks both languages. It processes the page request and fetches the data from the MySQL database (using SQL queries just like those you used to create a table of jokes in Chapter 2), then spits it out dynamically as the nicely formatted HTML page that the browser expects.

Just so it's clear and fresh in your mind, this is what will happen when a person visits a page on your database driven web site:

1. The visitor's web browser requests the web page using a standard URL.

2. The web server software (typically Apache) recognizes that the requested file is a PHP script, so the server fires up the PHP interpreter to execute the code contained in the file.

3. Certain PHP commands (which will be the focus of this chapter) connect to the MySQL database and request the content that belongs in the web page.

4. The MySQL database responds by sending the requested content to the PHP script.

5. The PHP script stores the content into one or more PHP variables, then uses echo statements to output the content as part of the web page.

6. The PHP interpreter finishes up by handing a copy of the HTML it has created to the web server.

7. The web server sends the HTML to the web browser as it would a plain HTML file, except that instead of coming directly from an HTML file, the page is the output provided by the PHP interpreter.

Connecting to MySQL with PHP

Before you can retrieve content out of your MySQL database for inclusion in a web page, you must know how to establish a connection to MySQL from inside a PHP script. Back in Chapter 2, you used a program called `mysql` that allowed you to make such a connection from the command prompt. Just as that program could connect directly to a running MySQL server, so too can the PHP interpreter; support for connecting to MySQL is built right into the language in the form of a library of built-in functions.

The built-in function `mysqli_connect` establishes a connection to a MySQL server:

```
mysqli_connect(hostname, username, password)
```

You may remember from Chapter 3 that PHP functions usually return a value when they're called. The `mysqli_connect` function, for example, returns a **link identifier** that identifies the connection that has been established. Since we intend to make use of the connection, we should hold onto this value. Here's an example of how we might connect to our MySQL server:

chapter4/connect/index.php *(excerpt)*

```
$link = mysqli_connect('localhost', 'root', 'password');
```

As described above, the values of the three function parameters may differ for your MySQL server; at the very least, you'll need to substitute in the root password you established for your MySQL server. What's important to see here is that the value returned by `mysqli_connect` is stored in a variable named `$link`.

As the MySQL server is a completely separate piece of software from the web server, we must consider the possibility that the server may be unavailable or inaccessible due to a network outage, or because the username/password combination you provided is rejected by the server. In such cases, the `mysqli_connect` function returns `FALSE`, instead of a connection identifier, as no connection is established. This allows us to react to such failures using an `if` statement:

chapter4/connect/index.php *(excerpt)*

```php
$link = mysqli_connect('localhost', 'root', 'password');
if (!$link)
{
  $output = 'Unable to connect to the database server.';
  include 'output.html.php';
  exit();
}
```

The condition in this `if` statement uses the not operator (`!`) to make the condition true when `$link` has a value of `false` (that is, when the connection attempt has failed). If the connection succeeds, `$link` will have a value that's considered true, which will make `!$link` false. In short, the body of the `if` statement is executed only if the connection fails.

Within the body of the `if` statement, we set the variable `$output` to contain a message about what went wrong. We then include the template **output.html.php**. This is a generic template that simply outputs the value of the `$output` variable:

chapter4/connect/output.html.php

```html
<!DOCTYPE html PUBLIC "-//W3C//DTD XHTML 1.0 Strict//EN"
    "http://www.w3.org/TR/xhtml1/DTD/xhtml1-strict.dtd">
<html xmlns="http://www.w3.org/1999/xhtml" xml:lang="en" lang="en">
  <head>
    <title>PHP Output</title>
    <meta http-equiv="content-type"
        content="text/html; charset=utf-8"/>
  </head>
  <body>
    <p>
      <?php echo $output; ?>
    </p>
  </body>
</html>
```

Finally, after outputting the message, the body of the `if` statement calls the built-in `exit` function.

`exit` is the first example in this book of a function that can be called with no parameters. When called this way, all this function does is cause PHP to stop executing the script at this point. This ensures that the rest of the code in our controller (which in most cases will depend on a successful database connection) will not be executed if the connection has failed.

Assuming the connection succeeds, however, you need to configure it before use. As I mentioned briefly in Chapter 3, you should use UTF-8 encoded text in your web sites to maximize the range of characters that your users will have at their disposal when filling in forms on your site. By default, when PHP connects to MySQL, it once again uses the simpler ISO-8859-1 encoding instead of UTF-8. You must therefore follow up your `mysqli_connect` code with a call to `mysqli_set_charset`—another built-in PHP function:

```
mysqli_set_charset($link, 'utf8')
```

Notice we use the `$link` variable that contains the MySQL link identifier to tell the function which database connection to use. This function returns `true` when it's successful and `false` if an error occurs. Once again, it's prudent to use an `if` statement to handle errors:

```
                                          chapter4/connect/index.php (excerpt)

if (!mysqli_set_charset($link, 'utf8'))
{
  $output = 'Unable to set database connection encoding.';
  include 'output.html.php';
  exit();
}
```

Note that this time, instead of assigning the result of the function to a variable and then checking if the variable is true or false, I have simply used the function call itself as the condition. This may look a little strange, but it's a very commonly used shortcut. To check whether the condition is true or false, PHP executes the function and then checks its return value—exactly what we need to happen.

As in Chapter 2 when you connected to the MySQL server using the **mysql** program, once you've established a connection the usual next step is to select the database with which you want to work. Let's say you want to work with the joke database you created in Chapter 2. This database was called `ijdb`. Selecting that database in PHP is just a matter of another function call:

```
mysqli_select_db($link, 'ijdb');
```

`mysqli_select_db` simply sets the selected database (`'ijdb'`) for the specified database connection (`$link`). Yet again, it's best to guard against errors with an `if` statement:

chapter4/connect/index.php *(excerpt)*

```php
if (!mysqli_select_db($link, 'ijdb'))
{
  $output = 'Unable to locate the joke database.';
  include 'output.html.php';
  exit();
}
```

To polish off this example, let's display a status message that indicates when everything has gone right. Here's the complete code of our controller:

chapter4/connect/index.php

```php
<?php
$link = mysqli_connect('localhost', 'root', 'password');
if (!$link)
{
  $output = 'Unable to connect to the database server.';
  include 'output.html.php';
  exit();
}

if (!mysqli_set_charset($link, 'utf8'))
{
  $output = 'Unable to set database connection encoding.';
  include 'output.html.php';
  exit();
}
```

```
if (!mysqli_select_db($link, 'ijdb'))
{
  $output = 'Unable to locate the joke database.';
  include 'output.html.php';
  exit();
}

$output = 'Database connection established.';
include 'output.html.php';
?>
```

Fire up this example in your browser (if you put the **index.php** and **output.html.php** files in a directory named **connect** on your web server, the URL will be like http://localhost/connect/). If your MySQL server is up and running and everything works the way it should, you should see the message indicating success in Figure 4.2.

Figure 4.2. A successful connection

If PHP is unable to connect to your MySQL server, or if the username and password you provided are incorrect, you'll instead see a similar screen to that in Figure 4.3. To make sure your error handling code is working properly, you might want to misspell your password intentionally to test it out.

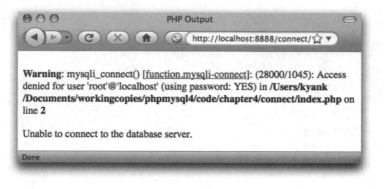

Figure 4.3. A connection failure

What PHP Error?

Depending on your web server's PHP configuration, you may or may not see the first paragraph shown in Figure 4.3. This warning message is automatically generated by PHP if it's configured to display errors. These detailed errors can be invaluable tools for diagnosing problems with your code during development. Since you'd probably prefer to keep this kind of technical information hidden once your site is live on the Web, it's common to switch off these errors on production servers.

If you installed Apache yourself, chances are this message will be displayed. If you're using a bundled Apache solution (like WampServer or MAMP), PHP error display may be switched off by default. To display these errors (they're especially helpful in development when you're trying to determine the cause of a problem), you need to open your server's **php.ini** file and set the `display_errors` option to On. You can access WampServer's **php.ini** file from the system tray menu. MAMP's **php.ini** file is in the **/Applications/MAMP/conf/php5** folder on your system.

If PHP connects to your MySQL server and then fails to find the `ijdb` database, you'll see a similar message to Figure 4.4. Once again, you should probably test your error handling code by intentionally misspelling your database name.

Figure 4.4. A connection failure

With a connection established and a database selected, you're ready to begin using the data stored in the database.

PHP Automatically Disconnects

You might be wondering what happens to the connection with the MySQL server after the script has finished executing. While PHP does have a function for disconnecting from the server (`mysqli_close`), PHP will automatically close any open database connections when they're no longer needed, so you can usually just let PHP clean up after you.

Sending SQL Queries with PHP

In Chapter 2, we connected to the MySQL database server using a program called `mysql` that allowed us to type SQL queries (commands) and view the results of those queries immediately. In PHP, a similar mechanism exists: the `mysqli_query` function.

```
mysqli_query(link, query)
```

Here *query* is a string that contains the SQL query you want to execute. As with `mysqli_select_db`, you must also provide the MySQL link identifier returned by `mysqli_connect`.

What this function returns will depend on the type of query being sent. For most SQL queries, `mysqli_query` returns either `true` or `false` to indicate success or failure respectively. Consider the following example, which attempts to create the `joke` table we created in Chapter 2:

chapter4/createtable/index.php *(excerpt)*

```php
$sql = 'CREATE TABLE joke (
      id INT NOT NULL AUTO_INCREMENT PRIMARY KEY,
      joketext TEXT,
      jokedate DATE NOT NULL
    ) DEFAULT CHARACTER SET utf8';
if (!mysqli_query($link, $sql))
{
  $output = 'Error creating joke table: ' . mysqli_error($link);
  include 'output.html.php';
  exit();
}

$output = 'Joke table successfully created.';
include 'output.html.php';
```

Note once again we use the same `if` statement technique to handle possible errors produced by the query. This example also uses the `mysqli_error` function to retrieve a detailed error message from the MySQL server. Figure 4.5 shows the error that's displayed when the `joke` table already exists, for example.

Figure 4.5. The CREATE TABLE query fails because the table already exists

For DELETE, INSERT, and UPDATE queries (which serve to modify stored data), MySQL also keeps track of the number of table rows (entries) that were affected by the query. Consider the SQL command below, which we used in Chapter 2 to set the dates of all jokes that contained the word "chicken":

chapter4/updatechicken/index.php *(excerpt)*

```
$sql = 'UPDATE joke SET jokedate="2010-04-01"
    WHERE joketext LIKE "%chicken%"';
if (!mysqli_query($link, $sql))
{
  $output = 'Error performing update: ' . mysqli_error($link);
  include 'output.html.php';
  exit();
}
```

When we execute this query, we can use the `mysql_affected_rows` function to view the number of rows that were affected by this update:

chapter4/updatechicken/index.php *(excerpt)*

```
$output = 'Updated ' . mysqli_affected_rows($link) . ' rows.';
include 'output.html.php';
```

Figure 4.6 shows the output of this example, assuming you only have one "chicken" joke in your database.

Figure 4.6. The number of database records updated is displayed

If you refresh the page to run the same query again, you should see the message change as shown in Figure 4.7 to indicate that no rows were updated, since the new date being applied to the jokes is the same as the existing date.

Figure 4.7. MySQL lets you know you're wasting its time

SELECT queries are treated a little differently as they can retrieve a lot of data, and
PHP provides ways to handle that information.

Handling SELECT Result Sets

For most SQL queries, the mysqli_query function returns either true (success) or
false (failure). For SELECT queries, more information is needed. You'll recall that
SELECT queries are used to view stored data in the database. In addition to indicating
whether the query succeeded or failed, PHP must also receive the results of the
query. Thus, when it processes a SELECT query, mysqli_query returns a **result set**,
which contains a list of all the rows (entries) returned from the query. false is still
returned if the query fails for any reason:

chapter4/listjokes/index.php *(excerpt)*

```
$result = mysqli_query($link, 'SELECT joketext FROM joke');
if (!$result)
{
  $error = 'Error fetching jokes: ' . mysqli_error($link);
  include 'error.html.php';
  exit();
}
```

As before, errors are displayed using a very simple PHP template:

chapter4/listjokes/error.html.php

```
<!DOCTYPE html PUBLIC "-//W3C//DTD XHTML 1.0 Strict//EN"
    "http://www.w3.org/TR/xhtml1/DTD/xhtml1-strict.dtd">
<html xmlns="http://www.w3.org/1999/xhtml" xml:lang="en" lang="en">
  <head>
    <title>PHP Error</title>
```

```
      <meta http-equiv="content-type"
          content="text/html; charset=utf-8"/>
    </head>
    <body>
      <p>
        <?php echo $error; ?>
      </p>
    </body>
  </html>
```

Provided that no error was encountered in processing the query, the above code will store a result set into the variable $result. This result set contains the text of all the jokes stored in the joke table. As there's no practical limit on the number of jokes in the database, that result set can be quite big.

I mentioned back in Chapter 3 that the while loop is a useful control structure for dealing with large amounts of data. Here's an outline of the code that will process the rows in a result set one at a time:

```
while ($row = mysqli_fetch_array($result))
{
  // process the row...
}
```

The condition for the while loop is probably different to the conditions you're used to, so let me explain how it works. Consider the condition as a statement all by itself:

```
$row = mysqli_fetch_array($result);
```

The mysqli_fetch_array function accepts a result set as a parameter (stored in the $result variable in this case), and returns the next row in the result set as an array (we discussed arrays in Chapter 3). When there are no more rows in the result set, mysqli_fetch_array instead returns false.

Now, the above statement assigns a value to the $row variable, but, at the same time, the statement as a whole takes on that same value. This is what lets you use the statement as a condition in the while loop. Since a while loop will keep looping until its condition evaluates to false, this loop will occur as many times as there are rows in the result set, with $row taking on the value of the next row each time the loop executes. All that's left to figure out is how to retrieve the values out of the $row variable each time the loop runs.

Rows of a result set returned by mysqli_fetch_array are represented as associative arrays. The indices are named after the table columns in the result set. If $row is a row in our result set, then $row['joketext'] is the value in the joketext column of that row.

Our goal in this code is to store away the text of all the jokes so we can display them in a PHP template. The best way to do this is to store each joke as a new item in an array, $jokes:

chapter4/listjokes/index.php *(excerpt)*

```php
while ($row = mysqli_fetch_array($result))
{
  $jokes[] = $row['joketext'];
}
```

With the jokes pulled out of the database, we can now pass them along to a PHP template (**jokes.html.php**) for display.

To summarize, here's the complete code of the controller for this example:

chapter4/listjokes/index.php

```php
<?php
$link = mysqli_connect('localhost', 'root', 'password');
if (!$link)
{
  $error = 'Unable to connect to the database server.';
  include 'error.html.php';
  exit();
}

if (!mysqli_set_charset($link, 'utf8'))
{
  $error = 'Unable to set database connection encoding.';
  include 'error.html.php';
  exit();
}

if (!mysqli_select_db($link, 'ijdb'))
```

```
{
  $error = 'Unable to locate the joke database.';
  include 'error.html.php';
  exit();
}

$result = mysqli_query($link, 'SELECT joketext FROM joke');
if (!$result)
{
  $error = 'Error fetching jokes: ' . mysqli_error($link);
  include 'error.html.php';
  exit();
}

while ($row = mysqli_fetch_array($result))
{
  $jokes[] = $row['joketext'];
}

include 'jokes.html.php';
?>
```

All that's left to complete this example is to write the **jokes.html.php** template.

In this template, for the first time we need to display the contents of an array, rather than just a simple variable. The most common way to process an array in PHP is to use a loop. We have already seen `while` loops and `for` loops; another type of loop, which is particularly helpful for processing arrays, is the `foreach` loop:

```
foreach (array as $item)
{
  // process each $item
}
```

Instead of a condition, the parentheses at the top of a `foreach` loop contain an array, followed by the keyword `as`, and then the name of a new variable that will be used to store each item of the array in turn. The body of the loop is then executed once for each item in the array; each time, that item is stored in the specified variable so that the code can access it directly.

It's common to use a `foreach` loop in a PHP template to display each item of an array in turn. Here's how this might look for our `$jokes` array:

```php
<?php  .
foreach ($jokes as $joke)
{
?>
  <!-- Code to output each $joke -->
<?php
}
?>
```

With this blend of PHP code to describe the loop and HTML code to display it, this code looks rather untidy. Because of this, it's common to use an alternative way of writing the `foreach` loop when it's used in a template:

```php
foreach (array as $item):
  // process each $item
endforeach;
```

Here's how this form of the code looks in a template:

```php
<?php foreach ($jokes as $joke): ?>
  <!-- Code to output each $joke -->
<?php endforeach; ?>
```

With this new tool in hand, we can write our template to display the list of jokes:

chapter4/listjokes/jokes.html.php

```php
<!DOCTYPE html PUBLIC "-//W3C//DTD XHTML 1.0 Strict//EN"
    "http://www.w3.org/TR/xhtml1/DTD/xhtml1-strict.dtd">
<html xmlns="http://www.w3.org/1999/xhtml" xml:lang="en" lang="en">
  <head>
    <title>List of Jokes</title>
    <meta http-equiv="content-type"
        content="text/html; charset=utf-8"/>
  </head>
  <body>
    <p>Here are all the jokes in the database:</p>
    <?php foreach ($jokes as $joke): ?>
      <blockquote><p>
        <?php echo htmlspecialchars($joke, ENT_QUOTES, 'UTF-8'); ?>
      </p></blockquote>
```

```
    <?php endforeach; ?>
  </body>
</html>
```

Each joke is displayed in a paragraph (<p>) contained within a block quote (<blockquote>), since we're effectively quoting the author of each joke in this page.

Because jokes might conceivably contain characters that could be interpreted as HTML code (for example, <, >, or &), we must use htmlspecialchars to ensure that these are translated into HTML character entities (that is, <, >, and &) so that they're displayed correctly.

Figure 4.8 shows what this page looks like once you've added a couple of jokes to the database.

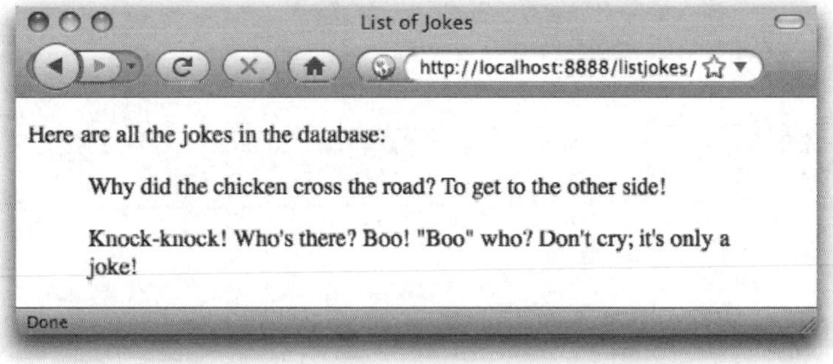

Figure 4.8. All my best material—in one place!

Inserting Data into the Database

In this section, I'll demonstrate how to use the tools at your disposal to enable site visitors to add their own jokes to the database.

If you want to let visitors to your site type in new jokes, you'll obviously need a form. Here's a template for a form that will fit the bill:

```
chapter4/addjoke/form.html.php (excerpt)

<!DOCTYPE html PUBLIC "-//W3C//DTD XHTML 1.0 Strict//EN"
    "http://www.w3.org/TR/xhtml1/DTD/xhtml1-strict.dtd">
<html xmlns="http://www.w3.org/1999/xhtml" xml:lang="en" lang="en">
  <head>
    <title>Add Joke</title>
    <meta http-equiv="content-type"
        content="text/html; charset=utf-8"/>
    <style type="text/css">
    textarea {
      display: block;
      width: 100%;
    }
    </style>
  </head>
  <body>
    <form action="?" method="post">
      <div>
        <label for="joketext">Type your joke here:</label>
        <textarea id="joketext" name="joketext" rows="3" cols="40">
➥</textarea>
      </div>
      <div><input type="submit" value="Add"/></div>
    </form>
  </body>
</html>
```

As we've seen before, when submitted this form will request the same PHP script that generated the form—the controller script (**index.php**). You'll notice, however, that instead of leaving the action attribute empty (""), we set its value to ?. As we'll see in a moment, the URL used to display the form in this example will feature a query string, and setting the action to ? strips that query string off the URL when submitting the form.

Figure 4.9 shows what this form looks like in a browser.

Figure 4.9. Another nugget of comic genius is added to the database

When this form is submitted, the request will include a variable, `joketext`, that contains the text of the joke as typed into the text area. This variable will then appear in the `$_POST` and `$_REQUEST` arrays created by PHP.

Let's tie this form into the preceding example, which displayed the list of jokes in the database. Add a link to the top of the list that invites the user to add a joke:

chapter4/addjoke/jokes.html.php *(excerpt)*

```
<body>
  <p><a href="?addjoke">Add your own joke</a></p>
  <p>Here are all the jokes in the database:</p>
```

Like the form, this link points back to the very same PHP script used to generate this page, but this time it adds a query string (`?addjoke`), indicating the user's intention to add a new joke. Our controller can detect this query string and use it as a signal to display the "Add Joke" form instead of the list of jokes.

Let's make the necessary changes to the controller now:

chapter4/addjoke/index.php *(excerpt)*

```
if (isset($_GET['addjoke']))
{
  include 'form.html.php';
  exit();
}
```

This opening `if` statement checks if the query string contains a variable named `addjoke`. This is how we detect that the user clicked the new link. Even though there is no value specified by the query string (`?addjoke`) for the `addjoke` variable, it does create it, which we can detect with `isset($_GET['addjoke'])`.

When we detect this variable, we display the form by including **form.html.php**, and then exit.

Once the user fills out the form and submits it, that form submission results in another request to this controller. This we detect by checking if `$_POST['joketext']` is set:

chapter4/addjoke/index.php *(excerpt)*

```
if (isset($_POST['joketext']))
{
```

To insert the submitted joke into the database, we must run an `INSERT` query using the value stored in `$_POST['joketext']` to fill in the `joketext` column of the `joke` table. This might lead you to write some code like this:

```
$sql = 'INSERT INTO joke SET
    joketext="' . $_POST['joketext'] . '",
    jokedate="today's date"';
```

There is a serious problem with this code, however: the contents of `$_POST['joketext']` are entirely under the control of the user who submitted the form. If a malicious user were to type just the right sort of SQL code into the form, this script would feed it to your MySQL server without question. This type of attack is called an **SQL injection attack**, and in the early days of PHP it was one of the most common security holes that hackers found and exploited in PHP-based web sites.

These attacks were so feared, in fact, that the team behind PHP added some built-in protection against SQL injections to the language that remains enabled by default in many PHP installations today. Called **magic quotes**, this protective feature of PHP automatically analyzes all values submitted by the browser and inserts backslashes (\) in front of any *dangerous* characters, like apostrophes—which can cause problems if they're included in an SQL query inadvertently.

The problem with the **magic quotes** feature is that it causes as many problems as it prevents. Firstly, the characters that it detects and the method it uses to sanitize them (prefixing them with a backslash) are only valid in some circumstances. Depending on the character encoding of your site, and the database server you're using, these measures may be completely ineffective.

Secondly, when a submitted value is used for some purpose *other* than creating an SQL query, those backslashes can be really bothersome. I mentioned this briefly in Chapter 2 when, in the welcome message example, the magic quotes feature would insert a spurious backslash into the user's last name if it contained an apostrophe.

In short, magic quotes was a bad idea, so much so that it's scheduled to be removed from PHP in version 6. In the meantime, however, you have to deal with the problems it creates in your code. The easiest way to do this is to detect if magic quotes is enabled on your web server and, if it is, to *undo* the modifications it has made to the submitted values.[1] Thankfully, the PHP Manual[2] provides a snippet of code that will do exactly this:

chapter4/addjoke/index.php *(excerpt)*

```php
if (get_magic_quotes_gpc())
{
  function stripslashes_deep($value)
  {
    $value = is_array($value) ?
        array_map('stripslashes_deep', $value) :
        stripslashes($value);

    return $value;
  }

  $_POST = array_map('stripslashes_deep', $_POST);
  $_GET = array_map('stripslashes_deep', $_GET);
  $_COOKIE = array_map('stripslashes_deep', $_COOKIE);
  $_REQUEST = array_map('stripslashes_deep', $_REQUEST);
}
```

---

[1] You can disable magic quotes—and save your web server a lot of work—by setting the `magic_quotes_gpc` option in your **php.ini** file to `Off`. To make sure your code still functions if this setting is changed, however, you should still deal with magic quotes in your code when it's enabled.

[2] http://www.php.net/manual/en/security.magicquotes.disabling.php

Avoid wasting time trying to understand the inner workings of this code; to keep the code short, it uses several advanced PHP features that we've yet to see—and one or two others that are beyond the scope of this book. Rather, just drop this code into the top of your controller—and indeed any other PHP script that will receive user input in the form of query variables or a form submission (or, as we'll learn in Chapter 9, browser cookies). And be assured; from this point forward, I'll remind you whenever this code is required by an example.[3]

With the damage done by magic quotes reversed, you must now prepare those values that you *do* intend to use in your SQL query. Just as it provides `htmlspecialchars` for outputting user-submitted values into HTML code, PHP provides a function that prepares a user-submitted value so that you can use it safely in your SQL query: `mysqli_real_escape_string`. Not the most elegant name, but it does the trick. Here's how you use it:

```
$joketext = mysqli_real_escape_string($link, $_POST['joketext']);
$sql = 'INSERT INTO joke SET
    joketext="' . $joketext . '",
    jokedate="today's date"';
```

This code first uses `mysqli_real_escape_string` to store a "query safe" version of the contents of `$_POST['joketext']` in the new variable `$joketext`. It then uses this variable to insert the submitted value into the `INSERT` query as the value of the `joketext` column.

The lingering question in this code is how to assign today's date to the `jokedate` field. We *could* write some fancy PHP code to generate today's date in the *YYYY-MM-DD* form that MySQL requires, but it turns out MySQL itself has a function to do this: `CURDATE`:

```
$joketext = mysqli_real_escape_string($link, $_POST['joketext']);
$sql = 'INSERT INTO joke SET
    joketext="' . $joketext . '",
    jokedate=CURDATE()';
```

---

[3] In Chapter 6 I'll show you how to manage the burden of repeatedly including this code snippet in your controller code.

The MySQL function CURDATE is used here to assign the current date as the value of the jokedate column. MySQL actually has dozens of these functions, but we'll introduce them only as required. Appendix B provides a reference that describes all commonly used MySQL functions.

Now that we have our query, we can complete the if statement we started above to handle submissions of the "Add Joke" form. We can execute our INSERT query by using the mysqli_query function:

```
                                          chapter4/addjoke/index.php (excerpt)

if (isset($_POST['joketext']))
{
  $joketext = mysqli_real_escape_string($link, $_POST['joketext']);
  $sql = 'INSERT INTO joke SET
      joketext="' . $joketext . '",
      jokedate=CURDATE()';
  if (!mysqli_query($link, $sql))
  {
    $error = 'Error adding submitted joke: ' . mysqli_error($link);
    include 'error.html.php';
    exit();
  }

  header('Location: .');
  exit();
}
```

But wait! This if statement has one more new trick up its sleeve. Once we've added the new joke to the database, instead of displaying the PHP template as previously, we want to redirect the user's browser back to the list of jokes. That way they are able to see the newly added joke among them. That's what the two lines highlighted in bold at the end of the if statement above do.

Your first instinct in order to achieve the desired result might be to allow the controller, after adding the new joke to the database, simply to fetch the list of jokes from the database and display the list using the **jokes.html.php** template as usual. The problem with doing this is that the resulting page, from the browser's perspective, would be the effect of having submitted the "Add Joke" form. If the user were then to refresh the page, the browser would resubmit that form, causing another copy of the new joke to be added to the database! This is rarely the desired behaviour.

Instead, we want the browser to treat the updated list of jokes as a normal web page, able to be reloaded without resubmitting the form. The way to do this is to answer the browser's form submission with an **HTTP redirect**[4]—a special response that tells the browser "the page you're looking for is over *here*."

The PHP `header` function provides the means of sending special server responses like this one, by letting you insert special **headers** into the response sent to the browser. In order to signal a redirect, you must send a `Location` header with the URL of the page to which you wish to direct the browser:

```
header('Location: URL');
```

In this case, we want to send the browser back to the very same page—our controller. We're asking the browser to submit another request—this time, without a form submission attached to it—rather than sending the browser to another location. Since we want to point the browser at our controller (**index.php**) using the URL of the parent directory, we can simply tell the browser to reload the current directory, which is expressed as a period (.).

Thus, the two lines that redirect the browser back to our controller after adding the new joke to the database:

chapter4/addjoke/index.php *(excerpt)*

```
  header('Location: .');
  exit();
}
```

---

[4] HTTP stands for HyperText Transfer Protocol, and is the language that describes the request/response communications that are exchanged between the visitor's web browser and your web server.

$_SERVER['PHP_SELF'] is the URL of the current page

Another common means of obtaining the URL of the current page in PHP is with $_SERVER['PHP_SELF'].

Like $_GET, $_POST, and $_REQUEST, $_SERVER is an array variable that is automatically created by PHP. $_SERVER contains a whole bunch of information supplied by your web server. In particular, $_SERVER['PHP_SELF'] will always be set to the URL of the PHP script that your web server used to generate the current page.

Unfortunately, because the web server automatically translates a request for http://localhost/addjoke/ to a request for http://localhost/addjoke/index.php, $_SERVER['PHP_SELF'] will contain the latter URL. Redirecting the browser to . lets us preserve the shorter, more memorable form of the URL.

For this reason, I have avoided using $_SERVER['PHP SELF'] in this book. Since it's so commonly used in basic PHP examples around the Web, however, I thought you might like to know what it does.

The rest of the controller is responsible for displaying the list of jokes as before. Here's the complete code of the controller:

chapter4/addjoke/index.php

```php
<?php
if (get_magic_quotes_gpc())
{
  function stripslashes_deep($value)
  {
    $value = is_array($value) ?
        array_map('stripslashes_deep', $value) :
        stripslashes($value);

    return $value;
  }

  $_POST = array_map('stripslashes_deep', $_POST);
  $_GET = array_map('stripslashes_deep', $_GET);
  $_COOKIE = array_map('stripslashes_deep', $_COOKIE);
  $_REQUEST = array_map('stripslashes_deep', $_REQUEST);
}
```

```php
if (isset($_GET['addjoke']))
{
  include 'form.html.php';
  exit();
}

$link = mysqli_connect('localhost', 'root', 'password');
if (!$link)
{
  $error = 'Unable to connect to the database server.';
  include 'error.html.php';
  exit();
}

if (!mysqli_set_charset($link, 'utf8'))
{
  $output = 'Unable to set database connection encoding.';
  include 'output.html.php';
  exit();
}

if (!mysqli_select_db($link, 'ijdb'))
{
  $error = 'Unable to locate the joke database.';
  include 'error.html.php';
  exit();
}

if (isset($_POST['joketext']))
{
  $joketext = mysqli_real_escape_string($link, $_POST['joketext']);
  $sql = 'INSERT INTO joke SET
      joketext="' . $joketext . '",
      jokedate=CURDATE()';
  if (!mysqli_query($link, $sql))
  {
    $error = 'Error adding submitted joke: ' . mysqli_error($link);
    include 'error.html.php';
    exit();
  }

  header('Location: .');
  exit();
}
```

```
$result = mysqli_query($link, 'SELECT joketext FROM joke');
if (!$result)
{
  $error = 'Error fetching jokes: ' . mysqli_error($link);
  include 'error.html.php';
  exit();
}

while ($row = mysqli_fetch_array($result))
{
  $jokes[] = $row['joketext'];
}

include 'jokes.html.php';
?>
```

As you review this code to make sure it all makes sense to you, note that the calls to `mysqli_connect` and `mysqli_select_db` must come before any of the code that runs database queries. A database connection is unnecessary to display the "Add Joke" form, however, so that code can come at the very top of the controller script.

Load this up and add a new joke or two to the database via your browser. The resulting page should look like Figure 4.10.

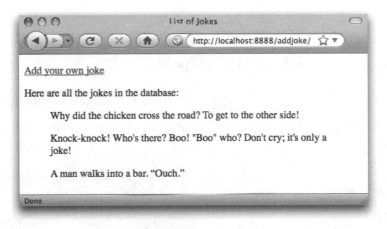

Figure 4.10. Look, Ma! No SQL!

There you have it! With a single controller (**index.php**) pulling the strings, you're able to view existing jokes in, and add new jokes to, your MySQL database.

Deleting Data from the Database

In this section, we'll make one final enhancement to our joke database site. We'll place next to each joke on the page a button labeled **Delete** that, when clicked, will remove that joke from the database and display the updated joke list.

If you like a challenge, you might want to take a stab at writing this feature yourself before you read on to see my solution. Although we're implementing a brand new feature, we'll mainly be using the same tools that we have for the previous examples in this chapter. Here are a few hints to start you off:

■ You'll still be able to do it all with a single controller script (**index.php**).

■ You'll need to use the SQL DELETE command, which I introduced in Chapter 2.

■ To delete a particular joke in your controller, you'll need to identify it uniquely. The id column in the joke table was created to serve this purpose. You're going to have to pass the ID of the joke to be deleted with the request to delete a joke. The easiest way to do this is to use a hidden form field.

At the very least, take a few moments to think about how you would approach this. When you're ready to see the solution, read on!

To begin with, we need to modify the SELECT query that fetches the list of jokes from the database. In addition to the joketext column, we must also fetch the id column, so we can identify each joke uniquely:

chapter4/deletejoke/index.php *(excerpt)*

```
$result = mysqli_query($link, 'SELECT id, joketext FROM joke');
if (!$result)
{
  $error = 'Error fetching jokes: ' . mysqli_error($link);
  include 'error.html.php';
  exit();
}
```

We must also modify the while loop that stores the database results in the $jokes array. Instead of simply storing the text of each joke as an item in the array, we must store both the ID and text of each joke. One way to do this is to make each item in the $jokes array an array in its own right:

chapter4/deletejoke/index.php *(excerpt)*

```
while ($row = mysqli_fetch_array($result))
{
  $jokes[] = array('id' => $row['id'], 'text' => $row['joketext']);
}
```

Once this `while` loop runs its course, we'll have the `$jokes` array, each item of which is an associative array with two items: the ID of the joke and its text. For each joke (`$jokes[n]`), we can therefore retrieve its ID (`$jokes[n]['id']`) and its text (`$jokes[n]['text']`).

Our next step, then, should be to update the **jokes.html.php** template to retrieve each joke's text from this new array structure, and also to provide a **Delete** button for each joke:

chapter4/deletejoke/jokes.html.php *(excerpt)*

```
<?php foreach ($jokes as $joke): ?>
  <form action="?deletejoke" method="post"> ❶
    <blockquote>
      <p>
        <?php echo htmlspecialchars($joke['text'], ENT_QUOTES, ❷
            'UTF-8'); ?>
        <input type="hidden" name="id" value="<?php
            echo $joke['id']; ?>"/> ❸
        <input type="submit" value="Delete"/> ❹
      </p>
    </blockquote>
  </form> ❺
<?php endforeach; ?>
```

Here are the highlights of this updated code:

 Each joke will be displayed in a form, which, if submitted, will delete that joke. We signal this to our controller using the `?deletejoke` query string in the `action` attribute.

❷ Since each joke in the `$jokes` array is now represented by a two-item array instead of a simple string, we must update this line to retrieve the text of the joke. We do this using `$joke['text']` instead of just `$joke`.

3 When we submit the form to delete this joke, we wish to send along the ID of the joke to be deleted. To do this, we need a form field containing the joke's ID, but this is a field we'd prefer to keep hidden from the user. We therefore using a hidden form field (`<input type="hidden"/>`). The name of this field is id, and its value is the ID of the joke to be deleted (`$joke['id']`).

Unlike the text of the joke, the ID is not a user-submitted value, so there's no need to worry about making it HTML-safe with htmlspecialchars. We can rest assured it will be a number, since it's automatically generated by MySQL for the id column when the joke is added to the database.

4 This submit button (`<input type="submit"/>`) submits the form when clicked. Its value attribute gives it a label of Delete.

5 Finally, we close the form for this joke.

This Markup Could Be Better

If you know your HTML, you're probably thinking those `<input/>` tags belong outside of the blockquote element, since they aren't a part of the quoted text (the joke).

Strictly speaking, that's true: the form and its inputs should really be either before or after the blockquote. Unfortunately, to make that tag structure display clearly requires a little Cascading Style Sheets (CSS) code that's really beyond the scope of this book.

Rather than attempt to teach you CSS layout techniques in a book about PHP and MySQL, I've decided to go with this imperfect markup. If you plan to use this code in the real world, you should invest some time into learning CSS (or securing the services of a person who does) so that you can take complete control of your HTML markup without worrying about the CSS code required to make it look nice.

Figure 4.11 shows what the joke list looks like with the **Delete** buttons added.

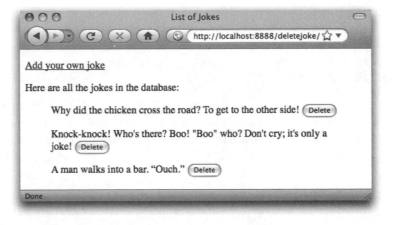

Figure 4.11. Each button will delete its respective joke

All that remains to make this new feature work is to update the controller so that it can process the form submission that results from clicking one of our new **Delete** buttons:

chapter4/deletejoke/index.php *(excerpt)*

```
if (isset($_GET['deletejoke']))
{
  $id = mysqli_real_escape_string($link, $_POST['id']);
  $sql = "DELETE FROM joke WHERE id='$id'";
  if (!mysqli_query($link, $sql))
  {
    $error = 'Error deleting joke: ' . mysqli_error($link);
    include 'error.html.php';
    exit();
  }

  header('Location: .');
  exit();
}
```

This chunk of code works exactly like the one we added to process the "Add Joke" code earlier in this chapter. We start by using `mysqli_real_escape_string` to sanitize the submitted value of `$_POST['id']` before using it in a database query[5]—this time, a `DELETE` query. Once that query is executed, we use the PHP

---

[5] You might think it's unnecessary to sanitize this value, since it's produced by a hidden form field that the user is unable to see. In fact, however, *all* form fields—even hidden ones—are ultimately under the

`header` function to ask the browser to send a new request to view the updated list of jokes.

Why Not a Link?

If you tackled this example yourself, your first instinct might have been to provide a **Delete** hyperlink for each joke, instead of going to the trouble of writing an entire HTML form containing a **Delete** button for each joke on the page. Indeed, the code for such a link would be much simpler:

```php
<?php foreach ($jokes as $joke): ?>
  <blockquote>
    <p>
      <?php echo htmlspecialchars($joke['text'], ENT_QUOTES,
          'UTF-8'); ?>
      <a href="?deletejoke&amp;id=<?php echo $joke['id'];
          ?>">Delete</a>
    </p>
  </blockquote>
<?php endforeach; ?>
```

In short, hyperlinks should never be used to perform *actions* (like deleting a joke); hyperlinks should only be used to provide a link to some related content. The same goes for forms with `method="get"`, which should only be used to perform queries of existing data. Actions should only ever be performed as a result of a form with `method="post"` being submitted.

The reason is that forms with `method="post"` are treated differently by browsers and related software. If you submit a form with `method="post"` and then click the **Refresh** button in your browser, for example, the browser will ask if you're certain you wish to resubmit the form. Browsers have no similar protection against resubmission when it comes to links and forms with `method="get"`.

Similarly, web accelerator software (and some modern browsers) will automatically follow hyperlinks present on a page in the background, so that the target pages will be available for immediate display if the user clicks one of those links. If your site deleted a joke as a result of a hyperlink being followed, you could find your jokes getting deleted automatically by your users' browsers!

---

user's control. There are widely distributed browser add-ons, for example, that will make hidden form fields visible and available for editing by the user. Remember: any value submitted by the browser is ultimately suspect when it comes to protecting your site's security.

Here's the complete code of the finished controller. If you have any questions, make sure to post them in the SitePoint Forums![6]

```
                                            chapter4/deletejoke/index.php
<?php
if (get_magic_quotes_gpc())
{
  function stripslashes_deep($value)
  {
    $value = is_array($value) ?
        array_map('stripslashes_deep', $value) :
        stripslashes($value);

    return $value;
  }

  $_POST = array_map('stripslashes_deep', $_POST);
  $_GET = array_map('stripslashes_deep', $_GET);
  $_COOKIE = array_map('stripslashes_deep', $_COOKIE);
  $_REQUEST = array_map('stripslashes_deep', $_REQUEST);
}

if (isset($_GET['addjoke']))
{
  include 'form.html.php';
  exit();
}

$link = mysqli_connect('localhost', 'root', 'password');
if (!$link)
{
  $error = 'Unable to connect to the database server.';
  include 'error.html.php';
  exit();
}

if (!mysqli_set_charset($link, 'utf8'))
{
  $output = 'Unable to set database connection encoding.';
  include 'output.html.php';
  exit();
}
```

```php
if (!mysqli_select_db($link, 'ijdb'))
{
  $error = 'Unable to locate the joke database.';
  include 'error.html.php';
  exit();
}

if (isset($_POST['joketext']))
{
  $joketext = mysqli_real_escape_string($link, $_POST['joketext']);
  $sql = 'INSERT INTO joke SET
      joketext="' . $joketext . '",
      jokedate=CURDATE()';
  if (!mysqli_query($link, $sql))
  {
    $error = 'Error adding submitted joke: ' . mysqli_error($link);
    include 'error.html.php';
    exit();
  }

  header('Location: .');
  exit();
}

if (isset($_GET['deletejoke']))
{
  $id = mysqli_real_escape_string($link, $_POST['id']);
  $sql = "DELETE FROM joke WHERE id='$id'";
  if (!mysqli_query($link, $sql))
  {
    $error = 'Error deleting joke: ' . mysqli_error($link);
    include 'error.html.php';
    exit();
  }

  header('Location: .');
  exit();
}

$result = mysqli_query($link, 'SELECT id, joketext FROM joke');
if (!$result)
{
  $error = 'Error fetching jokes: ' . mysqli_error($link);
  include 'error.html.php';
```

```
  exit();
}

while ($row = mysqli_fetch_array($result))
{
  $jokes[] = array('id' => $row['id'], 'text' => $row['joketext']);
}

include 'jokes.html.php';
?>
```

Mission Accomplished

In this chapter, you learned some new PHP functions that allow you to interface with a MySQL database server. Using these functions, you built your first database driven web site, which published the ijdb database online, and allowed visitors to add jokes to it and delete jokes from it.

In a way, you could say this chapter achieved the stated mission of this book, to teach you how to build a database driven web site. Of course, the example in this chapter contains only the bare essentials. In the rest of this book, I'll show you how to flesh out the skeleton you learned to build in this chapter.

In Chapter 5, we go back to the MySQL command line. We'll learn how to use relational database principles and advanced SQL queries to represent more complex types of information, and give our visitors credit for the jokes they add!

Relational Database Design

Since Chapter 2, we've worked with a very simple database of jokes, which is composed of a single table named, appropriately enough, joke. While this database has served us well as an introduction to MySQL databases, there's more to relational database design than can be understood from this simple example. In this chapter, we'll expand on this database, and learn a few new features of MySQL, in an effort to realize and appreciate the real power that relational databases have to offer.

Be forewarned that I will cover several topics only in an informal, non-rigorous sort of way. As any computer science major will tell you, database design is a serious area of research, with tested and mathematically provable principles that, while useful, are beyond the scope of this text.

For more complete coverage of database design concepts, and SQL in general, pick up a copy of *Simply SQL*[1] (Melbourne: SitePoint, 2008). If you're *really* into learning the hard principles behind relational databases, *Database In Depth*[2] (Sebastopol: O'Reilly, 2005) is a worthwhile read. And if you want even more information, stop by http://www.datamodel.org/ for a list of good books, as well as several useful re-

---

[1] http://www.sitepoint.com/books/sql1/

[2] http://oreilly.com/catalog/9780596100124/

sources on the subject. In particular, check out *Rules of Data Normalization* in the Data Modelling section of the site.

Giving Credit Where Credit is Due

To start off, let's recall the structure of our `joke` table. It contains three columns: `id`, `joketext`, and `jokedate`. Together, these columns allow us to identify jokes (`id`), and keep track of their text (`joketext`) and the date they were entered (`jokedate`). For your reference, here's the SQL code that creates this table and inserts a couple of entries:

```
                                                    chapter5/sql/jokes1.sql
# Code to create a simple joke table

CREATE TABLE joke (
  id INT NOT NULL AUTO_INCREMENT PRIMARY KEY,
  joketext TEXT,
  jokedate DATE NOT NULL
) DEFAULT CHARACTER SET utf8;


# Adding jokes to the table

INSERT INTO joke SET
joketext = 'Why did the chicken cross the road? To get to the other
➡ side!',
jokedate = '2009-04-01';

INSERT INTO joke
(joketext, jokedate) VALUES (
'Knock-knock! Who\'s there? Boo! "Boo" who? Don\'t cry; it\'s only a
➡ joke!',
"2009-04-01"
);
```

Now, let's say we wanted to track another piece of information about our jokes: the names of the people who submitted them. It would seem natural to want to add a new column to our `joke` table for this. The SQL `ALTER TABLE` command (which we've yet to see) lets us do exactly that. Log into your MySQL server using the **mysql** command-line program as in Chapter 2, select your database (`ijdb` if you used the name suggested in that chapter), then type this command:

```
mysql> ALTER TABLE joke ADD COLUMN
    -> authorname VARCHAR(255);
```

This code adds a column called authorname to your table. The type declared is a **variable-length character string** of up to 255 characters (VARCHAR(255))—plenty of space for even very esoteric names. Let's also add a column for the authors' email addresses:

```
mysql> ALTER TABLE joke ADD COLUMN
    -> authoremail VARCHAR(255);
```

For more information about the ALTER TABLE command, see Appendix A. Just to make sure the two columns were added properly, we should ask MySQL to describe the table to us:

```
mysql> DESCRIBE joke;
+-------------+--------------+------+-----+---------+------------
| Field       | Type         | Null | Key | Default | Extra
+-------------+--------------+------+-----+---------+------------
| id          | int(11)      | NO   | PRI | NULL    | auto_increm
| joketext    | text         | YES  |     | NULL    |
| jokedate    | date         | NO   |     |         |
| authorname  | varchar(255) | YES  |     | NULL    |
| authoremail | varchar(255) | YES  |     | NULL    |
+-------------+--------------+------+-----+---------+------------
5 rows in set (0.00 sec)
```

Looks good, right? Obviously, we would need to make changes to the HTML and PHP form code we wrote in Chapter 4 that allowed us to add new jokes to the database. Using UPDATE queries, we could now add author details to all the jokes in the table. But before we're carried away with these changes, we need to stop and consider whether this new table design was the right choice here. In this case, it turns out to be a poor choice.

Rule of Thumb: Keep Entities Separate

As your knowledge of database driven web sites continues to grow, you may decide that a personal joke list is too limited. In fact, you might begin to receive more submitted jokes than you have original jokes of your own. Let's say you decide to launch a web site where people from all over the world can share jokes with each other. To add the author's name and email address to each joke certainly makes a lot of sense, but the method we used above leads to several potential problems:

■ What if a frequent contributor to your site named Joan Smith changed her email address? She might begin to submit new jokes using the new address, but her old address would still be attached to all the jokes she'd submitted in the past. Looking at your database, you might simply think there were two different people named Joan Smith who had submitted jokes. If she were especially thoughtful, she might inform you of the change of address, and you might try to update all the old jokes with the new address, but if you missed just one joke, your database would still contain incorrect information. Database design experts refer to this sort of problem as an **update anomaly**.

■ It would be natural for you to rely on your database to provide a list of all the people who've ever submitted jokes to your site. In fact, you could easily obtain a mailing list using the following query:

```
mysql> SELECT DISTINCT authorname, authoremail
    -> FROM joke;
```

The word DISTINCT in the above query stops MySQL from outputting duplicate result rows. For example, if Joan Smith submitted twenty jokes to your site, using the DISTINCT option would cause her name to only appear once in the list instead of twenty times.

Then, if for some reason, you decided to remove all the jokes that a particular author had submitted to your site, you'd remove any record of this person from the database in the process, and you'd no longer be able to email him or her with information about your site! As your mailing list might be a major source of income for your site, it's unwise to go throwing away an author's email address just because you disliked the jokes that person had submitted to your site. Database design experts call this a **delete anomaly**.

■ You have no guarantee that Joan Smith will enter her name the same way each time—consider the variations: Joan Smith; J. Smith; Smith, Joan—you catch my drift. This would make keeping track of a particular author exceedingly difficult, especially if Joan Smith also had several email addresses she liked to use.

These problems—and more—can be dealt with very easily using established database design principles. Instead of storing the information for the authors in the joke table, let's create an entirely new table for our list of authors. Since we used a column called id in the joke table to identify each of our jokes with a unique number, we'll use an identically-named column in our new table to identify our authors. We can then use those author IDs in our joke table to associate authors with their jokes. The complete database layout is shown in Figure 5.1.

joke

id	joketext	jokedate	authorid
1	Why did the chicken ...	2009-04-01	1
2	Knock-knock! Who's ...	2009-04-01	1
3	A man walks into a bar ...	2009-05-16	2

author

id	name	email
1	Kevin Yank	kevin@sitepoint.com
2	Joan Smith	joan@example.com

Figure 5.1. The authorid field associates each row in joke with a row in author

What these two tables show are three jokes and two authors. The authorid column of the joke table establishes a **relationship** between the two tables, indicating that Kevin Yank submitted jokes 1 and 2 and Joan Smith submitted joke 3. Notice also that, since each author now only appears once in the database, and appears independently of the jokes submitted, we've avoided all the problems outlined above.

The most important characteristic of this database design, however, is that, since we're storing information about two types of *things* (jokes and authors), it's most appropriate to have two tables. This is a rule of thumb that you should always keep in mind when designing a database: *each type of entity (or "thing") about which you want to be able to store information should be given its own table.*

To set up the above database from scratch is fairly simple (involving just two CREATE TABLE queries), but since we'd like to make these changes in a nondestructive manner (i.e. without losing any of our precious knock-knock jokes), we'll use the ALTER TABLE command again. First, we remove the author-related columns in the joke table:

```
mysql> ALTER TABLE joke DROP COLUMN authorname;
Query OK, 0 rows affected (0.00 sec)
Records: 2  Duplicates: 0  Warnings: 0

mysql> ALTER TABLE joke DROP COLUMN authoremail;
Query OK, 0 rows affected (0.00 sec)
Records: 2  Duplicates: 0  Warnings: 0
```

Now, we create our new table:

```
mysql> CREATE TABLE author (
    ->    id INT NOT NULL AUTO_INCREMENT PRIMARY KEY,
    ->    name VARCHAR(255),
    ->    email VARCHAR(255)
    -> ) DEFAULT CHARACTER SET utf8;
```

Finally, we add the authorid column to our joke table:

```
mysql> ALTER TABLE joke ADD COLUMN authorid INT;
```

If you prefer, here are the CREATE TABLE commands that will create the two tables from scratch:

chapter5/sql/2tables.sql *(excerpt)*

```
# Code to create a simple joke table that stores an author ID

CREATE TABLE joke (
  id INT NOT NULL AUTO_INCREMENT PRIMARY KEY,
  joketext TEXT,
  jokedate DATE NOT NULL,
  authorid INT
) DEFAULT CHARACTER SET utf8;

# Code to create a simple author table
```

```
CREATE TABLE author (
  id INT NOT NULL AUTO_INCREMENT PRIMARY KEY,
  name VARCHAR(255),
  email VARCHAR(255)
) DEFAULT CHARACTER SET utf8;
```

All that's left is to add some authors to the new table, and assign authors to all the existing jokes in the database by filling in the authorid column.[3] Go ahead and do this now if you like—it should give you some practice with INSERT and UPDATE queries. If you're rebuilding the database from scratch, however, here's a series of INSERT queries that will do the trick:

chapter5/sql/2tables.sql (excerpt)

```
# Adding authors to the database
# We specify the IDs so they are known when we add the jokes below.

INSERT INTO author SET
  id = 1,
  name = 'Kevin Yank',
  email = 'kevin@sitepoint.com';

INSERT INTO author (id, name, email)
VALUES (2, 'Joan Smith', 'joan@example.com');

# Adding jokes to the database

INSERT INTO joke SET
  joketext = 'Why did the chicken cross the road? To get to the othe
➥r side!',
  jokedate = '2009-04-01',
  authorid = 1;

INSERT INTO joke (joketext, jokedate, authorid)
VALUES (
  'Knock-knock! Who\'s there? Boo! "Boo" who? Don\'t cry; it\'s only
➥ a joke!',
  '2009-04-01',
  1
);
```

---

[3] For now, you'll have to do this manually. But rest assured, in Chapter 7 we'll see how PHP can insert entries with the correct IDs automatically, reflecting the relationships between them.

```
INSERT INTO joke (joketext, jokedate, authorid)
VALUES (
  'A man walks into a bar. "Ouch."',
  '2009-04-01',
  2
);
```

SELECT with Multiple Tables

With your data now separated into two tables, it may seem that you're complicating the process of data retrieval. Consider, for example, our original goal: to display a list of jokes with the name and email address of the author next to each joke. In the single-table solution, you could gain all the information you needed to produce such a list using a single SELECT query in your PHP code:

```
$result = mysqli_query($link,
    'SELECT id, joketext, authorname, authoremail FROM joke');
if (!$result)
{
  $error = 'Error fetching jokes: ' . mysqli_error($link);
  include 'error.html.php';
  exit();
}

while ($row = mysqli_fetch_array($result))
{
  $jokes[] = array('id' => $row['id'], 'text' => $row['joketext'],
      'name' => $row['authorname'], 'email' => $row['authoremail']);
}
```

In the new system, this would, at first, no longer seem possible. As the details about the author of each joke are no longer stored in the joke table, you might think that you'd have to fetch those details separately for each joke you wanted to display. The code to perform this task would involve a call to mysqli_query for each and every joke to be displayed. This would be messy and slow. As your database of jokes increased in size, the overhead of all those queries would drag down the performance of your site in a big way.

With all this taken into account, it would seem that the "old way" was actually the better solution, despite its weaknesses. Fortunately, relational databases like MySQL are designed to make it easy to work with data stored in multiple tables! Using a new form of the SELECT statement, called a **join**, you can have the best of both worlds. Joins allow you to treat related data in multiple tables as if they were stored in a single table. Here's what the syntax of a simple join looks like:

```
mysql> SELECT columns
    -> FROM table1 INNER JOIN table2
    ->   ON condition(s) for data to be related;
```

In your case, the columns you're interested in are id and joketext in the joke table, and name and email in the author table. The condition for an entry in the joke table to be related to an entry in the author table is that the value of the authorid column in the joke table is equal to the value of the id column in the author table.

Here's an example of a join (the first two queries simply show you what's contained in the two tables—they're unnecessary):

```
mysql> SELECT id, LEFT(joketext, 20), authorid FROM joke;
+----+----------------------+----------+
| id | LEFT(joketext, 20)   | authorid |
+----+----------------------+----------+
|  1 | Why did the chicken  |        1 |
|  2 | Knock knock. Who's t |        1 |
|  3 | A man walks into a b |        2 |
+----+----------------------+----------+
3 rows in set (0.00 sec)

mysql> SELECT * FROM author;
+----+------------+---------------------+
| id | name       | email               |
+----+------------+---------------------+
|  1 | Kevin Yank | kevin@sitepoint.com |
|  2 | Joan Smith | joan@example.com    |
+----+------------+---------------------+
2 rows in set (0.00 sec)
```

```
mysql> SELECT joke.id, LEFT(joketext, 20), name, email
    -> FROM joke INNER JOIN author
    ->   ON authorid = author.id;
+----+----------------------+-------------+----------------------+
| id | LEFT(joketext, 20)   | name        | email                |
+----+----------------------+-------------+----------------------+
|  1 | Why did the chicken  | Kevin Yank  | kevin@sitepoint.com  |
|  2 | Knock-knock! Who's t | Kevin Yank  | kevin@sitepoint.com  |
|  3 | A man walks into a b | Joan Smith  | joan@example.com     |
+----+----------------------+-------------+----------------------+
3 rows in set (0.00 sec)
```

See? The results of the third SELECT, which is a join, group the values stored in the two tables into a single table of results, with related data correctly appearing together. Even though the data is stored in two tables, you can still access all the information you need to produce the joke list on your web page with a single database query. Note in the query that, since there are columns named id in both tables, you must specify the name of the table when you refer to either id column. The joke table's id is referred to as joke.id, while the author table's id column is author.id. If the table name is unspecified, MySQL won't know which id you're referring to, and will produce this error:

```
mysql> SELECT id, LEFT(joketext, 20), name, email
    -> FROM joke INNER JOIN author
    ->   ON authorid = id;
ERROR 1052 (23000): Column: 'id' in field list is ambiguous
```

Now that you know how to access the data stored in your two tables efficiently, you can rewrite the code for your joke list to take advantage of joins:

```
                                         chapter5/jokes/index.php (excerpt)

$result = mysqli_query($link,
    'SELECT joke.id, joketext, name, email
    FROM joke INNER JOIN author
      ON authorid = author.id');
if (!$result)
{
  $error = 'Error fetching jokes: ' . mysqli_error($link);
  include 'error.html.php';
  exit();
}

while ($row = mysqli_fetch_array($result))
{
  $jokes[] = array('id' => $row['id'], 'text' => $row['joketext'],
      'name' => $row['name'], 'email' => $row['email']);
}

include 'jokes.html.php';
?>
```

You can then update your template to display the author information for each joke:

```
                                      chapter5/jokes/jokes.html.php (excerpt)

<?php foreach ($jokes as $joke): ?>
  <form action="?deletejoke" method="post">
    <blockquote>
      <p>
        <?php echo htmlspecialchars($joke['text'], ENT_QUOTES,
            'UTF-8'); ?>
        <input type="hidden" name="id" value="<?php
            echo $joke['id']; ?>"/>
        <input type="submit" value="Delete"/>
        (by <a href="mailto:<?php
            echo htmlspecialchars($joke['email'], ENT_QUOTES,
                'UTF-8'); ?>"><?php
            echo htmlspecialchars($joke['name'], ENT_QUOTES,
                'UTF-8'); ?></a>)
      </p>
    </blockquote>
  </form>
<?php endforeach; ?>
```

The resulting display is shown in Figure 5.2.

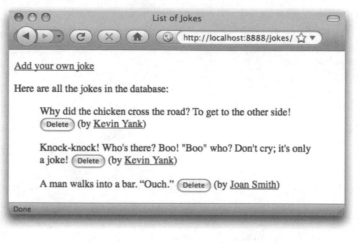

Figure 5.2. I wrote all the best ones myself

The more you work with databases, the more you'll come to realize the power of combining data contained in separate tables into a single table of results. Consider, for example, the following query, which displays a list of all jokes written by Joan Smith:

```
mysql> SELECT joketext
    -> FROM joke INNER JOIN author
    ->   ON authorid = author.id
    -> WHERE name = "Joan Smith";
+------------------------------------+
| joketext                           |
+------------------------------------+
| A man walks into a bar. "Ouch."    |
+------------------------------------+
1 row in set (0.00 sec)
```

The results that are output from the above query come only from the joke table, but the query uses a join to let it search for jokes based on a value stored in the author table. There will be plenty more examples of clever queries like this throughout the book, but this example alone illustrates that the practical applications of joins are many and varied and, in almost all cases, can save you a lot of work!

Simple Relationships

The best type of database layout for a given situation is usually dictated by the type of relationship that exists between the data that it needs to store. In this section, I'll examine the typical relationship types, and explain how best to represent them in a relational database.

In the case of a simple **one-to-one relationship**, a single table is all you'll need. An example of a one-to-one relationship that you've seen so far is the email address of each author in our joke database. Since there will be one email address for each author, and one author for each email address, there's no reason to split the addresses into a separate table.[4]

A **many-to-one relationship** is a little more complicated, but you've already seen one of these as well. Each joke in our database is associated with just one author, but many jokes may have been written by that one author. This joke–author relationship is many-to-one. I've already covered the problems that result from storing the information associated with a joke's author in the same table as the joke itself. In brief, it can result in many copies of the same data, which are difficult to keep synchronized, and waste space. If we split the data into two tables, and use an ID column to link the two together (which will make joins possible as shown above), all these problems disappear.

A **one-to-many relationship** is simply a many-to-one relationship seen from the opposite direction. Since the joke–author relationship is many-to-one, the author–joke relationship is one-to-many (there is one author for, potentially, many jokes). This is easy to see in theory, but when you're coming at a problem from the opposite direction, it's less obvious. In the case of jokes and authors, we started with a library of jokes (the many) and then wanted to assign an author to each of them (the one). Let's now look at a hypothetical design problem where we start with the one and want to add the many.

Say we wanted to allow each of the authors in our database (the one) to have multiple email addresses (the many). When an inexperienced person in database design ap-

---

[4] There are exceptions to this rule. For example, if a single table grows very large with lots of columns, some of which are rarely used in **SELECT** queries, it can make sense to split those columns out into their own table. This can improve the performance of queries on the now smaller table.

proaches a one-to-many relationship like this one, the first thought is often to try to store multiple values in a single database field, as shown in Figure 5.3.

author

id	name	email
1	Kevin Yank	kevin@sitepoint.com, kyank@example.com
2	Joan Smith	joan@example.com, jsmith@example.com

Figure 5.3. Never overload a table field to store multiple values, as is done here

While this would work, to retrieve a single email address from the database, we'd need to break up the string by searching for commas (or whatever special character you chose to use as a separator)—a not-so-simple and potentially time-consuming operation. Try to imagine the PHP code necessary to remove one particular email address from one particular author! In addition, you'd need to allow for much longer values in the `email` column, which could result in wasted disk space, because the majority of authors would have just one email address.

Now take a step back, and realize this one-to-many relationship is just the same as the many-to-one relationship we faced between jokes and authors. The solution, therefore, is also the same: split the entities (in this case, email addresses) into their own table. The resulting database structure is shown in Figure 5.4.

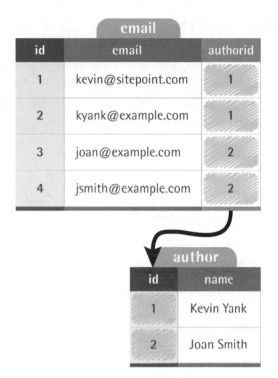

Figure 5.4. The authorid field associates each row of email with one row of author

Using a join with this structure, we can easily list the email addresses associated with a particular author:

```
mysql> SELECT email
    -> FROM author INNER JOIN email
    ->   ON authorid = author.id
    -> WHERE name = "Kevin Yank";
+----------------------+
| email                |
+----------------------+
| kevin@sitepoint.com  |
| kyank@example.com    |
+----------------------+
2 rows in set (0.00 sec)
```

Many-to-Many Relationships

Okay, you now have a steadily-growing database of jokes published on your web site. It's growing so quickly, in fact, that the number of jokes has become unmanageable! People who visit your site are faced with a mammoth page that contains hundreds of jokes listed without any structure whatsoever. We need to make a change.

You decide to place your jokes into categories such as Knock-Knock Jokes, Crossing the Road Jokes, Lawyer Jokes, and Political Jokes. Remembering our rule of thumb from earlier, you identify joke categories as a different type of entity, and create a new table for them:

```
mysql> CREATE TABLE category (
    ->    id INT NOT NULL AUTO_INCREMENT PRIMARY KEY,
    ->    name VARCHAR(255)
    -> ) DEFAULT CHARACTER SET utf8;
Query OK, 0 rows affected (0.00 sec)
```

Now you come to the daunting task of assigning categories to your jokes. It occurs to you that a "political" joke might also be a "crossing the road" joke, and a "knock-knock" joke might also be a "lawyer" joke. A single joke might belong to many categories, and each category will contain many jokes. This is a **many-to-many** relationship.

Once again, many inexperienced developers begin to think of ways to store several values in a single column—because the obvious solution is to add a `category` column to the `joke` table and use it to list the IDs of those categories to which each joke belongs. A second rule of thumb would be useful here: *if you need to store multiple values in a single field, your design is probably flawed.*

The correct way to represent a many-to-many relationship is to use a **lookup table**. This is a table that contains no actual data, but which lists pairs of entries that are related. Figure 5.5 shows what the database design would look like for our joke categories.

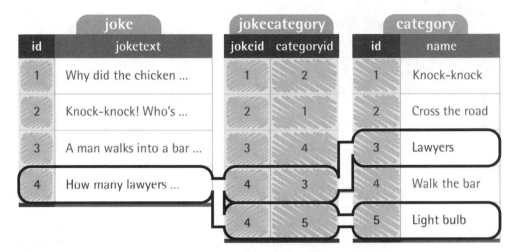

Figure 5.5. The `jokecategory` table associates pairs of rows from the `joke` and `category` tables

The `jokecategory` table associates joke IDs (`jokeid`) with category IDs (`categoryid`). In this example, we can see that the joke that starts with "How many lawyers ..." belongs to both the Lawyers and Light bulb categories.

A lookup table is created in much the same way as is any other table. The difference lies in the choice of the primary key. Every table we've created so far has had a column named `id` that was designated to be the PRIMARY KEY when the table was created. Designating a column as a primary key tells MySQL to disallow two entries in that column to have the same value. It also speeds up join operations based on that column.

In the case of a lookup table, there is no single column that we want to force to have unique values. Each joke ID may appear more than once, as a joke may belong to more than one category, and each category ID may appear more than once, as a category may contain many jokes. What we want to prevent is the same *pair* of values to appear in the table twice. And, since the sole purpose of this table is to facilitate joins, the speed benefits offered by a primary key would come in very handy. For this reason, we usually create lookup tables with a multi-column primary key as follows:

```
mysql> CREATE TABLE jokecategory (
    ->    jokeid INT NOT NULL,
    ->    categoryid INT NOT NULL,
    ->    PRIMARY KEY (jokeid, categoryid)
    -> ) DEFAULT CHARACTER SET utf8;
```

This creates a table in which the `jokeid` and `categoryid` columns together form
the primary key. This enforces the uniqueness that's appropriate to a lookup table,
preventing a particular joke from being assigned to a specific category more than
once, and speeds up joins that make use of this table.

Now that your lookup table is in place and contains category assignments, you can
use joins to create several interesting and very practical queries. This query lists all
jokes in the Knock-knock category:

```
mysql> SELECT joketext
    -> FROM joke INNER JOIN jokecategory
    ->   ON joke.id = jokeid
    -> INNER JOIN category
    ->   ON categoryid = category.id
    -> WHERE name = "Knock-knock";
```

As you can see, this query uses *two* joins. First, it takes the `joke` table and joins it
to the `jokecategory` table; then it takes that joined data and joins it to the `category`
table. As your database structure becomes more complex, multi-join queries like
this one become common.

The following query lists the categories that contain jokes beginning with "How
many lawyers ...":

```
mysql> SELECT name
    -> FROM joke INNER JOIN jokecategory
    ->   ON joke.id = jokeid
    -> INNER JOIN category
    ->   ON categoryid = category.id
    -> WHERE joketext LIKE "How many lawyers%";
```

And this query, which also makes use of our `author` table to join together the contents of *four tables*, lists the names of all authors who have written knock-knock
jokes:

```
mysql> SELECT author.name
    -> FROM joke INNER JOIN author
    ->    ON authorid = author.id
    -> INNER JOIN jokecategory
    ->    ON joke.id = jokeid
    -> INNER JOIN category
    ->    ON categoryid = category.id
    -> WHERE category.name = "Knock-knock";
```

One for Many, and Many for One

In this chapter, I explained the fundamentals of good database design, and we learned how MySQL and, for that matter, all relational database management systems provide support for the representation of different types of relationships between entities. From your initial understanding of one-to-one relationships, you should now have expanded your knowledge to include many-to-one, one-to-many, and many-to-many relationships.

In the process, you learned a few new features of common SQL commands. In particular, you learned how to use a SELECT query to join data spread across multiple tables into a single set of results.

With the increased expressiveness that multiple database tables bring, you're now equipped to extend the simple "joke list" site you assembled in Chapter 4 to include authors and categories, and that's exactly what Chapter 7 will be all about. Before you tackle this project, however, you should take some time to add to your PHP skills. Just as you spent this chapter learning some of the finer points of MySQL database design, Chapter 6 will teach you some of the subtleties of PHP programming—which will make the job of building a more complete joke database site much more fun.

Chapter

6

Structured PHP Programming

Before we plow headlong into the next enhancements of our joke database, let's spend a little time honing your "PHP-fu." Specifically, I want to show you a few techniques to better **structure your code**.

Structured coding techniques are useful in all but the simplest of PHP projects. Already in Chapter 3, you've learned how to split up your PHP code into multiple files: a controller and a set of associated templates. This lets you keep the server-side logic of your site separate from the HTML code used to display the dynamic content generated by that logic. In order to do this, you learned how to use the PHP `include` command.

The PHP language offers many such facilities to help you add structure to your code. The most powerful of these is undoubtedly its support for object-oriented programming (OOP), which is explored in depth in *The PHP Anthology: 101 Essential Tips, Tricks & Hacks, 2nd Edition*[1] (Melbourne: SitePoint, 2007). OOP is a big topic, and requires you to drastically change the way you think about solving problems

---

[1] http://www.sitepoint.com/books/phpant2/

in PHP. Thankfully, the more basic features of PHP already offer many opportunities for structuring your code.

In this chapter, I'll explore some *simple* ways to keep your code manageable and maintainable without requiring you to become a total programming wizard (though you might like to be that anyway!).

Include Files

Often, even very simple PHP-based web sites need the same piece of code in several places. You already learned to use the PHP `include` command to load a PHP template from inside your controller; it turns out you can use the same feature to save yourself from having to write the same code again and again.

Include files (also known as just **includes**) contain snippets of PHP code that you can then load into your other PHP scripts instead of having to retype them.

Including HTML Content

The concept of include files came long before PHP. If you're an old codger like me (which, in the web world, means you're over 25), you may have experimented with **Server-Side Includes** (SSIs). A feature of just about every web server out there, SSIs let you put commonly used snippets of HTML (and JavaScript, and CSS) into include files that you can then use in multiple pages.

In PHP, include files most commonly contain either pure PHP code or, in the case of PHP templates, a mixture of HTML and PHP code. But you don't *have* to put PHP code in your include files. If you like, an include file can contain strictly static HTML. This is most useful for sharing common design elements across your site, such as a copyright notice to appear at the bottom of every page:

chapter6/static-footer/footer.inc.html.php

```
<div id="footer">
  The contents of this webpage are copyright &copy; 1998 - 2009
  Example Pty. Ltd. All Rights Reserved.
</div>
```

This file is a **template fragment**—an include file to be used by PHP templates. To distinguish this type of file from the other files in your project, I recommend giving it a name ending with **.inc.html.php**.

You can then use this fragment in any of your PHP templates:

chapter6/static-footer/samplepage.html.php

```
<!DOCTYPE html PUBLIC "-//W3C//DTD XHTML 1.0 Strict//EN"
    "http://www.w3.org/TR/xhtml1/DTD/xhtml1-strict.dtd">
<html xmlns="http://www.w3.org/1999/xhtml" xml:lang="en" lang="en">
  <head>
    <title>A Sample Page</title>
    <meta http-equiv="content-type"
        content="text/html; charset=utf-8"/>
  </head>
  <body>
    <p id="main">
      This page uses a static include to display a standard
      copyright notice below.
    </p>
    <?php include 'footer.inc.html.php'; ?>
  </body>
</html>
```

Finally, here's the controller that loads this template:

chapter6/static-footer/index.php

```
<?php
include 'samplepage.html.php';
?>
```

Figure 6.1 shows what the page looks like in the browser.

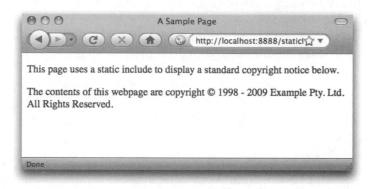

Figure 6.1. A static include displays the site's copyright notice

Now, each year all you need to do to update your copyright notice is to edit **footer.inc.html.php**. No more time-consuming and error-prone find-and-replace operations!

Of course, if you *really* want to make your life easy, you can just let PHP do the work for you:

chapter6/dynamic-footer/footer.inc.html.php

```
<p id="footer">
  The contents of this webpage are copyright &copy; 1998 -
  <?php echo date('Y'); ?> Example Pty. Ltd. All Rights
  Reserved.
</p>
```

Including PHP Code

On database driven web sites, almost every controller script must establish a database connection as its first order of business. As we've already seen, the code for doing this is fairly substantial:

```
$link = mysqli_connect('localhost', 'root', 'password');
if (!$link)
{
  $error = 'Unable to connect to the database server.';
  include 'error.html.php';
  exit();
}

if (!mysqli_set_charset($link, 'utf8'))
{
  $output = 'Unable to set database connection encoding.';
  include 'output.html.php';
  exit();
}

if (!mysqli_select_db($link, 'ijdb'))
{
  $error = 'Unable to locate the joke database.';
  include 'error.html.php';
  exit();
}
```

At some twenty-one lines long, it's only a slightly cumbersome chunk of code, but having to type it at the top of every controller script can become annoying in a hurry. Many new PHP developers will often omit essential error checking (for example, by leaving out the three if statements in the above) to save typing, which can result in a lot of lost time looking for the cause when an error *does* occur. Others will make heavy use of the clipboard to copy pieces of code like this from existing scripts for use in new ones. Some even use features of their text editor software to store useful pieces of code like this as snippets for frequent use.

But what happens when the database password, or some other detail of the code changes? Suddenly you're on a treasure hunt to find every occurrence of the code in your site to make the necessary change—a task that can be especially frustrating if you've used several variations of the code that you need to track down and update.

Figure 6.2 illustrates how include files can help in this situation. Instead of repeating the code fragment in every file that needs it, write it just once in a separate file, known as an **include file**. That file can then be **included** in any other PHP files that need to use it!

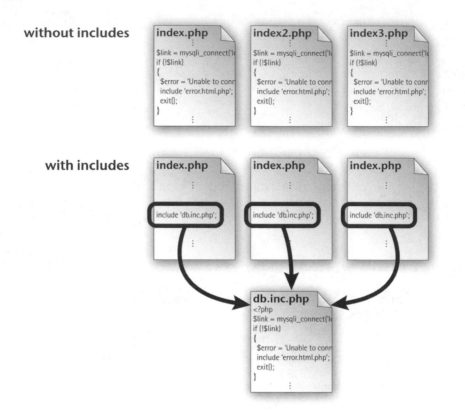

Figure 6.2. Include files allow several scripts to share common code

Let's apply this technique to create the database connection in our joke list example to see how this works in detail. First, create a file called **db.inc.php**[2] and place the database connection code inside it.

---

[2] The current convention is to name include files with a **.inc.php** extension. This allows you easily to identify them among ordinary PHP scripts, while at the same time ensuring that they're identified and processed as PHP scripts by the web server and the development tools you use. In practice, you can name include files however you like. Previously, it was common to simply give include files an **.inc** extension; but unless the web server was specifically configured to process such files as PHP scripts or to protect them from being downloaded, users who guessed the names of your include files could download them as plain text and gain access to sensitive information (such as database passwords) that appeared in the source code.

```
chapter6/jokes/db.inc.php

<?php
$link = mysqli_connect('localhost', 'root', 'password');
if (!$link)
{
  $error = 'Unable to connect to the database server.';
  include 'error.html.php';
  exit();
}

if (!mysqli_set_charset($link, 'utf8'))
{
  $output = 'Unable to set database connection encoding.';
  include 'output.html.php';
  exit();
}

if (!mysqli_select_db($link, 'ijdb'))
{
  $error = 'Unable to locate the joke database.';
  include 'error.html.php';
  exit();
}
?>
```

As you can see, include files are just like normal PHP files, but typically they contain
snippets of code that are only useful within the context of a larger script. Now you
can put this **db.inc.php** file to use in your controller:

```
chapter6/jokes/index.php

<?php
if (get_magic_quotes_gpc())
{
  function stripslashes_deep($value)
  {
    $value = is_array($value) ?
        array_map('stripslashes_deep', $value) :
        stripslashes($value);

    return $value;
  }
```

```php
  $_POST = array_map('stripslashes_deep', $_POST);
  $_GET = array_map('stripslashes_deep', $_GET);
  $_COOKIE = array_map('stripslashes_deep', $_COOKIE);
  $_REQUEST = array_map('stripslashes_deep', $_REQUEST);
}

if (isset($_GET['addjoke']))
{
  include 'form.html.php';
  exit();
}

if (isset($_POST['joketext']))
{
  include 'db.inc.php';

  $joketext = mysqli_real_escape_string($link, $_POST['joketext']);
  $sql = 'INSERT INTO joke SET
      joketext="' . $joketext . '",
      jokedate=CURDATE()';
  if (!mysqli_query($link, $sql))
  {
    $error = 'Error adding submitted joke: ' . mysqli_error($link);
    include 'error.html.php';
    exit();
  }

  header('Location: .');
  exit();
}

if (isset($_GET['deletejoke']))
{
  include 'db.inc.php';

  $id = mysqli_real_escape_string($link, $_POST['id']);
  $sql = "DELETE FROM joke WHERE id='$id'";
  if (!mysqli_query($link, $sql))
  {
    $error = 'Error deleting joke: ' . mysqli_error($link);
    include 'error.html.php';
    exit();
  }

  header('Location: .');
```

```php
  exit();
}

include 'db.inc.php';

$result = mysqli_query($link, 'SELECT id, joketext FROM joke');
if (!$result)
{
  $error = 'Error fetching jokes: ' . mysqli_error($link);
  include 'error.html.php';
  exit();
}

while ($row = mysqli_fetch_array($result))
{
  $jokes[] = array('id' => $row['id'], 'text' => $row['joketext']);
}

include 'jokes.html.php';
?>
```

As you can see, wherever our controller needs a database connection, we can obtain it simply by including the **db.Inc.php** file with an `include` statement. And because the code to do this is a simple one-liner, we can make our code more readable by using a separate `include` statement just before each `mysqli_query` in our controller. Previously, we established a database connection at the top of the controller, whether the code that followed would end up needing one or not.

When PHP encounters an `include` statement, it puts the current script on hold and runs the specified PHP script. When it's finished, it returns to the original script and picks up where it left off.

Include files are the simplest way to structure PHP code. Because of their simplicity, they're also the most widely used method. Even very simple web applications can benefit greatly from the use of include files.

Types of Includes

The `include` statement we've used so far is actually only one of four statements that you can use to include another PHP file in a currently running script:

- `include`
- `require`
- `include_once`
- `require_once`

`include` and `require` are almost identical. The only difference between them is what happens when the specified file is unable to be included (that is, if it does not exist, or if the web server doesn't have permission to read it). With `include`, a warning is displayed[3] and the script continues to run. With `require`, an error is displayed and the script stops.

In general, therefore, you should use `require` whenever the main script is unable to work without the script to be included. I do recommend using `include` whenever possible, however. Even if the **db.inc.php** file for your site is unable to be loaded, for example, you might still want to let the script for your front page continue to load. None of the content from the database will display, but the user might be able to use the **Contact Us** link at the bottom of the page to let you know about the problem!

`include_once` and `require_once` work just like `include` and `require`, respectively—but if the specified file has already been included (using *any* of the four statements described here) at least once for the current page request, the statement will be ignored. This is handy for include files that perform a task that only needs to be done once, like connecting to the database.

Figure 6.3 shows `include_once` in action. In the figure, **index.php** includes two files: **categories.inc.php** and **top10.inc.php**. Both of these files use `include_once` to include **db.inc.php**, as they both need a database connection in order to do their job. As

---

[3] In production environments, warnings and errors are usually disabled in **php.ini**. In such environments, a failed `include` has no visible effect (aside from the lack of whatever content would normally have been generated by the include file), while a failed `require` causes the page to stop at the point of failure. When a failed `require` occurs before any content is sent to the browser, the unlucky user will see nothing but a blank page!

shown, PHP will ignore the attempt to include **db.inc.php** in **top10.inc.php** because the file was already included in **categories.inc.php**. As a result, only one database connection is created.

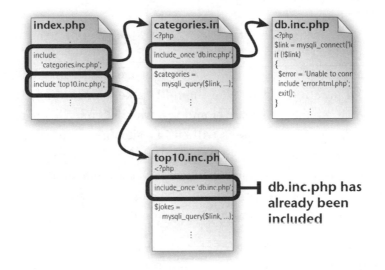

Figure 6.3. Use `include_once` to avoid opening a second database connection

`include_once` and `require_once` are also useful for loading function libraries, as we'll see in the section called "Custom Functions and Function Libraries".

Shared Include Files

In all of the examples I've shown you so far, I've assumed that the include file is located in the same directory on your web server as the file(s) that use it. Often, this is an invalid assumption! On many sites, you'll want to share include files among scripts that span potentially complex directory structures. A solid candidate for a shared include file would be the database connection include, **db.inc.php**.

So the question is, when the include file is in a *different* directory, how does a PHP script find it? The most obvious method is to specify the location of the include file as an **absolute path**. Here's how this would look on a Windows server:[4]

---

[4] I recommend always using forward slashes in your paths, even when you're working with a Windows server. PHP is smart enough to do the conversion for you, and using forward slashes saves you from having to type double-backslashes (\ \ ) to represent single backslashes in PHP strings.

```
<?php include 'C:/Program Files/Apache Software Foundation/Apache2.2
➥/htdocs/includes/db.inc.php'; ?>
```

And here's the code on a Linux server:

```
<?php include '/usr/local/apache2/htdocs/includes/db.inc.php'; ?>
```

While this method will work, it's undesirable because it ties your site's code to your web server configuration. Ideally, you should be able to drop your PHP-based web site onto any PHP-enabled web server and just watch it run. This is particularly important because many developers will build a site on one server, then deploy it publicly on a different server. This is impractical if your code refers to drives and directories that are specific to one particular server. And, even if you *do* have the luxury of working on a single server, you'll be kicking yourself if you ever need to move your web site to another drive/directory on that server.

A better method is to let PHP keep track of the **document root**[5] of your web server, then specify the path from that location. In any PHP script, you can get the document root of your web server using $_SERVER['DOCUMENT_ROOT']. As I briefly explained in Chapter 4, $_SERVER is an array variable that's automatically created by PHP, just like $_GET, $_POST, and $_REQUEST. $_SERVER contains a whole bunch of information supplied by your web server, including $_SERVER['DOCUMENT_ROOT'].

Here's an example:

```
<?php include $_SERVER['DOCUMENT_ROOT'] . '/includes/db.inc.php'; ?>
```

This will work on Windows, Mac, and Linux servers based on Apache and Internet Information Services (IIS).[6]

---

[5] The document root is the directory on your server that corresponds to the root directory of your web site. For example, to make **index.php** available at **http://www.example.com/index.php**, you would have to place it in the document root directory on the www.example.com web server.

[6] The one place where you can't count on $_SERVER['DOCUMENT_ROOT'] is on a server running the Common Gateway Interface (CGI) version of PHP. The CGI specification does not require the web server to inform PHP of the document root directory for the site, so this value will usually be absent on such configurations. Thankfully, CGI installations of PHP are increasingly rare, and should certainly be avoided in production environments. If you followed the installation instructions for PHP in this book, you can rest assured that $_SERVER['DOCUMENT_ROOT'] will work.

Another excellent candidate for a shared include file is the snippet of code that we've used to reverse the changes to submitted values made by PHP's misguided magic quotes feature, which we looked at in Chapter 4. Simply drop this code into its own file:

chapter6/includes/magicquotes.inc.php

```php
<?php
if (get_magic_quotes_gpc())
{
  function stripslashes_deep($value)
  {
    $value = is_array($value) ?
        array_map('stripslashes_deep', $value) :
        stripslashes($value);

    return $value;
  }

  $_POST = array_map('stripslashes_deep', $_POST);
  $_GET = array_map('stripslashes_deep', $_GET);
  $_COOKIE = array_map('stripslashes_deep', $_COOKIE);
  $_REQUEST = array_map('stripslashes_deep', $_REQUEST);
}
?>
```

From this point on, you can use this include file to remove the effects of magic quotes with a single line at the top of your controller scripts:

```php
<?php
include $_SERVER['DOCUMENT_ROOT'] . '/includes/magicquotes.inc.php';
```

I'll use the two shared include files discussed in this section—the database connection script and the magic quotes removal script—in many of the examples from this point forward in the book.

Custom Functions and Function Libraries

By this point, you're probably quite comfortable with the idea of **functions**. A function is a feature of PHP that you can invoke at will, usually providing one or more **parameters** (or **arguments**) for it to use, and often receiving a **return value** back as a result. You can use PHP's vast library of functions to do just about anything a PHP script could ever be asked to do, from connecting to a database (`mysqli_connect`) to generating graphics on the fly (`imagecreatetruecolor`[7]).

But what you may be unaware of is that you can create functions of your own! **Custom functions**, once defined, work just like PHP's built-in functions, and they can do anything a normal PHP script can do.

Let's start with a really simple example. Say you had a PHP script that needed to calculate the area of a rectangle given its width (3) and height (5). Thinking back to your basic geometry classes in school, you should recall that the area of a rectangle is its width multiplied by its height:

```
$area = 3 * 5;
```

But it'd be nicer to have a function called `area` that simply calculated the area of a rectangle given its dimensions:

chapter6/calculate-area/index.php *(excerpt)*

```
$area = area(3, 5);
```

As it happens, PHP is without a built-in `area` function, but clever PHP programmers like you and me can just roll up our sleeves and write the function ourselves:

chapter6/calculate-area/area-function.inc.php

```php
<?php
function area($width, $height)
{
  return $width * $height;
}
?>
```

---

[7] http://www.php.net/imagecreatetruecolor

This include file defines a single custom function: `area`. The `<?php` and `?>` markers are probably the only lines that look familiar to you in this code. What we have here is a **function declaration**; let me break it down for you a line at a time:

function area($width, $height)

The keyword `function` tells PHP that we wish to declare a new function for use in the current script. Then, we supply the function with a name (in this case, `area`). Function names operate under the same rules as variable names—they're case-sensitive, must start with a letter or an underscore (_), and may contain letters, numbers, and underscores—except of course that there is no dollar sign prefix. Instead, function names are always followed by a set of parentheses ((…)), which may or may not be empty.

The parentheses that follow a function name enclose the list of parameters that the function will accept. You should already be familiar with this from your experience with PHP's built-in functions. For example, when you use `mysqli_connect` to connect to your database, you provide the host name, user name, and password for the connection as parameters within the parentheses.

When declaring a custom function, instead of giving a list of values for the parameters, you give a list of variable names. In this example, we list two variables: `$width` and `$height`. When the function is called, it will therefore expect to be given two parameters. The value of the first parameter will be assigned to `$width`, while the value of the second will be assigned to `$height`. Those variables can then be used to perform the calculation within the function.

{

Speaking of calculations, the rest of the function declaration is the code that performs the calculation—or does whatever else the function is supposed to do. That code must be enclosed in a set of braces ({…}).

return $width * $height;

You can think of the code within those braces as a miniature PHP script. This function is a simple one, because it contains just a single statement: a `return` statement.

A `return` statement can be used in the code of a function to jump back into the main script immediately. When the PHP interpreter hits a `return` statement, it immediately stops running the code of this function and goes back to where the function was called. It's sort of an ejection seat for functions!

In addition to breaking out of the function, the `return` statement lets you specify a value for the function to *return* to the code that called it. In this case, the value we're returning is `$x * $y`—the result of multiplying the first parameter by the second.

```
}
```

The closing brace marks the end of the function declaration.

In order to use this function, we must first include the file containing this function declaration:

chapter6/calculate-area/index.php

```php
<?php
include_once 'area-function.inc.php';

$area = area(3, 5);

include 'output.html.php';
?>
```

Technically, you could write the function declaration within the controller script itself, but by putting it in an include file you can reuse the function in other scripts much more easily. It's tidier, too. To use the function in the include file, a PHP script need only include it with `include_once` (or `require_once` if the function is critical to the script).

Avoid using `include` or `require` to load include files that contain functions; as explained in the section called "Types of Includes", that would risk defining the functions in the library more than once and covering the user's screen with PHP warnings.

It's standard practice (but not required!) to include your function libraries at the top of the script, so you can quickly see which include files containing functions are used by any particular script.

What we have here is the beginnings of a **function library**—an include file that contains declarations for a group of related functions. If you wanted to, you could add a whole bunch of functions to this include file to perform all sorts of geometrical calculations.

Variable Scope and Global Access

One big difference between custom functions and include files is the concept of **variable scope**. Any variable that exists in the main script will also be available, and can be changed in the include file. While this is useful sometimes, more often it's a pain in the neck. Unintentionally overwriting one of the main script's variables in an include file is a common cause of error—and one that can take a long time to track down and fix! To avoid such problems, you need to remember the variable names in the script you're working on and any that exist in the include files your script uses.

Functions protect you from such problems. Variables created inside a function (including any argument variables) exist only within that function, and disappear when the function is complete. In programmer-speak, the **scope** of these variables is the function—they're said to have **function scope**. In contrast, variables created in the main script outside of any function, are unavailable inside of functions. The scope of these variables is the main script, and they're said to have **global scope**.

Okay, but beyond the fancy names, what does this really *mean* for us? It means that you can have a variable called, say, $width in your main script, and another variable called $width in your function, and PHP will treat them as two entirely separate variables! Perhaps more usefully, you can have two different functions, each using the same variable names, and they'll have no effect on each other because their variables are kept separate by their scope!

On some occasions you may actually *want* to use a global-scope variable (**global variable** for short) inside one of your functions. For example, the **db.inc.php** file creates a database connection for use by your script and stores it in the global variable $link. You might then want to use this variable in a function that needed to access the database.

Disregarding variable scope, here's how you may write such a function:

```
chapter6/totaljokes-error/totaljokes-function.inc.php
```

```php
<?php
include_once $_SERVER['DOCUMENT_ROOT'] . '/includes/db.inc.php';

function totaljokes()
{
  $result = mysqli_query($link, 'SELECT COUNT(*) FROM joke');
  if (!$result)
  {
    $error = 'Database error counting jokes!';
    include 'error.html.php';
    exit();
  }

  $row = mysqli_fetch_array($result);

  return $row[0];
}
?>
```

Shared Database Include in Use!

Note the first line of this controller script uses a shared copy of the **db.inc.php** file in the **includes** directory as discussed above in the section called "Shared Include Files". Make sure you've placed a copy of this file (and the associated **error.html.php** file that it uses to display errors) in the **includes** directory in your server's document root; otherwise, PHP will complain that it's unable to find the **db.inc.php** file.

The problem here is that the global variable $link, shown in bold, is unavailable within the scope of the function. If you attempt to call this function as it is, you'll receive the errors shown in Figure 6.4.

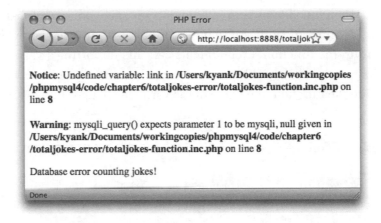

Figure 6.4. The `totaljokes` function is unable to access `$link`

Now, of course, you could just add a parameter to the `totaljokes` function and send it the connection identifier that way, but having to pass the identifier to every function that needs database access would become quite tedious.

Instead, let's use the global variable directly within our function. There are two ways to do this. The first is to **import** the global variable into the function's scope:

```
                                    chapter6/totaljokes-global1/totaljokes-function.inc.php
<?php
include_once $_SERVER['DOCUMENT_ROOT'] . '/includes/db.inc.php';

function totaljokes()
{
  global $link;

  $result = mysqli_query($link, 'SELECT COUNT(*) FROM joke');
  if (!$result)
  {
    $error = 'Database error counting jokes!';
    include 'error.html.php';
    exit();
  }

  $row = mysqli_fetch_array($result);

  return $row[0];
}
?>
```

The global statement, shown here in bold, lets you give a list of global variables (separated by commas, if you want to import more than one) that you want to make available within the function. Programmers call this importing a variable. This is different from passing the variable as a parameter, because if you modify an imported variable inside the function, the value of the variable changes outside the function, too.

The alternative to importing the variable is to use the $GLOBALS array:

```
chapter6/totaljokes-global2/totaljokes-function.inc.php
```

```php
<?php
include_once $_SERVER['DOCUMENT_ROOT'] . '/includes/db.inc.php';

function totaljokes()
{
  $result = mysqli_query($GLOBALS['link'],
      'SELECT COUNT(*) FROM joke');
  if (!$result)
  {
    $error = 'Database error counting jokes!';
    include 'error.html.php';
    exit();
  }

  $row = mysqli_fetch_array($result);

  return $row[0];
}
?>
```

As you can see, all we've done here is replace $link with $GLOBALS['link']. The special PHP array $GLOBALS is available across all scopes (for this reason, it's known as a **super-global**), and contains an entry for every variable in the global scope. You can therefore access any global variable within a function as $GLOBALS['*name*'], where *name* is the name of the global variable (without a dollar sign). The advantage of using $GLOBALS is that you can still create a function-scope variable called $link if you want.

Other special PHP arrays that are super-global, and are therefore accessible inside functions, include $_SERVER, $_GET, $_POST, $_COOKIE, $_FILES, $_ENV, $_REQUEST, and $_SESSION. See the PHP Manual[8] for full details.

Structure in Practice: Template Helpers

To cap this chapter off, let's make a start on a function library you can actually use.

There are few functions more tedious to call in the PHP language than htmlspecialchars. As I explained in Chapter 3, every time you wish to output some piece of text that was submitted by a user, you need to use htmlspecialchars to prevent hackers from inserting malicious code into your page.

For example, this is the code we've used to output user-submitted jokes in our joke list examples so far:

chapter6/jokes/jokes.html.php *(excerpt)*

```php
<?php echo htmlspecialchars($joke['text'], ENT_QUOTES, 'UTF-8'); ?>
```

As well as htmlspecialchars being an uncommonly long function name, it takes three arguments—two of which are always the same on any given site!

Because outputting text as HTML is such a common task in PHP template code, let's write a much shorter function that does this for us:

chapter6/includes/helpers.inc.php *(excerpt)*

```php
<?php
function html($text)
{
  return htmlspecialchars($text, ENT_QUOTES, 'UTF-8');
}
```

With this custom html function, we can call htmlspecialchars with a lot less typing!

```php
<?php echo html($joke['text']); ?>
```

---

[8] http://www.php.net/manual/en/language.variables.predefined.php

We can take this even further by writing a second custom function, `htmlout`, that takes the value generated by the first and outputs it:

chapter6/includes/helpers.inc.php *(excerpt)*

```php
<?php
function html($text)
{
  return htmlspecialchars($text, ENT_QUOTES, 'UTF-8');
}

function htmlout($text)
{
  echo html($text);
}
?>
```

I like to call these little convenience functions that make writing templates easier **template helpers**. Here's what our joke listing template looks like when we use these helpers:

chapter6/jokes-helpers/jokes.html.php

```php
<?php include_once $_SERVER['DOCUMENT_ROOT'] .
    '/includes/helpers.inc.php'; ?>
<!DOCTYPE html PUBLIC "-//W3C//DTD XHTML 1.0 Strict//EN"
    "http://www.w3.org/TR/xhtml1/DTD/xhtml1-strict.dtd">
<html xmlns="http://www.w3.org/1999/xhtml" xml:lang="en" lang="en">
  <head>
    <title>List of Jokes</title>
    <meta http-equiv="content-type"
        content="text/html; charset=utf-8"/>
  </head>
  <body>
    <p><a href="?addjoke">Add your own joke</a></p>
    <p>Here are all the jokes in the database:</p>
    <?php foreach ($jokes as $joke): ?>
      <form action="?deletejoke" method="post">
        <blockquote>
          <p>
            <?php htmlout($joke['text']); ?>
            <input type="hidden" name="id" value="<?php
                echo $joke['id']; ?>"/>
            <input type="submit" value="Delete"/>
```

```
      </p>
    </blockquote>
  </form>
<?php endforeach; ?>
</body>
</html>
```

Helpers Belong in the Shared **includes** Directory

Like **db.inc.php** and **magicquotes.inc.php**, the **helpers.inc.php** file belongs in the shared **includes** directory under your server's document root, as described in the section called "Shared Include Files".

As you write templates with more and more user-submitted content in them, these little gems will come in very handy indeed!

While you're at it, update the controller script to use the shared includes **db.inc.php** and **magicquotes.inc.php**:

chapter6/jokes-helpers/index.php

```php
<?php
include_once $_SERVER['DOCUMENT_ROOT'] .
    '/includes/magicquotes.inc.php';

if (isset($_GET['addjoke']))
{
  include 'form.html.php';
  exit();
}

if (isset($_POST['joketext']))
{
  include $_SERVER['DOCUMENT_ROOT'] . '/includes/db.inc.php';

  $joketext = mysqli_real_escape_string($link, $_POST['joketext']);
  $sql = 'INSERT INTO joke SET
      joketext="' . $joketext . '",
      jokedate=CURDATE()';
  if (!mysqli_query($link, $sql))
  {
    $error = 'Error adding submitted joke: ' . mysqli_error($link);
    include 'error.html.php';
```

```php
    exit();
  }

  header('Location: .');
  exit();
}

if (isset($_GET['deletejoke']))
{
  include $_SERVER['DOCUMENT_ROOT'] . '/includes/db.inc.php';

  $id = mysqli_real_escape_string($link, $_POST['id']);
  $sql = "DELETE FROM joke WHERE id='$id'";
  if (!mysqli_query($link, $sql))
  {
    $error = 'Error deleting joke: ' . mysqli_error($link);
    include 'error.html.php';
    exit();
  }

  header('Location: .');
  exit();
}

include $_SERVER['DOCUMENT_ROOT'] . '/includes/db.inc.php';

$result = mysqli_query($link, 'SELECT id, joketext FROM joke');
if (!$result)
{
  $error = 'Error fetching jokes: ' . mysqli_error($link);
  include 'error.html.php';
  exit();
}

while ($row = mysqli_fetch_array($result))
{
  $jokes[] = array('id' => $row['id'], 'text' => $row['joketext']);
}

include 'jokes.html.php';
?>
```

The Best Way

In this chapter, I've helped you to rise above the basic questions of what PHP can do for you, and begin to look for the *best* way to code a solution. Sure, you can approach many simple scripts as lists of actions you want PHP to do for you, but when you tackle site-wide issues such as database connections, shared navigation elements, visitor statistics, and access control systems, it really pays off to structure your code carefully.

We've now explored a couple of simple but effective devices for writing structured PHP code. Include files let you reuse a single piece of code across multiple pages of your site, greatly reducing the burden when you need to make changes. Writing your own functions to put in these include files lets you build powerful libraries of functions that can perform tasks as needed and return values to the scripts that call them. These new techniques will pay off in a big way in the rest of this book.

If you want to take the next step into structuring your PHP code, you'll want to explore PHP's object-oriented programming (OOP) features. The PHP Manual[9] has some useful information on the subject, but for a more complete guide you'll want to check out *The PHP Anthology: 101 Essential Tips, Tricks & Hacks, 2nd Edition*[10] (Melbourne: SitePoint, 2007).

In Chapter 7, you'll use all the knowledge you have gained so far, plus a few new tricks, to build a content management system in PHP. The aim of such a system is to provide a customized, secure, web-based interface that enables you to manage the contents of your site's database, instead of requiring you to type everything by hand on the MySQL command line.

---

[9] http://www.php.net/oop5
[10] http://www.sitepoint.com/books/phpant2/

Chapter

A Content Management System

To make the leap from a web page that displays information stored in a database to a completely database driven web site, we need to add a **content management system (CMS)**. Such a system usually takes the form of a series of web pages, access to which is restricted to users who are authorized to make changes to the site. These pages provide a database administration interface that allows a user to view and change the information that's stored in the database without bothering with the mundane details of SQL queries.

We built the beginnings of a CMS at the end of Chapter 4, where we allowed site visitors to add jokes to—and delete jokes from—the database using a web-based form and a **Delete** button, respectively. While impressive, these are features that you'd normally exclude from the interface presented to casual site visitors. For example, you'd want to prevent visitors from adding offensive material to your web site without your knowledge. And you *definitely* don't want just anyone to be able to delete jokes from your site.

By relegating those *dangerous* features to the restricted-access site administration pages, you avoid the risk of exposing your data to the average user, and you maintain the power to manage the contents of your database without having to memorize

SQL queries. In this chapter, we'll expand on the capabilities of our joke management system to take advantage of the enhancements we made to our database in Chapter 5. Specifically, we'll allow a site administrator to manage authors and categories, and assign these to appropriate jokes.

As we've seen, these administration pages must be protected by an appropriate access restriction scheme. One way to do this would be to configure your web server to protect the relevant PHP files by prompting users for valid usernames and passwords. On Apache servers, you can do this with an **.htaccess** file that lists authorized users.

Another method protects the administration pages with PHP itself. This option is generally more flexible and produces a much slicker result, but it takes a bit more work to set up. I'll show you how it's done in Chapter 9.

For now, let's focus on building the pages that will make up your CMS.

The Front Page

At the end of Chapter 5, your database contained tables for three types of entities: jokes, authors, and joke categories. This database layout is represented in Figure 7.1. Note that we're sticking with our original assumption that we'll have one email address per author.

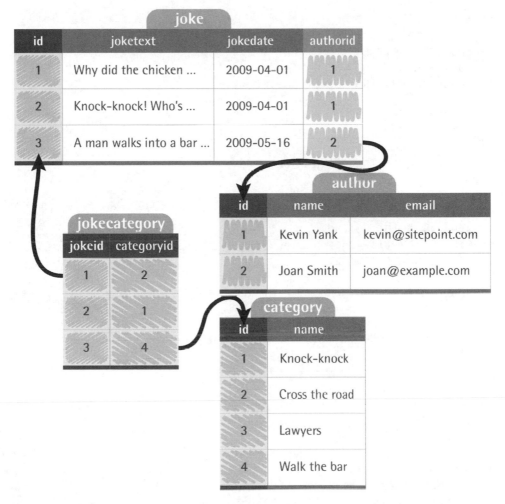

Figure 7.1. The structure of the finished ijdb database contains three entities

If you need to recreate this table structure from scratch, here are the SQL queries to do so, along with some sample data:

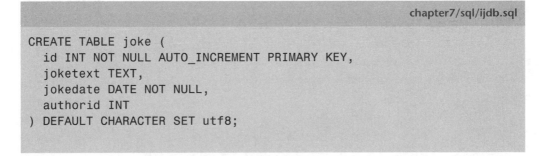

chapter7/sql/ijdb.sql

```
CREATE TABLE joke (
  id INT NOT NULL AUTO_INCREMENT PRIMARY KEY,
  joketext TEXT,
  jokedate DATE NOT NULL,
  authorid INT
) DEFAULT CHARACTER SET utf8;
```

```
CREATE TABLE author (
  id INT NOT NULL AUTO_INCREMENT PRIMARY KEY,
  name VARCHAR(255),
  email VARCHAR(255)
) DEFAULT CHARACTER SET utf8;

CREATE TABLE category (
  id INT NOT NULL AUTO_INCREMENT PRIMARY KEY,
  name VARCHAR(255)
) DEFAULT CHARACTER SET utf8;

CREATE TABLE jokecategory (
  jokeid INT NOT NULL,
  categoryid INT NOT NULL,
  PRIMARY KEY (jokeid, categoryid)
) DEFAULT CHARACTER SET utf8;

# Sample data
# We specify the IDs so they are known when we add related entries

INSERT INTO author (id, name, email) VALUES
(1, 'Kevin Yank', 'kevin@sitepoint.com'),
(2, 'Joan Smith', 'joan@example.com');

INSERT INTO joke (id, joketext, jokedate, authorid) VALUES
(1, 'Why did the chicken cross the road? To get to the other side!',
➡ '2009-04-01', 1),
(2, 'Knock-knock! Who\'s there? Boo! "Boo" who? Don\'t cry; it\'s on
➡ly a joke!', '2009-04-01', 1),
(3, 'A man walks into a bar. "Ouch."', '2009-04-01', 2),
(4, 'How many lawyers does it take to screw in a lightbulb? I can\'t
➡ say for fear of being sued.', '2009-04-01', 2);

INSERT INTO category (id, name) VALUES
(1, 'Knock-knock'),
(2, 'Cross the road'),
(3, 'Lawyers'),
(4, 'Walk the bar');

INSERT INTO jokecategory (jokeid, categoryid) VALUES
(1, 2),
(2, 1),
(3, 4),
(4, 3);
```

The front page of the content management system, therefore, will contain links to pages that manage these three entities. The following simple HTML code produces the index page shown in Figure 7.2:

chapter7/admin/index.html

```
<!DOCTYPE html PUBLIC "-//W3C//DTD XHTML 1.0 Strict//EN"
    "http://www.w3.org/TR/xhtml1/DTD/xhtml1-strict.dtd">
<html xmlns="http://www.w3.org/1999/xhtml" xml:lang="en" lang="en">
  <head>
    <title>Joke CMS</title>
    <meta http-equiv="content-type"
        content="text/html; charset=utf-8"/>
  </head>
  <body>
    <h1>Joke Management System</h1>
    <ul>
      <li><a href="jokes/">Manage Jokes</a></li>
      <li><a href="authors/">Manage Authors</a></li>
      <li><a href="categories/">Manage Joke Categories</a></li>
    </ul>
  </body>
</html>
```

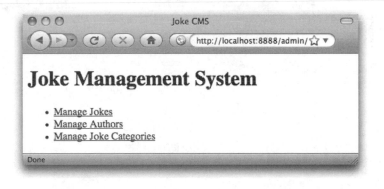

Figure 7.2. The Joke CMS index page offers three links

Each of these links points to a different subdirectory in our code: **jokes**, **authors**, and **categories**. Each of these directories will contain the controller (**index.php**) and associated templates needed to manage the corresponding entities in our database.

Managing Authors

Let's begin with the code that will handle adding new authors, and deleting and editing existing ones. All of this code will go in the **authors** subdirectory.

The first information we'll present to an administrator who needs to manage authors is a list of all authors currently stored in the database. Code-wise, this is the same as listing the jokes in the database. As we'll want to allow administrators to delete and edit existing authors, we'll include buttons for these actions next to each author's name. Just like the **Delete** buttons we added at the end of Chapter 4, these buttons will send the ID of the associated author, so that the controller knows which author the administrator wishes to edit or delete. Finally, we'll provide an **Add new author** link that leads to a form similar in operation to the **Add your own joke** link we created in Chapter 4.

Here's the controller code to do this:

```
                                    chapter7/admin/authors/index.php (excerpt)

// Display author list
include $_SERVER['DOCUMENT_ROOT'] . '/includes/db.inc.php';
$result = mysqli_query($link, 'SELECT id, name FROM author');
if (!$result)
{
  $error = 'Error fetching authors from database!';
  include 'error.html.php';
  exit();
}

while ($row = mysqli_fetch_array($result))
{
  $authors[] = array('id' => $row['id'], 'name' => $row['name']);
}

include 'authors.html.php';
?>
```

There should be no surprises for you in this code, but do note that the database connection is created using the shared include file (**db.inc.php**) stored in the **includes** directory under the document root.

Here's the template that this code uses to display the list of authors:

chapter7/admin/authors/authors.html.php *(excerpt)*

```php
<?php include_once $_SERVER['DOCUMENT_ROOT'] .
    '/includes/helpers.inc.php'; ?>
<!DOCTYPE html PUBLIC "-//W3C//DTD XHTML 1.0 Strict//EN"
    "http://www.w3.org/TR/xhtml1/DTD/xhtml1-strict.dtd">
<html xmlns="http://www.w3.org/1999/xhtml" xml:lang="en" lang="en">
  <head>
    <title>Manage Authors</title>
    <meta http-equiv="content-type"
        content="text/html; charset=utf-8"/>
  </head>
  <body>
    <h1>Manage Authors</h1>
    <p><a href="?add">Add new author</a></p>
    <ul>
      <?php foreach ($authors as $author): ?>
        <li>
          <form action="" method="post">
            <div>
              <?php htmlout($author['name']); ?>
              <input type="hidden" name="id" value="<?php
                  echo $author['id']; ?>"/>
              <input type="submit" name="action" value="Edit"/>
              <input type="submit" name="action" value="Delete"/>
            </div>
          </form>
        </li>
      <?php endforeach; ?>
    </ul>
    <p><a href="..">Return to JMS home</a></p>
  </body>
</html>
```

Again, this code should be fairly familiar to you by now. A few points of interest:

① This template will use the same shared include file we developed in Chapter 6 to make outputting values safely with **htmlspecialchars** less tedious.

② This link sends a query string (?add) to our controller so that it can tell when the user wants to add a new author.

③ Notice the empty `action` attribute. When submitted, this `form` will be asking our controller either to edit the author or to delete the author. In Chapter 4, we used a query string (?deletejoke) in the action attribute to signal the action to be performed to our controller. Since the action to be performed will be up to the user in this example, we'll use a different method of communicating it to the controller.

4 Here we use our custom htmlout function to output each author's name safely.

5 This form contains two submit buttons: one to edit the author and another to delete the author. We'll give each button the same name attribute value (action) so that our controller will be able to tell which button was clicked just by checking the submitted value for that name ($_POST['action']).

Figure 7.3 shows the list of authors produced by this template.

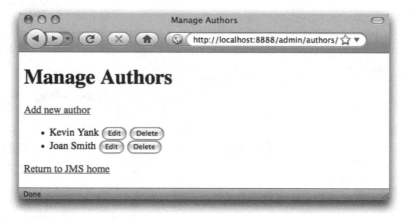

Figure 7.3. The maintenance of author details begins with the Manage Authors interface

Deleting Authors

When the user clicks one of the **Delete** buttons, our controller should remove the corresponding author from the database, using the author's ID that's submitted with the form.

As we've seen before, this is frighteningly easy to do, but there's added complexity here. Remember that our joke table has an authorid column that indicates the author responsible for any given joke. When we remove an author from the database, we must also remove any references to that author in other tables. Otherwise, our database might contain jokes associated with nonexistent authors.

We have three possible ways to handle this situation:

- Prohibit users from deleting authors that are associated with jokes in the database.

- When we delete an author, also delete any jokes attributed to the author.

- When we delete an author, set the `authorid` of any jokes attributed to the author to `NULL`, to indicate that they have no author.

When we take measures like these to preserve the relationships in our database, we are said to be protecting the database's **referential integrity**. MySQL, like most database servers, supports a feature called **foreign key constraints** that can do this automatically. By setting up these constraints, you can instruct MySQL to take any of the steps listed above, in order to keep your data properly related.

To take advantage of this feature, however, you must create your database using the more advanced **InnoDB table format**, rather than the simple **MyISAM table format** that MySQL creates by default. While more feature-rich, InnoDB tables can be slower because of the added overhead of those features. In simple applications like this one, the best result is usually achieved by letting the application code (in this case, the PHP script) take care of maintaining referential integrity. For more information on foreign key constraints, there's a useful explanation in the book *Simply SQL*[1] by Rudy Limeback (Melbourne: SitePoint, 2008). Otherwise, see the MySQL Reference Manual.[2]

Since most authors would prefer us to give credit when using their jokes, we'll choose the second option above. This also saves us from having to handle jokes with `NULL` values in their `authorid` column when we display our library of jokes.

Since we'll be deleting jokes, there's yet another layer of complexity to consider. Jokes may be assigned to categories by means of entries in the `jokecategory` table. When we delete jokes, we must also make sure that such entries are removed from the database. In summary, our controller will delete an author, any jokes belonging to that author, and any category assignments that pertain to those jokes.

The code to do all this is rather lengthy, as you might imagine. Take your time to read through it and make sure you understand how it works:

---

[1] http://www.sitepoint.com/books/sql1/

[2] http://dev.mysql.com/doc/mysql/en/ANSI_diff_Foreign_Keys.html

```php
if (isset($_POST['action']) and $_POST['action'] == 'Delete')
{
  include $_SERVER['DOCUMENT_ROOT'] . '/includes/db.inc.php';
  $id = mysqli_real_escape_string($link, $_POST['id']);

  // Get jokes belonging to author
  $sql = "SELECT id FROM joke WHERE authorid='$id'";
  $result = mysqli_query($link, $sql);
  if (!$result)
  {
    $error = 'Error getting list of jokes to delete.';
    include 'error.html.php';
    exit();
  }

  // For each joke
  while ($row = mysqli_fetch_array($result))
  {
    $jokeId = $row[0];

    // Delete joke category entries
    $sql = "DELETE FROM jokecategory WHERE jokeid='$jokeId'";
    if (!mysqli_query($link, $sql))
    {
      $error = 'Error deleting category entries for joke.';
      include 'error.html.php';
      exit();
    }
  }

  // Delete jokes belonging to author
  $sql = "DELETE FROM joke WHERE authorid='$id'";
  if (!mysqli_query($link, $sql))
  {
    $error = 'Error deleting jokes for author.';
    include 'error.html.php';
    exit();
  }

  // Delete the author
  $sql = "DELETE FROM author WHERE id='$id'";
  if (!mysqli_query($link, $sql))
  {
```

```
    $error = 'Error deleting author.';
    include 'error.html.php';
    exit();
  }

  header('Location: .');
  exit();
}
```

The one element of the above code that may seem unfamiliar is the `if` statement that triggers it all:

chapter7/admin/authors/index.php *(excerpt)*

```
if (isset($_POST['action']) and $_POST['action'] == 'Delete')
```

As we saw in the previous section, the user asks for an author to be deleted by clicking the **Delete** button next to the author name. Since the button's `name` attribute is set to `action`, we can detect this button click by checking if `$_POST['action']` is set, and if so, check if its value is `'Delete'`.

If you're coding along, go ahead and try deleting one of the authors from your database. Verify that any associated jokes and category entries are also deleted.

As a challenge, try adding a confirmation prompt to this process. If you have yet to dive in and try some coding, use the code in the code archive for this chapter as a starting point. Modify your controller to respond to the **Delete** button by simply displaying another template, this one prompting the user to confirm the action. When the user submits the form in *this* page, it should trigger the code in the controller that actually deletes the data. This second form will also have to submit in a hidden field the ID of the author to be deleted.

Adding and Editing Authors

You could implement the **Add new author** link at the top of the author list page the same way you did the **Add your own joke** link in Chapter 4. Instead of prompting the user for the text of the joke, you would instead prompt for the author's name and email address.

But our author management page includes a new, related feature: the ability to edit *existing* authors. Since both features will require the user to fill in a similar form, let's tackle both at once and kill two birds with one stone. Here's the code for the form template that will be used for both adding and editing authors:

chapter7/admin/authors/form.html.php

```php
<?php include_once $_SERVER['DOCUMENT_ROOT'] .
    '/includes/helpers.inc.php'; ?>
<!DOCTYPE html PUBLIC "-//W3C//DTD XHTML 1.0 Strict//EN"
    "http://www.w3.org/TR/xhtml1/DTD/xhtml1-strict.dtd">
<html xmlns="http://www.w3.org/1999/xhtml" xml:lang="en" lang="en">
  <head>
    <title><?php htmlout($pagetitle); ?></title>
    <meta http-equiv="content-type"
        content="text/html; charset=utf-8"/>
  </head>
  <body>
    <h1><?php htmlout($pagetitle); ?></h1>
    <form action="?<?php htmlout($action); ?>" method="post">
      <div>
        <label for="name">Name: <input type="text" name="name"
            id="name" value="<?php htmlout($name); ?>"/></label>
      </div>
      <div>
        <label for="email">Email: <input type="text" name="email"
            id="email" value="<?php htmlout($email); ?>"/></label>
      </div>
      <div>
        <input type="hidden" name="id" value="<?php
            htmlout($id); ?>"/>
        <input type="submit" value="<?php htmlout($button); ?>"/>
      </div>
    </form>
  </body>
</html>
```

Note the six PHP variables that are inserted into the content of this page:

$pagetitle   Sets the title and top-level heading (<h1>) for this page.

$action   Sets the value passed in the query string when the form is submitted.

$name   Sets the initial value of the form field for the author's name.

$email   Sets the initial value of the form field for the author's email address.

$id   Sets the value of the hidden form field for the author's database ID.

$button   Sets the label of the form's submit button.

These variables enable us to use the form for two different purposes: for creating new authors and for editing existing ones. Table 7.1 shows the values we'd like to assign to each of these variables in each instance.

Table 7.1. Variable values for dual-mode author form

Template variable	New author value	Existing author value
$pagetitle	'New Author'	'Edit Author'
$action	addform	editform
$name	' ' (empty string)	existing name
$email	' ' (empty string)	existing email address
$id	' ' (empty string)	existing author ID
$button	'Add author'	'Update author'

So, here's the controller code that loads the form in "new author mode" when the **Add new author** link is clicked:

chapter7/admin/authors/index.php *(excerpt)*

```php
<?php
include_once $_SERVER['DOCUMENT_ROOT'] .
    '/includes/magicquotes.inc.php';

if (isset($_GET['add']))
{
  $pagetitle = 'New Author';
  $action = 'addform';
  $name = '';
  $email = '';
  $id = '';
  $button = 'Add author';

  include 'form.html.php';
  exit();
}
```

When the user submits the form in this mode, you can detect it by watching for
$_GET['addform']:

chapter7/admin/authors/index.php *(excerpt)*

```php
if (isset($_GET['addform']))
{
  include $_SERVER['DOCUMENT_ROOT'] . '/includes/db.inc.php';

  $name = mysqli_real_escape_string($link, $_POST['name']);
  $email = mysqli_real_escape_string($link, $_POST['email']);
  $sql = "INSERT INTO author SET
      name='$name',
      email='$email'";
  if (!mysqli_query($link, $sql))
  {
    $error = 'Error adding submitted author.';
    include 'error.html.php';
    exit();
  }

  header('Location: .');
  exit();
}
```

When the user clicks one of the **Edit** buttons in the author list you can use the same
form, but this time you need to load the author's existing details from the database:

chapter7/admin/authors/index.php *(excerpt)*

```php
if (isset($_POST['action']) and $_POST['action'] == 'Edit')
{
  include $_SERVER['DOCUMENT_ROOT'] . '/includes/db.inc.php';

  $id = mysqli_real_escape_string($link, $_POST['id']);
  $sql = "SELECT id, name, email FROM author WHERE id='$id'";
  $result = mysqli_query($link, $sql);
  if (!$result)
  {
    $error = 'Error fetching author details.';
    include 'error.html.php';
    exit();
  }
  $row = mysqli_fetch_array($result);
```

```
    $pagetitle = 'Edit Author';
    $action = 'editform';
    $name = $row['name'];
    $email = $row['email'];
    $id = $row['id'];
    $button = 'Update author';

    include 'form.html.php';
    exit();
}
```

You can detect the form submitted in this mode by watching for $_GET['editform'].
The code for processing this form submission is very similar to how you add a new
author, but instead of issuing an INSERT query, it issues an UPDATE query:

chapter7/admin/authors/index.php (excerpt)

```
if (isset($_GET['editform']))
{
  include $_SERVER['DOCUMENT_ROOT'] . '/includes/db.inc.php';

  $id = mysqli_real_escape_string($link, $_POST['id']);
  $name = mysqli_real_escape_string($link, $_POST['name']);
  $email = mysqli_real_escape_string($link, $_POST['email']);
  $sql = "UPDATE author SET
      name='$name',
      email='$email'
      WHERE id='$id'";
  if (!mysqli_query($link, $sql))
  {
    $error = 'Error updating submitted author.';
    include 'error.html.php';
    exit();
  }

  header('Location: .');
  exit();
}
```

That'll do the trick! Go ahead and try the completed author management system,
which includes our new dual-mode form template shown in Figure 7.4. Make sure
you can add, edit, and delete authors smoothly. If you see any error messages, go

back and make sure you typed the code exactly as it appears here. If you become stuck, try using the completed code from the code archive and then compare it with your own.

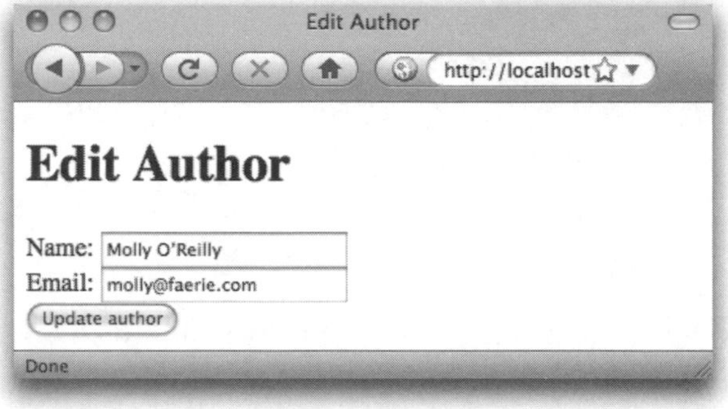

Figure 7.4. I'll bet she's funny ...

Managing Categories

The roles of the authors and joke categories in the database really are very similar. They both reside in tables of their own, and they both serve to group jokes together in some way. As a result, categories can be handled with code very similar to what we just developed for authors, but with one important exception.

When we delete a category, we must avoid simultaneously deleting any jokes that belong to that category, because those jokes may also belong to other categories. We could check each joke to see if it belonged to any other categories, and only delete those that did not, but rather than engage in such a time-consuming process, let's allow for the possibility of including jokes in our database that don't belong to any category at all. These jokes would be invisible to our site visitors, but would remain in the database in case we wanted to assign them to a category later on.

Thus, to delete a category, we also need to delete any entries in the `jokecategory` table that refer to that category:

chapter7/admin/categories/index.php *(excerpt)*

```
// Delete joke associations with this category
$sql = "DELETE FROM jokecategory WHERE categoryid='$id'";
if (!mysqli_query($link, $sql))
{
```

```php
    $error = 'Error removing jokes from category.';
    include 'error.html.php';
    exit();
  }

  // Delete the category
  $sql = "DELETE FROM category WHERE id='$id'";
  if (!mysqli_query($link, $sql))
  {
    $error = 'Error deleting category.';
    include 'error.html.php';
    exit();
  }
```

Other than this one detail, category management is functionally identical to author management. The complete code for the four files involved follows. This code also relies on the shared include files **db.inc.php**, **magicquotes.inc.php**, and **helpers.inc.php** introduced in Chapter 6:

chapter7/admin/categories/index.php

```php
<?php
include_once $_SERVER['DOCUMENT_ROOT'] .
    '/includes/magicquotes.inc.php';

if (isset($_GET['add']))
{
  $pagetitle = 'New Category';
  $action = 'addform';
  $name = '';
  $id = '';
  $button = 'Add category';

  include 'form.html.php';
  exit();
}

if (isset($_GET['addform']))
{
  include $_SERVER['DOCUMENT_ROOT'] . '/includes/db.inc.php';

  $name = mysqli_real_escape_string($link, $_POST['name']);
  $sql = "INSERT INTO category SET
      name='$name'";
```

```php
  if (!mysqli_query($link, $sql))
  {
    $error = 'Error adding submitted category.';
    include 'error.html.php';
    exit();
  }

  header('Location: .');
  exit();
}

if (isset($_POST['action']) and $_POST['action'] == 'Edit')
{
  include $_SERVER['DOCUMENT_ROOT'] . '/includes/db.inc.php';

  $id = mysqli_real_escape_string($link, $_POST['id']);
  $sql = "SELECT id, name FROM category WHERE id='$id'";
  $result = mysqli_query($link, $sql);
  if (!$result)
  {
    $error = 'Error fetching category details.';
    include 'error.html.php';
    exit();
  }
  $row = mysqli_fetch_array($result);

  $pagetitle = 'Edit Category';
  $action = 'editform';
  $name = $row['name'];
  $id = $row['id'];
  $button = 'Update category';

  include 'form.html.php';
  exit();
}

if (isset($_GET['editform']))
{
  include $_SERVER['DOCUMENT_ROOT'] . '/includes/db.inc.php';

  $id = mysqli_real_escape_string($link, $_POST['id']);
  $name = mysqli_real_escape_string($link, $_POST['name']);
  $sql = "UPDATE category SET
      name='$name'
      WHERE id='$id'";
```

```php
  if (!mysqli_query($link, $sql))
  {
    $error = 'Error updating submitted category.' .
        mysqli_error($link);
    include 'error.html.php';
    exit();
  }

  header('Location: .');
  exit();
}

if (isset($_POST['action']) and $_POST['action'] == 'Delete')
{
  include $_SERVER['DOCUMENT_ROOT'] . '/includes/db.inc.php';
  $id = mysqli_real_escape_string($link, $_POST['id']);

  // Delete joke associations with this category
  $sql = "DELETE FROM jokecategory WHERE categoryid='$id'";
  if (!mysqli_query($link, $sql))
  {
    $error = 'Error removing jokes from category.';
    include 'error.html.php';
    exit();
  }

  // Delete the category
  $sql = "DELETE FROM category WHERE id='$id'";
  if (!mysqli_query($link, $sql))
  {
    $error = 'Error deleting category.';
    include 'error.html.php';
    exit();
  }

  header('Location: .');
  exit();
}

// Display category list
include $_SERVER['DOCUMENT_ROOT'] . '/includes/db.inc.php';
$result = mysqli_query($link, 'SELECT id, name FROM category');
if (!$result)
{
  $error = 'Error fetching categories from database!';
```

```php
  include 'error.html.php';
  exit();
}

while ($row = mysqli_fetch_array($result))
{
  $categories[] = array('id' => $row['id'], 'name' => $row['name']);
}

include 'categories.html.php';
?>
```

chapter7/admin/categories/categories.html.php

```php
<?php include_once $_SERVER['DOCUMENT_ROOT'] .
    '/includes/helpers.inc.php'; ?>
<!DOCTYPE html PUBLIC "-//W3C//DTD XHTML 1.0 Strict//EN"
    "http://www.w3.org/TR/xhtml1/DTD/xhtml1-strict.dtd">
<html xmlns="http://www.w3.org/1999/xhtml" xml:lang="en" lang="en">
  <head>
    <title>Manage Categories</title>
    <meta http-equiv="content-type"
        content="text/html; charset=utf-8"/>
  </head>
  <body>
    <h1>Manage Categories</h1>
    <p><a href="?add">Add new category</a></p>
    <ul>
      <?php foreach ($categories as $category): ?>
        <li>
          <form action="" method="post">
            <div>
              <?php htmlout($category['name']); ?>
              <input type="hidden" name="id" value="<?php
                  echo $category['id']; ?>"/>
              <input type="submit" name="action" value="Edit"/>
              <input type="submit" name="action" value="Delete"/>
            </div>
          </form>
        </li>
      <?php endforeach; ?>
    </ul>
    <p><a href="..">Return to JMS home</a></p>
  </body>
</html>
```

```php
<?php include_once $_SERVER['DOCUMENT_ROOT'] .
    '/includes/helpers.inc.php'; ?>
<!DOCTYPE html PUBLIC "-//W3C//DTD XHTML 1.0 Strict//EN"
    "http://www.w3.org/TR/xhtml1/DTD/xhtml1-strict.dtd">
<html xmlns="http://www.w3.org/1999/xhtml" xml:lang="en" lang="en">
  <head>
    <title><?php htmlout($pagetitle); ?></title>
    <meta http-equiv="content-type"
        content="text/html; charset=utf-8"/>
  </head>
  <body>
    <h1><?php htmlout($pagetitle); ?></h1>
    <form action="?<?php htmlout($action); ?>" method="post">
      <div>
        <label for="name">Name: <input type="text" name="name"
            id="name" value="<?php htmlout($name); ?>"/></label>
      </div>
      <div>
        <input type="hidden" name="id" value="<?php
            htmlout($id); ?>"/>
        <input type="submit" value="<?php htmlout($button); ?>"/>
      </div>
    </form>
  </body>
</html>
```

```php
<!DOCTYPE html PUBLIC "-//W3C//DTD XHTML 1.0 Strict//EN"
    "http://www.w3.org/TR/xhtml1/DTD/xhtml1-strict.dtd">
<html xmlns="http://www.w3.org/1999/xhtml" xml:lang="en" lang="en">
  <head>
    <title>PHP Error</title>
    <meta http-equiv="content-type"
        content="text/html; charset=utf-8"/>
  </head>
  <body>
    <p>
      <?php echo $error; ?>
    </p>
  </body>
</html>
```

Managing Jokes

Along with adding, deleting, and modifying jokes in our database, we also need to be able to assign categories and authors to our jokes. Furthermore, we're likely to have many more jokes than authors or categories. To try to display a complete list of jokes, as we did for the authors and categories, could result in an unmanageably long list with no easy way to spot the joke we're after. We need to create a more intelligent method of browsing our library of jokes.

Searching for Jokes

Sometimes, we may know the category, author, or some of the text in a joke with which we want to work, so let's support all of these methods for finding jokes in our database. When we're done, it should work like a simple search engine.

The form that prompts the administrator for information about the desired joke must present lists of categories and authors. Let's start with the controller code that fetches these details from the database:

chapter7/admin/jokes/index.php *(excerpt)*

```
// Display search form
include $_SERVER['DOCUMENT_ROOT'] . '/includes/db.inc.php';
$result = mysqli_query($link, 'SELECT id, name FROM author');
if (!$result)
{
  $error = 'Error fetching authors from database!';
  include 'error.html.php';
  exit();
}

while ($row = mysqli_fetch_array($result))
{
  $authors[] = array('id' => $row['id'], 'name' => $row['name']);
}

$result = mysqli_query($link, 'SELECT id, name FROM category');
if (!$result)
{
  $error = 'Error fetching categories from database!';
  include 'error.html.php';
  exit();
```

```
}

while ($row = mysqli_fetch_array($result))
{
  $categories[] = array('id' => $row['id'], 'name' => $row['name']);
}

include 'searchform.html.php';
?>
```

This code builds two arrays for use by the **searchform.html.php** template: $authors and $categories. We'll use each of these arrays to build a drop-down list in our search form:

```
                                     chapter7/admin/jokes/searchform.html.php
<?php include_once $_SERVER['DOCUMENT_ROOT'] .
    '/includes/helpers.inc.php'; ?>
<!DOCTYPE html PUBLIC "-//W3C//DTD XHTML 1.0 Strict//EN"
    "http://www.w3.org/TR/xhtml1/DTD/xhtml1-strict.dtd">
<html xmlns="http://www.w3.org/1999/xhtml" xml:lang="en" lang="en">
  <head>
    <title>Manage Jokes</title>
    <meta http-equiv="content-type"
        content="text/html; charset=utf-8"/>
  </head>
  <body>
    <h1>Manage Jokes</h1>
    <p><a href="?add">Add new joke</a></p>
    <form action="" method="get">
      <p>View jokes satisfying the following criteria:</p>
      <div>
        <label for="author">By author:</label>
        <select name="author" id="author">
          <option value="">Any author</option>
          <?php foreach ($authors as $author): ?>
            <option value="<?php htmlout($author['id']); ?>"><?php
                htmlout($author['name']); ?></option>
          <?php endforeach; ?>
        </select>
      </div>
      <div>
        <label for="category">By category:</label>
        <select name="category" id="category">
```

```
          <option value="">Any category</option>
          <?php foreach ($categories as $category): ?>
            <option value="<?php htmlout($category['id']); ?>"><?php
                htmlout($category['name']); ?></option>
          <?php endforeach; ?>
        </select>
      </div>
      <div>
        <label for="text">Containing text:</label>
        <input type="text" name="text" id="text"/>
      </div>
      <div>
        <input type="hidden" name="action" value="search"/>
        <input type="submit" value="Search"/>
      </div>
    </form>
    <p><a href="..">Return to JMS home</a></p>
  </body>
</html>
```

As you can see, in each select list, we generate a series of option items using a PHP foreach loop. The value of each option is the author's or category's ID, and the text label of each option is the author's or category's name. Each of the drop-downs begins with an option with no value, which can be left alone to leave the corresponding field out of the search criteria.

Also note that the form's method attribute is set to get, so that it's possible to bookmark the results of a search, since the form values will be submitted in the URL query string. You should generally apply this technique to any search form you write.

The finished form appears in Figure 7.5.

It's up to the controller to use the values submitted by this form to build a list of jokes that satisfies the criteria specified. Obviously, this will be done with a SELECT query, but the exact nature of that query will depend on the search criteria specified. Because the building of this SELECT statement is a fairly complicated process, let's work through the controller code responsible a little at a time.

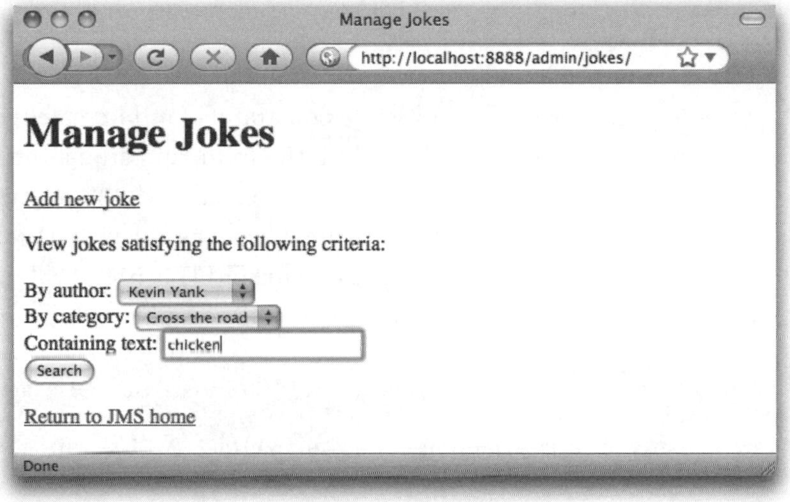

Figure 7.5. Search for a classic

To start, we define a few strings that, when strung together, form the SELECT query we'd need if no search criteria whatsoever had been selected in the form:

```
                                    chapter7/admin/jokes/index.php (excerpt)

if (isset($_GET['action']) and $_GET['action'] == 'search')
{
  include $_SERVER['DOCUMENT_ROOT'] . '/includes/db.inc.php';

  // The basic SELECT statement
  $select = 'SELECT id, joketext';
  $from   = ' FROM joke';
  $where  = ' WHERE TRUE';
```

You might find the WHERE clause in the above code a little confusing. The idea here is for us to be able to build on this basic SELECT statement, depending on the criteria selected in the form. These criteria will require us to add to the FROM and WHERE clauses (portions) of the SELECT query. But, if no criteria were specified (that is, the administrator wanted a list of all jokes in the database), there would be no need for a WHERE clause at all! Because it's difficult to add to a WHERE clause that's nonexistent, we needed to come up with a "do nothing" WHERE clause that will have no effect on the results unless added to. Since TRUE is always true, WHERE TRUE fits the bill nicely.[3]

Our next task is to check each of the possible constraints (author, category, and search text) that may have been submitted with the form, and adjust the three components of our SQL query accordingly. First, we deal with the possibility that an author was specified. The blank option in the form was given a value of "", so, if the value of that form field (stored in $_GET['author']) is not equal to '' (the empty string), then an author has been specified, and we must adjust our query:

chapter7/admin/jokes/index.php *(excerpt)*

```php
$authorid = mysqli_real_escape_string($link, $_GET['author']);
if ($authorid != '') // An author is selected
{
  $where .= " AND authorid='$authorid'";
}
```

As we've seen before, .= (the **append operator**) is used to tack a new string onto the end of an existing one. In this case, we add to the WHERE clause the condition that the authorid in the joke table must match the author ID selected in the form ($authorid).

Next, we handle the specification of a joke category:

chapter7/admin/jokes/index.php *(excerpt)*

```php
$categoryid = mysqli_real_escape_string($link,$_GET['category']);
if ($categoryid != '') // A category is selected
{
  $from  .= ' INNER JOIN jokecategory ON id = jokeid';
  $where .= " AND categoryid='$categoryid'";
}
```

As the categories associated with a particular joke are stored in the jokecategory table, we need to add this table to the query to create a join. To do this, we simply tack INNER JOIN jokecategory ON id = jokeid onto the end of the $from variable.

---

[3] In fact, the "do nothing" WHERE clause could just be WHERE 1, since MySQL considers any positive number true. Feel free to change it if you think that's easier.

This joins the two tables on the condition that the `id` column (in the `joke` table) matches the `jokeid` column (in `jokecategory`).

With the join in place, we can then apply the criterion specified in the form submission—that the joke belongs to the specified category. By adding to the `$where` variable, we can require the `categoryid` column (in `jokecategory`) to match the category ID selected in the form (`$categoryid`).

Handling search text is fairly simple thanks to the `LIKE` SQL operator that we learned way back in Chapter 2:

chapter7/admin/jokes/index.php *(excerpt)*

```php
$text = mysqli_real_escape_string($link, $_GET['text']);
if ($text != '') // Some search text was specified
{
  $where .= " AND joketext LIKE '%$text%'";
}
```

Now that we've built our SQL query, we can use it to retrieve and display our jokes:

chapter7/admin/jokes/index.php *(excerpt)*

```php
$result = mysqli_query($link, $select . $from . $where);
if (!$result)
{
  $error = 'Error fetching jokes.';
  include 'error.html.php';
  exit();
}

while ($row = mysqli_fetch_array($result))
{
  $jokes[] = array('id' => $row['id'], 'text' => $row['joketext']);
}

include 'jokes.html.php';
exit();
}
```

The template to display these jokes will include **Edit** and **Delete** buttons for each joke. To keep the page as organized as possible, it will structure the results using an HTML table:

```php
<?php include_once $_SERVER['DOCUMENT_ROOT'] .
    '/includes/helpers.inc.php'; ?>
<!DOCTYPE html PUBLIC "-//W3C//DTD XHTML 1.0 Strict//EN"
    "http://www.w3.org/TR/xhtml1/DTD/xhtml1-strict.dtd">
<html xmlns="http://www.w3.org/1999/xhtml" xml:lang="en" lang="en">
  <head>
    <title>Manage Jokes: Search Results</title>
    <meta http-equiv="content-type"
        content="text/html; charset=utf-8"/>
  </head>
  <body>
    <h1>Search Results</h1>
    <?php if (isset($jokes)): ?>
      <table>
        <tr><th>Joke Text</th><th>Options</th></tr>
        <?php foreach ($jokes as $joke): ?>
        <tr valign="top">
          <td><?php htmlout($joke['text']); ?></td>
          <td>
            <form action="?" method="post">
              <div>
                <input type="hidden" name="id" value="<?php
                    htmlout($joke['id']); ?>"/>
                <input type="submit" name="action" value="Edit"/>
                <input type="submit" name="action" value="Delete"/>
              </div>
            </form>
          </td>
        </tr>
        <?php endforeach; ?>
      </table>
    <?php endif; ?>
    <p><a href="?">New search</a></p>
    <p><a href="..">Return to JMS home</a></p>
  </body>
</html>
```

The search results will display as shown in Figure 7.6.

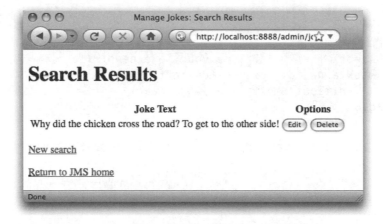

Figure 7.6. A classic is found

If you're up for a challenge, try adding a little code to this template to handle gracefully the case where no jokes satisfy the criteria specified in the search form. Right now, the template simply outputs nothing where the search results table should be.

Adding and Editing Jokes

At the top of the joke search form, we had our usual link to create a new joke:

chapter7/admin/jokes/searchform.html.php *(excerpt)*

```
<p><a href="?add">Add new joke</a></p>
```

Let's implement this feature now. The code will be very similar to that we used to create new authors and categories; however, in addition to specifying the joke text, the page must allow an administrator to assign an author and categories to a joke.

As with authors and categories, we can use the same form template both for creating new jokes and for editing existing jokes. Let's take a look at each of the important elements of this form. We begin with a standard text area into which we can type the text of the joke. If we're editing an existing joke, we'll populate this field with the existing joke text ($text):

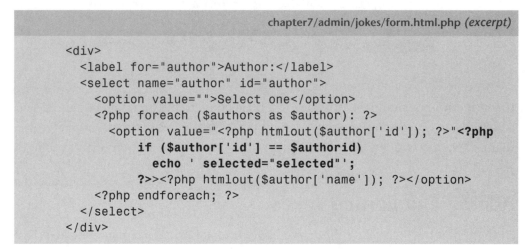

```
chapter7/admin/jokes/form.html.php (excerpt)

<div>
  <label for="text">Type your joke here:</label>
  <textarea id="text" name="text" rows="3" cols="40"><?php
    htmlout($text); ?></textarea>
</div>
```

Next, we'll prompt the administrator to select the author who wrote the joke:

```
chapter7/admin/jokes/form.html.php (excerpt)

<div>
  <label for="author">Author:</label>
  <select name="author" id="author">
    <option value="">Select one</option>
    <?php foreach ($authors as $author): ?>
      <option value="<?php htmlout($author['id']); ?>"<?php
          if ($author['id'] == $authorid)
            echo ' selected="selected"';
          ?>><?php htmlout($author['name']); ?></option>
    <?php endforeach; ?>
  </select>
</div>
```

Again, we've seen this kind of drop-down before (for example, in the joke search form), but the important difference is that we want to control the initial selection in the drop-down menu when we're editing an existing joke. The code in bold inserts into the `<option>` tag the attribute `selected="selected"` if the ID of the corresponding author (`$author['id']`) matches the author ID of the existing joke (`$authorid`).

Next, we need to prompt the administrator to select the categories to which the joke should belong. A drop-down list is unsuitable for this, because we want the administrator to be able to select *multiple* categories. Thus, we'll use a series of checkboxes (`<input type="checkbox"/>`)—one for each category. Since we have no way to know in advance the number of checkboxes we'll need, the matter of setting their `name` attribute becomes an interesting challenge.

What we'll do is use a *single* variable for all the checkboxes; thus, all the checkboxes will have the same name. To be able to receive multiple values from a single variable name, we must make that variable an **array**. Recall from Chapter 3 that an array is a single variable with compartments, each of which can hold a value. To submit a form element as part of an array variable, we simply add a pair of square brackets to the end of the name attribute (making it categories[] in this case).[4]

With all of our checkboxes named the same, we'll need a way to identify which particular checkboxes have been selected. To this end, we assign a different value to each checkbox—the ID of the corresponding category in the database. Thus, the form submits an array that contains the IDs of all the categories to which the new joke should be added.

Again, since we need to handle editing an existing joke, we'll include some code to output selected="selected" if the joke already belongs to the corresponding category. This we'll indicate in our controller by setting $category['selected'] to TRUE:

```
chapter7/admin/jokes/form.html.php (excerpt)

<fieldset>
  <legend>Categories:</legend>
  <?php foreach ($categories as $category): ?>
    <div><label for="category<?php htmlout($category['id']);
        ?>"><input type="checkbox" name="categories[]"
        id="category<?php htmlout($category['id']); ?>"
        value="<?php htmlout($category['id']); ?>"<?php
        if ($category['selected'])
        {
          echo ' checked="checked"';
        }
        ?>/><?php htmlout($category['name']); ?></label></div>
  <?php endforeach; ?>
</fieldset>
```

Other than these details, the form will work just like the other add/edit forms we have built. Here's the complete code:

---

[4] Another way to submit an array is with a <select multiple="multiple"> tag. Again, you'd set the name attribute to end with square brackets. What will be submitted is an array of all the option values selected from the list by the user. Feel free to experiment with this approach by modifying this form to present the categories as a list of option elements.

```php
<?php include_once $_SERVER['DOCUMENT_ROOT'] .
    '/includes/helpers.inc.php'; ?>
<!DOCTYPE html PUBLIC "-//W3C//DTD XHTML 1.0 Strict//EN"
    "http://www.w3.org/TR/xhtml1/DTD/xhtml1-strict.dtd">
<html xmlns="http://www.w3.org/1999/xhtml" xml:lang="en" lang="en">
  <head>
    <title><?php htmlout($pagetitle); ?></title>
    <meta http-equiv="content-type"
        content="text/html; charset=utf-8"/>
    <style type="text/css">
    textarea {
      display: block;
      width: 100%;
    }
    </style>
  </head>
  <body>
    <h1><?php htmlout($pagetitle); ?></h1>
    <form action="?<?php htmlout($action); ?>" method="post">
      <div>
        <label for="text">Type your joke here:</label>
        <textarea id="text" name="text" rows="3" cols="40"><?php
            htmlout($text); ?></textarea>
      </div>
      <div>
        <label for="author">Author:</label>
        <select name="author" id="author">
          <option value="">Select one</option>
          <?php foreach ($authors as $author): ?>
            <option value="<?php htmlout($author['id']); ?>"<?php
                if ($author['id'] == $authorid)
                  echo ' selected="selected"';
                ?>><?php htmlout($author['name']); ?></option>
          <?php endforeach; ?>
        </select>
      </div>
      <fieldset>
        <legend>Categories:</legend>
        <?php foreach ($categories as $category): ?>
          <div><label for="category<?php htmlout($category['id']);
              ?>"><input type="checkbox" name="categories[]"
              id="category<?php htmlout($category['id']); ?>"
              value="<?php htmlout($category['id']); ?>"<?php
```

```
              if ($category['selected'])
              {
                echo ' checked="checked"';
              }
              ?>/><?php htmlout($category['name']); ?></label></div>
        <?php endforeach; ?>
      </fieldset>
      <div>
        <input type="hidden" name="id" value="<?php
            htmlout($id); ?>"/>
        <input type="submit" value="<?php htmlout($button); ?>"/>
      </div>
    </form>
  </body>
</html>
```

Figure 7.7 shows what this form will look like.

Figure 7.7. The hits just keep on coming

Let's now turn our attention back to the controller, which will display and then handle the submission of this form in both of its modes.

When the user clicks the **Add new joke** link, we need to display the form with all of its fields blank. None of this code should be unfamiliar. Take your time, look over it, and make sure it all makes sense to you. If you're unsure what a particular variable is for, go find it in the form template and identify its purpose:

chapter7/admin/jokes/index.php *(excerpt)*

```php
<?php
include_once $_SERVER['DOCUMENT_ROOT'] .
    '/includes/magicquotes.inc.php';

if (isset($_GET['add']))
{
  $pagetitle = 'New Joke';
  $action = 'addform';
  $text = '';
  $authorid = '';
  $id = '';
  $button = 'Add joke';

  include $_SERVER['DOCUMENT_ROOT'] . '/includes/db.inc.php';

  // Build the list of authors
  $sql = "SELECT id, name FROM author";
  $result = mysqli_query($link, $sql);
  if (!$result)
  {
    $error = 'Error fetching list of authors.';
    include 'error.html.php';
    exit();
  }

  while ($row = mysqli_fetch_array($result))
  {
    $authors[] = array('id' => $row['id'], 'name' => $row['name']);
  }

  // Build the list of categories
  $sql = "SELECT id, name FROM category";
  $result = mysqli_query($link, $sql);
  if (!$result)
  {
    $error = 'Error fetching list of categories.';
    include 'error.html.php';
    exit();
```

```
    }
    while ($row = mysqli_fetch_array($result))
    {
      $categories[] = array(
          'id' => $row['id'],
          'name' => $row['name'],
          'selected' => FALSE);
    }

    include 'form.html.php';
    exit();
}
```

Note especially that we're setting the `selected` item in each of the arrays stored in the $categories array to FALSE. As a result, none of the category checkboxes in the form will be selected by default.

When the user clicks the **Edit** button next to an existing joke, the controller must instead load the form with its fields populated with the existing values. This code is similar in structure to the code we used to generate the empty form:

chapter7/admin/jokes/index.php (excerpt)

```
if (isset($_POST['action']) and $_POST['action'] == 'Edit')
{
  include $_SERVER['DOCUMENT_ROOT'] . '/includes/db.inc.php';

  $id = mysqli_real_escape_string($link, $_POST['id']);
  $sql = "SELECT id, joketext, authorid FROM joke WHERE id='$id'";
  $result = mysqli_query($link, $sql);
  if (!$result)
  {
    $error = 'Error fetching joke details.';
    include 'error.html.php';
    exit();
  }
  $row = mysqli_fetch_array($result);

  $pagetitle = 'Edit Joke';
  $action = 'editform';
  $text = $row['joketext'];
  $authorid = $row['authorid'];
```

```php
$id = $row['id'];
$button = 'Update joke';

// Build the list of authors
$sql = "SELECT id, name FROM author";
$result = mysqli_query($link, $sql);
if (!$result)
{
  $error = 'Error fetching list of authors.';
  include 'error.html.php';
  exit();
}

while ($row = mysqli_fetch_array($result))
{
  $authors[] = array('id' => $row['id'], 'name' => $row['name']);
}

// Get list of categories containing this joke
$sql = "SELECT categoryid FROM jokecategory WHERE jokeid='$id'";
$result = mysqli_query($link, $sql);
if (!$result)
{
  $error = 'Error fetching list of selected categories.';
  include 'error.html.php';
  exit();
}

while ($row = mysqli_fetch_array($result))
{
  $selectedCategories[] = $row['categoryid'];
}

// Build the list of all categories
$sql = "SELECT id, name FROM category";
$result = mysqli_query($link, $sql);
if (!$result)
{
  $error = 'Error fetching list of categories.';
  include 'error.html.php';
  exit();
}

while ($row = mysqli_fetch_array($result))
{
```

❶ (marker at `$sql = "SELECT categoryid FROM jokecategory WHERE jokeid='$id'";`)

❷ (marker at `$selectedCategories[] = $row['categoryid'];`)

```
    $categories[] = array(
        'id' => $row['id'],
        'name' => $row['name'],
        'selected' => in_array($row['id'], $selectedCategories)); 3
  }

  include 'form.html.php';
  exit();
}
```

In addition to fetching the details of the joke (ID, text, and author ID), this code fetches a list of categories to which the joke in question belongs:

1 The SELECT query is straightforward, since it's simply fetching records from the jokecategory lookup table. It grabs all of the category IDs associated with the joke ID for the joke that the user wishes to edit.

2 This while loop stores all of the selected category IDs into an array variable, $selectedCategories.

 And here's the big trick: while building the list of *all* categories for the form to display as checkboxes, we check each category's ID to see if it's listed in our $selectedCategories array. The built-in function in_array does this for us automatically. We store the return value (either TRUE or FALSE) in the 'selected' item of the array that represents each category. This value will then be used by the form template (as we've already seen) to select the appropriate checkboxes.

That takes care of generating the form in each of its two modes; now let's look at the controller code that processes the form submissions.

Since we're submitting an array for the first time (the list of selected category checkboxes), the code that processes this form will feature a couple of new tricks as well. It starts off fairly simply as we add the joke to the joke table. As an author is required, we make sure that $_POST['author'] contains a value. This prevents the administrator from choosing the **Select One** option in the author select list (that choice has a value of "", the empty string):

```
                                    chapter7/admin/jokes/index.php (excerpt)

if (isset($_GET['addform']))
{
  include $_SERVER['DOCUMENT_ROOT'] . '/includes/db.inc.php';

  $text = mysqli_real_escape_string($link, $_POST['text']);
  $author = mysqli_real_escape_string($link, $_POST['author']);

  if ($author == '')
  {
    $error = 'You must choose an author for this joke.
        Click &lsquo;back&rsquo; and try again.';
    include 'error.html.php';
    exit();
  }

  $sql = "INSERT INTO joke SET
      joketext='$text',
      jokedate=CURDATE(),
      authorid='$author'";
  if (!mysqli_query($link, $sql))
  {
    $error = 'Error adding submitted joke.';
    include 'error.html.php';
    exit();
  }

  $jokeid = mysqli_insert_id($link);
```

The last line in the above code uses a function that we've yet to see: mysqli_insert_id. This function returns the number assigned to the last inserted entry by the AUTO_INCREMENT feature in MySQL. In other words, it retrieves the ID of the newly inserted joke, which we'll need momentarily.

The code that adds the entries to jokecategory based on which checkboxes were checked is probably unclear to you. First of all, we've never seen how a checkbox passes its value to a PHP variable before. Also, we need to deal with the fact that these particular checkboxes will submit into an array variable.

A typical checkbox will pass its value to a PHP variable if it's checked, and will do nothing when it's unchecked. Checkboxes without assigned values pass 'on' as the value of their corresponding variables when they're checked. However, we've assigned values to our checkboxes (the category IDs), so this is not an issue.

The fact that these checkboxes submit into an array actually adds quite a measure of convenience to our code. In essence, what we'll receive from the submitted form is either:

- an array of category IDs to which we'll add the joke
- nothing at all (if none of the checkboxes were checked)

In the latter case, we have nothing to do—no categories were selected, so we have nothing to add to the jokecategory table. If we *do* have an array of category IDs to process, however, we'll use a foreach loop to issue an INSERT query for each ID:

```
                                  chapter7/admin/jokes/index.php (excerpt)
if (isset($_POST['categories']))
{
  foreach ($_POST['categories'] as $category)
  {
    $categoryid = mysqli_real_escape_string($link, $category);
    $sql = "INSERT INTO jokecategory SET
        jokeid='$jokeid',
        categoryid='$categoryid'";
    if (!mysqli_query($link, $sql))
    {
      $error = 'Error inserting joke into selected category.';
      include 'error.html.php';
      exit();
    }
  }
}

header('Location: .');
exit();
}
```

Note the use of the $jokeid variable, which we obtained from mysqli_insert_id above.

That takes care of adding new jokes. The form processing code for editing existing jokes is predictably similar, with two important differences:

■ It uses an UPDATE query instead of an INSERT query to store the joke's details in the joke table.

■ It removes all existing entries for the joke from the jokecategory table before INSERTing entries for the selected checkboxes in the form.

Here's the code. Take the time to read through it and make sure it all makes sense to you:

chapter7/admin/jokes/index.php *(excerpt)*

```
if (isset($_GET['editform']))
{
  include $_SERVER['DOCUMENT_ROOT'] . '/includes/db.inc.php';

  $text = mysqli_real_escape_string($link, $_POST['text']);
  $author = mysqli_real_escape_string($link, $_POST['author']);
  $id = mysqli_real_escape_string($link, $_POST['id']);

  if ($author == '')
  {
    $error = 'You must choose an author for this joke.
        Click &lsquo;back&rsquo; and try again.';
    include 'error.html.php';
    exit();
  }

  $sql = "UPDATE joke SET
      joketext='$text',
      authorid='$author'
      WHERE id='$id'";
  if (!mysqli_query($link, $sql))
  {
    $error = 'Error updating submitted joke.';
    include 'error.html.php';
    exit();
  }

  $sql = "DELETE FROM jokecategory WHERE jokeid='$id'";
  if (!mysqli_query($link, $sql))
  {
    $error = 'Error removing obsolete joke category entries.';
    include 'error.html.php';
    exit();
```

```
    }

  if (isset($_POST['categories']))
  {
    foreach ($_POST['categories'] as $category)
    {
      $categoryid = mysqli_real_escape_string($link, $category);
      $sql = "INSERT INTO jokecategory SET
          jokeid='$id',
          categoryid='$categoryid'";
      if (!mysqli_query($link, $sql))
      {
        $error = 'Error inserting joke into selected category.';
        include 'error.html.php';
        exit();
      }
    }
  }

  header('Location: .');
  exit();
}
```

Deleting Jokes

The last feature we need to implement is the **Delete** button displayed next to each joke. The controller code responsible for this feature mirrors the code we wrote for the author and category **Delete** buttons, with only minor adjustments. For example, besides deleting the selected joke from the joke table, it must also remove any entries in the jokecategory table for that joke.

Here's the code. There's nothing new here, but take some time to browse through it and make sure you're comfortable with everything that's going on:

chapter7/admin/jokes/index.php *(excerpt)*

```
if (isset($_POST['action']) and $_POST['action'] == 'Delete')
{
  include $_SERVER['DOCUMENT_ROOT'] . '/includes/db.inc.php';
  $id = mysqli_real_escape_string($link, $_POST['id']);

  // Delete category assignments for this joke
  $sql = "DELETE FROM jokecategory WHERE jokeid='$id'";
```

```php
if (!mysqli_query($link, $sql))
{
  $error = 'Error removing joke from categories.';
  include 'error.html.php';
  exit();
}

// Delete the joke
$sql = "DELETE FROM joke WHERE id='$id'";
if (!mysqli_query($link, $sql))
{
  $error = 'Error deleting joke.';
  include 'error.html.php';
  exit();
}

header('Location: .');
exit();
}
```

Summary

There are a few minor tasks of which our content management system is still incapable. For example, it's unable to provide a listing of just the jokes that don't belong to *any* category—which could be very handy as the number of jokes in the database grows. You might also like to sort the joke lists by various criteria. These particular capabilities require a few more advanced SQL tricks that we'll see in Chapter 11.

If we ignore these little details for the moment, you'll see that you now have a system that allows a person without SQL or database knowledge to administer your database of jokes with ease! Together with a set of PHP-powered pages through which regular site visitors can view the jokes, this content management system allows us to set up a complete database driven web site that can be maintained by a user with absolutely no database knowledge. And if you think that sounds like a valuable commodity to businesses looking to be on the Web today, you're right!

In fact, only one aspect of our site requires users to have special knowledge (beyond the use of a web browser): content formatting. If we wanted to enable administrators to include rich text formatting in the jokes they entered, we could invite them to type the necessary HTML code directly into the **New Joke** form. To preserve that formatting, we would then `echo` out the content of our jokes "raw" instead of using our `htmlout` function.

This is unacceptable for two reasons: first, we'd have to stop accepting joke submissions from the general public, otherwise we'd be opening the door to attackers submitting harmful code in their jokes; our site would then display these unfiltered, since we'd no longer be passing our content through `htmlspecialchars`.

Second, as we stated way back in the introduction to this book, one of the most desirable features of a database driven web site is that people can be responsible for adding content despite being unfamiliar with technical *mumbo jumbo* like HTML. If we require knowledge of HTML for a task as simple as dividing a joke into paragraphs, or applying italics to a word or two, we'll have failed to achieve our goal.

In Chapter 8, I'll show you how to use some of the features of PHP that make it simpler for your users to format content without knowing the ins and outs of HTML. We'll also revisit the **Submit your own joke** form, and discover how we can safely accept content submissions from casual site visitors.

Content Formatting with Regular Expressions

We're almost there! We've designed a database to store jokes, organized them into categories, and tracked their authors. We've learned how to create a web page that displays this library of jokes to site visitors. We've even developed a set of web pages that a site administrator can use to manage the joke library without having to know anything about databases.

In so doing, we've built a site that frees the resident webmaster from continually having to plug new content into tired HTML page templates, and from maintaining an unmanageable mass of HTML files. The HTML is now kept completely separate from the data it displays. If you want to redesign the site, you simply have to make the changes to the HTML contained in the PHP templates that you've constructed. A change to one file (for example, modifying the footer) is immediately reflected in the page layouts of all pages in the site. Only one task still requires the knowledge of HTML: **content formatting**.

On any but the simplest of web sites, it will be necessary to allow content (in our case study, jokes) to include some sort of formatting. In a simple case, this might merely be the ability to break text into paragraphs. Often, however, content providers will expect facilities such as **bold** or *italic* text, hyperlinks, and so on.

Supporting these requirements with our current code is deceptively easy. In the past couple of chapters, we've used `htmlout` to output user-submitted content:

> chapter6/jokes-helpers/jokes.html.php *(excerpt)*

```php
<?php htmlout($joke['text']); ?>
```

If, instead, we just `echo` out the raw content pulled from the database, we can enable administrators to include formatting in the form of HTML code in the joke text:

```php
<?php echo $joke['text']; ?>
```

Following this simple change, a site administrator could include HTML tags that would have their usual effect on the joke text when inserted into a page.

But is this really what we want? Left unchecked, content providers can do a lot of damage by including HTML code in the content they add to your site's database. Particularly if your system will be enabling non-technical users to submit content, you'll find that invalid, obsolete, and otherwise inappropriate code will gradually infest the pristine web site you set out to build. With one stray tag, a well-meaning user could tear apart the layout of your site.

In this chapter, you'll learn about several new PHP functions that specialize in finding and replacing patterns of text in your site's content. I'll show you how to use these capabilities to provide for your users a simpler markup language that's better suited to content formatting. By the time we've finished, we'll have completed a content management system that anyone with a web browser can use—no knowledge of HTML required.

Regular Expressions

To implement our own markup language, we'll have to write some PHP code to spot our custom tags in the text of jokes and replace them with their HTML equivalents. For tackling this sort of task, PHP includes extensive support for regular expressions. A **regular expression** is a string of text that describes a pattern that may occur in text content like our jokes.

The language of regular expression is cryptic enough that, once you master it, you may feel as if you're able to weave magical incantations with the code that you write. To begin with, however, let's start with some very simple regular expressions.

This is a regular expression that searches for the text "PHP" (without the quotes):

```
/PHP/
```

Fairly simple, you would say? It's the text for which you want to search surrounded by a pair of matching delimiters. Traditionally, slashes (/) are used as regular expression delimiters, but another common choice is the hash character (#). You can actually use any character as a delimiter except letters, numbers, or backslashes (\). I'll use slashes for all the regular expressions in this chapter.

To use a regular expression, you must be familiar with the regular expression functions available in PHP. preg_match is the most basic, and can be used to determine whether a regular expression is **matched** by a particular text string.

Consider this code:

chapter8/preg_match1/index.php

```php
<?php
$text = 'PHP rules!';

if (preg_match('/PHP/', $text))
{
  $output = '$text contains the string &ldquo;PHP&rdquo;.';
}
else
{
  $output = '$text does not contain the string &ldquo;PHP&rdquo;.';
}

include 'output.html.php';
?>
```

In this example, the regular expression finds a match because the string stored in the variable $text contains "PHP." This example will therefore output the message shown in Figure 8.1 (note that the single quotes around the strings in the code prevent PHP from filling in the value of the variable $text).

Figure 8.1. The regular expression finds a match

By default, regular expressions are case sensitive; that is, lowercase characters in the expression only match lowercase characters in the string, and uppercase characters only match uppercase characters. If you want to perform a case-insensitive search instead, you can use a pattern modifier to make the regular expression ignore case.

Pattern modifiers are single-character flags following the ending delimiter of the expression. The modifier for performing a case-insensitive match is i. So while /PHP/ will only match strings that contain "PHP", /PHP/i will match strings that contain "PHP", "php", or even "pHp".

Here's an example to illustrate this:

chapter8/preg_match2/index.php

```php
<?php
$text = 'What is Php?';

if (preg_match('/PHP/i', $text))
{
  $output = '$text contains the string &ldquo;PHP&rdquo;.';
}
else
{
  $output = '$text does not contain the string &ldquo;PHP&rdquo;.';
}

include 'output.html.php';
?>
```

Again, as shown in Figure 8.2 this outputs the same message, despite the string actually containing "Php".

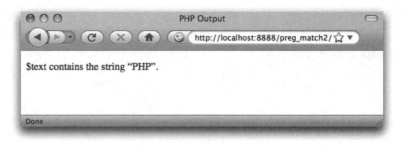

Figure 8.2. No need to be picky …

Regular expressions are almost a programming language unto themselves. A dazzling variety of characters have a special significance when they appear in a regular expression. Using these special characters, you can describe in great detail the pattern of characters for which a PHP function like preg_match will search.

When you first encounter it, regular expression syntax can be downright confusing and difficult to remember, so if you intend to make extensive use of it, a good reference might come in handy. The PHP Manual includes a very decent regular expression reference.[1]

Let's work our way through a few examples to learn the basic regular expression syntax.

First of all, a caret (^) may be used to indicate the start of the string, while a dollar sign ($) is used to indicate its end:

/PHP/	Matches "PHP rules!" and "What is PHP?"
/^PHP/	Matches "PHP rules!" but not "What is PHP?"
/PHP$/	Matches "I love PHP" but not "What is PHP?"
/^PHP$/	Matches "PHP" but nothing else.

Obviously, you may sometimes want to use ^, $, or other special characters to represent the corresponding character in the search string, rather than the special meaning ascribed to these characters in regular expression syntax. To remove the special meaning of a character, prefix it with a backslash:

/\$\$\$/	Matches "Show me the $$$!" but not "$10".

---

[1] http://php.net/manual/en/regexp.reference.php

Square brackets can be used to define a set of characters that may match. For example, the following regular expression will match any string that contains any digit from 1 to 5 inclusive:

`/[12345]/`   Matches "1a" and "39", but not "a" or "76".

If the character list within the square brackets is preceded with a caret (^), the set will match anything *but* the characters listed:

`/[^12345]/`   Matches "1a" and "39", but not "1", or "54".

Ranges of numbers and letters may also be specified:

`/[1-5]/`   Equivalent to `/[12345]/`.
`/^[a-z]$/`   Matches any single lowercase letter.
`/^[^a-z]$/`   Matches any single character *except* a lowercase letter.
`/[0-9a-zA-Z]/` Matches any string with a letter or number.

The characters ?, +, and * also have special meanings. Specifically, ? means "the preceding character is optional, " + means "one or more of the previous character," and * means "zero or more of the previous character."

`/bana?na/`   Matches "banana" and "banna",
                   but not "banaana".
`/bana+na/`   Matches "banana" and "banaana",
                   but not "banna".
`/bana*na/`   Matches "banna", "banana", and "banaaana",
                   but not "bnana".
`/^[a-zA-Z]+$/` Matches any string of one or more
                   letters and nothing else.

Parentheses may be used to group strings together to apply ?, +, or * to them as a whole:

`/ba(na)+na/`   Matches "banana" and "banananana",
                   but not "bana" or "banaana".

You can provide a number of alternatives within parentheses, separated by pipes (|):

`/ba(na|ni)+/`   Matches "bana" and "banina",
                  but not "naniba".

And finally, a period (.) matches any character except a new line:

`/^.+$/`   Matches any string of one or more characters with no line breaks.

There are more special codes and syntax tricks for regular expressions, all of which should be covered in any reference, such as that mentioned above. For now, we have more than enough for our purposes.

String Replacement with Regular Expressions

We can detect the presence of our custom tags in a joke's text using `preg_match` with the regular expression syntax we've just learned. However, what we need to do is pinpoint those tags and replace them with appropriate HTML tags. To achieve this, we need to look at another regular expression function offered by PHP: `preg_replace`.

`preg_replace`, like `preg_match`, accepts a regular expression and a string of text, and attempts to match the regular expression in the string. In addition, `preg_replace` takes a second string of text, and replaces every match of the regular expression with that string.

The syntax for `preg_replace` is as follows:

```
$newString = preg_replace(regExp, replaceWith, oldString);
```

Here, *regExp* is the regular expression, and *replaceWith* is the string that will replace matches to *regExp* in *oldString*. The function returns the new string with all the replacements made. In the above, this newly generated string is stored in `$newString`.

We're now ready to build our custom markup language.

Boldface and Italic Text

In Chapter 6, we wrote a helper function, `htmlout` for outputting arbitrary text as HTML. This function is housed in a shared include file, **helpers.inc.php**. Since we'll now want to output text containing our custom tags as HTML, let's add a new helper function to this file for this purpose:

```
chapter8/includes/helpers.inc.php (excerpt)

function bbcode2html($text)
{
  $text = html($text);

  : Convert custom tags to HTML

  return $text;
}
```

The markup language we'll support is commonly called **BBCode** (short for Bulletin Board Code), and is used in many web-based discussion forums. Since this helper function will convert BBCode to HTML, it's named `bbcode2html`.

The first action this function performs is to use the `html` helper function to convert any HTML code present in the text into HTML text. We want to avoid any HTML code appearing in the output except that which is generated by our own custom tags. Let's now look at the code that will do just that.

Let's start by implementing tags that create **bold** and *italic* text. Let's say we want `[B]` to mark the start of bold text and `[/B]` to mark the end of bold text. Obviously, you must replace `[B]` with `<strong>` and `[/B]` with `</strong>`.[2] To achieve this, simply apply `preg_replace`:[3]

---

[2] You may be more accustomed to using `<b>` and `<i>` tags for bold and italic text; however, I've chosen to respect the most recent HTML standards, which recommend using the more meaningful `<strong>` and `<em>` tags, respectively. If bold text doesn't necessarily indicate strong emphasis in your content, and italic text doesn't necessarily indicate emphasis, you should use `<b>` and `<i>` instead.

[3] Experienced PHP developers may object to this use of regular expressions. Yes, regular expressions are probably overkill for this simple example, and yes, a single regular expression for both tags would be more appropriate than two separate expressions. I'll address both of these issues later in this chapter.

```
$text = preg_replace('/\[B]/i', '<strong>', $text);
$text = preg_replace('/\[\/B]/i', '</strong>', $text);
```

Notice that, because [normally indicates the start of a set of acceptable characters in a regular expression, we put a backslash before it in order to remove its special meaning.

Similarly, we must escape the forward slash in the [/b] tag with a backslash, to prevent it from being mistaken for the delimiter that marks the end of the regular expression.

Without a matching [, the] loses its special meaning, so it's unnecessary to escape it, although you could put a backslash in front of it as well if you wanted to be thorough.

Also notice that, since we're using the i modifier on each of the two regular expressions to make them case insensitive, both [B] and [b] (as well as [/B] and [/b]) will work as tags in our custom markup language.

Italic text can be achieved in the same way:

```
$text = preg_replace('/\[I]/i', '<em>', $text);
$text = preg_replace('/\[\/I]/i', '</em>', $text);
```

Paragraphs

While we could create tags for paragraphs just as we did for bold and italic text above, a simpler approach makes more sense. Since your users will type the content into a form field that allows them to format text using the **Enter** key, we'll take a single new line to indicate a line break (<br />) and a double new line to indicate a new paragraph (</p><p>).

You can represent a new line character in a regular expression as \n. Other *whitespace* characters you can write this way include a carriage return (\r) and a tab space (\t).

Exactly which characters are inserted into text when the user hits **Enter** is dependant on the operating system in use. In general, Windows computers represent a line break as a carriage-return/new-line pair (\r\n), whereas older Mac computers represent it as a single carriage return character (\r). Only recent Macs and Linux computers use a single new line character (\n) to indicate a new line.[4]

To deal with these different line-break styles, any of which may be submitted by the browser, we must do some conversion:

```
// Convert Windows (\r\n) to Unix (\n)
$text = preg_replace('/\r\n/', "\n", $text);
// Convert Macintosh (\r) to Unix (\n)
$text = preg_replace('/\r/', "\n", $text);
```

 Regular Expressions in Double Quoted Strings

All of the regular expressions we've seen so far in this chapter have been expressed as single-quoted PHP strings. The automatic variable substitution provided by PHP strings is sometimes more convenient, but they can cause headaches when used with regular expressions.

Double-quoted PHP strings and regular expressions share a number of special character escape codes. "\n" is a PHP string containing a new line character. Likewise, /\n/ is a regular expression that will match any string containing a new line character. We can represent this regular expression as a single-quoted PHP string ('/\n/'), and all is well, because the code \n has no special meaning in a single-quoted PHP string.

If we were to use a double-quoted string to represent this regular expression, we'd have to write "/\\n/"—with a double-backslash. The double-backslash tells PHP to include an actual backslash in the string, rather than combining it with the n that follows it to represent a new line character. This string will therefore generate the desired regular expression, /\n/.

Because of the added complexity it introduces, it's best to avoid using double-quoted strings when writing regular expressions. Note, however, that I *have* used double quotes for the replacement strings ("\n") passed as the second parameter to `preg_replace`. In this case, we actually do want to create a string containing a new line character, so a double-quoted string does the job perfectly.

---

[4] In fact, the type of line breaks used can vary between software programs on the same computer. If you've ever opened a text file in Notepad to see all the line breaks missing, then you've experienced the frustration this can cause. Advanced text editors used by programmers usually let you specify the type of line breaks to use when saving a text file.

With our line breaks all converted to new line characters, we can convert them to paragraph breaks (when they occur in pairs) and line breaks (when they occur alone):

```
// Paragraphs
$text = '<p>' . preg_replace('/\n\n/', '</p><p>', $text) . '</p>';
// Line breaks
$text = preg_replace('/\n/', '<br/>', $text);
```

Note the addition of <p> and </p> tags surrounding the joke text. Because our jokes may contain paragraph breaks, we must make sure the joke text is output within the context of a paragraph to begin with.

This code does the trick: the line breaks in the next will now become the natural line- and paragraph-breaks expected by the user, removing the requirement to learn custom tags to create this simple formatting.

It turns out, however, that there's a simpler way to achieve the same result in this case—there's no need to use regular expressions at all! PHP's str_replace function works a lot like preg_replace, except that it only searches for strings—instead of regular expression patterns:

```
$newString = str_replace(searchFor, replaceWith, oldString);
```

We can therefore rewrite our line-breaking code as follows:

```
                                        chapter8/includes/helpers.inc.php (excerpt)

// Convert Windows (\r\n) to Unix (\n)
$text = str_replace("\r\n", "\n", $text);
// Convert Macintosh (\r) to Unix (\n)
$text = str_replace("\r", "\n", $text);

// Paragraphs
$text = '<p>' . str_replace("\n\n", '</p><p>', $text) . '</p>';
// Line breaks
$text = str_replace("\n", '<br/>', $text);
```

str_replace is much more efficient than preg_replace because there's no need for it to interpret your search string for regular expression codes. Whenever str_replace (or str_ireplace, if you need a case-insensitive search) can do the job, you should use it instead of preg_replace.

You might be tempted to go back and rewrite the code for processing [B] and [I] tags with str_replace. Hold off on this for now—in just a few pages I'll show you another technique that will enable you to make *that* code even better!

Hyperlinks

While supporting the inclusion of hyperlinks in the text of jokes may seem unnecessary, this feature makes plenty of sense in other applications. Hyperlinks are a little more complicated than the simple conversion of a fixed code fragment into an HTML tag. We need to be able to output a URL, as well as the text that should appear as the link.

Another feature of preg_replace comes into play here. If you surround a portion of the regular expression with parentheses, you can **capture** the corresponding portion of the matched text and use it in the replacement string. To do this, you'll use the code $*n*, where *n* is 1 for the first parenthesized portion of the regular expression, 2 for the second, and so on, up to **99** for the 99th. Consider this example:

```
$text = 'banana';
$text = preg_replace('/(.*)(nana)/', '$2$1', $text);
echo $text; // outputs "nanaba"
```

In the above, $1 is replaced with ba in the replacement string, which corresponds to (.*) (zero or more non-new line characters) in the regular expression. $2 is replaced by nana, which corresponds to (nana) in the regular expression.

We can use the same principle to create our hyperlinks. Let's begin with a simple form of link, where the text of the link is the same as the URL. We want to support this syntax:

```
Visit [URL]http://sitepoint.com/[/URL].
```

The corresponding HTML code, which we want to output, is as follows:

```
Visit <a href="http://sitepoint.com/">http://sitepoint.com/</a>.
```

First, we need a regular expression that will match links of this form. The regular expression is as follows:

```
/\[URL][-a-z0-9._~:\/?#@!$&'()*+,;=%]+\[\/URL]/i
```

This is a rather complicated regular expression. You can see how regular expressions have gained a reputation for being indecipherable! Let me break it down for you:

/

As with all of our regular expressions, we choose to mark its beginning with a slash.

\[URL]

This matches the opening [URL] tag. Since square brackets have a special meaning in regular expressions, we must escape the opening square bracket with a backslash to have it interpreted literally.

[-a-z0-9._~:\/?#@!$&'()*+,;=%]+

This will match any URL.[5] The square brackets contain a list of characters that may appear in a URL, which is followed by a + to indicate that one or more of these acceptable characters must be present.

Within a square-bracketed list of characters, many of the characters that normally have a special meaning within regular expressions lose that meaning. ., ?, +, *, (, and) are all listed here without the need to be escaped by backslashes. The only character that *does* need to be escaped in this list is the slash (/), which must be written as \/ to prevent it being mistaken for the end-of-regular-expression delimiter.

Note also that to include the hyphen (-) in the list of characters, you have to list it first. Otherwise, it would have been taken to indicate a range of characters (as in a-z and 0-9).

\[\/URL]

This matches the closing [/URL] tag. Both the opening square bracket and the slash must be escaped with backslashes.

---

[5] It will also match some strings that are invalid URLs, but it's close enough for our purposes. If you're especially intrigued by regular expressions, you might want to check out RFC 3986, the official standard for URLs. Appendix B of this specification demonstrates how to parse a URL with a rather impressive regular expression.

/i

> We mark the end of the regular expression with a slash, followed by the case-insensitivity flag, i.

To output our link, we'll need to capture the URL and output it both as the `href` attribute of the `<a>` tag, and as the text of the link. To capture the URL, we surround the corresponding portion of our regular expression with parentheses:

```
/\[URL]([-a-z0-9._~:\/?#@!$&'()*+,;=%]+)\[\/URL]/i
```

We can therefore convert the link with the following PHP code:

```
$text = preg_replace(
    '/\[URL]([-a-z0-9._~:\/?#@!$&\'()*+,;=%]+)\[\/URL]/i',
    '<a href="$1">$1</a>', $text);
```

As you can see, $1 is used twice in the replacement string to substitute the captured URL in both places.

Note that because we're expressing our regular expression as a single-quoted PHP string, you have to escape the single quote that appears in the list of acceptable characters with a backslash.

We'd also like to support hyperlinks for which the link text differs from the URL. Such a link will look like this:

```
Check out [URL=http://www.php.net/]PHP[/URL].
```

Here's the regular expression for this form of link:

```
/\[URL=([-a-z0-9._~:\/?#@!$&'()*+,;=%]+)]([^[]+)\[\/URL]/i
```

Squint at it for a little while, and see if you can figure out how it works. Grab your pen and break it into parts if you need to. If you have a highlighter pen handy, you might use it to highlight the two pairs of parentheses (()) used to capture portions of the matched string—the link URL ($1) and the link text ($2).

This expression describes the link text as one or more characters, none of which is an opening square bracket ([^[]+).

Here's how to use this regular expression to perform the desired substitution:

```
$text = preg_replace(
    '/\[URL=([-a-z0-9._~:\/?#@!$&\'()*+,;=%]+)]([^[]+)\[\/URL]/i',
    '<a href="$1">$2</a>', $text);
```

Matching Tags

A nice side-effect of the regular expressions we developed to read hyperlinks is that they'll only find matched pairs of [URL] and [/URL] tags. A [URL] tag missing its [/URL] or vice versa will be undetected, and will appear unchanged in the finished document, allowing the person updating the site to spot the error and fix it.

In contrast, the PHP code we developed for bold and italic text in the section called "Boldface and Italic Text" will convert unmatched [B] and [I] tags into unmatched HTML tags! This can lead to ugly situations in which, for example, the entire text of a joke starting from an unmatched tag will be displayed in bold—possibly even spilling into subsequent content on the page.

We can rewrite our code for bold and italic text in the same style we used for hyperlinks. This solves the problem by only processing matched pairs of tags:

```
$text = preg_replace('/\[B]([^[]+)\[\/B]/i',
    '<strong>$1</strong>', $text);

$text = preg_replace('/\[I]([^[]+)\[\/I]/i', '<em>$1</em>',
    $text);
```

We've still some more work to do, however.

One weakness of these regular expressions is that they represent the content between the tags as a series of characters that lack an opening square bracket ([^\[]+). As a result, nested tags (tags within tags) will fail to work correctly with this code.

Ideally, we'd like to be able to tell the regular expression to capture characters following the opening tag until it reaches a matching closing tag. Unfortunately, the regular expression symbols + (one or more) and * (zero or more) are what we call **greedy**, which means they'll match as many characters as they can. Consider this example:

```
This text contains [B]two[/B] bold [B]words[/B]!
```

Now, if we left unrestricted the range of characters that could appear between opening and closing tags, we might come up with a regular expression like this one:

```
/\[B](.+)\[\/B]/i
```

Nice and simple, right? Unfortunately, because the + is greedy, the regular expression will match only one pair of tags in the above example—and it's a different pair to what you might expect! Here are the results:

```
This text contains <strong>two[/B] bold[B]words</strong>!
```

As you can see, the greedy + plowed right through the first closing tag and the second opening tag to find the second closing tag in its attempt to match as many characters as possible. What we need in order to support nested tags are *non-greedy* versions of + and *.

Thankfully, regular expressions *do* provide non-greedy variants of these control characters! The non-greedy version of + is +?, and the non-greedy version of * is *?. With these, we can produce improved versions of our code for processing [B] and [I] tags:

chapter8/includes/helpers.inc.php *(excerpt)*

```
// [B]old
$text = preg_replace('/\[B](.+?)\[\/B]/i', '<strong>$1</strong>',
    $text);

// [I]talic
$text = preg_replace('/\[I](.+?)\[\/I]/i', '<em>$1</em>', $text);
```

We can give the same treatment to our hyperlink processing code:

chapter8/includes/helpers.inc.php *(excerpt)*

```
// [URL]link[/URL]
$text = preg_replace(
    '/\[URL]([-a-z0-9._~:\/?#@!$&\'()*+,;=%]+)\[\/URL]/i',
    '<a href="$1">$1</a>', $text);
```

```
// [URL=url]link[/URL]
$text = preg_replace(
    '/\[URL=([-a-zO-9._~:\/?#@!$&\'()*+,;=%]+)](.+?)\[\/URL]/i',
    '<a href="$1">$2</a>', $text);
```

Putting It All Together

Here's our finished helper function for converting BBCode to HTML:

chapter8/includes/helpers.inc.php (excerpt)

```php
function bbcode2html($text)
{
  $text = html($text);

  // [B]old
  $text = preg_replace('/\[B](.+?)\[\/B]/i',
      '<strong>$1</strong>', $text);

  // [I]talic
  $text = preg_replace('/\[I](.+?)\[\/I]/i', '<em>$1</em>', $text);

  // Convert Windows (\r\n) to Unix (\n)
  $text = str_replace("\r\n", "\n", $text);
  // Convert Macintosh (\r) to Unix (\n)
  $text = str_replace("\r", "\n", $text);

  // Paragraphs
  $text = '<p>' . str_replace("\n\n", '</p><p>', $text) . '</p>';
  // Line breaks
  $text = str_replace("\n", '<br/>', $text);

  // [URL]link[/URL]
  $text = preg_replace(
      '/\[URL]([-a-zO-9._~:\/?#@!$&\'()*+,;=%]+)\[\/URL]/i',
      '<a href="$1">$1</a>', $text);

  // [URL=url]link[/URL]
  $text = preg_replace(
      '/\[URL=([-a-zO-9._~:\/?#@!$&\'()*+,;=%]+)](.+?)\[\/URL]/i',
      '<a href="$1">$2</a>', $text);
```

```
    return $text;
}
```

For added convenience when using this in a PHP template, we'll add a `bbcodeout` function that calls `bbcode2html` and then echoes out the result:

chapter8/includes/helpers.inc.php *(excerpt)*

```php
function bbcodeout($text)
{
  echo bbcode2html($text);
}
```

We can then use this helper in our two templates that output joke text. First, in the admin pages, we have the joke search results template:

chapter8/admin/jokes/jokes.html.php

```php
<?php include_once $_SERVER['DOCUMENT_ROOT'] .
    '/includes/helpers.inc.php'; ?>
<!DOCTYPE html PUBLIC "-//W3C//DTD XHTML 1.0 Strict//EN"
    "http://www.w3.org/TR/xhtml1/DTD/xhtml1-strict.dtd">
<html xmlns="http://www.w3.org/1999/xhtml" xml:lang="en" lang="en">
  <head>
    <title>Manage Jokes: Search Results</title>
    <meta http-equiv="content-type"
        content="text/html; charset=utf-8"/>
  </head>
  <body>
    <h1>Search Results</h1>
    <?php if (isset($jokes)): ?>
      <table>
        <tr><th>Joke Text</th><th>Options</th></tr>
        <?php foreach ($jokes as $joke): ?>
        <tr valign="top">
          <td><?php bbcodeout($joke['text']); ?></td>
          <td>
            <form action="?" method="post">
              <div>
                <input type="hidden" name="id" value="<?php
                    htmlout($joke['id']); ?>"/>
                <input type="submit" name="action" value="Edit"/>
                <input type="submit" name="action" value="Delete"/>
```

```
        </div>
      </form>
    </td>
  </tr>
  <?php endforeach; ?>
  </table>
  <?php endif; ?>
  <p><a href="?">New search</a></p>
  <p><a href="..">Return to JMS home</a></p>
  </body>
</html>
```

Second, we have the public joke list page:

chapter8/Jokes/jokes.html.php

```
<?php include_once $_SERVER['DOCUMENT_ROOT'] .
    '/includes/helpers.inc.php'; ?>
<!DOCTYPE html PUBLIC "-//W3C//DTD XHTML 1.0 Strict//EN"
    "http://www.w3.org/TR/xhtml1/DTD/xhtml1-strict.dtd">
<html xmlns="http://www.w3.org/1999/xhtml" xml:lang="en" lang="en">
  <head>
    <title>List of Jokes</title>
    <meta http-equiv="content-type"
        content="text/html; charset=utf-8"/>
  </head>
  <body>
    <p><a href="?addjoke">Add your own joke</a></p>
    <p>Here are all the jokes in the database:</p>
    <?php foreach ($jokes as $joke): ?>
      <form action="?deletejoke" method="post">
        <blockquote>
          <p>
            <?php bbcodeout($joke['text']); ?>
            <input type="hidden" name="id" value="<?php
                echo $joke['id']; ?>"/>
            <input type="submit" value="Delete"/>
          </p>
        </blockquote>
      </form>
    <?php endforeach; ?>
  </body>
</html>
```

With these changes made, take your new markup language for a spin! Edit a few of your jokes to contain BBCode tags and verify that the formatting is correctly displayed.

Real World Content Submission

It seems a shame to have spent so much time and effort on a content management system that's so easy to use, when the only people who are actually *allowed* to use it are the site administrators. Furthermore, while it's extremely convenient for an administrator to be able to avoid having to edit HTML to make updates to the site's content, submitted documents still need to be transcribed into the "Add new joke" form, and any formatted text converted into the custom formatting language we developed above—a tedious and mind-numbing task to say the least.

What if we put the "Add new joke" form in the hands of casual site visitors? If you recall, we actually did this in Chapter 4 when we provided a form through which users could submit their own jokes. At the time, this was simply a device that demonstrated how INSERT statements could be made from within PHP scripts. We excluded it in the code we developed from scratch in this chapter because of the inherent security risks involved. After all, who wants to open the content of a site for just anyone to tamper with?

In the next chapter, you'll turn your joke database into a web site that could survive in the real world by introducing access control. Most importantly, you'll limit access to the admin pages for the site to authorized users only. But perhaps more excitingly, you'll place some limits on what *normal* users can get away with.

Chapter

Cookies, Sessions, and Access Control

Cookies and sessions are two of those mysterious technologies that are almost always made out to be more intimidating and complex than they really are. In this chapter, I'll debunk those myths by explaining in simple language what they are, how they work, and what they can do for you. I'll also provide practical examples to demonstrate each.

Finally, we'll use these new tools to provide sophisticated access control to the administration features of your Internet Joke Database site.

Cookies

Most computer programs these days preserve some form of **state** when you close them. Whether it be the position of the application window, or the names of the last five files that you worked with, the settings are usually stored in a small file on your system, so they can be read back the next time the program is run. When web developers took web design to the next level, and moved from static pages to complete, interactive, online applications, there was a need for similar functionality in web browsers—so cookies were born.

A **cookie** is a name-value pair associated with a given web site, and stored on the computer that runs the client (browser). Once a cookie is set by a web site, all future page requests to that same site will also include the cookie until it **expires**, or becomes out of date. Other web sites are unable to access the cookies set by your site, and vice versa, so, contrary to popular belief, they're a relatively safe place to store personal information. Cookies in and of themselves are incapable of compromising a user's privacy.

Illustrated in Figure 9.1 is the life cycle of a PHP-generated cookie.

1 First, a web browser requests a URL that corresponds to a PHP script. Within that script is a call to the `setcookie` function that's built into PHP.

2 The page produced by the PHP script is sent back to the browser, along with an HTTP `set-cookie` header that contains the name (for example, `mycookie`) and value of the cookie to be set.

3 When it receives this HTTP header, the browser creates and stores the specified value as a cookie named `mycookie`.

4 Subsequent page requests to that web site contain an HTTP `cookie` header that sends the name/value pair (`mycookie=value`) to the script requested.

5 Upon receipt of a page request with a cookie header, PHP automatically creates an entry in the `$_COOKIE` array with the name of the cookie (`$_COOKIE['mycookie']`) and its value.

In other words, the PHP `setcookie` function lets you set a variable that will automatically be set by subsequent page requests from the same browser. Before we examine an actual example, let's take a close look at the `setcookie` function:

```
setcookie(name[, value[, expiryTime[, path[, domain[, secure[,
    httpOnly]]]]]])
```

Square Brackets Indicate Optional Code

The square brackets ([...]) in the above code indicate portions of the code that are optional. Leave out the square brackets when using the syntax in your code.

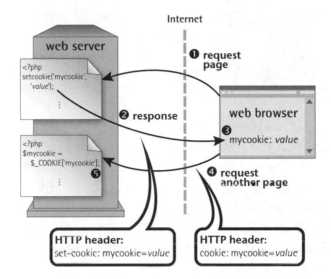

Figure 9.1. The life cycle of a cookie

Like the `header` function we saw in Chapter 4, the `setcookie` function adds HTTP headers to the page, and thus *must be called before any of the actual page content is sent*. Any attempt to call `setcookie` after page content has been sent to the browser will produce a PHP error message. Typically, therefore, you will use these functions in your controller script before any actual output is sent (by an included PHP template, for example).

The only required parameter for this function is *name*, which specifies the name of the cookie. Calling `setcookie` with only the *name* parameter will actually delete the cookie that's stored on the browser, if it exists. The *value* parameter allows you to create a new cookie, or modify the value stored in an existing one.

By default, cookies will remain stored by the browser, and thus will continue to be sent with page requests, until the browser is closed by the user. If you want the cookie to persist beyond the current browser session, you must set the *expiryTime* parameter to specify the number of seconds from January 1, 1970 to the time at which you want the cookie to be deleted automatically. The current time in this format can be obtained using the PHP `time` function. Thus, a cookie could be set to expire in one hour, for example, by setting *expiryTime* to `time() + 3600`. To delete a cookie that has a preset expiry time, change this expiry time to represent a point in the past (such as one year ago: `time() - 3600 * 24 * 365`). Here's an example:

```
// Set a cookie to expire in 1 year
setcookie('mycookie', 'somevalue', time() + 3600 * 24 * 365);

// Delete it
setcookie('mycookie', '', time() − 3600 * 24 * 365);
```

The *path* parameter lets you restrict access to the cookie to a given path on your server. For instance, if you set a path of '/~kyank/' for a cookie, only requests for pages in the **~kyank** directory (and its subdirectories) will include the cookie as part of the request. Note the trailing /, which prevents other scripts in other directories beginning with /~kyank (such as /**kyankfake**/) from accessing the cookie. This is helpful if you're sharing a server with other users, and each user has a web home directory. It allows you to set cookies without exposing your visitors' data to the scripts of other users on your server.

The *domain* parameter serves a similar purpose; it restricts the cookie's access to a given domain. By default, a cookie will be returned only to the host from which it was originally sent. Large companies, however, commonly have several host names for their web presence (for example, www.example.com and support.example.com). To create a cookie that's accessible by pages on both servers, you would set the *domain* parameter to '.example.com'. Note the leading ., which prevents another site at fakeexample.com from accessing your cookies on the basis that their domain ends with example.com.

The *secure* parameter, when set to 1, indicates that the cookie should be sent only with page requests that happen over a secure (SSL) connection (that is, with a URL that starts with https://).

The *httpOnly* parameter, when set to 1, tells the browser to prevent JavaScript code on your site from seeing the cookie that you're setting. Normally, the JavaScript code you include in your site can read the cookies that have been set by the server for the current page. While this can be useful in some cases, it also puts the data stored in your cookies at risk should an attacker figure out a way to inject malicious JavaScript code into your site. This code could then read your users' potentially sensitive cookie data and do unspeakable things with it. If you set *httpOnly* to 1, the cookie you're setting will be sent to your PHP scripts as usual, but will be invisible to JavaScript code running on your site.

While all parameters except *name* are optional, you must specify values for earlier parameters if you want to specify values for later ones. For instance, to call `setcookie` with a *domain* value, you also need to specify a value for the *expiryTime* parameter. To omit parameters that require a value, you can set string parameters (*value*, *path*, *domain*) to `' '` (the empty string) and numerical parameters (*expiryTime*, *secure*) to `0`.

Let's now look at an example of cookies in use. Imagine you want to display a special welcome message to people on their first visit to your site. You could use a cookie to count the number of times a user had been to your site before, and only display the message when the cookie was not set. Here's the code:

```
                                              chapter9/cookiecounter/index.php
<?php

if (!isset($_COOKIE['visits']))
{
  $_COOKIE['visits'] = 0;
}
$visits = $_COOKIE['visits'] + 1;
setcookie('visits', $visits, time() + 3600 * 24 * 365);

include 'welcome.html.php';

?>
```

This code starts by checking if `$_COOKIE['visits']` is set. If it isn't, it means the `visits` cookie has yet to be set in the user's browser. To handle this special case, we set `$_COOKIE['visits']` to `0`. The rest of our code can then safely assume that `$_COOKIE['visits']` contains the number of previous visits the user has made to the site.

Next, to work out the number of *this* visit, we take `$_COOKIE['visits']` and add 1. This variable, `$visits`, will be used by our PHP template.

Finally, we use `setcookie` to set the `visits` cookie to reflect the new number of visits. We set this cookie to expire in one year's time.

With all the work done, our controller includes the PHP template **welcome.html.php**:

chapter9/cookiecounter/welcome.html.php

```
<!DOCTYPE html PUBLIC "-//W3C//DTD XHTML 1.0 Strict//EN"
    "http://www.w3.org/TR/xhtml1/DTD/xhtml1-strict.dtd">
<html xmlns="http://www.w3.org/1999/xhtml" xml:lang="en" lang="en">
  <head>
    <title>Cookie counter</title>
    <meta http-equiv="content-type"
        content="text/html; charset=utf-8"/>
  </head>
  <body>
    <p>
      <?php
      if ($visits > 1)
      {
        echo "This is visit number $visits.";
      }
      else
      {
        // First visit
        echo 'Welcome to my web site! Click here for a tour!';
      }
      ?>
    </p>
  </body>
</html>
```

Figure 9.2 shows what this example looks like the first time a browser visits the page. Subsequent visits look like Figure 9.3.

Figure 9.2. The first visit

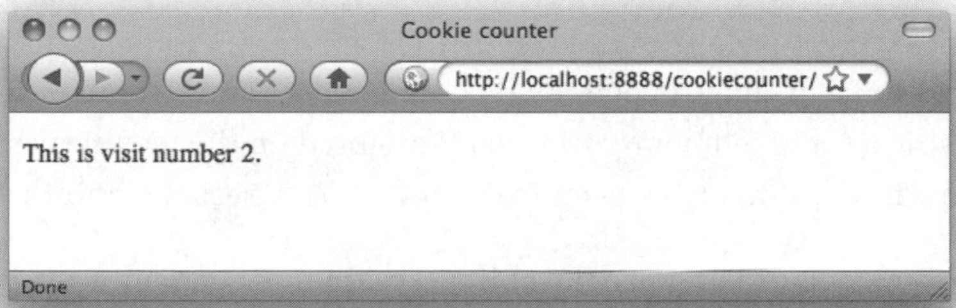

Figure 9.3. The second visit

Before you go overboard using cookies, be aware that browsers place a limit on the number and size of cookies allowed per web site. Some browsers will start deleting old cookies to make room for new ones after you've set 20 cookies from your site. Other browsers will allow up to 50 cookies per site, but will *reject* new cookies beyond this limit. Browsers also enforce a maximum combined size for all cookies from all web sites, so an especially cookie-heavy site might cause your own site's cookies to be deleted.

For these reasons, you should do your best to keep the number and size of the cookies your site creates to a minimum.

PHP Sessions

Because of the limitations I've just described, cookies are inappropriate for storing large amounts of information. If you run an ecommerce web site that uses cookies to store the items in a user's shopping cart as the user makes his or her way through your site, this can be a big problem—the bigger a customer's order, the more likely it will run afoul of a browser's cookie restrictions.

Sessions were developed in PHP as the solution to this issue. Instead of storing all your (possibly large) data as cookies in the web browser, sessions let you store the data on your web server. The only value that's stored in the browser is a single cookie that contains the user's **session ID**—a variable for which PHP watches on subsequent page requests, and uses to load the stored data that's associated with that session.

Unless configured otherwise, a PHP session automatically sets in the user's browser a cookie that contains the session ID—a long string of letters and numbers that serves to identify that user uniquely for the duration of that visit to your site. The browser then sends that cookie along with every request for a page from your site, so that PHP can determine to which of potentially numerous sessions-in-progress the request belongs. Using a set of temporary files that are stored on the web server, PHP keeps track of the variables that have been registered in each session, and their values.

Before you can go ahead and use the spiffy session-management features in PHP, you need to ensure that the relevant section of your **php.ini** file has been set up properly. If you're using a server that belongs to your web host, it's probably safe to assume this has been done for you. Otherwise, open your **php.ini** file in a text editor and look for the section marked [`Session`] (say *that* ten times fast!). Beneath it, you'll find around 20 options that begin with the word `session`. Most of them are just fine as they are, but here are a few crucial ones you'll want to check:

```
session.save_handler      = files
session.save_path         = "C:\WINDOWS\TEMP"
session.use_cookies       = 1
```

`session.save_path` tells PHP where to create the temporary files used to track sessions. It must be set to a directory that exists on the system, or you'll receive ugly error messages when you try to create a session on one of your pages. On Mac OS X and Linux systems, **/tmp** is a popular choice. In Windows, you could use **C:\WINDOWS\TEMP**, or some other directory if you prefer (I use **D:\PHP\SESSIONS**). With these adjustments made, restart your web server software to allow the changes to take effect.

You're now ready to start working with PHP sessions. But before we jump into an example, let's quickly look at the most common session management functions in PHP. To tell PHP to look for a session ID, or to start a new session if none is found, you simply call `session_start`. If an existing session ID is found when this function is called, PHP restores the variables that belong to that session. Since this function attempts to create a cookie, it must come before any page content is sent to the browser, just as we saw for `setcookie` above:

```
session_start();
```

To create a session variable, which will be available on all pages in the site when accessed by the current user, simply set a value in the special $_SESSION array. For example, the following will store the variable called password in the current session:

```
$_SESSION['password'] = 'mypassword';
```

To remove a variable from the current session, use PHP's unset function:

```
unset($_SESSION['password']);
```

Finally, should you want to end the current session and delete all registered variables in the process, you can clear all the stored values and use session_destroy:

```
$_SESSION = array();
session_destroy();
```

For more detailed information on these and the other session-management functions in PHP, see the relevant section of the PHP Manual.[1]

Now that we have these basic functions under our belt, let's put them to work in a simple example.

A Simple Shopping Cart

This example will consist of a controller script feeding two PHP templates:

- a product catalog, through which you can add items to your shopping cart
- a checkout page, which displays the contents of the user's shopping cart for confirmation

From the checkout page, the order could then be submitted to a processing system that would handle the details of payment acceptance and shipping arrangements. That system is beyond the scope of this book, but if you'd like to try one I'd recommend playing with PayPal,[2] which is quite easy to set up. The developer documentation[3] should be well within reach of your PHP skills at this point.

---

[1] http://www.php.net/session

[2] http://www.paypal.com/

[3] https://developer.paypal.com/

Let's start with the controller code that sets up the list of items we'll have for sale in our online store. For each item, we wish to list a description and a price per unit. For this example, we'll code these details as a PHP array. In a real-world system, you would probably store these details in a database, but I'm using this method so we can focus on the session code. You should already know all you need to put together a database driven product catalog, so if you're feeling ambitious, go ahead and write it now!

Here's the code for our list of products:

chapter9/shoppingcart/index.php *(excerpt)*

```php
<?php
include_once $_SERVER['DOCUMENT_ROOT'] .
    '/includes/magicquotes.inc.php';

$items = array(
    array('id' => '1', 'desc' => 'Canadian-Australian Dictionary',
        'price' => 24.95),
    array('id' => '2', 'desc' => 'As-new parachute (never opened)',
        'price' => 1000),
    array('id' => '3', 'desc' => 'Songs of the Goldfish (2CD set)',
        'price' => 19.99),
    array('id' => '4', 'desc' => 'Simply JavaScript (SitePoint)',
        'price' => 39.95));
```

Each item in this array is itself an associative array of three items: a unique item ID, the item description, and the price. It's no coincidence that this looks like an array of results we might build from querying a database.

Now, we're going to store the list of items the user placed in the shopping cart in yet another array. Because we'll need this variable to persist throughout a user's visit to your site, we'll store it using PHP sessions. Here's the code that's responsible:

chapter9/shoppingcart/index.php *(excerpt)*

```php
session_start();
if (!isset($_SESSION['cart']))
{
  $_SESSION['cart'] = array();
}
```

`session_start` either starts a new session (and sets the session ID cookie), or restores the variables registered in the existing session, if one exists. The code then checks if `$_SESSION['cart']` exists, and, if it doesn't, initializes it to an empty array to represent the empty cart.

That's all we need to display a product catalog, using a PHP template:

```php
include 'catalog.html.php';
```

Let's look at the code for this template:

```php
<?php include_once $_SERVER['DOCUMENT_ROOT'] .
    '/includes/helpers.inc.php'; ?>
<!DOCTYPE html PUBLIC "-//W3C//DTD XHTML 1.0 Strict//EN"
    "http://www.w3.org/TR/xhtml1/DTD/xhtml1-strict.dtd">
<html xmlns="http://www.w3.org/1999/xhtml" xml:lang="en" lang="en">
  <head>
    <title>Product catalog</title>
    <meta http-equiv="content-type"
        content="text/html; charset=utf-8" />
    <style type="text/css">
    table {
      border-collapse: collapse;
    }
    td, th {
      border: 1px solid black;
    }
    </style>
  </head>
  <body>
    <p>Your shopping cart contains <?php
        echo count($_SESSION['cart']); ?> items.</p> ❶
    <p><a href="?cart">View your cart</a></p> ❷
    <table border="1">
      <thead>
        <tr>
          <th>Item Description</th>
          <th>Price</th>
        </tr>
      </thead>
```

```
    <tbody>
      <?php foreach ($items as $item): ?>
        <tr>
          <td><?php htmlout($item['desc']); ?></td>
          <td>
            $<?php echo number_format($item['price'], 2); ?> ❸
          </td>
          <td>
            <form action="" method="post"> ❹
              <div>
                <input type="hidden" name="id" value="<?php
                    htmlout($item['id']); ?>"/>
                <input type="submit" name="action" value="Buy"/>
              </div>
            </form>
          </td>
        </tr>
      <?php endforeach; ?>
    </tbody>
  </table>
  <p>All prices are in imaginary dollars.</p>
</body>
</html>
```

Here are the highlights:

❶   We use the built-in PHP function count to output the number of items in the array stored in the $_SESSION['cart'].

❷   We provide a link to let the user view the contents of the shopping cart. In a system that provided checkout facilities, you might label this link **Proceed to Checkout**.

❸   We use PHP's built-in number_format function to display the prices with two digits after the decimal point (see the PHP Manual[4] for more information about this function).

❹   For each item in the catalog, we provide a form with a **Buy** button that submits the unique ID of the item.

Figure 9.4 shows the product catalog produced by this template.

---

[4] http://www.php.net/number_format

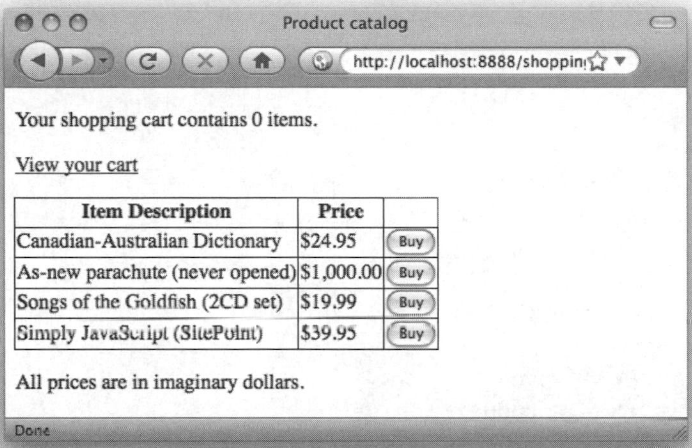

Figure 9.4. The completed product catalog

Now, when a user clicks one of the **Buy** buttons, our controller will receive a form submission with $_POST['action'] set to 'Buy'. Here's how we process this in the controller:

```
                                    chapter9/shoppingcart/index.php (excerpt)

if (isset($_POST['action']) and $_POST['action'] == 'Buy')
{
  // Add item to the end of the $_SESSION['cart'] array
  $_SESSION['cart'][] = $_POST['id'];
  header('Location: .');
  exit();
}
```

We add the product ID of the item to the $_SESSION['cart'] array before redirecting the browser back to the same page, but without a query string, thereby ensuring that refreshing the page avoids repeatedly adding the item to the cart.

When the user clicks the **View your cart** link, our controller will receive a request with $_GET['cart'] set. Here's how our controller will handle this:

```php
if (isset($_GET['cart']))
{
  $cart = array();
  $total = 0;
  foreach ($_SESSION['cart'] as $id)
  {
    foreach ($items as $product)
    {
      if ($product['id'] == $id)
      {
        $cart[] = $product;
        $total += $product['price'];
        break;
      }
    }
  }

  include 'cart.html.php';
  exit();
}
```

What this code does is build an array ($cart) much like the $items array, except that the items in $cart reflect the items the user has added to the shopping cart. To do this, it uses two nested foreach loops. The first loops through the IDs in $_SESSION['cart']. For each of these IDs, it uses the second foreach loop to search through the $items array looking for a product whose ID ($product['id']) is equal to the $id from the cart. When it finds the product, it adds it to the $cart array.

At the same time, this code tallies the total price of the items in the shopping cart. Each time the second foreach loop finds the product in the cart, it adds its price ($product['price']) to the $total.

The break command tells PHP to stop executing the second foreach loop, since it has found the product for which it has been searching.

Once the $cart array is built, we load the second of our two PHP templates, **cart.html.php**.

The code for **cart.html.php** is very similar to the product catalog template. All it does is list the items in the $cart array instead of the $items array. It also outputs the total in the footer of the table:

```php
<?php include_once $_SERVER['DOCUMENT_ROOT'] .
    '/includes/helpers.inc.php'; ?>
<!DOCTYPE html PUBLIC "-//W3C//DTD XHTML 1.0 Strict//EN"
    "http://www.w3.org/TR/xhtml1/DTD/xhtml1-strict.dtd">
<html xmlns="http://www.w3.org/1999/xhtml" xml:lang="en" lang="en">
  <head>
    <title>Shopping cart</title>
    <meta http-equiv="content-type"
        content="text/html; charset=utf-8" />
    <style type="text/css">
    table {
      border-collapse: collapse;
    }
    td, th {
      border: 1px solid black;
    }
    </style>
  </head>
  <body>
    <h1>Your Shopping Cart</h1>
    <?php if (count($cart) > 0): ?>
    <table>
      <thead>
        <tr>
          <th>Item Description</th>
          <th>Price</th>
        </tr>
      </thead>
      <tfoot>
        <tr>
          <td>Total:</td>
          <td>$<?php echo number_format($total, 2); ?></td>
        </tr>
      </tfoot>
      <tbody>
        <?php foreach ($cart as $item): ?>
          <tr>
            <td><?php htmlout($item['desc']); ?></td>
            <td>
```

```
            $<?php echo number_format($item['price'], 2); ?>
          </td>
        </tr>
      <?php endforeach; ?>
    </tbody>
  </table>
  <?php else: ?>
  <p>Your cart is empty!</p>
  <?php endif; ?>
  <form action="?" method="post">
    <p>
      <a href="?">Continue shopping</a> or
      <input type="submit" name="action" value="Empty cart"/>
    </p>
  </form>
  </body>
</html>
```

Once you have filled your cart with goodies, Figure 9.5 shows the output of this template.

Figure 9.5. A full cart

This template also provides an **Empty cart** button that causes the controller script to unset the $_SESSION['cart'] variable, which results in a new, empty shopping cart. Here's the code:

```
                                  chapter9/shoppingcart/index.php (excerpt)
if (isset($_POST['action']) and $_POST['action'] == 'Empty cart')
{
  // Empty the $_SESSION['cart'] array
  unset($_SESSION['cart']);
  header('Location: ?cart');
  exit();
}
```

And Figure 9.6 shows what the cart looks like once emptied.

Figure 9.6. Avoid going home empty-handed!

That's it! Here's the complete code for the controller, with all the pieces assembled:

```
                                  chapter9/shoppingcart/index.php
<?php

$items = array(
    array('id' => '1', 'desc' => 'Canadian-Australian Dictionary',
        'price' => 24.95),
    array('id' => '2', 'desc' => 'As-new parachute (never opened)',
        'price' => 1000),
    array('id' => '3', 'desc' => 'Songs of the Goldfish (2CD set)',
        'price' => 19.99),
    array('id' => '4', 'desc' => 'Simply JavaScript (SitePoint)',
        'price' => 39.95));

session_start();
```

```php
if (!isset($_SESSION['cart']))
{
  $_SESSION['cart'] = array();
}

if (isset($_POST['action']) and $_POST['action'] == 'Buy')
{
  // Add item to the end of the $_SESSION['cart'] array
  $_SESSION['cart'][] = $_POST['id'];
  header('Location: .');
  exit();
}

if (isset($_POST['action']) and $_POST['action'] == 'Empty cart')
{
  // Empty the $_SESSION['cart'] array
  unset($_SESSION['cart']);
  header('Location: ?cart');
  exit();
}

if (isset($_GET['cart']))
{
  $cart = array();
  $total = 0;
  foreach ($_SESSION['cart'] as $id)
  {
    foreach ($items as $product)
    {
      if ($product['id'] == $id)
      {
        $cart[] = $product;
        $total += $product['price'];
        break;
      }
    }
  }

  include 'cart.html.php';
  exit();
}

include 'catalog.html.php';

?>
```

Access Control

One of the most common reasons for building a database driven web site is that it allows the site owner to update the site from any web browser, anywhere! But, in a world where roaming bands of jubilant hackers will fill your site with viruses and pornography, you need to stop and think about the security of your administration pages.

At the very least, you'll want to require username and password authentication before a visitor to your site can access the administration area. There are two main ways of doing this:

- configure your web server software to require a valid login for the relevant pages
- use PHP to prompt the user and check the login credentials as appropriate

If you have access to your web server's configuration, the first option is often the easiest to set up, but the second is by far the more flexible. With PHP, you can design your own login form, and even embed it into the layout of your site if you wish. PHP also makes it easy to change the credentials required to gain access, or manage a database of authorized users, each with their own credentials and privileges.

In this section, you'll enhance your joke database site to protect sensitive features with username/password-based authentication. In order to control which users can do what, you'll build a sophisticated **role-based access control** system.

"What does all this have to do with cookies and sessions?" you might wonder. Well, rather than prompting your users for login credentials every time they wish to view a sensitive page or perform a sensitive action, you can use PHP sessions to hold onto those credentials throughout their visit to your site.

Database Design

Depending on the type of application you're working on, you may need to create a new database table to store the list of authorized users and their passwords. In the case of the joke database site, you already have a table to do the job—the `author` table:

```
mysql> DESCRIBE author;
+-------+--------------+------+-----+---------+----------------+
| Field | Type         | Null | Key | Default | Extra          |
+-------+--------------+------+-----+---------+----------------+
| id    | int(11)      | NO   | PRI | NULL    | auto_increment |
| name  | varchar(255) | YES  |     | NULL    |                |
| email | varchar(255) | YES  |     | NULL    |                |
+-------+--------------+------+-----+---------+----------------+
3 rows in set (0.03 sec)
```

Rather than track authors and users separately, let's extend this existing database table so that authors can log into your site. Some authors in the database may never log in, and may exist only to give credit for jokes. Other authors may never write a joke, existing only to give a person administrative access to the site. But for those users who may do both, it will be more elegant to have their details stored in this one table, rather than spread across two different tables.

We can actually use each author's email address as a username. To do this, we'll want to ensure that each author in the database has a unique email address. We can do this with an ALTER TABLE ADD UNIQUE command:[5]

```
mysql> ALTER TABLE author ADD UNIQUE (email);
Query OK, 3 rows affected (0.76 sec)
Records: 3  Duplicates: 0  Warnings: 0
```

With this change made, MySQL will now generate an error if you try to create a new author with the same email address as an existing author.

Now, all this table needs is an extra column to store each author's password:

```
mysql> ALTER TABLE author ADD COLUMN password CHAR(32);
Query OK, 3 rows affected (0.54 sec)
Records: 3  Duplicates: 0  Warnings: 0
```

---

[5] In this chapter I'll show you the SQL commands needed to modify the database we've built up to this point. If you need to recreate the database from scratch, the necessary commands are provided in the **ijdb.sql** file in the code archive for this chapter.

Note that we refrain from using the `NOT NULL` modifier on this column, so some authors may have no password. When we write the PHP code that uses this column, we'll simply prevent authors with no password from logging in.

Note the column type: `CHAR(32)`. It's a big no-no to store users' actual passwords in your database. Many users share a bad habit of reusing the same password across many different web sites. It's an expected courtesy, therefore, as a site administrator, to *scramble* the passwords your users give you, so that even if your database were stolen out from under you, those passwords would be useless to an attacker trying to gain access to your users' accounts on other web sites.

A typical method of scrambling passwords is to use the **md5** function built into PHP:

```
$scrambled = md5($password . 'ijdb');
```

Adding `'ijdb'` to the end of the password supplied by the user before scrambling it ensures that the scrambled password in your site's database is different to the scrambled version of the same password in another site's database. Security experts call this **salt**, as in "add a dash of salt before you scramble the eggs."

A Note from the Security Experts

Security experts will tell you that using the same salt for every password in your database is asking for trouble, since an attacker who's able to figure out your salt (say by obtaining a copy of your site's code) will be one step closer to being able to guess the original passwords based on the scrambled versions in your database. Of course, those same security experts will tell you that, rather than write your own password-handling code, you should rely on a proven solution developed by security experts like themselves.

This example provides a basic level of security with plenty of room for improvement if you're interested in doing a little research.

The **md5** function creates a string exactly 32 characters long made up of apparently random letters and numbers. Although the same password will always generate the same string of 32 characters, it's effectively impossible to guess the password that was used to generate a given 32-character string. By storing only these strings in your database, you'll be able to check if a user has entered the correct password.

Unlike the VARCHAR column type, a column of type CHAR(32) will only store values exactly 32 characters long. This added regularity makes your database perform faster. Since the md5 function always generates a string 32 characters long, we can safely take advantage of this speed boost.

It turns out that MySQL has an MD5 function that performs the same task. Go ahead and store a password for your own author entry—or create one from scratch if you need to—now:

```
mysql> UPDATE author SET password = MD5('passwordijdb')
    -> WHERE id = 1;
Query OK, 1 row affected (0.04 sec)
Rows matched: 1  Changed: 1  Warnings: 0
```

Note that you have to tack on to your desired password the same suffix ('ijdb' in this example) that you're using in your PHP code.

Next, we need to store the list of sensitive actions each author is permitted to do. While you *could* simply give every logged-in user *carte blanche*—blanket permission to do absolutely anything—on most sites it will make greater sense to have more granular control over what each user's able to do.

Let's build a new table that will contain a list of **roles** that you'll be able to assign to each of your authors. Each author may have one or more of these roles assigned to them. An author who's assigned the role of Content Editor, for example, would be able to edit jokes in your CMS. This type of system is called **role-based access control**:

```
mysql> CREATE TABLE role (
    ->    id VARCHAR(255) NOT NULL PRIMARY KEY,
    ->    description VARCHAR(255)
    -> ) DEFAULT CHARACTER SET utf8;
Query OK, 0 rows affected (0.04 sec)
```

Each role will have a short string ID and a longer description. Let's fill in a few roles now:

```
mysql> INSERT INTO role (id, description) VALUES
    -> ('Content Editor', 'Add, remove, and edit jokes'),
    -> ('Account Administrator', 'Add, remove, and edit authors'),
```

```
      -> ('Site Administrator', 'Add, remove, and edit categories');
Query OK, 3 rows affected (0.06 sec)
Records: 3  Duplicates: 0  Warnings: 0
```

Finally, we'll need a lookup table to assign roles to users in a many-to-many relationship:

```
mysql> CREATE TABLE authorrole (
    ->    authorid INT NOT NULL,
    ->    roleid VARCHAR(255) NOT NULL,
    ->    PRIMARY KEY (authorid, roleid)
    -> ) DEFAULT CHARACTER SET utf8;
Query OK, 0 rows affected (0.03 sec)
```

While you're at it, assign yourself the Account Administrator role:

```
mysql> INSERT INTO authorrole (authorid, roleid) VALUES
    -> (1, 'Account Administrator');
Query OK, 1 row affected (0.00 sec)
```

That takes care of the database. Now let's turn our attention to the PHP code that will use these new database structures.

Controller Code

Obviously, access control is a feature that will be very handy in many different PHP projects. Therefore, like our database connection code and our view helpers, it makes sense to write as much of our access control code as a shared include file, so that we can then reuse in future projects.

Rather than try to guess what functions our shared include file should contain, let's start by modifying our controller code as if we already had the include file written.

You'll recall that our administration pages start with with an ordinary HTML page that displays the menu shown in Figure 9.7.

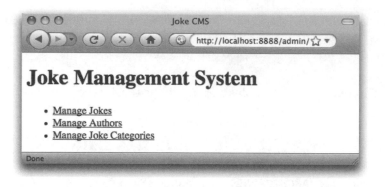

Figure 9.7. No protection required on this page

Your instinct might be to protect this page, but in fact it contains no sensitive information, so we can safely leave it alone. Each of the three links, however, point to a PHP controller script that performs all sorts of sensitive operations:

/admin/jokes/index.php   Searches for, displays, adds, edits, and removes jokes from the system. Only users with the Content Editor role should be able to perform these actions.

/admin/authors/index.php   Lists, adds, edits, and removes authors from the system. Users with the Account Administrator role only should be able to perform these actions.

/admin/categories/index.php   Lists, adds, edits, and removes categories from the system. Only users with the Site Administrator role should be able to perform these actions.

Each of these controllers, therefore, should check if the user is currently logged in and is assigned the required role before proceeding. If the user has yet to log in, it should display a login form. If the user is logged in, but lacks the required role, it should display an appropriate error message.

If we imagine that we already have functions to achieve all these actions, here's what the code might look like:

chapter9/admin/authors/index.php *(excerpt)*

```php
<?php
include_once $_SERVER['DOCUMENT_ROOT'] .
    '/includes/magicquotes.inc.php';

require_once $_SERVER['DOCUMENT_ROOT'] . '/includes/access.inc.php';

if (!userIsLoggedIn())
{
  include '../login.html.php';
  exit();
}

if (!userHasRole('Account Administrator'))
{
  $error = 'Only Account Administrators may access this page.';
  include '../accessdenied.html.php';
  exit();
}
```
: *The rest of the controller code is unchanged.*

We add the similar code to each of our other two controllers, but with the appropriate role specified for each:

chapter9/admin/categories/index.php *(excerpt)*

```php
<?php
include_once $_SERVER['DOCUMENT_ROOT'] .
    '/includes/magicquotes.inc.php';

require_once $_SERVER['DOCUMENT_ROOT'] . '/includes/access.inc.php';

if (!userIsLoggedIn())
{
  include '../login.html.php';
  exit();
}

if (!userHasRole('Site Administrator'))
{
  $error = 'Only Site Administrators may access this page.';
  include '../accessdenied.html.php';
  exit();
```

```
}

⋮ The rest of the controller code is unchanged.
```

chapter9/admin/jokes/index.php *(excerpt)*

```php
<?php
include_once $_SERVER['DOCUMENT_ROOT'] .
    '/includes/magicquotes.inc.php';

require_once $_SERVER['DOCUMENT_ROOT'] . '/includes/access.inc.php';

if (!userIsLoggedIn())
{
  include '../login.html.php';
  exit();
}

if (!userHasRole('Content Editor'))
{
  $error = 'Only Content Editors may access this page.';
  include '../accessdenied.html.php';
  exit();
}

⋮ The rest of the controller code is unchanged.
```

From each of these blocks of code, we can see that we have the following tasks ahead of us:

■ Write the login form, **login.html.php**.

■ Write the "access denied" error page, **accessdenied.html.php**.

■ Write the shared include file **access.inc.php**, containing the following functions:

userIsLoggedIn   Checks if the user's already logged in, or if the user has just submitted the login form with a correct email address and password.

userHasRole   Checks if the user who's logged in has been assigned the specified role in the database.

Since the login form and the error page will be shared by all three of our controllers, we'll put them in the **admin** directory alongside **index.html**.

The code for the error page is completely straightforward. All it does is output the $error variable set by the controller:

chapter9/admin/accessdenied.html.php

```php
<?php include_once $_SERVER['DOCUMENT_ROOT'] .
    '/includes/helpers.inc.php'; ?>
<!DOCTYPE html PUBLIC "-//W3C//DTD XHTML 1.0 Strict//EN"
    "http://www.w3.org/TR/xhtml1/DTD/xhtml1-strict.dtd">
<html xmlns="http://www.w3.org/1999/xhtml" xml:lang="en" lang="en">
  <head>
    <title>Access Denied</title>
    <meta http-equiv="content-type"
        content="text/html; charset=utf-8"/>
  </head>
  <body>
    <h1>Access Denied</h1>
    <p><?php echo htmlout($error); ?></p>
  </body>
</html>
```

The login form takes a little more thought. Here's the code:

chapter9/admin/login.html.php

```php
<?php include_once $_SERVER['DOCUMENT_ROOT'] .
    '/includes/helpers.inc.php'; ?>
<!DOCTYPE html PUBLIC "-//W3C//DTD XHTML 1.0 Strict//EN"
    "http://www.w3.org/TR/xhtml1/DTD/xhtml1-strict.dtd">
<html xmlns="http://www.w3.org/1999/xhtml" xml:lang="en" lang="en">
  <head>
    <title>Log In</title>
    <meta http-equiv="content-type"
        content="text/html; charset=utf-8"/>
  </head>
  <body>
    <h1>Log In</h1>
    <p>Please log in to view the page that you requested.</p>
    <?php if (isset($loginError)): ?> ❶
      <p><?php echo htmlout($loginError); ?></p>
    <?php endif; ?>
```

```
    <form action="" method="post"> ❷
      <div>
        <label for="email">Email: <input type="text" name="email"
          id="email"/></label>
      </div>
      <div>
        <label for="password">Password: <input type="password" ❸
          name="password" id="password"/></label>
      </div>
      <div>
        <input type="hidden" name="action" value="login"/> ❹
        <input type="submit" value="Log in"/>
      </div>
    </form>
    <p><a href="/admin/">Return to JMS home</a></p> ❺
  </body>
</html>
```

The form takes an email address and a password, as you might expect.

 If the user submits the login form with an incorrect email address or password, the user will be denied access, simply being presented with the login form again. We need a way to tell the user what went wrong in this situation; this template will check if a variable named $loginError exists, and if so, will display it above the form.

❷ The <form> tag has an empty action attribute, so this form will be submitted back to the same URL that produced this form. Thus, if the user's login attempt is successful, the controller will display the page that the browser originally requested.

❸ Notice the second <input/> tag has its type attribute set to password. This tells the browser to hide the value that the user types in, to shield the password from prying eyes.

❹ This hidden field will be submitted with the form, to act as a signal to the userIsLoggedIn function that the user has submitted this form in an attempt to log in. You might be tempted simply to put the name="action attribute on the submit button's <input/> tag and watch for that—but if the user submits the form by hitting **Enter** while editing one of the two text fields, the submit button will not be submitted with the form. Using a hidden field like this ensures that the `action` variable will be submitted no matter how the form submission is triggered.

 A user might request a protected page by accident, or might be unaware that a page is protected until they see the login form. We therefore provide a link back to an unprotected page as a way out.

This form will take care of people logging in, but we also want to provide a way for a logged-in user to log out. Just as our `userIsLoggedIn` function will detect submissions of the login form to log users in, we can also make it detect the submission of a logout form to log users out. Let's add this form to the bottom of each of our protected pages:

```
chapter9/admin/logout.inc.html.php

<form action="" method="post">
  <div>
    <input type="hidden" name="action" value="logout"/>
    <input type="hidden" name="goto" value="/admin/"/>
    <input type="submit" value="Log out"/>
  </div>
</form>
```

Again, we use a hidden `action` field to signal the user's intentions. The `goto` field indicates where we wish to send the user that's just logged out.

To add this form to each of our protected pages, simply add the necessary `include` command to the bottom of each template:

```
chapter9/admin/authors/authors.html.php (excerpt)

    ⋮
    <p><a href="..">Return to JMS home</a></p>
    <?php include '../logout.inc.html.php'; ?>
  </body>
</html>
```

```
                                 chapter9/admin/authors/categories.html.php (excerpt)

    ⋮
  <p><a href="..">Return to JMS home</a></p>
  <?php include '../logout.inc.html.php'; ?>
  </body>
</html>
```

```
                                 chapter9/admin/authors/searchform.html.php (excerpt)

    ⋮
  <p><a href="..">Return to JMS home</a></p>
  <?php include '../logout.inc.html.php'; ?>
  </body>
</html>
```

```
                                   chapter9/admin/authors/jokes.html.php (excerpt)

    ⋮
  <p><a href="..">Return to JMS home</a></p>
  <?php include '../logout.inc.html.php'; ?>
  </body>
</html>
```

Function Library

Finally, we can look at writing the shared include file, **access.inc.php**. The code above demands a lot from this humble file, but having written all the code that depends on it ahead of time, we have a fairly good idea of what it needs to do.

Let's review. This file must define two custom functions:

userIsLoggedIn   This function should return TRUE if the user is logged in, or FALSE otherwise.

This function should also detect and handle a couple of special cases:

▪ If the current request contains a submission of the login form, as indicated by the hidden field in the form (which sets $_POST['action'] to 'login'), it should check if the submitted username and password are correct. If they are, it should log in the user and return TRUE. Otherwise, it should set the global variable $loginError to an appropriate error message, and return FALSE.

■ If the current request contains a submission of the logout form, as indicated by the hidden field in the form (which sets $_POST['action'] to 'logout'), it should log out the user and redirect the browser to the URL specified by $_POST['goto'].

userHasRole   This function should look in the database and check if the currently logged-in user has been assigned the role that's passed to this function. If the role has been assigned, this function should return TRUE; if not, it should return FALSE.

Let's work through these two functions a few lines at a time:

chapter9/includes/access.inc.php *(excerpt)*

```php
<?php

function userIsLoggedIn()
{
  if (isset($_POST['action']) and $_POST['action'] == 'login')
  {
```

We start with the userIsLoggedIn function. The first deed it does is check if the login form has been submitted:

chapter9/includes/access.inc.php *(excerpt)*

```php
    if (!isset($_POST['email']) or $_POST['email'] == '' or
        !isset($_POST['password']) or $_POST['password'] == '')
    {
      $GLOBALS['loginError'] = 'Please fill in both fields';
      return FALSE;
    }
```

Next, before we go looking in the database, we should make sure that the user has filled in a value for both the email address and password. If either of these was not submitted, or was submitted as an empty string, we set the global $loginError

variable (using the special `$GLOBALS` array we looked at in Chapter 6) and return
FALSE.

Now that we have checked that an email address and password were actually submitted, we can look for a matching author in the database. The first task we need
to do is scramble the submitted password to match the scrambled version that will
be stored in the database:

chapter9/includes/access.inc.php *(excerpt)*

```php
$password = md5($_POST['password'] . 'ijdb');
```

Next, we'll query the database for a matching author record. Since this is an under-
taking we'll need to do more than once in this code, we'll write another custom
function to do it:

chapter9/includes/access.inc.php *(excerpt)*

```php
function databaseContainsAuthor($email, $password)
{
  include 'db.inc.php';

  $email = mysqli_real_escape_string($link, $email);
  $password = mysqli_real_escape_string($link, $password);

  $sql = "SELECT COUNT(*) FROM author
      WHERE email='$email' AND password='$password'";
  $result = mysqli_query($link, $sql);
  if (!$result)
  {
    $error = 'Error searching for author.';
    include 'error.html.php';
    exit();
  }
  $row = mysqli_fetch_array($result);

  if ($row[0] > 0)
  {
    return TRUE;
  }
  else
  {
```

```
        return FALSE;
    }
}
```

This code should be quite familiar to you by now. We start by connecting to the database using our shared **db.inc.php** include file.[6] We then use `mysqli_real_escape_string` to prepare our two submitted values—the email address and the scrambled password—for use in a database query. We then execute a database query that will count the number of records in the `author` table that have a matching email address and password. If the number returned is greater than zero, we return `TRUE`; if not, we return `FALSE`.

If the database query fails for some reason, we use an `error.html.php` template to display an error message to the user, so make sure you drop this into the **includes** directory alongside the **access.inc.php** file:

chapter9/includes/error.html.php

```
<!DOCTYPE html PUBLIC "-//W3C//DTD XHTML 1.0 Strict//EN"
    "http://www.w3.org/TR/xhtml1/DTD/xhtml1-strict.dtd">
<html xmlns="http://www.w3.org/1999/xhtml" xml:lang="en" lang="en">
  <head>
    <title>PHP Error</title>
    <meta http-equiv="content-type"
        content="text/html; charset=utf-8"/>
  </head>
  <body>
    <p>
      <?php echo $error; ?>
    </p>
  </body>
</html>
```

Now, back in the `userIsLoggedIn` function, we can call our new `databaseContainsAuthor` function:

---

[6] We use `include` instead of `include_once` here, since the `$link` variable that **db.inc.php** creates will be unavailable outside this function. Code elsewhere in our application that requires a database connection will therefore have to include **db.inc.php** again.

```
                              chapter9/includes/access.inc.php (excerpt)

    if (databaseContainsAuthor($_POST['email'], $password))
    {
```

If the database contains a matching author, it means the user filled out the login form correctly and we have to log in the user. But what exactly does "log in the user" mean? There are two approaches to this, both of which involve using PHP sessions:

- You can log in the user by setting a session variable as a "flag" (for example, $_SESSION['loggedIn'] = TRUE). On future requests, you can just check if this variable is set. If it is, the user is logged in, and the isUserLoggedIn function can return TRUE.

- You can store the "flag" variable as well as the submitted email address and scrambled password in two additional session variables. On future requests, you can check if these variables are set. If they are, you can use the databaseContainsAuthor function to check if they still match an author stored in the database. If they do, the isUserLoggedIn function can return TRUE.

The first option offers greater performance, since the user's credentials are only checked once—when the login form is submitted. The second option offers greater security, since the user's credentials are checked against the database every time a sensitive page is requested.

In general, the more secure option is preferable, since it allows you to remove authors from the site even while they're logged in. Otherwise, once a user is logged in, they'll stay logged in for as long as their PHP session remains active. That's a steep price to pay for a little extra performance.

So, here's the code for the second option:

```
                              chapter9/includes/access.inc.php (excerpt)

    session_start();
    $_SESSION['loggedIn'] = TRUE;
    $_SESSION['email'] = $_POST['email'];
    $_SESSION['password'] = $password;
    return TRUE;
  }
```

And finally, of course, if the user submits a login form with incorrect values, we need to ensure the user is logged out, set an appropriate error message, and return FALSE.

```php
    else
    {
      session_start();
      unset($_SESSION['loggedIn']);
      unset($_SESSION['email']);
      unset($_SESSION['password']);
      $GLOBALS['loginError'] =
          'The specified email address or password was incorrect.';
      return FALSE;
    }
}
```

That takes care of processing the login form. The second special case we need to handle is the logout form. This one's much simpler—so much so that the code should be self-explanatory:

```php
if (isset($_POST['action']) and $_POST['action'] == 'logout')
{
  session_start();
  unset($_SESSION['loggedIn']);
  unset($_SESSION['email']);
  unset($_SESSION['password']);
  header('Location: ' . $_POST['goto']);
  exit();
}
```

Finally, if neither of the two special cases are detected, we simply check if the user is logged in using the session variables we have already discussed:

```php
session_start();
if (isset($_SESSION['loggedIn']))
{
  return databaseContainsAuthor($_SESSION['email'],
```

```
        $_SESSION['password']);
    }
}
```

That takes care of `userIsLoggedIn`. Now let's look at `userHasRole`. This function really just performs a complex database query: Given an author's email address (stored in the session), and a role ID (passed to the function), we need to check if the specified author has been assigned that role. This query will involve three different database tables, so let's look at the SQL code in isolation:

```
SELECT COUNT(*) FROM author
INNER JOIN authorrole ON author.id = authorid
INNER JOIN role ON roleid = role.id
WHERE email = email AND role.id = roleID
```

We join the `author` table to the `authorrole` table by matching up the `author` table's `id` field with the `authorrole` table's `authorid` field. We then join *those* with the `role` table by matching up the `authorrole` table's `roleid` field with the `role` table's `id` field. Finally, with our three tables joined, we use the `WHERE` clause to look for records with the email address and role ID for which we're looking.

From there, it's just a matter of writing the PHP code to execute this query and interpret the results:

chapter9/includes/access.inc.php (excerpt)

```php
function userHasRole($role)
{
  include 'db.inc.php';

  $email = mysqli_real_escape_string($link, $_SESSION['email']);
  $role = mysqli_real_escape_string($link, $role);

  $sql = "SELECT COUNT(*) FROM author
      INNER JOIN authorrole ON author.id = authorid
      INNER JOIN role ON roleid = role.id
      WHERE email = '$email' AND role.id='$role'";
  $result = mysqli_query($link, $sql);
  if (!$result)
  {
    $error = 'Error searching for author roles.';
```

```php
    include 'error.html.php';
    exit();
  }
  $row = mysqli_fetch_array($result);

  if ($row[0] > 0)
  {
    return TRUE;
  }
  else
  {
    return FALSE;
  }
}
```

Understand all that? Save your changes, and try visiting some of the protected pages. If you gave yourself the Account Administrator role as I suggested above, you should be able to visit and use the **Manage Authors** section of the admin pages. The other sections should display the appropriate "access denied" errors. Also try clicking the **Log out** button on any of the protected admin pages. These should return you to the admin index, and prompt you to log in again if you try to access a protected page afterwards.

If you have any problems, check your code using whatever error messages you see as a guide. For easy reference, here's the completed **access.inc.php** file:

chapter9/includes/access.inc.php

```php
<?php

function userIsLoggedIn()
{
  if (isset($_POST['action']) and $_POST['action'] == 'login')
  {
    if (!isset($_POST['email']) or $_POST['email'] == '' or
      !isset($_POST['password']) or $_POST['password'] == '')
    {
      $GLOBALS['loginError'] = 'Please fill in both fields';
      return FALSE;
    }

    $password = md5($_POST['password'] . 'ijdb');
```

```php
    if (databaseContainsAuthor($_POST['email'], $password))
    {
      session_start();
      $_SESSION['loggedIn'] = TRUE;
      $_SESSION['email'] = $_POST['email'];
      $_SESSION['password'] = $password;
      return TRUE;
    }
    else
    {
      session_start();
      unset($_SESSION['loggedIn']);
      unset($_SESSION['email']);
      unset($_SESSION['password']);
      $GLOBALS['loginError'] =
          'The specified email address or password was incorrect.';
      return FALSE;
    }
  }

  if (isset($_POST['action']) and $_POST['action'] == 'logout')
  {
    session_start();
    unset($_SESSION['loggedIn']);
    unset($_SESSION['email']);
    unset($_SESSION['password']);
    header('Location: ' . $_POST['goto']);
    exit();
  }

  session_start();
  if (isset($_SESSION['loggedIn']))
  {
    return databaseContainsAuthor($_SESSION['email'],
        $_SESSION['password']);
  }
}

function databaseContainsAuthor($email, $password)
{
  include 'db.inc.php';

  $email = mysqli_real_escape_string($link, $email);
  $password = mysqli_real_escape_string($link, $password);
```

```php
  $sql = "SELECT COUNT(*) FROM author
      WHERE email='$email' AND password='$password'";
  $result = mysqli_query($link, $sql);
  if (!$result)
  {
    $error = 'Error searching for author.';
    include 'error.html.php';
    exit();
  }
  $row = mysqli_fetch_array($result);

  if ($row[0] > 0)
  {
    return TRUE;
  }
  else
  {
    return FALSE;
  }
}

function userHasRole($role)
{
  include 'db.inc.php';

  $email = mysqli_real_escape_string($link, $_SESSION['email']);
  $role = mysqli_real_escape_string($link, $role);

  $sql = "SELECT COUNT(*) FROM author
      INNER JOIN authorrole ON author.id = authorid
      INNER JOIN role ON roleid = role.id
      WHERE email = '$email' AND role.id='$role'";
  $result = mysqli_query($link, $sql);
  if (!$result)
  {
    $error = 'Error searching for author roles.';
    include 'error.html.php';
    exit();
  }
  $row = mysqli_fetch_array($result);

  if ($row[0] > 0)
  {
    return TRUE;
  }
```

```
  else
  {
    return FALSE;
  }
}

?>
```

Managing Passwords and Roles

Now that we've added passwords and roles to the database, we should update our author admin pages so that they can manipulate these aspects of authors.

First, let's add to the author add/edit form a **Set password** field, as well as a set of checkboxes for choosing the roles that the user should be assigned:

chapter9/admin/authors/form.html.php

```php
<?php include_once $_SERVER['DOCUMENT_ROOT'] .
    '/includes/helpers.inc.php'; ?>
<!DOCTYPE html PUBLIC "-//W3C//DTD XHTML 1.0 Strict//EN"
    "http://www.w3.org/TR/xhtml1/DTD/xhtml1-strict.dtd">
<html xmlns="http://www.w3.org/1999/xhtml" xml:lang="en" lang="en">
  <head>
    <title><?php htmlout($pagetitle); ?></title>
    <meta http-equiv="content-type"
        content="text/html; charset=utf-8"/>
  </head>
  <body>
    <h1><?php htmlout($pagetitle); ?></h1>
    <form action="?<?php htmlout($action); ?>" method="post">
      <div>
        <label for="name">Name: <input type="text" name="name"
            id="name" value="<?php htmlout($name); ?>"/></label>
      </div>
      <div>
        <label for="email">Email: <input type="text" name="email"
            id="email" value="<?php htmlout($email); ?>"/></label>
      </div>
      <div>
        <label for="password">Set password: <input type="password"
            name="password" id="password"/></label>
      </div>
      <fieldset>
```

```
        <legend>Roles:</legend>
        <?php for ($i = 0; $i < count($roles); $i++): ?>
          <div>
            <label for="role<?php echo $i; ?>"><input
              type="checkbox" name="roles[]"
              id="role<?php echo $i; ?>"
              value="<?php htmlout($roles[$i]['id']); ?>"<?php
              if ($roles[$i]['selected'])
              {
                echo ' checked="checked"';
              }
              ?>/><?php htmlout($roles[$i]['id']); ?></label>:
            <?php htmlout($roles[$i]['description']); ?>
          </div>
        <?php endfor; ?>
      </fieldset>
      <div>
        <input type="hidden" name="id" value="<?php
            htmlout($id); ?>"/>
        <input type="submit" value="<?php htmlout($button); ?>"/>
      </div>
    </form>
  </body>
</html>
```

The **Set password** field is a little special because, when it's left blank, it should cause the controller to leave the user's current password alone. Remember that, because we store only scrambled passwords in the database, we're unable to display a user's existing password in the form for editing.

The role checkboxes are a lot like the category checkboxes we created for the joke add/edit form in Chapter 7, with one notable difference. Since we're using strings instead of numbers for our role IDs in the database, we're unable to use the IDs to generate the <input> tags' id attributes. The id attribute can't contain spaces. We therefore have to go a little out of our way to generate a unique number for each role. Instead of using a foreach loop to step through our array of roles, we use an old-fashioned for loop instead:

chapter9/admin/authors/form.html.php *(excerpt)*

```
<?php for ($i = 0; $i < count($roles); $i++): ?>
```

The counter variable $i starts at 0 and each time through the loop it's incremented by one. We can therefore access each role within the loop as $roles[$i], and we can also use $i to build our unique id attributes:

chapter9/admin/authors/form.html.php *(excerpt)*

```
        id="role<?php echo $i; ?>"
```

Now you can update the controller to handle these new fields. The code for the password field is straightforward, and the code for the role checkboxes is nearly identical to what we wrote to process joke categories. I've highlighted the changes in bold below. Take a look, and satisfy yourself that you understand everything that's going on:

chapter9/admin/authors/index.php

```php
<?php
include_once $_SERVER['DOCUMENT_ROOT'] .
    '/includes/magicquotes.inc.php';

require_once $_SERVER['DOCUMENT_ROOT'] . '/includes/access.inc.php';

if (!userIsLoggedIn())
{
  include '../login.html.php';
  exit();
}

if (!userHasRole('Account Administrator'))
{
  $error = 'Only Account Administrators may access this page.';
  include '../accessdenied.html.php';
  exit();
}

if (isset($_GET['add']))
{
  include $_SERVER['DOCUMENT_ROOT'] . '/includes/db.inc.php';

  $pagetitle = 'New Author';
  $action = 'addform';
  $name = '';
  $email = '';
```

```php
$id = '';
$button = 'Add author';

// Build the list of roles
$sql = "SELECT id, description FROM role";
$result = mysqli_query($link, $sql);
if (!$result)
{
  $error = 'Error fetching list of roles.';
  include 'error.html.php';
  exit();
}

while ($row = mysqli_fetch_array($result))
{
  $roles[] = array(
      'id' => $row['id'],
      'description' => $row['description'],
      'selected' => FALSE);
}

include 'form.html.php';
exit();
}

if (isset($_GET['addform']))
{
  include $_SERVER['DOCUMENT_ROOT'] . '/includes/db.inc.php';

  $name = mysqli_real_escape_string($link, $_POST['name']);
  $email = mysqli_real_escape_string($link, $_POST['email']);
  $sql = "INSERT INTO author SET
      name='$name',
      email='$email'";
  if (!mysqli_query($link, $sql))
  {
    $error = 'Error adding submitted author.';
    include 'error.html.php';
    exit();
  }

  $authorid = mysqli_insert_id($link);

  if ($_POST['password'] != '')
  {
```

```php
    $password = md5($_POST['password'] . 'ijdb');
    $password = mysqli_real_escape_string($link, $password);
    $sql = "UPDATE author SET
        password = '$password'
        WHERE id = '$authorid'";
    if (!mysqli_query($link, $sql))
    {
      $error = 'Error setting author password.';
      include 'error.html.php';
      exit();
    }
  }

  if (isset($_POST['roles']))
  {
    foreach ($_POST['roles'] as $role)
    {
      $roleid = mysqli_real_escape_string($link, $role);
      $sql = "INSERT INTO authorrole SET
          authorid='$authorid',
          roleid='$roleid'";
      if (!mysqli_query($link, $sql))
      {
        $error = 'Error assigning selected role to author.';
        include 'error.html.php';
        exit();
      }
    }
  }

  header('Location: .');
  exit();
}

if (isset($_POST['action']) and $_POST['action'] == 'Edit')
{
  include $_SERVER['DOCUMENT_ROOT'] . '/includes/db.inc.php';

  $id = mysqli_real_escape_string($link, $_POST['id']);
  $sql = "SELECT id, name, email FROM author WHERE id='$id'";
  $result = mysqli_query($link, $sql);
  if (!$result)
  {
    $error = 'Error fetching author details.';
    include 'error.html.php';
```

```php
    exit();
}
$row = mysqli_fetch_array($result);

$pagetitle = 'Edit Author';
$action = 'editform';
$name = $row['name'];
$email = $row['email'];
$id = $row['id'];
$button = 'Update author';

// Get list of roles assigned to this author
$sql = "SELECT roleid FROM authorrole WHERE authorid='$id'";
$result = mysqli_query($link, $sql);
if (!$result)
{
  $error = 'Error fetching list of assigned roles.';
  include 'error.html.php';
  exit();
}

$selectedRoles = array();
while ($row = mysqli_fetch_array($result))
{
  $selectedRoles[] = $row['roleid'];
}

// Build the list of all roles
$sql = "SELECT id, description FROM role";
$result = mysqli_query($link, $sql);
if (!$result)
{
  $error = 'Error fetching list of roles.';
  include 'error.html.php';
  exit();
}

while ($row = mysqli_fetch_array($result))
{
  $roles[] = array(
      'id' => $row['id'],
      'description' => $row['description'],
      'selected' => in_array($row['id'], $selectedRoles));
}
```

```php
    include 'form.html.php';
    exit();
}

if (isset($_GET['editform']))
{
  include $_SERVER['DOCUMENT_ROOT'] . '/includes/db.inc.php';

  $id = mysqli_real_escape_string($link, $_POST['id']);
  $name = mysqli_real_escape_string($link, $_POST['name']);
  $email = mysqli_real_escape_string($link, $_POST['email']);
  $sql = "UPDATE author SET
      name='$name',
      email='$email'
      WHERE id='$id'";
  if (!mysqli_query($link, $sql))
  {
    $error = 'Error updating submitted author.';
    include 'error.html.php';
    exit();
  }

  if ($_POST['password'] != '')
  {
    $password = md5($_POST['password'] . 'ijdb');
    $password = mysqli_real_escape_string($link, $password);
    $sql = "UPDATE author SET
        password = '$password'
        WHERE id = '$id'";
    if (!mysqli_query($link, $sql))
    {
      $error = 'Error setting author password.';
      include 'error.html.php';
      exit();
    }
  }

  $sql = "DELETE FROM authorrole WHERE authorid='$id'";
  if (!mysqli_query($link, $sql))
  {
    $error = 'Error removing obsolete author role entries.';
    include 'error.html.php';
    exit();
  }
```

```php
  if (isset($_POST['roles']))
  {
    foreach ($_POST['roles'] as $role)
    {
      $roleid = mysqli_real_escape_string($link, $role);
      $sql = "INSERT INTO authorrole SET
          authorid='$id',
          roleid='$roleid'";
      if (!mysqli_query($link, $sql))
      {
        $error = 'Error assigning selected role to author.';
        include 'error.html.php';
        exit();
      }
    }
  }

  header('Location: .');
  exit();
}

if (isset($_POST['action']) and $_POST['action'] == 'Delete')
{
  include $_SERVER['DOCUMENT_ROOT'] . '/includes/db.inc.php';
  $id = mysqli_real_escape_string($link, $_POST['id']);

  // Delete role assignments for this author
  $sql = "DELETE FROM authorrole WHERE authorid='$id'";
  if (!mysqli_query($link, $sql))
  {
    $error = 'Error removing author from roles.';
    include 'error.html.php';
    exit();
  }

  // Get jokes belonging to author
  $sql = "SELECT id FROM joke WHERE authorid='$id'";
  $result = mysqli_query($link, $sql);
  if (!$result)
  {
    $error = 'Error getting list of jokes to delete.';
    include 'error.html.php';
    exit();
  }
```

```php
  // For each joke
  while ($row = mysqli_fetch_array($result))
  {
    $jokeId = $row[0];

    // Delete joke category entries
    $sql = "DELETE FROM jokecategory WHERE jokeid='$jokeId'";
    if (!mysqli_query($link, $sql))
    {
      $error = 'Error deleting category entries for joke.';
      include 'error.html.php';
      exit();
    }
  }

  // Delete jokes belonging to author
  $sql = "DELETE FROM joke WHERE authorid='$id'";
  if (!mysqli_query($link, $sql))
  {
    $error = 'Error deleting jokes for author.';
    include 'error.html.php';
    exit();
  }

  // Delete the author
  $sql = "DELETE FROM author WHERE id='$id'";
  if (!mysqli_query($link, $sql))
  {
    $error = 'Error deleting author.';
    include 'error.html.php';
    exit();
  }

  header('Location: .');
  exit();
}

// Display author list
include $_SERVER['DOCUMENT_ROOT'] . '/includes/db.inc.php';
$result = mysqli_query($link, 'SELECT id, name FROM author');
if (!$result)
{
  $error = 'Error fetching authors from database!';
  include 'error.html.php';
  exit();
```

```php
}

while ($row = mysqli_fetch_array($result))
{
  $authors[] = array('id' => $row['id'], 'name' => $row['name']);
}

include 'authors.html.php';
?>
```

That's it! Take your enhancements for a spin and give yourself ultimate power by assigning yourself all the roles! Make sure everything works, otherwise fix it. Just for kicks, try changing your own password while you're logged in. You should be kicked out to the login form with the next link or button you click, where you can enter your new password to log back in.

A Challenge: Joke Moderation

It's all well and good to follow along with the code that I present, but it is quite another to write a significant new feature yourself. Now is a good time to try your hand at planning and building a significant new feature for the joke database web site.

For the past few chapters, we've been so focused on the administration pages, that the public side of the site has become a little out-of-date. When we last left it, the main page of our joke database site looked like Figure 9.8.

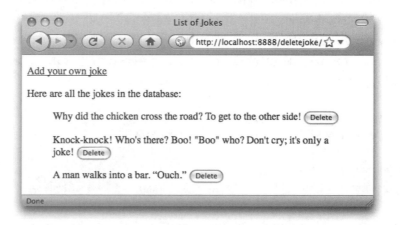

Figure 9.8. Feeling left behind?

Obviously, those **Delete** buttons must go, but what about that **Add your own joke** link? Currently, this link goes to the form shown in Figure 9.9.

Figure 9.9. Another nugget of comic genius is added to the database

When submitted, this form inserts a new joke into the database with no associated author or categories. Nevertheless, the joke is immediately displayed on the front page. Launch the site like this, and spammers will be filling up your database with junk in no time!

How would you deal with this problem? Remove the feature? Force authors to email their submissions to a content editor? Think about it: there must be a way to preserve this "easy submission" feature without having your front page filled with spam.

Is it necessary for new joke submissions to appear on the site immediately? What if you add a new column to the `joke` table called `visible` that could take one of two values: `'YES'` and `'NO'`? Newly submitted jokes could automatically be set to `'NO'`, and could be prevented from appearing on the site if you simply added `WHERE visible='YES'` to any query of the `joke` table for which the results are intended for public viewing. Jokes with `visible` set to `'NO'` would wait in the database for review by a Content Editor, who could edit each joke and assign it an author and categories before making it visible, or just delete it as unwanted.

To create a column that can contain either of two values, of which one is the default, you'll need a new MySQL column type called `ENUM`:

```
mysql> ALTER TABLE joke ADD COLUMN
    -> visible ENUM('NO', 'YES') NOT NULL;
```

Since we declared this column as required (`NOT NULL`), the first value listed within the parentheses (`'NO'` in this case) is the default value, which is assigned to new entries if no value is specified in the INSERT command. All that's left for you to do is modify the administration system, enabling Content Editors to make hidden jokes visible. A simple checkbox in the joke add/edit form should do the trick. You also may want to modify the joke search form to allow Content Editors to search only for visible or hidden jokes.

Newly submitted jokes will be without an author associated. How to deal with that I leave up to you. The **Add your own joke** form could prompt visitors to include contact information with their submissions, which Content Editors could then use to identify and assign authors to submitted jokes. A more challenging solution might be to invite authors to sign up, set a password, and then log in before submitting new jokes.

There's no right answer, but I challenge you to find a way to deal with the issue, and build that into your Internet Joke Database site. You have all the tools you need: set aside some time and see what you can build if you put your mind to it! If you get stuck, the SitePoint PHP Forum[7] is a friendly place to gain answers to your questions.

The Sky's the Limit

In this chapter, you learned about the two main methods of creating persistent variables—those variables that continue to exist from page to page in PHP. The first stores the variable in the visitor's browser in the form of a cookie. By default, cookies terminate at the end of the browser session, but by specifying an expiry time, they can be preserved indefinitely. Unfortunately, cookies are fairly unreliable because you have no way of knowing when the browser might delete your cookies, and because some users occasionally clear their cookies out of concern for their privacy.

Sessions, on the other hand, free you from all the limitations of cookies. They let you store an unlimited number of potentially large variables. Sessions are an essential building block in modern ecommerce applications, as we demonstrated in our simple shopping cart example. They're also a critical component of systems that provide access control, like the one we built for your joke content management system.

---

[7] http://www.sitepoint.com/forums/forumdisplay.php?f=34

At this point, you should be equipped with all the basic skills and concepts you need to build your very own database driven web site. While you may be tempted to skip the challenge of building a complete system for safely accepting public submissions, I encourage you to give it a try. You should already have all the skills necessary to build it, and there is no better way to learn than to make a few mistakes of your own to learn from. At the very least, set this challenge aside for now and come back to it when you've finished this book. If you can tackle it with confidence, you will have proven to yourself that you are now a qualified PHP and MySQL programmer.

If you've solved this challenge, try another! Want to let users rate the jokes on the site? How about letting joke authors make changes to their jokes, but with with the backup of requiring an administrator to approve the changes before they go live on the site? The power and complexity of the system is limited only by your imagination.

In the rest of this book, I'll cover more advanced topics that will help optimize your site's performance and solve some complex problems with less code. Oh, and of course we'll explore more exciting features of PHP and MySQL!

In Chapter 10, we'll take a step away from our joke database and have a close-up look at MySQL server maintenance and administration. We'll learn how to make backups of our database (a critical task for any web-based company), to administer MySQL users and their passwords, and to log into a MySQL server if you've forgotten your password.

Chapter

10

MySQL Administration

At the core of most well-designed, content driven sites is a relational database. In this book, we've used the MySQL Relational Database Management System (RDBMS) to create our database. MySQL is a popular choice among web developers—because it's free and because MySQL servers are fairly simple to set up. As I demonstrated in Chapter 1, armed with proper instructions, a new user can have a MySQL server up and running in less than 30 minutes—under ten if you practice a little!

If all you want is to have a MySQL server to play with a few examples and experiment a little, then the initial installation process we went through in Chapter 1 is likely to be all you'll need. If, on the other hand, you want to set up a database back end to a real live web site—perhaps a site upon which your company depends—then there are a few more fundamentals you'll need to learn how to do before you can rely on a MySQL server day-in and day-out.

First, as I promised in Chapter 2, I'll show you how to set up phpMyAdmin to browse, edit, and administer your databases using your web browser. Using phpMyAdmin is generally much easier than gaining access to a MySQL command prompt, particularly when working with a MySQL server running on another computer.

Next, we'll look at backups. Backing up data that's important to you or your business should be an essential item on any administrator's list of priorities. Unfortunately, because there are usually more interesting tasks in an administrator's role, backup procedures are mainly arranged once out of necessity and deemed "good enough" for all applications. If, until now, your answer to the question, "Should we back up our databases?" has been, "It's okay; they'll be backed up along with everything else," you really should read on. I'll show you why a generic file backup solution is inadequate for many MySQL installations, and I'll demonstrate the *right* way to back up and restore a MySQL database.

In Chapter 1, we set up the MySQL server so that you could connect as the special user "root" with a password you chose. This root MySQL user (which, incidentally, has nothing to do with the root user on Linux and similar systems) had read/write access to all databases and tables. In many organizations, it's necessary to create users whose access is limited to particular databases and tables, and to restrict that access in some way (for example, read-only access to a particular table). In this chapter, we'll also learn how to facilitate such restrictions using two new MySQL commands: GRANT and REVOKE.

Finally, in some situations, such as power outages, MySQL databases can become damaged. There are alternatives, however, to scrambling for your backups when this occurs. We'll finish off our review of MySQL database administration by learning how to use the MySQL database check and repair utility to fix simple database corruptions.

phpMyAdmin

Like most of the code in this book, phpMyAdmin[1] is a PHP script designed to communicate with a MySQL server to generate web pages on the fly. Rather than generating pleasing pages for your visitors, however, phpMyAdmin's job is to provide for you a web-based interface for administering your MySQL server.

phpMyAdmin will let you do almost anything you can do from the MySQL command prompt using a handy point-and-click interface, rather than by typing SQL queries by hand. Of course, if you want to perform a task that can only be expressed in

---

[1] http://www.phpmyadmin.net/

handwritten SQL, phpMyAdmin also offers a form for you to type that SQL code, and will execute it on your behalf and display the results.

Most commercial web hosts will actually give you access to a pre-configured copy of phpMyAdmin within your hosting plan's administration console. Also, if you set up your MySQL server using one of the all-in-one solutions (WampServer or MAMP), you'll find they also include a copy of phpMyAdmin; you'll need to update its configuration to include the MySQL root password you established in Chapter 1, though.

If there's no phpMyAdmin on your server, installing it yourself is relatively easy. Head over to the phpMyAdmin download page[2] and download the latest recommended version (3.1.3.2 as I write this) in a convenient format (**.zip** on Windows or Mac OS X, **.tar.gz** on Linux). Extract the file, and there'll be a directory called **phpMyAdmin-*version-language***. Rename it to **phpMyAdmin** and move it into the document root of your web server.

Using your text editor, create a new file named **config.inc.php** within the **phpMyAdmin** directory, and type the following code into it:

```php
<?php
$cfg['blowfish_secret'] = 'bhvhbv3577h3qguw83qdh37b2fnqelinbq38qhg';

$cfg['Servers'][1]['auth_type'] = 'cookie';
?>
```

Set the $cfg['blowfish_secret'] value to any jumble of letters and numbers. It's unnecessary to remember this value, it just needs to be difficult for a hacker to guess—so the closer to random you can make it, the better.

The second line configures your phpMyAdmin installation to connect to the MySQL server running on the same computer, and to prompt the user for a MySQL username and password. If your MySQL server is on a different computer, or if you wish to set up phpMyAdmin to log into the MySQL server automatically, the installation instructions that come with the software will make worthwhile reading. Just open the **Documentation.html** file in the **phpMyAdmin** directory using your browser of choice.

---

[2] http://www.phpmyadmin.net/home_page/downloads.php

With the configuration file in place, open your browser and load up
http://localhost/phpMyAdmin/ (or whatever URL will point to the **phpMyAdmin**
directory on your web server). You should be greeted by a login screen similar to
Figure 10.1.

Figure 10.1. phpMyAdmin's login screen

You can safely ignore the warning about the mcrypt extension if it appears. On most
servers, it's an optional PHP component that will greatly speed up phpMyAdmin
if installed, but phpMyAdmin will work fine without it.[3]

In the **Username** field, type **root**. In the **Password** field, type your MySQL server's
root password. Alternatively, if you're unaware of the root password for the MySQL
server to which you're connecting, type the username and password that you do
have; phpMyAdmin will then work with the same privileges that have been granted
to that MySQL user.

When you log in, you should see a similar screen to Figure 10.2.

---

[3] mcrypt is required on some 64-bit operating systems. phpMyAdmin will let you know if it's unable to
proceed without it, in which case you'll need to look into adding the mcrypt extension to your copy of
PHP. On Windows this may be as simple as uncommenting the `extension=php_mcrypt.dll` line
in your **php.ini** file, but on Mac OS X and Linux servers you'll need to install the libmcrypt software and
then recompile PHP—there are better ways to spend an afternoon!

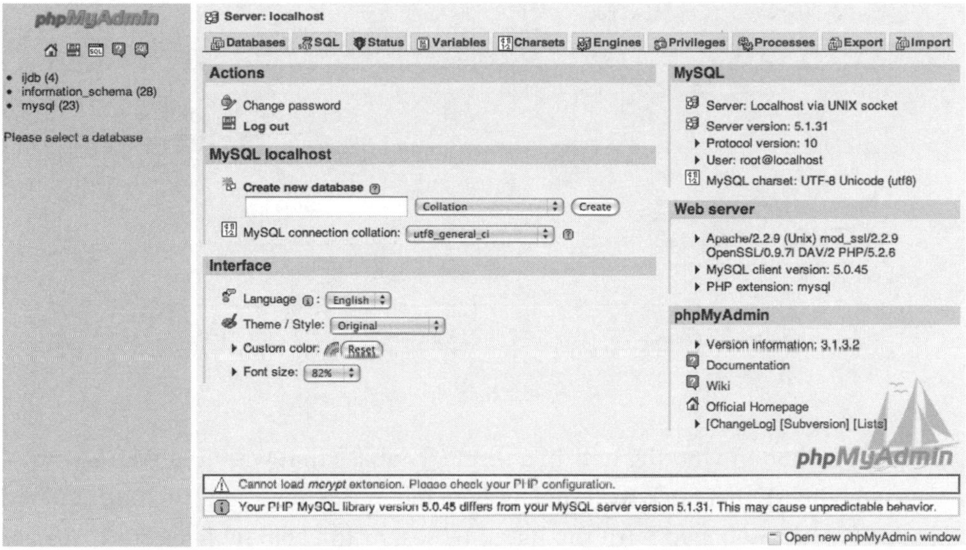

Figure 10.2. The interface may be a little intimidating, but be strong!

Try to avoid being intimidated by the dazzling array of options at your disposal. phpMyAdmin is complex, yes, but once you explore a little you'll feel right at home.

Start by looking at the list of databases on the left-hand side. If this is the server you used to develop the examples in this book, you should see the ijdb database listed among them. Otherwise, you can go ahead and create it now.

If you have the necessary privileges to create databases on this server, use the **Create new database** form in the middle of the screen to create a new database named ijdb. You can leave the **Collation** drop-down menu alone. When you click the **Create** button, phpMyAdmin will drop you in the new, empty ijdb database, with the message "No tables found in database" displayed on the screen, as in Figure 10.3.

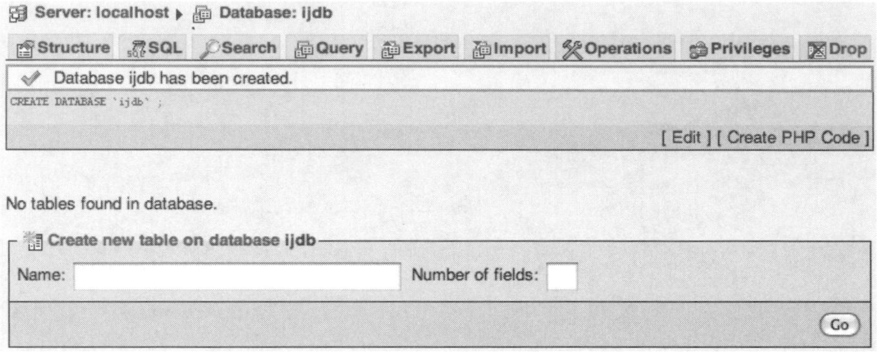

Figure 10.3. No tables found

If you're restricted to working within a single database that was created for you (say, by your web host), just click the database's name in the menu on the left-hand side. Again, you'll be presented with the list of tables, or the "No tables found" message if the database is empty.

Now you can use phpMyAdmin to create all the tables required by the Internet Joke Database web site. Click the **Import** tab at the top of the page, and then under **File to import**, browse to select the **chapter9/sql/ijdb.sql** file from the code archive for this book. Click the **Go** button at the bottom of the page, and phpMyAdmin will feed the contents of the file to your MySQL server, which will create the tables and sample data for the Internet Joke Database.

The tables should now be listed down the left-hand side of the page. Click any of the table names to browse its contents. With a table selected, explore each of the tabs in phpMyAdmin's interface. Much of what you see will make sense; some of it will not. If you're curious about a feature, try it out and see what happens (on a nonessential MySQL server, of course!). Just be careful of the **Empty** and **Drop** tabs, which will empty a table and delete a table or database, respectively.

Few PHP developers understand *every* part of a complex tool like phpMyAdmin, but even a basic understanding of its features will make it an extremely useful tool for administering your MySQL database.

Backing Up MySQL Databases

Like web servers, most MySQL servers are expected to remain online 24 hours a day, seven days a week. This makes backups of MySQL database files problematic. Because the MySQL server uses memory caches and buffers to improve the efficiency of updates to the database files stored on disk, these files may be in an inconsistent state at any given time. Since standard backup procedures involve merely copying system and data files, backups of MySQL data files are unreliable, as there's no guarantee that the files that are copied are in a fit state to be used as replacements in the event of a crash.

Furthermore, as many databases receive new information at all hours of the day, standard backups can provide only snapshots of database data. Any information stored in the database that's changed after the last backup will be lost in the event that the MySQL data files are destroyed or become unusable. In many situations, such as when a MySQL server is used to track customer orders on an ecommerce site, this is an unacceptable loss.

Facilities exist in MySQL to keep up-to-date backups that are largely unaffected by server activity at the time at which the backups are generated. Unfortunately, they require you to set up a backup scheme specifically for your MySQL data, completely apart from whatever backup measures you've established for the rest of your data. As with any good backup system, however, you'll appreciate it when the time comes to use it.

Database Backups Using `mysqldump`

In addition to **mysql**, the MySQL client, a MySQL installation comes with many useful utility programs. We've seen **mysqladmin**, which is responsible for the control and retrieval of information about an operational MySQL server, for example.

mysqldump is another such program. When run, it connects to a MySQL server (in much the same way as the **mysql** program or the PHP language does) and downloads the complete contents of the database(s) you specify. It then outputs these as a series of SQL CREATE TABLE and INSERT commands that, if run in an empty MySQL server, would recreate the MySQL database(s) with exactly the same contents as the original.

If you redirect the output of **mysqldump** to a file, you can store a snapshot of the database(s) as a backup. The following command (typed all on one line) connects to the MySQL server running on the local machine as user root with password *password*, and saves a backup of all databases into the file **full_backup.sql**:[4]

```
mysqldump -u root -ppassword --all-databases > full_backup.sql
```

To restore this database after a server crash, you would use this command:

```
mysql -u root -ppassword < full_backup.sql
```

This command connects to the MySQL server using the usual **mysql** program, and feeds in our backup file as a list of commands to be executed. If you prefer working at the MySQL command line client, you can use the source command to run the commands contained in the **full_backup.sql** file instead:

```
mysql> source full_backup.sql
```

The source Command is not SQL

source is a barely documented[5] command supported directly by the **mysql** client program, rather than an actual SQL command like CREATE DATABASE. You should, therefore, omit the semicolon at the end, as this will prevent the command from working properly.

In this way, we can use **mysqldump** to create backups of our databases. **mysqldump** connects to the MySQL server to perform backups, rather than by accessing directly the database files in the MySQL data directory. The backup it produces is guaranteed to be a valid copy of the databases, instead of merely a database files snapshot, which may be in a state of flux as long as the MySQL server is online.

But how do we bridge the gap between these snapshots to maintain a database backup that's always up to date? The solution is simple: instruct the server to keep a binary log.

---

[4] To run **mysqldump** and the other MySQL utility programs, you need to be in the **bin** directory of your MySQL installation, or that directory must be added to the system path. If you followed the installation instructions in Chapter 1, your system path should already be set up correctly.

[5] http://dev.mysql.com/doc/refman/5.1/en/batch-commands.html

Incremental Backups Using Binary Logs

As I mentioned above, many situations in which MySQL databases are used would make the loss of data—any data—unacceptable. In cases like these, we need a way to bridge the gaps between the backups we made using **mysqldump** as described above. The solution is to instruct the MySQL server to keep a **binary log**. A binary log is a record of all SQL queries that were received by the database, and which modified the contents of the database in some way. This includes INSERT, UPDATE, and CREATE TABLE statements (among others), but excludes SELECT statements.

The basic idea is that you should be able to restore the contents of the database at the very moment at which a disaster occurred. This restoration involves applying a backup (made using **mysqldump**), and then applying the contents of the binary logs that were generated after that backup was made.

You can also edit binary logs to undo mistakes that might have been made. For example, if a co-worker comes to you after accidentally issuing a DROP TABLE command, you can export your binary log to a text file and then edit that file to remove the command. You can then restore the database using your last backup and then running the edited binary log. In this way, you can even keep changes to other tables that were made *after* the accident. And, as a precaution, you should probably also revoke your co-worker's DROP privileges (see the next section to find out how).

When you launch a MySQL server from the command prompt, you can tell it to keep binary logs with the --log-bin switch. For example, on a Mac OS X system:

```
Machine:~ user$ sudo mysqld_safe --log-bin=binlog
```

The above command starts the MySQL server and tells it to create files named **binlog.000001**, **binlog.000002**, and so on, in the server's data directory (**/usr/local/mysql/data** on Mac OS X and Linux systems if you set up the server according to the instructions in Chapter 1). A new file will then be created each time the server flushes its log files; in practice, this occurs whenever the server is restarted. If you want to store your binary logs elsewhere (usually a good idea—if the disk that contains your data directory dies, you'd prefer your backups to survive!), you can specify the full path for the binary log files.

If you run your MySQL server full-time, you probably have your system set up to launch the MySQL server at startup. It can be difficult to add command-line options to the server in this case. A simpler way to have update logs created is to add the option to the MySQL configuration file, **my.cnf** (or **my.ini** on Windows servers).

Like **php.ini**, which controls your server's PHP configuration, **my.cnf** or **my.ini** is a simple text file with a list of options that control your MySQL server. By default, MySQL is installed without a configuration file, and simply runs with the default settings. In order to switch on binary logs, you'll need to create a **my.cnf** or **my.ini** file and set the correct option.

All-in-one Installations

In the following instructions, I'll assume you've installed a MySQL server yourself, from scratch. This is an especially good idea when building a real-world production server.

The all-in-one solutions like WampServer or MAMP come with a built-in MySQL configuration file already set up. While it's possible to go in and edit this file to modify the MySQL configuration and enable binary logging, you'd be better off taking a step back and setting up your own MySQL server from scratch.

Setting up binary logs for a development server is overkill anyway. If you want to back up your development server, simply shut it down and perform a backup of the MySQL data files while they're not in use.

On Windows, use Notepad or another text editor to create a file named **my.ini** in your MySQL installation directory (for example, **C:\Program Files\MySQL\MySQL Server 5.x**).

On Mac OS X or Linux, use your text editor of choice to create a text file named **my.cnf** with the necessary configuration settings, and then move it into your MySQL installation directory (**/usr/local/mysql**). You'll likely need administrator privileges to put the file there.

However you create the file, here's what it should contain:

```
[mysqld]
log-bin=/tmp/binlog
```

In this example I'm instructing the server to store its binary log files in the **/tmp** directory. In the real world, you'll want to pick a more suitable location (such as a secondary backup drive). On Mac OS X and Linux servers, it's important to make sure that whatever location you choose will be writable by the `mysql` user account that's used to run your MySQL server.

With your new configuration file in place, restart your MySQL server. From now on, the server will behave as if it were launched using the `--log-bin` option on the command line. To make sure, check the location you specified to verify that a new log file was created when the server started up.

Obviously, binary logs can take up a lot of space on an active server. For this reason, it's important to tell MySQL to delete obsolete binary logs whenever you perform a full backup using **mysqldump**:

```
mysqldump -u root -ppassword --all-databases --flush-logs
➡ --master-data=2 --delete-master-logs > backup.sql
```

The `--flush-logs` option tells the MySQL server to close the current binary log file and start a new one, as if the MySQL server had been restarted. The `--master-data=2` option instructs **mysqldump** to include a comment at the end of the **ijdb_backup.sql** file that indicates the name of the new binary log file; this will contain the first changes that are made to the database following the full backup. Finally, the `--delete-master-logs` command tells **mysqldump** to delete the binary log files that are no longer needed, now that a full backup has taken place.

In the event of a disaster, as long as you have a full backup and the binary log files that were generated since the backup was made, restoring your database should be fairly simple. Set up a new, empty MySQL server, then apply the full backup as described in the previous section. All that's left is to apply the binary logs using the **mysqlbinlog** utility included with your MySQL installation.

mysqbinlog's job is to convert the data format of MySQL binary logs into SQL commands that you can run on your database. Say you had two binary log files that you needed to apply after restoring your most recent full backup. You can generate an SQL text file from the two files using **mysqlbinlog**, and then apply that file to your MySQL server just as you would a file generated by **mysqldump**:

```
mysqlbinlog binlog.000041 binlog.000042 > binlog.sql
mysql -u root -ppassword < binlog.sql
```

MySQL Access Control

In Chapter 2, I mentioned that the database called mysql, which appears on every MySQL server, is used to keep track of users, their passwords, and what they are allowed to do. Until now, however, you've always logged into the server as the root user, which gives you access to all databases and tables.

If your MySQL server will only be accessed through PHP, and you're careful about who's given the password to the root MySQL account, then the root account may be sufficient for your needs. However, in cases where a MySQL server is shared among many users (for example, if a web host wishes to use a single MySQL server to provide a database to each of its users), it's usually a good idea to set up user accounts with more restricted access.

The MySQL access control system is fully documented in Chapter 5 of the MySQL Reference Manual.[6] In essence, user access is governed by the contents of five tables in the mysql database: user, db, host, tables_priv, and columns_priv. If you plan to edit these tables directly using INSERT, UPDATE, and DELETE statements, I'd suggest you read the relevant section of the MySQL manual first. But, for us mere mortals, MySQL has a simpler method to manage user access. Using GRANT and REVOKE—non-standard commands provided by MySQL—you can create users and set their privileges without worrying about the details of how they'll be represented in the tables mentioned above.

Granting Privileges

The GRANT command, which is used to create new users, assign user passwords, and add user privileges, looks like this:

```
mysql> GRANT privilege [(columns)] ON what
    -> TO user [IDENTIFIED BY 'password']
    -> [WITH GRANT OPTION];
```

---

[6] http://dev.mysql.com/doc/mysql/en/privilege_system.html

As you can see, there are a lot of blanks to be filled in with this command. Let's describe each of them in turn, then review some examples to gain an idea of how they work together.

privilege

is the privilege you wish to grant with this command. The privileges you can specify can be sorted into three groups:

Database/Table/Column privileges

ALTER	Modify existing tables (for example, add or remove columns) and indexes.
CREATE	Create new databases and tables.
DELETE	Delete table entries.
DROP	Delete tables and/or databases.
INDEX	Create and/or delete indexes.
INSERT	Add new table entries.
LOCK TABLES	Lock tables for which the user has SELECT privileges (see Chapter 11).
SELECT	View/search table entries.
SHOW DATABASES	View a list of available databases.
UPDATE	Modify existing table entries.

Global administrative privileges

FILE	Read and write files on the MySQL server machine.
PROCESS	View and/or kill server threads that belong to other users.
RELOAD	Reload the access control tables, flush the logs, and so on.
SHUTDOWN	Shut down the MySQL server.

Special privileges

ALL   The user is allowed to do anything (like root), except grant privileges.

USAGE   The user is only allowed to log in—nothing else.

Some of these privileges apply to features of MySQL that we've yet to see, but most should be familiar to you.

what

defines the areas of the database server to which the privileges apply.

- `*.*` means the privileges apply to all databases and tables.

- *dbName*.`*` means the privileges apply to all tables in the database called `db-Name`.

- *dbName*.*tblName* means the privileges apply only to the table called `tblName` in the database called `dbName`.

You can even specify privileges for individual table columns—simply place a list of the columns between the parentheses that follow the privileges to be granted (we'll see an example of this in a moment).

user

specifies the user to which these privileges should apply. In MySQL, a user is specified both by the username given at login, and the host name/IP address of the machine from which the user connects. The two values are separated by the @ sign (that is, *user@host*). Both values may contain the % wildcard character, but you need to put quotes around any value that does (for example, `kevin@"%"` will allow the username `kevin` to log in from any host and use the privileges you specify).

password

specifies the password that's required to connect the user to the MySQL server. As indicated by the square brackets above, the `IDENTIFIED BY 'password'` portion of the `GRANT` command is optional. Any password specified here will replace the existing password for that user. If no password is specified for a new user, a password will be unnecessary when connecting.

The optional WITH GRANT OPTION portion of the command specifies that the user be allowed to use the GRANT/REVOKE commands in order to allow identical privileges to another user. Be careful with this option—the repercussions are sometimes not obvious! A WITH GRANT OPTION user can give the option to other users in order to trade privileges.

Let's consider a few examples. To create a user named dbmgr that can connect from example.com with password managedb, as well as have full access to the database named ijdb only (including the ability to grant access to that database to other users), use this GRANT command:

```
mysql> GRANT ALL ON ijdb.*
    -> TO dbmgr@example.com
    -> IDENTIFIED BY 'managedb'
    -> WITH GRANT OPTION;
```

Subsequently, to change that user's password to funkychicken, use:

```
mysql> GRANT USAGE ON *.*
    -> TO dbmgr@example.com
    -> IDENTIFIED BY 'funkychicken';
```

Notice that no additional privileges have been granted (the USAGE privilege prohibits a user from doing anything besides log in), but the user's existing privileges remain unchanged.

Now, let's create a new user named jess, who'll connect from various machines in the example.com domain. Say she's responsible for updating the names and email addresses of authors in the database, but may need to refer to other database information at times. As a result, she'll have read-only (that is, SELECT) access to the ijdb database, but will be able to UPDATE the name and email columns of the author table. Here are the commands:

```
mysql> GRANT SELECT ON ijdb.*
    -> TO jess@"%.example.com"
    -> IDENTIFIED BY "jessrules";

mysql> GRANT UPDATE (name, email) ON ijdb.author
    -> TO jess@"%.example.com";
```

Notice that, in the first command, we used the % (wildcard) character in the host name to indicate the host from which jess could connect. Notice also that we've denied her the ability to pass her privileges to other users, as we omitted WITH GRANT OPTION from the end of the command. The second command demonstrates how privileges are granted for specific table columns—it lists the column(s), separated by commas, in parentheses after the privilege(s) being granted.

To see what privileges have been granted to a particular user, use the SHOW GRANTS command:

```
mysql> SHOW GRANTS FOR jess@"%.example.com"
```

This command outputs a list of GRANT commands that you could run to recreate this user from scratch.

Revoking Privileges

The REVOKE command, as you'd expect, is used to strip previously granted privileges from a user. The syntax for the command is as follows:

```
mysql> REVOKE privilege [(columns)]
    -> ON what FROM user;
```

All the fields in this command work just as they do in GRANT above.

To revoke the DROP privileges of a co-worker of Jess's (for instance, this person has demonstrated a habit of occasionally deleting tables and databases by mistake), you would use this command:

```
mysql> REVOKE DROP ON *.* FROM idiot@"%.example.com";
```

Revoking a user's login privileges is about the only task that requires a different command to GRANT and REVOKE. The following commands will definitely prevent a user from doing anything of consequence besides logging in:

```
mysql> REVOKE ALL PRIVILEGES ON *.* FROM idiot@"%.example.com";
mysql> REVOKE GRANT OPTION ON *.* FROM idiot@"%.example.com";
```

But, to remove a user completely, you'll need to use the DROP USER command:

```
mysql> DROP USER idiot@"%.example.com";
```

Access Control Tips

As a result of the way the access control system in MySQL works, there are a couple of idiosyncrasies of which you should be aware before you launch into user creation.

When you create users that can log into the MySQL server only from the computer on which that server is running (for example, you require them to log into the server and run the MySQL client from there, or to communicate using server-side scripts like PHP), you may ask yourself what the *user* part of the GRANT command should be. Imagine the server is running on www.example.com. Should you set up the user as *username*@www.example.com or *username*@localhost?

The answer is that both are unreliable to handle all connections. In theory, if, when connecting, the user specifies the host name either with the **mysql** client program, or with PHP's mysqli_connect function, that host name will have to match the entry in the access control system. However, as you probably want to avoid forcing your users to specify the host name a particular way (in fact, users of the **mysql** client are likely to want to steer clear of specifying the host name at all), it's best to use a workaround.

For users who need the ability to connect from the machine on which the MySQL server is running, it's best to create two user entries in the MySQL access system: one with the actual host name of the machine (*username*@www.example.com, for example), the other with localhost (for example, *username*@localhost). Of course, you'll have to grant/revoke all privileges to both of these user entries individually, but this is the only workaround that you can really rely upon.

Another problem commonly faced by MySQL administrators is that user entries whose host names contain wild cards (for example, jess@"%.example.com" above) may fail to work. When a failure occurs, it's usually due to the way MySQL prioritizes the entries in the access control system. Specifically, it orders entries so that more specific host names appear first (for example, www.example.com is absolutely specific, %.example.com is less specific, and % is totally unspecific).

In a fresh installation, the MySQL access control system contains two anonymous user entries (these allow connections to be made from the local host using any username—the two entries support connections from `localhost` and the server's actual host name, as described above), and two `root` user entries. The problem described above occurs when the anonymous user entries take precedence over our new entry because their host name is more specific.

Let's look at the abridged contents of the user table on `www.example.com`, our fictitious MySQL server, after we add Jess's entry. The rows are sorted in the order in which the MySQL server considers them when it validates a connection:

```
+-----------------+------+-----------------+
| Host            | User | Password        |
+-----------------+------+-----------------+
| localhost       | root | encrypted value |
| www.example.com | root | encrypted value |
| localhost       |      |                 |
| www.example.com |      |                 |
| %.example.com   | jess | encrypted value |
+-----------------+------+-----------------+
```

As you can see, since Jess's entry has the least specific host name, it comes last in the list. When Jess attempts to connect from `www.example.com`, the MySQL server matches her connection attempt to one of the anonymous user entries (a blank `User` value matches anyone). Since a password is unnecessary for these anonymous entries, and presumably Jess enters her password, MySQL rejects the connection attempt. Even if Jess managed to connect without a password, she would be given the very limited privileges that are assigned to anonymous users, as opposed to the privileges assigned to her entry in the access control system.

The solution to this problem is either to make your first order of business as a MySQL administrator the deletion of those anonymous user entries (`DELETE FROM mysql.user WHERE User=""`), or to give two more entries to all users who need to connect from localhost (that is, entries for `localhost` and the actual host name of the server):

```
+------------------+------+-----------------+
| Host             | User | Password        |
+------------------+------+-----------------+
| localhost        | root | encrypted value |
| www.example.com  | root | encrypted value |
| localhost        | jess | encrypted value |
| www.example.com  | jess | encrypted value |
| localhost        |      |                 |
| www.example.com  |      |                 |
| %.example.com    | jess | encrypted value |
+------------------+------+-----------------+
```

As it's excessive to maintain three user entries (and three sets of privileges) for each user, I recommend that you remove the anonymous users unless you have a particular need for them:

```
+------------------+------+-----------------+
| Host             | User | Password        |
+------------------+------+-----------------+
| localhost        | root | encrypted value |
| www.example.com  | root | encrypted value |
| %.example.com    | jess | encrypted value |
+------------------+------+-----------------+
```

Locked Out?

Like locking your keys in the car, forgetting your password after you've spent an hour installing and tweaking a new MySQL server can be an embarrassment—to say the least! Fortunately, if you have administrator access to the computer on which the MySQL server is running, or if you can log in as the user you set up to run the MySQL server (mysql if you followed the Linux installation instructions in Chapter 1), all is well. The following procedure will let you regain control of the server.

First, you must shut down the MySQL server. If you do this using **mysqladmin**, which requires your forgotten password, you'll instead need to kill the server process to shut it down. Under Windows, use Task Manager to find and end the MySQL process, or simply stop the MySQL service if you've installed it as such. Under Mac OS X and Linux, use the ps command, or look in the server's PID file in the MySQL data directory to determine the process ID of the MySQL server, then terminate it with this command:

```
kill pid
```

pid is the process ID of the MySQL server.

This should be enough to stop the server. Do *not* use `kill -9` unless absolutely necessary, as this may damage your table files. If you're forced to do so, however, the next section provides instructions on how to check and repair those files.

Now that the server's down, you can restart it by running **mysqld_safe** with the `--skip-grant-tables` command line option. This instructs the MySQL server to allow unrestricted access to anyone. Obviously, you'll want to run the server in this mode as infrequently as possible, to avoid the inherent security risks.

Once you're connected, change your root password to a memorable one:

```
mysql> UPDATE mysql.user SET Password=PASSWORD("newpassword")
    -> WHERE User="root";
```

Finally, disconnect, and instruct the MySQL server to reload the grant tables to begin requiring passwords:

```
mysqladmin flush-privileges
```

That does it—and nobody ever has to know what you did. As for locking your keys in your car, you're on your own there.

Checking and Repairing MySQL Data Files

In power outages, situations where you need to forcibly terminate (`kill -9`) the MySQL server process, or when Jess's friend `idiot@"%.example.com"` accidentally kicks the plug out of the wall, there's a risk that your MySQL data files may be damaged. This situation can arise if the server's in the middle of making changes to the files at the time of the disturbance, as the files may be left in a corrupt or in-consistent state. Since this type of damage can be subtle, it can go undetected for days, weeks, or even months. As a result, by the time you do finally discover the problem, all your backups may contain the same corruption.

Chapter 6 of the MySQL Reference Manual[7] describes the **myisamchk** utility that comes with MySQL, and how you can use it to check and repair your MySQL data files. While that chapter is recommended reading for anyone who wants to set up a heavy-duty preventative maintenance schedule for their MySQL server, we'll cover all the essentials here.

Before we go any further, though, it's important to realize that the **myisamchk** program expects to have sole access to the MySQL data files that it checks and modifies. If the MySQL server works with the files at the same time, and makes a modification to a file that **myisamchk** is in the middle of checking, **myisamchk** might incorrectly detect an error and try to fix it—which in turn could trip up the MySQL server! Thus, to avoid making the situation worse instead of better, it's usually a good idea to shut down the MySQL server while you're working on the data files. Alternatively, shut down the server just long enough to make a copy of the files, then do the work on the copies. When you're done, shut down the server again briefly to replace the files with the new ones, and perhaps apply any binary logs that were made in the interim.

The MySQL data directory is fairly easy to understand. It contains a subdirectory for each database, and each of these subdirectories contains the data files for the tables in the corresponding database. Each table is represented by three files that have the same name as the table, but three different extensions. The *tblName*.**frm** file is the table definition, which keeps track of the columns contained in the table, as well as their types. The *tblName*.**MYD** file contains all the table data. The *tblName*.**MYI** file contains any indexes for the table. For example, it might contain the lookup table that helps the table's primary key column speed up queries based on this table.

To check a table for errors, just run **myisamchk** (in the MySQL **bin** directory) and provide either the location of these files and the name of the table, or the name of the table index file:[8]

```
myisamchk /usr/local/mysql/data/dbName/tblName
myisamchk /usr/local/mysql/data/dbName/tblName.MYI
```

---

[7] http://dev.mysql.com/doc/mysql/en/table-maintenance.html

[8] Though omitted here to simplify the discussion, you'll likely need administrative privileges to access the MySQL data files on Mac OS X or Linux. Type `sudo myisamchk` instead of just `myisamchk`, in order to run **myisamchk** with administrator privileges.

Or, on Windows:

```
myisamchk "C:\Program Files"\MySQL\data\dbName\tblName"
myisamchk "C:\"Program Files"\MySQL\data\dbName\tblName.MYI"
```

Either of the above will perform a check of the specified table. To check all tables in the database, use a wild card:

```
myisamchk /usr/local/mysql/data/dbName/*.MYI
```

To check all tables in all databases, use two:

```
myisamchk /usr/local/mysql/data/*/*.MYI
```

Without any options, **myisamchk** performs a normal check of the table files. If you suspect problems with a table and a normal check fails to bring anything to light, you can perform a more thorough (but much slower!) check using the `--extend-check` option:

```
myisamchk --extend-check /path/to/tblName
```

Checking for errors is nondestructive, so there's no need to worry that you might make an existing problem worse if you perform a check on your data files. Repair operations, on the other hand, while usually safe, will make changes to your data files that are impossible to undo. For this reason, I strongly recommend that you make a copy of any damaged table files before you attempt to repair them. As usual, make sure your MySQL server is shut down before you make copies of live data files.

There are three types of repair that you can use to fix a problem with a damaged table. These should be tried in order with fresh copies of the data files each time (that is, don't try the second recovery method on a set of files that result from a failed attempt of the first recovery method). If at any point you receive an error message that indicates that a temporary file is unable to be created, delete the file to which the message refers and try again—the offending file is a remnant of a previous repair attempt.

The three repair methods can be executed as follows:

```
myisamchk --recover --quick /path/to/tblName
myisamchk --recover /path/to/tblName
myisamchk --safe-recover /path/to/tblName
```

The first is the quickest, and fixes the most common problems; the last is the slowest, and fixes a few problems that the other methods do not.

If these methods fail to resurrect a damaged table, there are a couple more tricks you can try before you give up:

- If you suspect that the table index file (*tblName*.MYI) is damaged beyond repair, or even missing entirely, it can be regenerated from scratch and used with your existing data (*tblName*.MYD) and table form (*tblName*.frm) files. To begin, make a copy of your table data (*tblName*.MYD) file. Restart your MySQL server and connect to it, then delete the contents of the table with the following command:

```
mysql> DELETE FROM tblName;
```

This command does more than just delete the contents of your table; it also creates a brand new index file for that table. Log out and shut down the server again, then copy your saved data file (*tblName*.MYD) over the new (empty) data file. Finally, perform a standard repair (the second method stated above), and use myisamchk to regenerate the index data based on the contents of the data and table form files.

- If your table form file (*tblName*.frm) is missing or damaged beyond repair, but you know the table well enough to reproduce the CREATE TABLE statement that defines it, you can generate a new .frm file and use it with your existing data and index files. If the index file is no good, use the above method to generate a new one afterwards. First, make a copy of your data and index files, then delete the originals and remove any record of the table from the data directory.

Start up the MySQL server and create a new table using exactly the same CREATE TABLE statement. Log out and shut down the server, then copy your two saved files over the top of the new, empty files. The new .frm file should work with them, but perform a standard table repair—the second method above—for good measure.

Better Safe than Sorry

Admittedly, this chapter hasn't been the usual nonstop, action-packed code-fest to which you may have become accustomed by now. But our concentration on these topics—the back up and restoration of MySQL data, the administration of the MySQL access control system, and table checking and repair—has armed you with the tools you'll need in order to set up a MySQL database server that will stand the test of time, as well as endure the constant traffic your site will attract during that period.

In Chapter 11, we'll return to the fun stuff and learn some advanced SQL techniques that can make a relational database server perform tricks you may never have thought possible.

Advanced SQL Queries

As you've worked through the construction of the Internet Joke Database web site, you've had opportunities to explore most aspects of Structured Query Language (SQL). From the basic form of a CREATE TABLE query, to the two syntaxes of INSERT queries, you probably know many of these commands by heart now.

In an effort to tie up some loose ends in this chapter, we'll look at a few more SQL tricks that we've yet to come across—some may have been a bit too advanced. As is typical, most of these will expand on your knowledge of what's already the most complex and potentially confusing SQL command available to you: the SELECT query.

Sorting SELECT Query Results

Long lists of information are always easier to use when they're presented in some kind of order. To find a single author in a list from your author table, for example, could become an exercise in frustration if you had more than a few dozen registered authors in your database. While at first it might appear that they're sorted in order of database insertion, with the oldest records first and the newest records last, you'll quickly notice that deleting records from the database leaves invisible gaps in this order; these gaps are filled by the insertion of newer entries.

Fortunately, there's another, optional part of the SELECT query that lets you specify a column by which your table of results can be sorted. Let's say you wanted to print out a listing of the entries in your author table for future reference. As you'll recall, this table has three columns: id, name, and email. Since id is really just a means to associating entries in this table with entries in the joke table, you'll usually list only the remaining two columns when you work with this table in isolation. Here's a short list of a table of authors:

```
mysql> SELECT name, email FROM author;
+-----------------+-----------------------+
| name            | email                 |
+-----------------+-----------------------+
| Kevin Yank      | kevin@sitepoint.com   |
| Jessica Graham  | jess@example.com      |
| Michael Yates   | yatesy@example.com    |
| Amy Mathieson   | amym@example.com      |
+-----------------+-----------------------+
```

As you can see, the entries are unsorted, which is fine for a short list like this; it would be easier, though, to find a particular author's email address (that of Amy Mathieson, for example) in a very long list of authors—say a few hundred or so—if the authors' names appeared in alphabetical order. Here's how you'd create that ordering:

```
mysql> SELECT name, email FROM author ORDER BY name;
+-----------------+-----------------------+
| name            | email                 |
+-----------------+-----------------------+
| Amy Mathieson   | amym@example.com      |
| Jessica Graham  | jess@example.com      |
| Kevin Yank      | kevin@sitepoint.com   |
| Michael Yates   | yatesy@example.com    |
+-----------------+-----------------------+
```

The entries now appear sorted alphabetically by their names. Just as you can add a WHERE clause to a SELECT statement to narrow down the list of results, you can also add an ORDER BY clause to specify a column by which a set of results should be sorted. Adding the keyword DESC after the name of the column allows you to sort the entries in descending order:

```
mysql> SELECT name, email FROM author ORDER BY name DESC;
+----------------+---------------------+
| name           | email               |
+----------------+---------------------+
| Michael Yates  | yatesy@example.com  |
| Kevin Yank     | kevin@sitepoint.com |
| Jessica Graham | jess@example.com    |
| Amy Mathieson  | amym@example.com    |
+----------------+---------------------+
```

You can actually use a comma-separated list of several column names in the ORDER BY clause to have MySQL sort the entries by the first column, then sort any sets of tied entries by the second, and so on. Any of the columns listed in the ORDER BY clause may use the DESC keyword to reverse the sort order.

Obviously, in a large table, MySQL must do a lot of work to sort the result set. You can ease this burden by setting up **indexes** for columns (or sets of columns) that you expect to use to sort result sets. When you index a column, the database invisibly creates and maintains a sorted list of the entries in that column, along with their locations in the table. Whenever you INSERT a new entry or UPDATE an existing entry, the database will update the index accordingly. When the database is asked to sort results based on that column, all it needs to do is to refer to the index for the pre-sorted list of entries.

To create an index, you can use a CREATE INDEX query or an ALTER TABLE ADD INDEX query. The following two queries are equivalent, and both create an index for the name column of the author table:

```
mysql> CREATE INDEX nameidx ON author (name);
Query OK, 4 rows affected (0.28 sec)
Records: 4  Duplicates: 0  Warnings: 0
```

```
mysql> ALTER TABLE author ADD INDEX nameidx (name);
Query OK, 4 rows affected (0.28 sec)
Records: 4  Duplicates: 0  Warnings: 0
```

In both query formats, you place in parentheses the list of columns you want to use for the index. In this example, you're creating an index for a single column.

Removing an index is equally easy, and can again be done with either of two query types:

```
mysql> DROP INDEX nameidx ON author;
Query OK, 4 rows affected (0.16 sec)
Records: 4  Duplicates: 0  Warnings: 0
```

```
mysql> ALTER TABLE author DROP INDEX nameidx;
Query OK, 4 rows affected (0.28 sec)
Records: 4  Duplicates: 0  Warnings: 0
```

All of these queries are described in Appendix A. A more detailed look at indexes and how they can be used to speed up queries can be found in the article *Optimizing your MySQL Application*[1] on sitepoint.com.

Setting LIMITs

Often, you might work with a large database table, but only be interested in a few entries within it. Let's say you wanted to track the popularity of different jokes on your site. You could add a column named `timesviewed` to your `joke` table. Start it with a value of zero for new jokes, and add one to the value of the requested joke every time the joke is viewed, to keep count of the number of times each joke in your database has been read.

The query that adds one to the `timesviewed` column of a joke with a given ID is as follows:

```
$sql = "UPDATE joke SET
    timesviewed = timesviewed + 1
    WHERE id='$id'";
if (!mysqli_query($link, $sql))
{
  $error = 'Error updating joke view count.';
```

---

[1] http://www.sitepoint.com/article/optimizing-mysql-application/

```
    include 'error.html.php';
    exit();
}
```

You might use this joke view counter to present a "Top 10 Jokes" list on the front page of your site, for example. Using `ORDER BY timesviewed DESC` to list the jokes from highest `timesviewed` to lowest, you would just have to pick the first ten values from the top of the list. But if you have thousands of jokes in your database, the retrieval of that entire list in order to obtain just ten results would be quite wasteful in terms of the processing time and server system resources, such as memory and CPU load, required.

However, if you use a `LIMIT` clause, you can specify a certain number of results to be returned. In this example, you need only the first ten:

```
$sql = "SELECT * FROM joke ORDER BY timesviewed DESC LIMIT 10";
```

Although it's much less interesting, you could eliminate the word `DESC` and retrieve the ten *least* popular jokes in the database.

Often, you want to let users view a long list of entries—for example, the results of a search—but wish to display only a few at a time.[2] Think of the last time you went looking through pages of search engine results to find a particular web site. You can use a `LIMIT` clause to do this sort of action—simply specify the result with which the list will begin, and the maximum number of results to display. The query below, for example, will list the 21st to 25th most popular jokes in the database:

```
$sql = "SELECT * FROM joke ORDER BY timesviewed DESC LIMIT 20, 5";
```

Remember, the first entry in the list of results is entry number zero. Thus, the 21st entry in the list is entry number 20.

LOCKing TABLES

Notice how, in the `UPDATE` query given above, and repeated here for convenience, we take the existing value of `timesviewed` and add one to it to set the new value:

---

[2] I have written an article that explores this technique in greater detail at sitepoint.com, entitled *Object Oriented PHP: Paging Result Sets* [http://www.sitepoint.com/article/php-paging-result-sets].

```
$sql = "UPDATE joke SET
    timesviewed = timesviewed + 1
    WHERE id='$id'";
```

If you'd been unaware that you were allowed to use this shortcut, you might have performed a separate SELECT to gain the current value, added one to it, then performed an UPDATE using that newly calculated value. Besides the fact that this would've required two queries instead of one, and thus would take about twice as long, there's a danger to using this method. What if, while that new value was being calculated, another person viewed the same joke? The PHP script would be run a second time for that new request. When it performed the SELECT to obtain the current value of timesviewed, it would retrieve the same value the first script did, because the value would yet to be updated. Both scripts would then add one to the same value, and write the new value into the table. See what happens? Two users view the joke, but the timesviewed counter increments by just one!

In some situations, this kind of fetch–calculate–update procedure is unavoidable, and the possibility of interference between simultaneous requests of this nature must be dealt with. Other situations in which this procedure might be necessary include cases in which you need to update several tables in response to a single action (for example, updating inventory and shipping tables in response to a sale on an ecommerce web site).

By **locking** the table or tables with which you're working in a multiple-query operation, you can obtain exclusive access for the duration of that operation, and prevent potentially damaging interference from concurrent operations. The syntax that locks a table is fairly simple:

```
LOCK TABLES tblName { READ | WRITE }
```

As shown, when you lock a table, you must specify whether you want a **read lock** or a **write lock**. The former prevents other processes from making changes to the table, but allows others to read the table. The latter stops all other access to the table.

When you're finished with a table you've locked, you must release the lock to give other processes access to the table again:

```
UNLOCK TABLES
```

A `LOCK TABLES` query implicitly releases whatever locks you may already have. Therefore, to safely perform a multi-table operation, you must lock all the tables you'll use with a single query. Here's what the PHP code might look like for the ecommerce application we mentioned above:

```
mysqli_query($link, 'LOCK TABLES inventory WRITE, shipping WRITE');

: Perform the operation…

mysqli_query($link, 'UNLOCK TABLES');
```

For simple databases that require the occasional multi-table operation, table locking, as described here, will do the trick. More demanding applications, however, can benefit from the increased performance and crash-proof nature of **transactions**.

Transactions in MySQL

Many high-end database servers (for example, Oracle, MS SQL Server, and so on) support a feature called **transactions**, which lets you perform complex, multi-query operations in a single, uninterrupted step. Consider what would happen if your server were struck by a power failure halfway through a database update in response to a client order. For example, the server might have crashed after it updated your `shipping` table, but before it updated your `inventory` table, in response to a customer's order.

Transactions allow a group of table updates such as this to be defined so that they all occur, or none of them will. You can also manually cancel a transaction halfway through if the logic of your application requires it.

MySQL 5 includes built-in support for **InnoDB tables**, which support transactions in addition to the foreign key constraints I mentioned in Chapter 7. A full discussion of transactions is outside the scope of this book; please refer to the MySQL Reference Manual for a full description of InnoDB tables[3] and transaction support.[4]

---

[3] http://dev.mysql.com/doc/mysql/en/innodb.html
[4] http://dev.mysql.com/doc/mysql/en/transactional-commands.html

Column and Table Name Aliases

In some situations, it may be more convenient to refer to MySQL columns and tables using different names. Let's take the example of a database used by an airline's online booking system; this example actually came up in the SitePoint Forums when I was first writing this book. The database structure can be found in **airline.sql** in the code archive if you want to follow along.

To represent the flights offered by the airline, the database contains two tables: `flight` and `city`. Each entry in the `flight` table represents an actual flight between two cities—the origin and destination of the flight. Obviously, `origincityid` and `destinationcityid` are columns in the `flight` table; other columns record information like the date and time of the flight, the type of aircraft, the flight numbers, and the various fares.

The `city` table contains a list of all the cities to which the airline flies. Thus, both the `origincityid` and `destinationcityid` columns in the `flight` table will just contain IDs referring to entries in the `city` table.

Now, consider these queries. To retrieve a list of flights with their origins, here's what you do:

```
mysql> SELECT flight.number, city.name
    -> FROM flight INNER JOIN city
    ->   ON flight.origincityid = city.id;
+--------+-----------+
| number | name      |
+--------+-----------+
| CP110  | Montreal  |
| QF2026 | Melbourne |
| CP226  | Sydney    |
| QF2027 | Sydney    |
+--------+-----------+
```

To obtain a list of flights with their destinations, the query is very similar:

```
mysql> SELECT flight.number, city.name
    -> FROM flight INNER JOIN city
    ->   ON flight.destinationcityid = city.id;
+--------+-----------+
```

```
| number  | name      |
+---------+-----------+
| CP226   | Montreal  |
| QF2027  | Melbourne |
| CP110   | Sydney    |
| QF2026  | Sydney    |
+---------+-----------+
```

Now, what if you wanted to list both the origin and destination of each flight with a single query? That's reasonable, right? Here's a query you might try:

```
mysql> SELECT flight.number, city.name, city.name
    -> FROM flight INNER JOIN city
    ->    ON flight.origincityid = city.id
    -> INNER JOIN city
    ->    ON flight.destinationcityid = city.id;
ERROR 1066 (42000): Not unique table/alias: 'city'
```

Why does this fail? Have another look at the query, and this time focus on what it actually says, rather than what you expect it to do. It tells MySQL to join the `flight`, `city`, and `city` (yes, twice!) tables. This attempt at joining the same table twice is what produces the error message you see above.

But even without this error, the query lacks sense. It attempts to list the flight number, city name, and city name (twice again!) of all entries obtained, by matching up the `origincityid` with the city id, and the `destinationcityid` with the city id. In other words, the `origincityid`, `destinationcityid`, and city id must all be equal! Even if this query worked, it would result in a list of all flights where the origin and the destination are the same! Unless your airline offers scenic flights, it's unlikely there'll be any entries that match this description.

What we need is a way to use the `city` table twice without confusing MySQL. We want to be able to return two different entries from the `city` table—one for the origin and one for the destination—for each result. If we had two copies of the table, one called `origin` and one called `destination`, this would be much easier to do, but why maintain two tables that contain the same list of cities? The solution is to give the `city` table two different **aliases** (temporary names) for the purposes of this query.

If we follow the name of a table with AS *alias* in the FROM portion of the SELECT query, we can give it a temporary name by which we can refer to it elsewhere in the query. Here's that first query again (to display flight numbers and origins only), but this time we've given the `city` table an alias: `origin`.

```
mysql> SELECT flight.number, origin.name
    -> FROM flight INNER JOIN city AS origin
    ->    ON flight.origincityid = origin.id;
+---------+-----------+
| number  | name      |
+---------+-----------+
| CP110   | Montreal  |
| QF2026  | Melbourne |
| CP226   | Sydney    |
| QF2027  | Sydney    |
+---------+-----------+
```

The query still works the same way, and the results remain unchanged—but, for long table names, it can save some typing. Consider, for example, if we had given aliases of f and o to `flight` and `origin`, respectively. The query would be much shorter as a result.

Let's now return to our problem query. If we refer to the `city` table twice, using different aliases, we can use a three-table join (in which two of the tables are actually one and the same) to achieve the effect we want:

```
mysql> SELECT flight.number, origin.name, destination.name
    -> FROM flight INNER JOIN city AS origin
    ->    ON flight.origincityid = origin.id
    -> INNER JOIN city AS destination
    ->    ON flight.destinationcityid = destination.id;
+---------+-----------+-----------+
| number  | name      | name      |
+---------+-----------+-----------+
| CP110   | Montreal  | Sydney    |
| QF2026  | Melbourne | Sydney    |
| CP226   | Sydney    | Montreal  |
| QF2027  | Sydney    | Melbourne |
+---------+-----------+-----------+
```

You can also define aliases for column names. We could use this, for example, to differentiate the two `name` columns in our result table above:

```
mysql> SELECT f.number, o.name AS origin, d.name AS destination
    -> FROM flight AS f INNER JOIN city AS o
    ->    ON f.origincityid = o.id
    -> INNER JOIN city AS d
    ->    ON f.destinationcityid = d.id;
+---------+-----------+-------------+
| number  | origin    | destination |
+---------+-----------+-------------+
| CP110   | Montreal  | Sydney      |
| QF2026  | Melbourne | Sydney      |
| CP226   | Sydney    | Montreal    |
| QF2027  | Sydney    | Melbourne   |
+---------+-----------+-------------+
```

You could use this same technique to add a messaging system to the Internet Joke Database web site, whereby one author could send a message to another author on the site. The table of sent messages would reference the author table twice—once for the sender of the message, and another for the recipient. If you're keen for a fresh challenge, try building this system!

GROUPing SELECT Results

In Chapter 2, you saw the following query, which tells you how many jokes are stored in your joke table:

```
mysql> SELECT COUNT(*) FROM joke;
+----------+
| COUNT(*) |
+----------+
|        4 |
+----------+
```

The MySQL function COUNT used in this query belongs to a special class of functions called **summary functions** or **group-by functions**, depending on where you look. A complete list of these functions is provided in Chapter 11 of the MySQL Manual[5] and in Appendix B. Unlike other functions, which affect each entry individually in the result of the SELECT query, summary functions group together all the results and return a single result. In the above example, for instance, COUNT returns the total number of result rows.

---

[5] http://dev.mysql.com/doc/mysql/en/group-by-functions.html

Let's say you wanted to display a list of authors along with the number of jokes they have to their names. Your first instinct might be to retrieve a list of all the authors' names and IDs, then use COUNT to count the number of results when you SELECT the jokes with each author's ID. The PHP code (presented without error handling, for simplicity) would look a little like this:

```
// Get a list of all the authors
$authors = mysqli_query($link, 'SELECT name, id FROM author');

// Process each author
while ($author = mysqli_fetch_array($authors))
{
  $name = $author['name'];
  $id = $author['id'];

  // Get count of jokes attributed to this author
  $result = mysqli_query($link,
      "SELECT COUNT(*) AS numjokes FROM joke WHERE authorid='$id'");
  $row = mysqli_fetch_array($result);
  $numjokes = $row['numjokes'];

  // Display the author & number of jokes
  $output = "$name ($numjokes jokes)";
}
```

Note the use of AS in the second query above to give a friendlier name (numjokes) to the result of COUNT(*).

This technique will work, but will require $n+1$ separate queries (where n is the number of authors in the database). Having the number of queries depend on a number of entries in the database is always worth avoiding, as a large number of authors would make this script unreasonably slow and resource-intensive. Fortunately, another advanced feature of SELECT comes to the rescue!

If you add a GROUP BY clause to a SELECT query, you can tell MySQL to group the query results into sets, the results in each set sharing a common value in the specified column. Summary functions like COUNT then operate on those groups—rather than the entire result set as a whole. The next query, for example, lists the number of jokes attributed to each author in the database:

```
mysql> SELECT author.name, COUNT(*) AS numjokes
    -> FROM joke INNER JOIN author
    ->   ON authorid = author.id
    -> GROUP BY authorid;
+----------------+----------+
| name           | numjokes |
+----------------+----------+
| Kevin Yank     |        3 |
| Jessica Graham |        1 |
+----------------+----------+
```

If you group the results by author ID (authorid), you receive a breakdown of results for each author. Note that you could have specified GROUP BY author.id and achieved the same result (since, as stipulated in the FROM clause, these columns must be equal). GROUP BY author.name would also work in most cases, but, since there's always the possibility, however slight, that two different authors might have the same name (in which case their results would be lumped together) it's best to stick to the ID columns, which are guaranteed to be unique for each author.

LEFT JOINs

You can see from the results above that Kevin Yank has three jokes to his name, and Jessica Graham has one. What these results conceal is that there's a third and fourth author, Amy Mathieson and Michael Yates, who have *no* jokes. Since there are no entries in the joke table with authorid values that match either author ID, there will be no results that satisfy the ON clause in the query above, and they are therefore excluded from the table of results.

About the only practical way to overcome this challenge with the tools we've seen so far would be to add another column to the author table and simply store the number of jokes attributed to each author in that column. Keeping that column up to date, however, would be a real pain, because we'd have to remember to update it every time a joke was added to, removed from, or changed (if, for example, the value of authorid was changed) in the joke table. To keep it all synchronized, we'd have to use LOCK TABLES whenever we made such changes, as well. Quite a mess, to say the least!

Besides the INNER JOINs we've used so far, MySQL provides another type of join.
Called a **left join**, it's designed for just this type of situation. To understand how
left joins differ from standard joins, we must first recall how inner joins work.

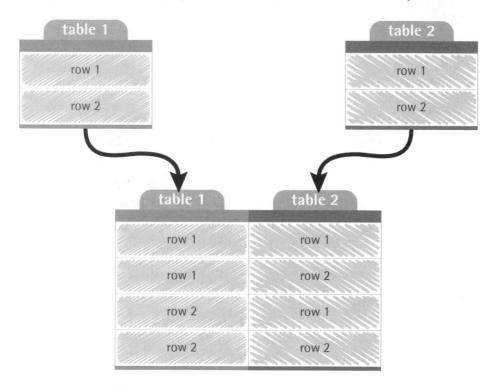

Figure 11.1. Inner joins take all possible combinations of rows

As shown in Figure 11.1, MySQL performs a standard join of two tables by listing
all possible combinations of the rows of those tables. In a simple case, a standard
join of two tables with two rows apiece will contain four rows: row 1 of table 1 with
row 1 of table 2, row 1 of table 1 with row 2 of table 2, row 2 of table 1 with row 1
of table 2, and row 2 of table 1 with row 2 of table 2. With all of these result rows
calculated, MySQL then looks to the ON condition for guidance on which rows
should actually be kept (for example, those where the id column from table 1
matches the authorid column from table 2).

The reason why the above solution is unsuitable for our purposes is that we'd like
to also include rows in table 1 (that is, author) that don't match any rows in table
2 (joke). A left join does exactly what we need—it forces a row to appear in the
results for each row in the first (left-hand) table, even if no matching entries are

found in the second (right-hand) table. Such **forced rows** are given NULL values for all of the columns in the right-hand table.

To perform a left join between two tables in MySQL, simply type LEFT JOIN instead of INNER JOIN within the FROM clause. Here's our revised query for listing authors and the number of jokes to their credit:

```
mysql> SELECT author.name, COUNT(*) AS numjokes
    -> FROM author LEFT JOIN joke
    ->    ON authorid = author.id
    -> GROUP BY author.id;
```

A couple of important points to note about this query:

▪ We must type author LEFT JOIN joke, rather than joke LEFT JOIN author.

   The order in which we list the tables to be joined is significant. A LEFT JOIN will only force all rows from the table on the *left* to appear in the results. In this example, we want every row in the author table to appear in the results.

▪ We must use GROUP BY author.id, rather than GROUP BY authorid.

   author.id is the id field of the author table, whereas authorid is the authorid field of the joke table. In all previous SELECT queries, our join has guaranteed that these would always have matching values, but when the LEFT JOIN creates a forced row based on a row in the author table that has no matching row in the joke table, it assigns a value of NULL to all the columns in the joke table. This includes the authorid field. If we used GROUP BY authorid, the query would group all our authors with no jokes together, since they all share an authorid value of NULL following the LEFT JOIN.[6]

---

[6] You may find you have to read this a few times to understand it. That's because this is by far the subtlest aspect of the SQL language that you'll find in this book.

If you type that query just right, you should achieve these results:

```
+-----------------+-----------+
| name            | numjokes  |
+-----------------+-----------+
| Kevin Yank      |        3  |
| Jessica Graham  |        1  |
| Michael Yates   |        1  |
| Amy Mathieson   |        1  |
+-----------------+-----------+
```

Wait just a minute! Suddenly Amy Mathieson and Michael Yates have one joke? That can't be right! In fact, it is—but only because the query is still wrong. COUNT(*) counts the number of rows returned for each author. If we look at the ungrouped results of the LEFT JOIN, we can see what's happened:

```
mysql> SELECT author.name, joke.id AS jokeid
    -> FROM author LEFT JOIN joke
    ->    ON authorid = author.id;
+-----------------+---------+
| name            | jokeid  |
+-----------------+---------+
| Kevin Yank      |      1  |
| Kevin Yank      |      2  |
| Kevin Yank      |      4  |
| Jessica Graham  |      3  |
| Michael Yates   |   NULL  |
| Amy Mathieson   |   NULL  |
+-----------------+---------+
```

See? Amy Mathieson and Michael Yates *do* have rows—the rows are forced because there are no matching rows in the right-hand table of the LEFT JOIN (joke). The fact that the joke ID value is NULL has no affect on COUNT(*)—it still counts it as a row. If, instead of *, you specify an actual column name (say, joke.id) for the COUNT function to look at, it will ignore NULL values in that column, and give us the count we want:

```
mysql> SELECT author.name, COUNT(joke.id) AS numjokes
    -> FROM author LEFT JOIN joke
    ->    ON authorid = author.id
    -> GROUP BY author.id;
```

```
+-----------------+-----------+
| name            | numjokes  |
+-----------------+-----------+
| Kevin Yank      |        3  |
| Jessica Graham  |        1  |
| Michael Yates   |        0  |
| Amy Mathieson   |        0  |
+-----------------+-----------+
```

Limiting Results with HAVING

What if we wanted a list of *only* those authors that had no jokes to their name? Once again, let's look at the query that many developers would try first:

```
mysql> SELECT author.name, COUNT(joke.id) AS numjokes
    -> FROM author LEFT JOIN joke
    ->   ON authorid = author.id
    -> WHERE numjokes = 0
    -> GROUP BY author.id;
ERROR 1054: Unknown column 'numjokes' in 'where clause'
```

By now, you're probably unfazed that it failed to work as expected. The reason why WHERE numjokes = 0 caused an error has to do with the way MySQL processes result sets. First, MySQL produces the raw, combined list of authors and jokes from the author and joke tables. Next, it processes the ON portion of the FROM clause and the WHERE clause so that only the relevant rows in the list are returned (in this case, rows that match authors with their jokes, and which have a numjokes value of 0). Finally, MySQL processes the GROUP BY clause by grouping the results according to their authorid, COUNTing the number of entries in each group that have non-NULL joke.id values, and producing the numjokes column as a result.

Notice that the numjokes column is actually created after the GROUP BY clause is processed, and *that* happens only after the WHERE clause does its stuff! Thus the error message above—the WHERE clause is looking for a numjokes column that is yet to exist.

If you wanted to exclude jokes that contained the word "chicken" from the count, you could use the WHERE clause without a problem, because that exclusion doesn't rely on a value that the GROUP BY clause is responsible for producing. Conditions that affect the results after grouping takes place, however, must appear in a special HAVING clause. Here's the corrected query:

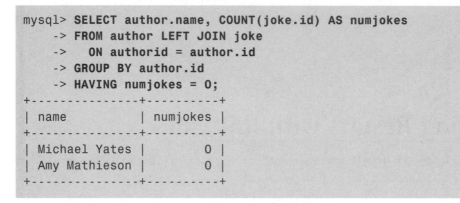

```
mysql> SELECT author.name, COUNT(joke.id) AS numjokes
    -> FROM author LEFT JOIN joke
    ->   ON authorid = author.id
    -> GROUP BY author.id
    -> HAVING numjokes = 0;
+----------------+----------+
| name           | numjokes |
+----------------+----------+
| Michael Yates  |        0 |
| Amy Mathieson  |        0 |
+----------------+----------+
```

Some conditions work both in the HAVING and the WHERE clauses. For example, if we wanted to exclude a particular author by name, we could do this by using author.name != 'Author Name' in either the WHERE or the HAVING clause; that's because, regardless of whether you filter out the author before or after you group the results, the same results are returned. In such cases, it's always best to use the WHERE clause, because MySQL is better at optimizing such queries internally so they happen faster.

Further Reading

In this chapter, you rounded out your knowledge of Structured Query Language (SQL), as supported by MySQL. We focused predominantly on features of SELECT that allow you to view information stored in a database with an unprecedented level of flexibility and power. With judicious use of the advanced features of SELECT, you can have MySQL do what it does best—and lighten the load on PHP in the process.

There are still a few isolated query types that we've yet to seen, and MySQL offers a whole library of built-in functions to do tasks like calculate dates and format text strings (see Appendix B). To become truly proficient with MySQL, you should also have a firm grasp on the various column types offered by MySQL. The TIMESTAMP type, for example, can be a real time-saver (no pun intended). All of these are fully documented in the MySQL Manual, and briefly covered in Appendix C.

For more detailed coverage of the features of SQL covered in this chapter—and a whole lot more that wasn't—I highly recommend the book *Simply SQL*[7] by Rudy Limeback (Melbourne: SitePoint, 2008).

---

[7] http://www.sitepoint.com/books/sql1/

Chapter

12

Binary Data

All the examples of database driven web sites we've seen so far have dealt with sites based around textual data. Jokes, authors, categories ... all of these elements can be fully represented with strings of text. But, what if you ran, say, an online digital photo gallery to which people could upload pictures taken with digital cameras? For this idea to work, we need to be able to let visitors to our site upload their photos, and we need to be able to keep track of them.

In this chapter, you will develop a system whereby users can upload binary files (images, documents ... whatever!) and have them stored on your web server for display on your site. There are several techniques you need to learn on the way, though, and I'll cover all of these in this chapter: working with files in PHP, handling uploaded files in PHP, and storing and retrieving binary data in MySQL.

As we learn to juggle files with PHP, we'll also take the opportunity to relieve some of the load on your web server with the help of semi-dynamic pages.

Semi-dynamic Pages

As the owner of a successful—or soon-to-be so—web site, site traffic is probably worth encouraging. Unfortunately, high site traffic is just the kind of thing that a web server administrator dreads—especially when that site's primarily composed of dynamically generated, database driven pages. Such pages take a great deal more horsepower from the computer that runs the web server software than do plain, old HTML files, because every page request is like a miniature program that runs on that computer.

While some pages of a database driven site must always display current-to-the-second data culled from the database, others do not. Consider the front page of a web site like sitepoint.com. Typically, it presents a sort of digest of what's new and fresh on the site. But how often does that information actually change? Once an hour? Once a *day*? And how important is it that visitors to your site see those changes the instant they occur? Would your site really suffer if changes took effect after a slight delay?

By converting high-traffic dynamic pages into **semi-dynamic** equivalents—static pages that are regenerated dynamically at regular intervals to freshen their content—you can significantly reduce the toll that the database driven components of your site take on your web server's performance.

Say you have a controller script, **index.php** that uses a PHP template to generate your front page, which provides a summary of new content on your site. Through examination of server logs, you'll probably find that this is one of the most requested pages on your site. If you ask yourself some of the questions above, you'll realize that there's no need to dynamically generate this page for every request. As long as it's updated every time new content is added to your site, it'll be as dynamic as it needs to be. Instead of using a controller script to handle every request for the front page of your site, you can use the PHP code instead to generate a static snapshot of the PHP template's output and put this snapshot online, in place of the dynamic version, as **index.html**.

This little trick will require some reading, writing, and juggling of files. PHP is perfectly capable of accomplishing this task, but we've yet to see the functions we'll need:

file_get_contents

This function opens a file and reads the contents, returning them in the form of a PHP string. The file can be stored on the server's hard disk, or PHP can load it from a URL just like a web browser would. If an error occurs, the function returns FALSE instead.

file_put_contents

This function opens a file and writes the specified data into it. You can optionally specify settings like whether the data should be added to the end of the existing file, rather than replacing the file completely (the default).[1]

file_exists

This function checks if a file with a specific name exists or not. If the file exists, the function returns TRUE; otherwise, it returns FALSE.

copy

This function performs a run-of-the-mill file copy operation.

unlink

This function deletes a file from the hard disk.

Do you see where we're headed? If not, I assure you—you will in a moment.

Let's begin with a dead simple controller script and template for displaying a list of the three most recent jokes in the databases of the Internet Joke Database, as we last left it in Chapter 9:

chapter12/recentjokes/controller.php

```php
<?php

include_once $_SERVER['DOCUMENT_ROOT'] . '/includes/db.inc.php';

$result = mysqli_query($link,
    'SELECT id, joketext FROM joke
    ORDER BY jokedate DESC
    LIMIT 3');
if (!$result)
{
```

---

[1] For full details of the available options, check out the PHP Manual [http://php.net/file_put_contents].

```
    $error = 'Error fetching jokes: ' . mysqli_error($link);
    include $_SERVER['DOCUMENT_ROOT'] . '/includes/error.html.php';
    exit();
}

while ($row = mysqli_fetch_array($result))
{
  $jokes[] = array('text' => $row['joketext']);
}

include 'jokes.html.php';

?>
```

chapter12/recentjokes/jokes.html.php

```
<?php include_once $_SERVER['DOCUMENT_ROOT'] .
    '/includes/helpers.inc.php'; ?>
<!DOCTYPE html PUBLIC "-//W3C//DTD XHTML 1.0 Strict//EN"
    "http://www.w3.org/TR/xhtml1/DTD/xhtml1-strict.dtd">
<html xmlns="http://www.w3.org/1999/xhtml" xml:lang="en" lang="en">
  <head>
    <title>Recent Jokes</title>
    <meta http-equiv="content-type"
        content="text/html; charset=utf-8"/>
    <link rel="canonical" href="/recentjokes/"/>
  </head>
  <body>
    <p>Here are the most recent jokes in the database:</p>
    <?php foreach ($jokes as $joke): ?>
      <div>
        <?php bbcodeout($joke['text']); ?>
      </div>
    <?php endforeach; ?>
  </body>
</html>
```

Normally, you would name the controller script **index.php**, so that a browser request for http://www.example.com/recentjokes/ would run the controller script and build the list of jokes on-the-fly. However, the controller is named **controller.php** in this case. A browser that knew this file name could still request the controller, but as indicated by the `<link rel="canonical"/>`[2] tag in the **jokes.html.php** template, we still expect most visitors to access the page as http://www.example.com/recentjokes/. Instead of triggering the controller, however, browsers that request this URL will hit a static version of the page that's been prepared in advance.

To generate this static version, we'll write another script: **generate.php**. It will be the responsibility of this script to load **controller.php**—the dynamic version of your front page, as a web browser would, then to write an up-to-date static snapshot of the page as **index.html**. If anything goes wrong in this process, you want to avoid the potential destruction of the existing version of **index.html**, so we'll make this script write the new static version into a temporary file (**tempindex.html**), then copy it over **index.html** if all is well.

We start out by setting some PHP variables to configure the URL of the PHP script we wish to load, the temporary filename to use in the process, and the name of the static page we wish to create:

chapter12/recentjokes/generate.php (excerpt)

```php
<?php
$srcurl = 'http://localhost/recentjokes/controller.php';
$tempfilename = $_SERVER['DOCUMENT_ROOT'] .
    '/recentjokes/tempindex.html';
$targetfilename = $_SERVER['DOCUMENT_ROOT'] .
    '/recentjokes/index.html';
```

$srcurl Must Be a URL

Resist the temptation to set `$srcurl` to the filename of **controller.php** on your web server. In order for this script to retrieve the page *produced* by the **controller.php** script, it must request the script using a URL that points to your web server. If you pointed the script directly at the file, it would receive the code of the **controller.php** script itself—rather than the HTML output it produces.

Now, to do the work. We start out by deleting the temporary file, in case it was previously left lying around by a failed execution of this script. We use `file_exists` to check if the file exists, then `unlink` to delete it if it does:

---

[2] For a full description of the `<link rel="canonical"/>` tag, check out the Google Webmaster Central Blog [http://googlewebmastercentral.blogspot.com/2009/02/specify-your-canonical.html].

```php
if (file_exists($tempfilename))
{
  unlink($tempfilename);
}
```

Now we can load the dynamic page (**controller.php**) by requesting its URL with `file_get_contents`. Since we're requesting the file as a URL, rather than directly using its file name, the PHP script will be processed by the web server before we receive it, so what we'll end up with is essentially a static HTML page:

```php
$html = file_get_contents($srcurl);
if (!$html)
{
  $error = "Unable to load $srcurl. Static page update aborted!";
  include $_SERVER['DOCUMENT_ROOT'] . '/includes/error.html.php';
  exit();
}
```

With the page contents tucked away in the `$html` variable, we now want to write them into a static HTML file. The `file_put_contents` function makes this a piece of cake:

```php
if (!file_put_contents($tempfilename, $html))
{
  $error =
      "Unable to write $tempfilename. Static page update aborted!";
  include $_SERVER['DOCUMENT_ROOT'] . '/includes/error.html.php';
  exit();
}
```

With the static page written into a temporary file, we now want to copy the temporary file over the previous version of the static file using `copy`. We can then delete the temporary file with `unlink`:

chapter12/recentjokes/generate.php (excerpt)

```
copy($tempfilename, $targetfilename);
unlink($tempfilename);
?>
```

Now, whenever **generate.php** is executed, a fresh copy of **index.html** will be generated from **controller.php**. Go ahead and request **generate.php** with your browser, then load the **recentjokes** directory (for example, http://localhost/recentjokes/). You should see the contents of the generated **index.html** file.

Errors Due to File Permissions

Particularly on Mac OS X and Linux servers, this script could be tripped up if it has insufficient privileges to copy and delete files in this directory on your server. If **generate.php** outputs errors that indicate this, you'll need to make the directory containing these files writable by your web server. Usually, this can be done with a simple chmod command:

```
chmod 777 /path/to/recentjokes
```

Check with your web host if you need help setting permissions to make a directory PHP-writable on your site.

Of course, it would be a pain to have to manually request the **generate.php** script whenever the content of your site changes. The easiest way to automate this process is to include the **generate.php** script from within the code of your site's content management system whenever a joke is added, updated, or removed from the site.

If a page is quite complex, it may be difficult to find all the right places within your content management system to regenerate its static version. Alternatively, you may simply wish to set up your server to run **generate.php** at regular intervals—say every hour. Under Windows, you can use the Task Scheduler to run **php.exe** (a standalone version of PHP included with the Windows PHP distribution) automatically every hour. Just create a batch file called **generate.bat** that contains this line of text:

chapter12/recentjokes/generate.bat

```
@C:\PHP\php.exe generate.php
```

Adjust the paths and filenames as necessary, then set up Task Scheduler to run **generate.bat** every hour. Done!

Under Mac OS X or Linux, you can do a similar thing with **cron**—a system-level utility that lets you define tasks to be run at regular intervals. Type `man crontab` at your system's Terminal prompt to read about how you can set up tasks for **cron**.

The task you'll set **cron** to run will be very similar to the Windows task discussed above. However, the standalone version of PHP that you'll need lacks the PHP Apache module we compiled way back in Chapter 1. You'll need to compile it separately, from the same package we used to compile the Apache module. Instructions are provided with the package and on the PHP web site,[3] but feel free to post in the SitePoint Forums if you need help!

For experienced **cron** users in a hurry, here's what the line in your **crontab** file should look like:

```
0 0-23 * * * php /path/to/generate.php > /dev/null
```

Handling File Uploads

Okay, we can now juggle files we've created ourselves, but the next piece of the puzzle is to accept files uploaded by visitors to your site, and handle them just as deftly.

We'll start with the basics: let's write an HTML form that allows users to upload files. HTML makes this quite easy with its `<input type="file"/>` tag. By default, however, only the name of the file selected by the user is sent. To have the file itself submitted with the form data, we need to add `enctype="multipart/form-data"` to the `<form>` tag:

```
<form action="index.php" method="post"
    enctype="multipart/form-data">
  <div><label id="upload">Select file to upload:
    <input type="file" id="upload" name="upload"/></label></div>
  <div>
    <input type="hidden" name="action" value="upload"/>
```

---

[3] http://www.php.net/

```
    <input type="submit" value="Submit"/>
  </div>
</form>
```

As we can see, a PHP script (**index.php**, in this case) will handle the data submitted with the form above. Information about uploaded files appears in a array called $_FILES that's automatically created by PHP. As you'd expect, an entry in this array called $_FILES['upload'] (from the name attribute of the <input/> tag) will contain information about the file uploaded in this example. However, instead of storing the contents of the uploaded file, $_FILES['upload'] contains yet another array. We therefore use a second set of square brackets to select the information we want:

$_FILES['*upload*']['tmp_name']

Provides the name of the file stored on the web server's hard disk in the system temporary file directory, unless another directory has been specified using the upload_tmp_dir setting in your **php.ini** file. This file is only kept as long as the PHP script responsible for handling the form submission is running. So, if you want to use the uploaded file later on (for example, store it for display on the site), you need to make a copy of it elsewhere. To do this, use the copy function described in the previous section.

$_FILES['*upload*']['name']

Provides the name of the file on the client machine before it was submitted. If you make a permanent copy of the temporary file, you might want to give it its original name instead of the automatically-generated temporary filename that's described above.

$_FILES['*upload*']['size']

Provides the size (in bytes) of the file.

$_FILES['*upload*']['type']

Provides the **MIME type** of the file (sometimes referred to as **file type** or **content type**, an identifier used to describe the file format, for example, text/plain, image/gif, and so on).

Remember, 'upload' is just the name attribute of the <input/> tag that submitted the file, so the actual array index will depend on that attribute.

You can use these variables to decide whether to accept or reject an uploaded file. For example, in a photo gallery we would only really be interested in JPEG and possibly GIF and PNG files. These files have MIME types of image/jpeg, image/gif, and image/png respectively, but to cater to differences between browsers,[4] you should use regular expressions to validate the uploaded file's type:

```
if (preg_match('/^image\/p?jpeg$/i', $_FILES['upload']['type']) or
    preg_match('/^image\/gif$/i', $_FILES['upload']['type']) or
    preg_match('/^image\/(x-)?png$/i', $_FILES['upload']['type']))
{
  ⋮ Handle the file…
}
else
{
  $error = 'Please submit a JPEG, GIF, or PNG image file.';
  include $_SERVER['DOCUMENT_ROOT'] . '/includes/error.html.php';
  exit();
}
```

See Chapter 8 for help with regular expression syntax.

While you can use a similar technique to disallow files that are too large (by checking the $_FILES['upload']['size'] variable), I'd advise against it. Before this value can be checked, the file is already uploaded and saved in the temporary directory. If you try to reject files because you have limited disk space and/or bandwidth, the fact that large files can still be uploaded, even though they're deleted almost immediately, may be a problem for you.

Instead, you can tell PHP in advance the maximum file size you wish to accept. There are two ways to do this. The first is to adjust the upload_max_filesize setting in your **php.ini** file. The default value is 2MB, so if you want to accept uploads larger than that, you'll immediately need to change that value.[5]

---

[4] The exact MIME type depends on the browser in use. Internet Explorer uses image/pjpeg for JPEG images and image/x-png for PNG images, while Firefox and other browsers use image/jpeg and image/png respectively.

[5] A second restriction, affecting the total size of form submissions, is enforced by the post_max_size setting in **php.ini**. Its default value is 8MB, so if you want to accept *really* big uploads, you'll need to modify that setting, too.

The second method is to include a hidden `<input/>` field in your form with the name `MAX_FILE_SIZE`, and the maximum file size you want to accept with this form as its `value`. For security reasons, this value can't exceed the `upload_max_filesize` setting in your **php.ini**, but it does provide a way for you to accept different maximum sizes on different pages. The following form, for example, will allow uploads of up to 1 kilobyte (1024 bytes):

```
<form action="upload.php" method="post"
    enctype="multipart/form-data">
  <p><label id="upload">Select file to upload:
  <input type="hidden" name="MAX_FILE_SIZE" value="1024"/>
    <input type="file" id="upload" name="upload"/></label></p>
  <p>
    <input type="hidden" name="action" value="upload"/>
    <input type="submit" value="Submit"/>
  </p>
</form>
```

Note that the hidden `MAX_FILE_SIZE` field must come before any `<input type="file"/>` tags in the form, so that PHP is apprised of this restriction before it receives any submitted files. Note also that this restriction can easily be circumvented by a malicious user who simply writes his or her own form without the `MAX_FILE_SIZE` field. For fail-safe security against large file uploads, use the `upload_max_filesize` setting in **php.ini**.

Assigning Unique Filenames

As I explained above, to keep an uploaded file, you need to copy it to another directory. And while you have access to the name of each uploaded file with its `$_FILE['upload']['name']` variable, you have no guarantee that two files with the same name will not be uploaded. In such a case, storage of the file with its original name may result in newer uploads overwriting older ones.

For this reason, you'll usually want to adopt a scheme that allows you to assign a unique filename to every uploaded file. Using the system time (which you can access using the PHP `time` function), you can easily produce a name based on the number of seconds since January 1, 1970. But what if two files happen to be uploaded within one second of each other? To help guard against this possibility, we'll also use the client's IP address (automatically stored in `$_SERVER['REMOTE_ADDR']` by PHP) in the filename. Since you're unlikely to receive two files from the same IP address within one second of each other, this is an acceptable solution for most purposes:

```
// Pick a file extension
if (preg_match('/^image\/p?jpeg$/i', $_FILES['upload']['type']))
{
  $ext = '.jpg';
}
else if (preg_match('/^image\/gif$/i', $_FILES['upload']['type']))
{
  $ext = '.gif';
}
else if (preg_match('/^image\/(x-)?png$/i',
    $_FILES['upload']['type']))
{
  $ext = '.png';
}
else
{
  $ext = '.unknown';
}

// The complete path/filename
$filename = 'C:/uploads/' . time() . $_SERVER['REMOTE_ADDR'] . $ext;

// Copy the file (if it is deemed safe)
if (!is_uploaded_file($_FILES['upload']['tmp_name']) or
    !copy($_FILES['upload']['tmp_name'], $filename))
{
  $error = "Could not  save file as $filename!";
  include $_SERVER['DOCUMENT_ROOT'] . '/includes/error.html.php';
  exit();
}
```

Important to note in the above code is the use of the is_uploaded_file function to check if the file is "safe." All this function does is return TRUE if the filename it's passed as a parameter ($_FILES['upload']['tmp_name'] in this case) was in fact uploaded as part of a form submission. If a malicious user loaded this script and manually specified a filename such as **/etc/passwd** (the system password store on Linux servers), and you had failed to use is_uploaded_file to check that $_FILES['upload'] really referred to an uploaded file, your script might be used to copy sensitive files on your server into a directory from which they would become publicly accessible over the Web! Thus, before you ever trust a PHP variable that you expect to contain the filename of an uploaded file, be sure to use `is_uploaded_file` to check it.

A second trick I have used in the above code is to combine `is_uploaded_file` and `copy` together as the condition of an `if` statement. If the result of `is_uploaded_file($_FILES['upload']['tmp_name'])` is FALSE (making `!is_uploaded_file($_FILES['upload']['tmp_name'])` TRUE), PHP will know immediately that the entire condition will be TRUE when it sees the or operator separating the two function calls. To save time, it will refrain from bothering to run `copy`, so the file won't be copied when `is_uploaded_file` returns FALSE. On the other hand, if `is_uploaded_file` returns TRUE, PHP goes ahead and copies the file. The result of `copy` then determines whether or not an error message is displayed. Similarly, if we'd used the and operator instead of or, a FALSE result in the first part of the condition would cause PHP to skip evaluating the second part. This characteristic of `if` statements is known as **short-circuit evaluation**, and works in other conditional structures such as `while` and `for` loops, too.

Finally, note in the above script that I've used UNIX-style forward slashes (/) in the path, despite it being a Windows path. If I'd used backslashes I'd have had to replace them with double-backslashes (\\) to avoid PHP interpreting them as escaped characters. However, PHP is smart enough to convert forward slashes in a file path to backslashes when it's running on a Windows system. Since we can also use single slashes (/) as usual on non-Windows systems, adopting forward slashes in general for file paths in PHP will make your scripts more portable.

Recording Uploaded Files in the Database

So, you've created a system whereby visitors can upload JPEG, GIF, and PNG images and have them saved on your server … but this book was supposed to be about database driven web sites—right? If we used the system as it stands now, the submitted images would need to be collected out of the folder in which they're saved, then added to the web site by hand! If you think back to the end of Chapter 9, when I suggested you develop a system that enabled site visitors to submit jokes and have them stored in the database ready for quick approval by a content administrator, you'll know there must be a better way!

MySQL has several column types that allow you to store binary data. In database parlance, these column types let us store **BLOBs (Binary Large OBjects)**. However, the storage of potentially large files in a relational database is often a bad idea. While there is convenience in having all the data located in one place, large files lead to large databases, and large databases lead to reduced performance and much larger backup files.

The best alternative is usually to store the *filenames* in the database. As long as you remember to delete files when you delete their corresponding entries in the database, everything should work just the way you need it to. Since we've seen all the SQL code involved in this time and again, I'll leave the details to you. As usual, the SitePoint Forum community is there to offer a helping hand if you need it.

In cases where you're dealing with relatively small files—for example, head shots for use in a staff directory—the storage of data in MySQL is quite practical. In the rest of this chapter, I'll demonstrate how to use PHP to store binary files uploaded over the Web in a MySQL database, and how to retrieve those files for download or display.

Binary Column Types

As with most database driven web applications, the first thing to consider is the layout of the database. To keep this example separate from the Internet Joke Database, I recommend creating a new database for it:

```
mysql> CREATE DATABASE filestore;
```

If you lack this freedom (for example, if you're working on a hosted MySQL server where you're only allowed a single database), go ahead and stick with your existing database.

For each of the files that's stored in our database, we'll store the filename, the MIME type (for example, `image/jpeg` for JPEG image files), a short description of the file, and the binary data itself. Here's the `CREATE TABLE` statement to create the table:

```
mysql> CREATE TABLE filestore (
    ->   id INT NOT NULL PRIMARY KEY AUTO_INCREMENT,
    ->   filename VARCHAR(255) NOT NULL,
    ->   mimetype VARCHAR(50) NOT NULL,
    ->   description VARCHAR(255) NOT NULL,
    ->   filedata MEDIUMBLOB
    -> ) DEFAULT CHARACTER SET utf8;
```

This code is also provided as **filestore.sql** in the code archive for this chapter.

Most of this syntax should be familiar to you; however, the MEDIUMBLOB column type is new. If you consult the MySQL Column Type Reference in Appendix C, you'll find that MEDIUMBLOB is the same as MEDIUMTEXT, except that it performs case-sensitive searches and sorts. In fact, from MySQL's point of view, there's no difference between binary data and blocks of text—both are just long strings of bytes to be stored in the database. MySQL just applies a bunch of extra rules to text column types to ensure that the expected sorting behavior and character encoding conversions are performed transparently.

Aside from the increased performance you gain from avoiding these extra rules, MySQL provides BLOB column types like MEDIUMBLOB to support situations in which you might need to compare the contents of one binary file with another. In such cases, you'd want the comparison to be case sensitive, as binary files may use byte patterns that are equivalent to alphabetical letters; for example, you'd want to distinguish the byte pattern that represents "A" from that which represents "a," which a MEDIUMTEXT column would consider equal.

MEDIUMBLOB is one of several BLOB column types designed to store variable-length binary data. These column types differ from one another only in two aspects: the maximum size of the data a particular value in the column can contain, and the number of bytes used to store the length of each data value. The different binary column types are listed with these details in Table 12.1.

Table 12.1. Binary Column Types in MySQL

Column type	Maximum size	Space required per entry
TINYBLOB	255B	Data size + 1 byte
BLOB	65KB	Data size + 2 bytes
MEDIUMBLOB	16.7MB	Data size + 3 bytes
LONGBLOB	4.3GB	Data size + 4 bytes

As you can see, the table we created above will be able to store files up to 16.7MB in size. If you think you'll need larger files, you can bump the filedata column up to a LONGBLOB. Each file will occupy one more byte in the database, because MySQL will require that extra byte in order to record larger file sizes, but you'll be able to store files up to 4.3GB in size—assuming that your operating system allows files of this size!

If you took my advice to create this table in a separate database, you'll need a new **db.inc.php** file to enable this example to connect to that database:

```
                                              chapter12/filestore/db.inc.php

<?php
$link = mysqli_connect('localhost', 'root', 'password');
if (!$link)
{
  $error = 'Unable to connect to the database server.';
  include 'error.html.php';
  exit();
}

if (!mysqli_set_charset($link, 'utf8'))
{
  $output = 'Unable to set database connection encoding.';
  include 'output.html.php';
  exit();
}

if (!mysqli_select_db($link, 'filestore'))
{
  $error = 'Unable to locate the filestore database.';
  include 'error.html.php';
  exit();
}
?>
```

Storing Files

With the database ready and waiting, the next step is to create a PHP controller script and template that lets users upload files and store them in the database. You can hold off copying the code in the next two sections—I'll present the completed code at the end of the chapter. Here's the code for the form—there should be no surprises here:

chapter12/filestore/files.html.php *(excerpt)*

```
<form action="" method="post" enctype="multipart/form-data">
  <div>
    <label for="upload">Upload File:
    <input type="file" id="upload" name="upload"/></label>
  </div>
  <div>
    <label for="desc">File Description:
    <input type="text" id="desc" name="desc"
        maxlength="255"/></label>
  </div>
  <div>
    <input type="hidden" name="action" value="upload"/>
    <input type="submit" value="Upload"/>
  </div>
</form>
```

As you should already know from your reading in this chapter, this form will create a temporary file on the server and store the name of that file in `$_FILES['upload']['tmp_name']`. It also creates `$_FILES['upload']['name']` (the original name of the file), `$_FILES['upload']['size']` (the file size in bytes), and `$_FILES['upload']['type']` (the MIME type of the file).

Inserting the file into the database is a relatively straightforward process: read the data from the temporary file into a PHP variable, then use that variable in a standard MySQL `INSERT` query. Again, we make use of `is_uploaded_file` to make sure the filename we use does, in fact, correspond to an uploaded file before we do any of this. Here's the code:

chapter12/filestore/index.php *(excerpt)*

```
<?php
include_once $_SERVER['DOCUMENT_ROOT'] .
    '/includes/magicquotes.inc.php';

if (isset($_POST['action']) and $_POST['action'] == 'upload')
{
  // Bail out if the file isn't really an upload
  if (!is_uploaded_file($_FILES['upload']['tmp_name']))
  {
    $error = 'There was no file uploaded!';
    include $_SERVER['DOCUMENT_ROOT'] . '/includes/error.html.php';
```

```
      exit();
   }
   $uploadfile = $_FILES['upload']['tmp_name'];
   $uploadname = $_FILES['upload']['name'];
   $uploadtype = $_FILES['upload']['type'];
   $uploaddesc = $_POST['desc'];
   $uploaddata = file_get_contents($uploadfile);

   include 'db.inc.php';

   // Prepare user-submitted values for safe database insert
   $uploadname = mysqli_real_escape_string($link, $uploadname);
   $uploadtype = mysqli_real_escape_string($link, $uploadtype);
   $uploaddesc = mysqli_real_escape_string($link, $uploaddesc);
   $uploaddata = mysqli_real_escape_string($link, $uploaddata);

   $sql = "INSERT INTO filestore SET
       filename = '$uploadname',
       mimetype = '$uploadtype',
       description = '$uploaddesc',
       filedata = '$uploaddata'";
   if (!mysqli_query($link, $sql))
   {
     $error = 'Database error storing file!';
     include $_SERVER['DOCUMENT_ROOT'] . '/includes/error.html.php';
     exit();
   }

   header('Location: .');
   exit();
}
```

Viewing Stored Files

Armed with the code that accepts file uploads and stores them in a database, you're halfway home. But you still need to be able to pull that data out of the database to use it. For our purposes, this will mean sending the file to a requesting browser.

Once again, this turns out to be a relatively straightforward process. We simply retrieve the data for the requested file from the database and send it to the web browser. The only tricky part is to send the browser information *about* the file:

the file size   so that the browser can display accurate download progress information to the user

the file type   so that the browser knows what to do with the data it receives—that is, display it as a web page, a text file, an image, or offer to save the file

the filename   without specifying this, the browser will assume all files downloaded from our script have the same filename as our controller script

All this information is sent to the browser using **HTTP headers**—lines of information that precede the transmission of the file data itself. As we've already seen, sending HTTP headers via PHP is quite easy using the `header` function, but as headers must be sent before plain content, any calls to this function must come before anything is outputted by your script.

The file size is specified with a `Content-length` header:

chapter12/filestore/index.php (excerpt)

```php
header('Content-length: ' . strlen($filedata));
```

`strlen` is a built-in PHP function that returns the length of the given string. Since binary data is just a string of bytes as far as PHP is concerned, you can use this function to count the length (in bytes) of the file data.

The file type is specified with a `Content-type` header:

chapter12/filestore/index.php (excerpt)

```php
header("Content-type: $mimetype");
```

Finally, the filename is specified with a `Content-disposition` header:

```php
header("Content-disposition: inline; filename=$filename");
```

You could use the code below to fetch a file with a given ID from the database, and send it to the browser:

```
include 'db.inc.php';

$id = mysqli_real_escape_string($link, $_GET['id']);

$sql = "SELECT filename, mimetype, filedata
    FROM filestore
    WHERE id = '$id'";
$result = mysqli_query($link, $sql);
if (!$result)
{
  $error = 'Database error fetching requested file.';
  include $_SERVER['DOCUMENT_ROOT'] . '/includes/error.html.php';
  exit();
}

$file = mysqli_fetch_array($result);
if (!$file)
{
  $error = 'File with specified ID not found in the database!';
  include $_SERVER['DOCUMENT_ROOT'] . '/includes/error.html.php';
  exit();
}

$filename = $file['filename'];
$mimetype = $file['mimetype'];
$filedata = $file['filedata'];

header("Content-disposition: inline; filename=$filename");
header("Content-type: $mimetype");
header('Content-length: ' . strlen($filedata));

echo $filedata;
exit();
```

One final trick we can add to this code is to allow a file to be downloaded, instead of viewed, if the user so desires. Web standards suggest that the way to do this is to send a Content-disposition of attachment instead of inline. Here's the modified code. It checks if $_GET['action'] equals 'download', which would indicate that this special file type should be sent:

```
include 'db.inc.php';

$id = mysqli_real_escape_string($link, $_GET['id']);
```

```
$sql = "SELECT filename, mimetype, filedata
    FROM filestore
    WHERE id = '$id'";
$result = mysqli_query($link, $sql);
if (!$result)
{
  $error = 'Database error fetching requested file.';
  include $_SERVER['DOCUMENT_ROOT'] . '/includes/error.html.php';
  exit();
}

$file = mysqli_fetch_array($result);
if (!$file)
{
  $error = 'File with specified ID not found in the database!';
  include $_SERVER['DOCUMENT_ROOT'] . '/includes/error.html.php';
  exit();
}

$filename = $file['filename'];
$mimetype = $file['mimetype'];
$filedata = $file['filedata'];
$disposition = 'inline';

if ($_GET['action'] == 'download')
{
  $disposition = 'attachment';
}

header("Content-disposition: $disposition; filename=$filename");
header("Content-type: $mimetype");
header('Content-length: ' . strlen($filedata));

echo $filedata;
exit();
```

Unfortunately, many older browsers generally ignore the Content-disposition header, deciding what to do with a file based on the Content-type header instead—especially when it comes after the Content-disposition header.

To achieve the desired download behavior in as many browsers as possible, make sure the Content-type header comes before the Content-disposition header, and replace the file's actual MIME type with a generic `Content-type` of `application/oct-et-stream` (which is required to force a download in older browsers):

```php
include 'db.inc.php';

$id = mysqli_real_escape_string($link, $_GET['id']);

$sql = "SELECT filename, mimetype, filedata
    FROM filestore
    WHERE id = '$id'";
$result = mysqli_query($link, $sql);
if (!$result)
{
  $error = 'Database error fetching requested file.';
  include $_SERVER['DOCUMENT_ROOT'] . '/includes/error.html.php';
  exit();
}

$file = mysqli_fetch_array($result);
if (!$file)
{
  $error = 'File with specified ID not found in the database!';
  include $_SERVER['DOCUMENT_ROOT'] . '/includes/error.html.php';
  exit();
}

$filename = $file['filename'];
$mimetype = $file['mimetype'];
$filedata = $file['filedata'];
$disposition = 'inline';

if ($_GET['action'] == 'download')
{
  $mimetype = 'application/octet-stream';
  $disposition = 'attachment';
}

// Content-type must come before Content-disposition
header("Content-type: $mimetype");
header("Content-disposition: $disposition; filename=$filename");
header('Content-length: ' . strlen($filedata));
```

```php
  echo $filedata;
  exit();
```

Putting It All Together

Below, you'll find the complete file store example. It combines all the elements given above with some simple code that will list the files in the database and allow them to be viewed, downloaded, or deleted. As always, this code is available in the code archive.

First, the controller script:

```php
                                           chapter12/filestore/index.php
<?php
if (isset($_POST['action']) and $_POST['action'] == 'upload')
{
  // Bail out if the file isn't really an upload
  if (!is_uploaded_file($_FILES['upload']['tmp_name']))
  {
    $error = 'There was no file uploaded!';
    include $_SERVER['DOCUMENT_ROOT'] . '/includes/error.html.php';
    exit();
  }
  $uploadfile = $_FILES['upload']['tmp_name'];
  $uploadname = $_FILES['upload']['name'];
  $uploadtype = $_FILES['upload']['type'];
  $uploaddesc = $_POST['desc'];
  $uploaddata = file_get_contents($uploadfile);

  include 'db.inc.php';

  // Prepare user-submitted values for safe database insert
  $uploadname = mysqli_real_escape_string($link, $uploadname);
  $uploadtype = mysqli_real_escape_string($link, $uploadtype);
  $uploaddesc = mysqli_real_escape_string($link, $uploaddesc);
  $uploaddata = mysqli_real_escape_string($link, $uploaddata);

  $sql = "INSERT INTO filestore SET
      filename = '$uploadname',
      mimetype = '$uploadtype',
      description = '$uploaddesc',
```

```
      filedata = '$uploaddata'";
  if (!mysqli_query($link, $sql))
  {
    $error = 'Database error storing file!';
    include $_SERVER['DOCUMENT_ROOT'] . '/includes/error.html.php';
    exit();
  }

  header('Location: .');
  exit();
}

if (isset($_GET['action']) and
    ($_GET['action'] == 'view' or $_GET['action'] == 'download') and
    isset($_GET['id']))
{
  include 'db.inc.php';

  $id = mysqli_real_escape_string($link, $_GET['id']);

  $sql = "SELECT filename, mimetype, filedata
      FROM filestore
      WHERE id = '$id'";
  $result = mysqli_query($link, $sql);
  if (!$result)
  {
    $error = 'Database error fetching requested file.';
    include $_SERVER['DOCUMENT_ROOT'] . '/includes/error.html.php';
    exit();
  }

  $file = mysqli_fetch_array($result);
  if (!$file)
  {
    $error = 'File with specified ID not found in the database!';
    include $_SERVER['DOCUMENT_ROOT'] . '/includes/error.html.php';
    exit();
  }

  $filename = $file['filename'];
  $mimetype = $file['mimetype'];
  $filedata = $file['filedata'];
  $disposition = 'inline';

  if ($_GET['action'] == 'download')
```

```php
  {
    $mimetype = 'application/x-download';
    $disposition = 'attachment';
  }

  // Content-type must come before Content-disposition
  header("Content-type: $mimetype");
  header("Content-disposition: $disposition; filename=$filename");
  header('Content-length: ' . strlen($filedata));

  echo $filedata;
  exit();
}

if (isset($_POST['action']) and $_POST['action'] == 'delete' and
    isset($_POST['id']))
{
  include 'db.inc.php';

  $id = mysqli_real_escape_string($link, $_POST['id']);

  $sql = "DELETE FROM filestore
      WHERE id = '$id'";
  if (!mysqli_query($link, $sql))
  {
    $error = 'Database error deleting requested file.';
    include $_SERVER['DOCUMENT_ROOT'] . '/includes/error.html.php';
    exit();
  }

  header('Location: .');
  exit();
}

include 'db.inc.php';

$sql = 'SELECT id, filename, mimetype, description
    FROM filestore';
$result = mysqli_query($link, $sql);
if (!$result)
{
  $error = 'Database error fetching stored files.';
  include $_SERVER['DOCUMENT_ROOT'] . '/includes/error.html.php';
  exit();
}
```

```php
$files = array();
while ($row = mysqli_fetch_array($result))
{
  $files[] = array(
      'id' => $row['id'],
      'filename' => $row['filename'],
      'mimetype' => $row['mimetype'],
      'description' => $row['description']);
}

include 'files.html.php';
?>
```

Next, the PHP template that includes the upload form and the list of files:

chapter12/filestore/files.html.php

```php
<?php include_once $_SERVER['DOCUMENT_ROOT'] .
    '/includes/helpers.inc.php'; ?>
<!DOCTYPE html PUBLIC "-//W3C//DTD XHTML 1.0 Strict//EN"
    "http://www.w3.org/TR/xhtml1/DTD/xhtml1-strict.dtd">
<html xmlns="http://www.w3.org/1999/xhtml" xml:lang="en" lang="en">
  <head>
    <title>PHP/MySQL File Repository</title>
    <meta http-equiv="content-type"
        content="text/html; charset=utf-8" />
  </head>
  <body>
    <h1>PHP/MySQL File Repository</h1>

    <form action="" method="post" enctype="multipart/form-data">
      <div>
        <label for="upload">Upload File:
        <input type="file" id="upload" name="upload"/></label>
      </div>
      <div>
        <label for="desc">File Description:
        <input type="text" id="desc" name="desc"
            maxlength="255"/></label>
      </div>
      <div>
        <input type="hidden" name="action" value="upload"/>
        <input type="submit" value="Upload"/>
      </div>
```

```
        </form>

        <?php if (count($files) > 0): ?>

        <p>The following files are stored in the database:</p>

        <table>
          <thead>
            <tr>
              <th>File name</th>
              <th>Type</th>
              <th>Description</th>
            </tr>
          </thead>
          <tbody>
            <?php foreach($files as $f): ?>
            <tr valign="top">
              <td>
                <a href="?action=view&amp;id=<?php htmlout($f['id']); ?>"
                   ><?php htmlout($f['filename']); ?></a>
              </td>
              <td><?php htmlout($f['mimetype']); ?></td>
              <td><?php htmlout($f['description']); ?></td>
              <td>
                <form action="" method="get">
                  <div>
                    <input type="hidden" name="action"
                        value="download"/>
                    <input type="hidden" name="id"
                        value="<?php htmlout($f['id']); ?>"/>
                    <input type="submit" value="Download"/>
                  </div>
                </form>
              </td>
              <td>
                <form action="" method="post">
                  <div>
                    <input type="hidden" name="action" value="delete"/>
                    <input type="hidden" name="id"
                        value="<?php htmlout($f['id']); ?>"/>
                    <input type="submit" value="Delete"/>
                  </div>
                </form>
              </td>
            </tr>
```

```
        <?php endforeach; ?>
      </tbody>
    </table>

    <?php endif; ?>
  </body>
</html>
```

And just to be thorough, the database connection include file:

```
                                        chapter12/filestore/db.inc.php
<?php
$link = mysqli_connect('localhost', 'root', 'password');
if (!$link)
{
  $error = 'Unable to connect to the database server.';
  include 'error.html.php';
  exit();
}

if (!mysqli_set_charset($link, 'utf8'))
{
  $output = 'Unable to set database connection encoding.';
  include 'output.html.php';
  exit();
}

if (!mysqli_select_db($link, 'filestore'))
{
  $error = 'Unable to locate the filestore database.';
  include 'error.html.php';
  exit();
}
?>
```

Note that this uses a different database (`filestore`) than the Internet Joke Database site. If you prefer to put the `filestore` table in the `ijdb` database along with everything else that's in there, you can just use the shared **db.inc.php** include file instead.

With all these files in place, and the database set up, fire up your browser and take a look. The empty repository should produce a page like the one in Figure 12.1.

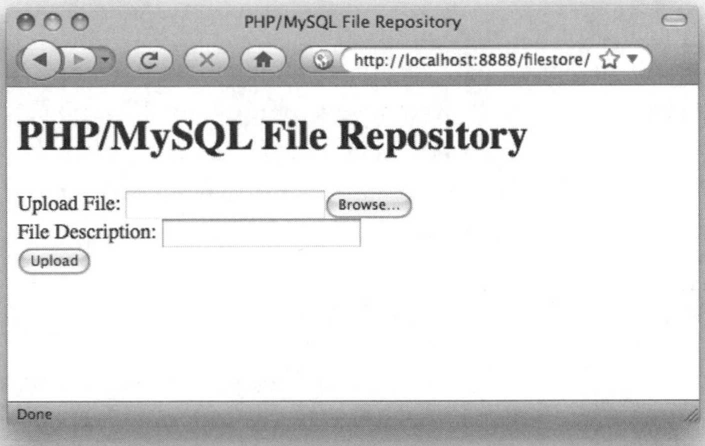

Figure 12.1. The Empty Repository

Upload a few files, and you should see them listed in a table, as shown in Figure 12.2.

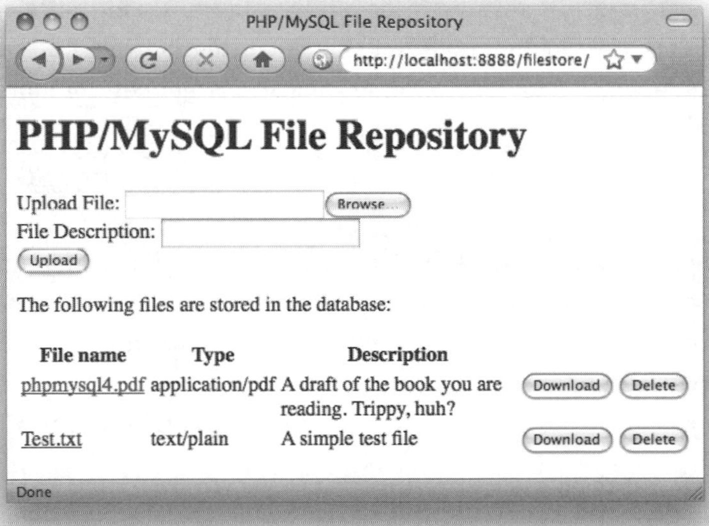

Figure 12.2. A couple of files on board

Click on a file's name, and it should be displayed in the browser (assuming the file is of a type that your browser supports). Also, try out the **Download** and **Delete** buttons provided for each file. They should work as you would expect.

This example demonstrates all the techniques you need in order to juggle binary files with PHP and MySQL, and I invite you to think of some creative uses of this code. Consider, for example, a file archive to which users must provide a username and password before they're allowed to view or download the files. If a user enters an incorrect username/password combination, your script can display an error page instead of sending the file data. Another possibility would be a script that sends different files depending on the details submitted by the form.

Large File Considerations

In systems like those developed above, large files present some unique challenges to the developer. I'll explain these here briefly, but fully developed solutions to these problems are beyond the scope of this book.

MySQL Packet Size

By default, MySQL rejects commands (packets) that are longer than 1MB. This default puts a reasonably severe limit on the maximum file size you can store, unless you're prepared to write your file data in 1MB chunks, using an INSERT followed by several UPDATEs. Increase the maximum packet size by setting the max_allowed_packet option in your **my.cnf** or **my.ini** file. Refer to the MySQL manual[6] for more information on this issue.

PHP Script Timeout

PHP is configured by default to kill PHP scripts that run for more than 30 seconds. For large downloads over slow connections, this limit will be reached fairly quickly! Use PHP's set_time_limit function to set an appropriate time limit for the download, or simply set the time limit to zero, which allows the script to run to completion, however long it takes. But only do this if you're positive your script will always terminate, and not run forever!

---

[6] http://dev.mysql.com/doc/refman/5.1/en/packet-too-large.html

The End

In this chapter, we completed our exploration of PHP and MySQL with a practical look at handling file uploads and storing binary data in MySQL databases. Admittedly, this is a rather arbitrary place to end this book; there are plenty of other aspects of PHP and MySQL that you could explore, some of which could be called no less basic or essential than binary data.

PHP in particular, with its "batteries included" philosophy of packing as much functionality as possible directly into the language in the form of built-in functions, could fill *ten* books this size. Exactly which aspects you'll need to learn before tackling any particular project will vary wildly. Having worked as a professional PHP developer for many years now, I have to admit that I remain unfamiliar with *most* of the functionality that PHP has to offer. There's just so much available to explore! That's why very few people bother to print out the PHP Manual[7] in its entirety!

By far the best way to cement your newfound knowledge of PHP and MySQL is to put it to work: build your own database driven web site from scratch using the techniques covered in this book. Publish it on the Web, and ask for feedback from real, live users. Chances are they'll push you to make improvements to the site that you may find you lack the knowhow to implement right away. These real-world requirements should direct your further exploration of PHP and MySQL—and there's plenty more to be learned!

A great resource on your adventures would be a copy of *The PHP Anthology: 101 Essential Tips, Tricks & Hacks, 2nd Edition*[8] (Melbourne: SitePoint, 2007). Beginning with an exploration of PHP's object oriented programming features, it then builds on that foundation to demonstrate efficient ways of tackling some of the problems we looked at in this book—and many more that we didn't.

If you end up tackling more than one project, you may find yourself writing the same pieces of code over and over again. Rather than spending time perfecting your

---

[7] http://php.net/docs.php
[8] http://www.sitepoint.com/books/phpant2/

own collection of shared include files, you might like to spend some time learning a PHP framework, such as Zend Framework,[9] CakePHP,[10] or Symfony.[11]

Each of these frameworks represents many thousands of hours' work by PHP experts who've developed ready-made solutions for the most common problems tackled by PHP developers. By using these solutions in your own projects, you can focus on writing the code to solve the problems that are unique to that project, and waste less time reinventing the wheel. Each framework has its own philosophy, strengths, and weaknesses, and finding the right one for you will take some work. If you plan on becoming a professional PHP developer, however, you'll find it time well spent.

However you proceed from this point, rest assured you're starting out with a solid grounding in the essentials. That's more than can be said for many developers working today! Take that advantage and use it.

Most importantly, go out there and write some code!

---

[9] http://framework.zend.com/
[10] http://cakephp.org/
[11] http://www.symfony-project.org/

Appendix A: MySQL Syntax Reference

This appendix describes the syntax of the majority of SQL statements implemented in MySQL, as of version 5.1.34 (current as of this writing).

The following conventions are used in this reference:

- Commands are listed in alphabetical order for easy reference.

- Optional components are surrounded by square brackets ([]).

- Lists of elements from which one element must be chosen are surrounded by braces ({}), with the elements separated by vertical bars (|).

- An ellipsis (...) means that the preceding element may be repeated.

The query syntax documented in this appendix has been simplified in several places by the omission of the alternative syntax, and of keywords that performed no function, but which were originally included for compatibility with other database systems. Query features having to do with some advanced features such as transactions have also been omitted. For a complete, up-to-date reference to supported MySQL syntax, see the MySQL Reference Manual.[1]

SQL Statements Implemented in MySQL

ALTER TABLE

```
ALTER [IGNORE] TABLE tbl_name action[, action …]
```

In this code, *action* refers to an action as defined below.

ALTER TABLE queries may be used to change the definition of a table without losing any of the information in that table (except in obvious cases, such as the deletion of a column). Here are the main actions that are possible:

---

[1] http://dev.mysql.com/doc/refman/5.1/en/

ADD [COLUMN] *create_definition* **[FIRST | AFTER** *column_name*]

This action adds a new column to the table. The syntax for *create_definition* is as described for the section called "CREATE TABLE". By default, the column will be added to the end of the table, but by specifying FIRST or AFTER *column_name*, you can place the column wherever you like. The optional word COLUMN performs no actual function—leave it off unless you particularly like to see it there.

ADD INDEX [*index_name***] (***index_col_name***, …)**

This action creates a new index to speed up searches based on the column(s) specified. It's usually a good idea to assign a name to your indices by specifying the *index_name*, otherwise, a default name based on the first column in the index will be used. When creating an index based on CHAR and/or VARCHAR columns, you can specify a number of characters to index as part of *index_col_name* (for example, myColumn(5) will index the first five characters of myColumn). This number must be specified when indexing BLOB and TEXT columns. For detailed information on indexes, see the MySQL Reference Manual,[2] or Mike Sullivan's excellent article *Optimizing your MySQL Application*[3] on SitePoint.

ADD FULLTEXT [*index_name***] (***index_col_name***, …)**

This action creates a full-text index on the column(s) specified. This special type of index allows you to perform complex searches for text in CHAR, VARCHAR, or TEXT columns using the MATCH MySQL function. For full details, see the MySQL Reference Manual.[4]

ADD PRIMARY KEY (*index_col_name***, …)**

This action creates an index for the specified row(s) with the name PRIMARY, identifying it as the primary key for the table. All values (or combinations of values) must be unique, as described for the ADD UNIQUE action below. This action will cause an error if a primary key already exists for this table. *index_col_name* is defined as it is for the ADD INDEX action above.

ADD UNIQUE [*index_name***] (***index_col_name***, …)**

This action creates an index on the specified columns, but with a twist: all values in the designated column—or all combinations of values, if more than

---

[2] http://dev.mysql.com/doc/mysql/en/Indexes.html

[3] http://www.sitepoint.com/article/optimizing-mysql-application

[4] http://dev.mysql.com/doc/mysql/en/fulltext-search.html

one column is included in the index—must be unique. The parameters *index_name* and *index_col_name* are defined as they are for the ADD INDEX action above.

ALTER [COLUMN] `col_name` {SET DEFAULT `value` | DROP DEFAULT}

This action assigns a new default value to a column (SET DEFAULT), or removes the existing default value (DROP DEFAULT). Again, the word COLUMN is completely optional, and has no effect.

CHANGE [COLUMN] `col_name create_definition`

This action replaces an existing column (*col_name*) with a new column, as defined by *create_definition* (the syntax of which is as specified for the section called "CREATE TABLE"). The data in the existing column is converted, if necessary, and placed in the new column. Note that *create_definition* includes a new column name, so this action may be used to rename a column. If you want to leave the name of the column unchanged, however, don't forget to include it twice (once for *col_name* and once for *create_definition*), or use the MODIFY action below.

DISABLE KEYS
ENABLE KEYS

When you insert a large number of records into a table, MySQL can spend a lot of time updating the index(es) of the table to reflect the new entries. Executing ALTER TABLE … DISABLE KEYS before you perform the inserts will instruct MySQL to postpone those index updates. Once the inserts are complete, execute ALTER TABLE … ENABLE KEYS to update the indexes for all the new entries at once. This will usually save time over performing the updates one at a time.

DROP [COLUMN] `col_name`

Fairly self-explanatory, this action completely removes a column from the table. The data in that column is irretrievable after this query completes, so be sure of the column name you specify. COLUMN, as usual, can be left off—it just makes the query sound better when read aloud.

DROP PRIMARY KEY
DROP INDEX `index_name`

These actions are quite self-explanatory: they remove from the table the primary key, and a specific index, respectively.

MODIFY [COLUMN] *create_definition*

Nearly identical to the CHANGE action above, this action lets you specify a new declaration for a column in the table, but assumes the name will remain the same. Thus, you simply have to re-declare the column with the same name in the *create_definition* parameter (as defined for the section called "CREATE TABLE"). As before, COLUMN is completely optional and does nothing. Although convenient, this action is not standard SQL syntax, and was added for compatibility with an identical extension in Oracle database servers.

ORDER BY *col_name*

This action lets you sort a table's entries by a particular column. However, as soon as new entries are added to the table, or existing entries modified, ordering can no longer be guaranteed. The only practical use of this action would be to increase performance of a table that you sorted regularly in a certain way in your application's SELECT queries. Under some circumstances, arranging the rows in (almost) the right order to begin with will make sorting quicker.

RENAME [TO] *new_tbl_name*

This action renames the table. The word TO is completely optional, and does nothing. Use it if you like it.

table_options

Using the same syntax as in the CREATE TABLE query, this action allows you to set and change advanced table options. These options are fully documented in the MySQL Reference Manual.[5]

ANALYZE TABLE

```
ANALYZE TABLE tbl_name[, tbl_name, …]
```

This function updates the information used by the SELECT query in the optimization of queries that take advantage of table indices. It pays in performance to run this query periodically on tables whose contents change a lot over time. The table(s) in question are locked "read-only" while the analysis runs.

---

[5] http://dev.mysql.com/doc/mysql/en/CREATE_TABLE.html

CREATE DATABASE

```
CREATE DATABASE [IF NOT EXISTS] db_name
```

This action simply creates a new database with the given name (*db_name*). This query will fail if the database already exists (unless IF NOT EXISTS is specified), or if you lack the required privileges.

CREATE INDEX

```
CREATE [UNIQUE | FULLTEXT] INDEX index_name ON tbl_name
    (col_name[(length)], …)
```

This query creates a new index on an existing table. It works identically to ALTER TABLE ADD {INDEX | UNIQUE | FULLTEXT}, described in the section called "ALTER TABLE".

CREATE TABLE

```
CREATE [TEMPORARY] TABLE [IF NOT EXISTS] [db_name.]tbl_name
    {   [(create_definition, …)]
        [table_options] [[IGNORE | REPLACE] select_statement]

    | LIKE [db_name.]old_tbl_name }
```

Where *create_definition* is:

```
{   col_name type [NOT NULL] [DEFAULT default_value]
        [AUTO_INCREMENT] [PRIMARY KEY]

    | PRIMARY KEY (index_col_name, …)

    | INDEX [index_name] (index_col_name, …)

    | FULLTEXT [index_name] (index_col_name, …)

    | UNIQUE [INDEX] [index_name] (index_col_name, …) }
```

In this code, *type* is a MySQL column type (see Appendix C), and *index_col_name* is as described for ALTER TABLE ADD INDEX in the section called "ALTER TABLE".

CREATE TABLE is used to create a new table called *tbl_name* in the current database (or in a specific database if *db_name* is specified). If TEMPORARY is specified, the table disappears upon termination of the connection by which it was created. A temporary table created with the same name as an existing table will hide the existing table from the current client session until the temporary table is deleted or the session ends; however, other clients will continue to see the original table.

Assuming TEMPORARY is not specified, this query will fail if a table with the given name already exists, unless IF NOT EXISTS is specified (in which case the query is ignored). A CREATE TABLE query will also fail if you lack the required privileges.

Most of the time, the name of the table will be followed by a series of column declarations (*create_definition* above). Each column definition includes the name and data type for the column, and any of the following options:

NOT NULL

This specifies that the column may not be left empty (NULL). Note that NULL is a special "no value" value, which is quite different from, say, an empty string (' '). A column of type VARCHAR, for instance, which is set NOT NULL may be set to ' ' but will not be NULL. Likewise, a NOT NULL column of type INT may contain zero (0), which is a value, but it may not contain NULL, as this is not a value.

DEFAULT *default_value*

DEFAULT lets you specify a value to be given to a column when no value is assigned in an INSERT statement. When this option is not specified, NULL columns (columns for which the NOT NULL option is not set) will be assigned a value of NULL when there is no value given in an INSERT statement. NOT NULL columns will instead be assigned a "default default value": an empty string (' '), zero (0), '0000-00-00', or a current timestamp, depending on the data type of the column.

AUTO_INCREMENT

As described in Chapter 2, an AUTO_INCREMENT column will automatically insert a number that is one greater than the current highest number in that column, when NULL is inserted. AUTO_INCREMENT columns must also be NOT NULL, and be either a PRIMARY KEY or UNIQUE.

PRIMARY KEY

This option specifies that the column in question should be the primary key for the table; that is, the values in the column must identify uniquely each of the rows in the table. This forces the values in this column to be unique, and speeds up searches for items based on this column by creating an index of the values it contains.

UNIQUE

Very similar to PRIMARY KEY, this option requires all values in the column to be unique and indexes the values for high speed searches.

In addition to column definitions, you can list additional indexes you wish to create on the table using the PRIMARY KEY, INDEX, and FULLTEXT forms of *create_definition*. See the descriptions of the equivalent forms of ALTER TABLE in the section called "ALTER TABLE" for details.

The *table_options* portion of the CREATE TABLE query is used to specify advanced properties of the table, and is described in detail in the MySQL Reference Manual.[6]

The *select_statement* portion of the CREATE TABLE query allows you to create a table from the results of a SELECT query (see the section called "SELECT"). When you create this table, it's unnecessary to declare separately the columns that correspond to those results. This type of query is useful if you want to obtain the result of a SELECT query, store it in a temporary table, and then perform a number of SELECT queries upon it.

Instead of defining a table from scratch, you can instead instruct MySQL to create the new table using the same structure as some other table. Rather than a list of *create_definition*s and the *table_options*, simply end the CREATE TABLE query with LIKE, followed by the name of the existing table.

DELETE

```
DELETE [LOW_PRIORITY] [QUICK] [IGNORE]
    {   FROM tbl_name
            [WHERE where_clause]
            [ORDER BY order_by_expr]
            [LIMIT rows]

    | tbl_name[, tbl_name …]
        FROM table_references
```

---

[6] http://dev.mysql.com/doc/mysql/en/create-table.html

```
          [WHERE where_clause]

    | FROM tbl_name[, tbl_name …]
        USING table_references
        [WHERE where_clause] }
```

The first form of this query deletes all rows from the specified table, unless the optional (but desirable) WHERE or LIMIT clauses are specified. The WHERE clause works the same way as its twin in the SELECT query (see the section called "SELECT"). The LIMIT clause simply lets you specify the maximum number of rows to be deleted. The ORDER BY clause lets you specify the order in which the entries are deleted, which, in combination with the LIMIT clause, allows you to do things like delete the ten oldest entries from the table.

The second and third forms are equivalent, and enable you to delete rows from multiple tables in a single operation, in much the same way as you can retrieve entries from multiple tables using a join in a SELECT query (see the section called "SELECT"). The *table_references* work the same way as they do for SELECT queries (you can create simple joins or outer joins), while the WHERE clause lets you narrow down the rows that are considered for deletion. The first list of tables (*tbl_name[, tbl_name, …]*), however, identifies from the *table_references* the tables from which rows will actually be deleted. In this way, you can use a complex join involving a number of tables to isolate a set of results, then delete the rows from only one of those tables.

The LOW_PRIORITY option causes the query to wait until there are no clients reading from the table before performing the operation. The QUICK option attempts to speed up lengthy delete operations by changing the way it updates the table's index(es). The IGNORE option instructs MySQL to refrain from reporting any errors that occur while the delete is performed.

DESCRIBE/DESC

```
{DESCRIBE | DESC} tbl_name [col_name | wild]
```

This command supplies information about the columns, a specific column (*col_name*), or any columns that match a pattern containing the wild cards % and _ (*wild*), that make up the specified table. The information returned includes the column name, its type, whether it accepts NULL as a value, whether the column has an index, the default value for the column, and any extra features it has (for example, AUTO_INCREMENT).

DROP DATABASE

```
DROP DATABASE [IF EXISTS] db_name
```

This is a dangerous command. It will immediately delete a database, along with all of its tables. This query will fail with an error if the database does not exist (unless IF EXISTS is specified, in which case it will fail silently), or if you lack the required privileges.

DROP INDEX

```
DROP INDEX index_name ON tbl_name
```

DROP INDEX has exactly the same effect as ALTER TABLE DROP INDEX, described in the section called "ALTER TABLE".

DROP TABLE

```
DROP TABLE [IF EXISTS] tbl_name[, tbl_name, …]
```

This query completely deletes one or more tables. *This is a dangerous query*, since the data can never be retrieved once this action is executed. Be very careful with it!

This query will fail with an error if the table doesn't exist (unless IF EXISTS is specified, in which case it will fail silently) or if you lack the required privileges.

EXPLAIN

The explain query has two very different forms. The first,

```
EXPLAIN tbl_name
```

is equivalent to DESCRIBE tbl_name or SHOW COLUMNS FROM tbl_name.

The second format,

```
EXPLAIN select_statement
```

where *select_statement* can be any valid SELECT query, will produce an explanation of how MySQL would determine the results of the SELECT statement. This query is useful for finding out where indexes will help speed up your SELECT queries, and also for determining if MySQL is performing multi-table queries in optimal order. See the STRAIGHT_JOIN option of the SELECT query in the section called "SELECT" for information on how to override the MySQL optimizer and control this order manually. See the MySQL Reference Manual[7] for complete information on how to interpret the results of an EXPLAIN query.

GRANT

```
GRANT priv_type [(column_list)], …
     ON {tbl_name | * | *.* | db_name.*}
     TO username [IDENTIFIED BY 'password'], …
     [WITH GRANT OPTION]
```

GRANT adds new access privileges to a user account, and creates a new account if the specified *username* does not yet exist, or changes the password if IDENTIFIED BY 'password' is used on an account that already has a password.

See the section called "MySQL Access Control" in Chapter 10 for a complete query description.

INSERT

```
INSERT [LOW_PRIORITY | DELAYED] [IGNORE] [INTO] tbl_name

    {   [(col_name, …)] VALUES (expression, …), …

      | SET col_name=expression, col_name=expression, …

      | [(col_name, …)] SELECT … }
```

---

[7] http://dev.mysql.com/doc/mysql/en/explain.html

The INSERT query is used to add new entries to a table. It supports three general options:

LOW_PRIORITY

The query will wait until there are no clients reading from the table before it proceeds.

DELAYED

The query completes immediately from the client's point of view, and the INSERT operation is performed in the background. This option is useful when you wish to insert a large number of rows without waiting for the operation to complete. Be aware that the client will not know the last inserted ID on an AUTO_INCREMENT column when a DELAYED insert is performed (for example, mysqli_insert_id in PHP will fail to work correctly).

IGNORE

Normally, when an insert operation causes a clash in a PRIMARY KEY or UNIQUE column, the insert fails and produces an error message. This option allows the insert to fail silently—the new row is not inserted, but no error message is displayed.

The word INTO is entirely optional, and has no effect on the operation of the query.

As you can see above, INSERT queries may take three forms. The first form lets you insert one or more rows by specifying the values for the table columns in parentheses. If the optional list of column names is omitted, then the list(s) of column values must include a value for every column in the table, in the order in which they appear in the table.

The second form of INSERT can be used only to insert a single row, but, very intuitively, it allows you to assign values to the columns in that row by giving them in *col_name=value* format.

In the third and final form of INSERT, the rows to be inserted result from a SELECT query. Again, if the list of column names is omitted, the result set of the SELECT must contain values for each and every column in the table, in the correct order. A SELECT query that makes up part of an insert statement may not contain an ORDER BY clause, and you're unable to use the table into which you are inserting in the FROM clause.

Columns to which you assign no value (for example, if you leave them out of the column list) are assigned their default. By default, inserting a NULL value into a NOT NULL field will also cause that field to be set to its default value; however, if MySQL is configured with the DONT_USE_DEFAULT_FIELDS option enabled, such an INSERT operation will cause an error. For this reason, it's best to avoid them.

LOAD DATA INFILE

```
LOAD DATA [LOW_PRIORITY | CONCURRENT] [LOCAL] INFILE
    'file_name.txt' [REPLACE | IGNORE] INTO TABLE tbl_name
    [FIELDS
      [TERMINATED BY 'string']
      [[OPTIONALLY] ENCLOSED BY 'char']
      [ESCAPED BY 'char'] ]
    [LINES [STARTING BY ''] [TERMINATED BY 'string']]
    [IGNORE number LINES]
    [(col_name, …)]
```

The LOAD DATA INFILE query is used to import data from a text file either on the MySQL server, or on the LOCAL (client) system (for example, a text file created with a SELECT INTO OUTFILE query). The syntax of this command is given above; however, I refer you to the MySQL Reference Manual[8] for a complete explanation of this query and the issues that surround its use.

LOCK/UNLOCK TABLES

```
LOCK TABLES
    tbl_name [AS alias] {READ [LOCAL] | [LOW_PRIORITY] WRITE},
    tbl_name …
```

```
UNLOCK TABLES
```

LOCK TABLES locks the specified table(s) so that the current connection has exclusive access to them, while other connections will have to wait until the lock is released. The lock can be released with UNLOCK TABLES, with another LOCK TABLES query, or with the closure of the current connection.

---

[8] http://dev.mysql.com/doc/mysql/en/load-data.html

A READ lock prevents the specified table(s) from being written by this, or any other connection. This allows you to make certain that the contents of a table (or set of tables) are unchanged for a certain period of time. READ LOCAL allows INSERT statements to continue to be processed on the table while the lock is held, but blocks UPDATEs and DELETEs as usual.

A WRITE lock prevents all other connections from reading or writing the specified table(s). It's useful when a series of INSERT or UPDATE queries must be performed together to maintain the integrity of the data model in the database. New support for **transactions** in MySQL provides more robust support for these types of "grouped queries" (see the sidebar in the section called "LOCKing TABLES" in Chapter 11 for details).

By default, a WRITE lock that is waiting for access to a table will take priority over any READ locks that may also be waiting. To specify that a WRITE lock should yield to all other READ lock requests, you can use the LOW_PRIORITY option. Be aware, however, that if there are always READ lock requests pending, a LOW_PRIORITY WRITE lock will never be allowed to proceed.

When locking tables, you must list the same aliases that you're going to use in the queries you'll be performing. If, for example, you are going to refer to the same table with two different aliases in one of your queries, you'll need to obtain a lock for each of those aliases beforehand.

For more information on locking tables, see the section called "LOCKing TABLES" in Chapter 11.

OPTIMIZE TABLE

```
OPTIMIZE TABLE tbl_name[, tbl_name, …]
```

Much like a hard disk partition becomes fragmented if existing files are deleted or resized, MySQL tables become fragmented over time as you delete rows and modify variable-length columns (such as VARCHAR or BLOB). This query performs the database equivalent of a defrag on the table, reorganizing the data it contains to eliminate wasted space.

It's important to note that a table is *locked* while an optimize operation occurs, so if your application relies on a large table being constantly available, that application will grind to a halt while the optimization takes place. In such cases, it's better to copy the table, optimize the copy, and then replace the old table with the newly optimized version using a RENAME query. Changes made to the original table in the interim will be lost, so this technique is only appropriate for some applications.

RENAME TABLE

```
RENAME TABLE tbl_name TO new_table_name[, tbl_name2 TO …, …]
```

This query quickly and conveniently renames one or more tables. This differs from ALTER TABLE tbl_name RENAME in that all the tables being renamed in the query are locked for the duration of the query, so that no other connected clients may access them. As the MySQL Reference Manual explains,[9] this assurance of atomicity lets you replace a table with an empty equivalent; for example, if you wanted to safely start a new table once a certain number of entries was reached:

```
CREATE TABLE new_table (…)
    RENAME TABLE old_table TO backup_table, new_table TO old_table;
```

You can also move a table from one database to another by specifying the table name as db_name.tbl_name, as long as both tables are stored on the same physical disk, which is usually the case.

You must have ALTER and DROP privileges on the original table—as well as CREATE and INSERT privileges on the new table—in order to perform this query. A RENAME TABLE query that fails to complete halfway through will automatically be reversed, so that the original state is restored.

REPLACE

```
REPLACE [LOW_PRIORITY | DELAYED] [INTO] tbl_name

    {   [(col_name, …)] VALUES (expression, …), …

      | [(col_name, …)] SELECT …

      | SET col_name=expression, col_name=expression, … }
```

---

[9] http://dev.mysql.com/doc/mysql/en/rename-table.html

REPLACE is identical to INSERT, except that if an inserted row clashes with an existing row in a PRIMARY KEY or UNIQUE column, the old entry is replaced with the new.

REVOKE

```
REVOKE priv_type [(column_list)], …
      ON {tbl_name | * | *.* | db_name.*}
      FROM user, …
```

This function removes access privileges from a user account. If all privileges are removed from an account, the user will still be able to log in, though unable to access any information.

See the section called "MySQL Access Control" in Chapter 10 for a complete description of this query.

SELECT

```
SELECT [select_options]
      select_expression, …
      [INTO {OUTFILE | DUMPFILE} 'file_name' export_options]
      [FROM table_references
        [WHERE where_definition]
        [GROUP BY {col_name | col_pos } [ASC | DESC], …]
        [HAVING where_definition]
        [ORDER BY {col_name | col_pos } [ASC | DESC], …]
        [LIMIT [offset,] rows]]
```

SELECT is the most complex query in SQL, and is used to perform all data retrieval operations. This query supports the following select_options, which may be specified in any sensible combination simply by listing them separated by spaces:

ALL
DISTINCT
DISTINCTROW

Any one of these options may be used to specify the treatment of duplicate rows in the result set. ALL (the default) specifies that all duplicate rows appear in the result set, while DISTINCT and DISTINCTROW (they have the same effect) specify that duplicate rows should be eliminated from the result set.

HIGH_PRIORITY

This option does exactly what it says—it assigns a high priority to the SELECT query. Normally, if a query is waiting to update a table, all read-only queries (such as SELECT) must yield to it. A SELECT HIGH_PRIORITY, however, will go first.

STRAIGHT_JOIN

Forces MySQL to join multiple tables specified in the *table_references* portion of the query in the order specified there. If you think MySQL's query optimizer is doing it the *slow* way, this argument lets you override it. For more information on joins, see the section called "Joins" below.

SQL_BUFFER_RESULT

This option forces MySQL to store the result set in a temporary table. This frees up the tables that were used in the query for use by other processes, while the result set is transmitted to the client.

SQL_CACHE

This option instructs MySQL to store the result of this query in the **query cache**, an area of memory set aside by the server to store the results of frequently-run queries so that no need to recalculate them from scratch if the contents of the relevant tables have not changed. MySQL can be configured so that only queries with the SQL_CACHE option are cached. If the query cache is disabled, this option will have no effect.

SQL_NO_CACHE

This option instructs MySQL to avoid storing the result of this query in the query cache (see the previous option). MySQL can be configured so that every query is cached unless it has the SQL_NO_CACHE option. If the query cache is disabled, this option will have no effect.

SQL_CALC_FOUND_ROWS

For use in conjunction with a LIMIT clause, this option calculates and sets aside the total number of rows that would be returned from the query if no LIMIT clause were present. You can then retrieve this number using SELECT FOUND_ROWS() (see Appendix B).

select_expression defines a column of the result set to be returned by the query. Typically, this is a table column name, and may be specified as *col_name*, *tbl_name.col_name*, or *db_name.tbl_name.col_name*, depending on how specific you need to be for MySQL to identify the column to which you are referring. *select_expression*s can refer to other expressions apart from the database column—simple mathematical formulas including column names as variables, and complex expressions calculated with MySQL functions may also be used. Here's an example of the latter, which will give the date one month from now in the form "January 1, 2010":

```
SELECT DATE_FORMAT(
      DATE_ADD(CURDATE(), INTERVAL 1 MONTH), '%M %D, %Y')
```

*select_expression*s may also contain an alias, or assigned name for the result column, if the expression is followed with [AS] `alias` (the AS is entirely optional). This expression must be used when referring to that column elsewhere in the query (for example, in WHERE and ORDER BY clauses), as follows:

```
SELECT jokedate AS jd FROM joke ORDER BY jd ASC
```

MySQL lets you use an INTO clause to output the results of a query into a file instead of returning them to the client. The most typical use of this clause is to export the contents of a table into a text file containing comma-separated values (CSV). Here's an example:

```
SELECT * INTO OUTFILE '/home/user/myTable.txt'
    FIELDS TERMINATED BY ',' OPTIONALLY ENCLOSED BY '"'
    LINES TERMINATED BY '\n'
    FROM myTable
```

The file to which the results are dumped must not exist beforehand, or this query will fail. This restriction prevents an SQL query from being used to overwrite critical operating system files. The created file will also be world-readable on systems that support file security, so consider this before you export sensitive data to a text file that anyone on the system can read.

DUMPFILE may be used instead of OUTFILE to write to the file only a single row, without row or column delimiters. It can be used, for example, to dump a BLOB stored in the table to a file (SELECT *blobCol* INTO DUMPFILE …). For complete information on the INTO clause, see the MySQL Reference Manual.[10] For information on reading data back from a text file, see the section called "LOAD DATA INFILE".

The FROM clause contains a list of tables from which the rows composing the result set should be formed, along with instructions on how they should be joined together. At its most basic, *table_references* is the name of a single database table, which may be assigned an alias with or without using AS as described for *select_expression* above. If you specify more than one table name, you're performing a **join**. These are discussed in the section called "Joins" below.

The *where_definition* in the WHERE clause sets the condition for a row to be included in the table of results sent in response to the SELECT query. This may be a simple condition (for example, id = 5), or a complex expression that makes use of MySQL functions and combines multiple conditions using Boolean operators (AND, OR, NOT).

The GROUP BY clause lets you specify one or more columns (by name, alias, or column position, where 1 is the first column in the result set) for which rows with equal values should be collapsed into single rows in the result set. This clause should usually be used in combination with the MySQL grouping functions such as COUNT, MAX, and AVG, described in Appendix B, to produce result columns that give summary information about the groups produced. By default, the grouped results are sorted in ascending order of the grouped column(s); however, the ASC or DESC argument may be added following each column reference to explicitly sort that column's results in ascending or descending order, respectively. Results are sorted by the first column listed, then tying sets of rows are sorted by the second, and so on.

Note that the WHERE clause is processed before GROUP BY grouping occurs, so conditions in the WHERE clause may not refer to columns that depend on the grouping operation. To impose conditions on the post-grouping result set, you should use the HAVING clause instead. This clause's syntax is identical to that of the WHERE clause, except the conditions specified here are processed just prior to returning the set of results, and are not optimized. For this reason, you should use the WHERE clause whenever possible. For more information on GROUP BY and the HAVING clause, see Chapter 11.

---

[10] http://dev.mysql.com/doc/mysql/en/select.html

The ORDER BY clause lets you sort results according to the values in one or more rows before they're returned. As for the GROUP BY clause, each column may be identified by a column name, alias, or position (where 1 is the first column in the result set), and each column may have an ASC or DESC argument to specify that sorting occurs in ascending or descending order, respectively (ascending is the default). Rows initially are sorted by the first column listed, then tying sets of rows are sorted by the second, and so on.

The LIMIT clause instructs the query to return only a portion of the results it would normally generate. In the simple case, LIMIT n returns only the first n rows of the complete result set. You can also specify an offset by using the form LIMIT x, n. In this case, up to n rows will be returned, beginning from the xth row of the complete result set. The first row corresponds to $x = 0$, the second to $x = 1$, and so on.

Joins

As described above, the FROM clause of a SELECT query lets you specify the tables that are combined to create the result set. When multiple tables are combined in this way, it's called a **join**. MySQL supports several types of joins, as defined by the following supported syntaxes for the *table_references* component of the FROM clause above:

```
table_ref
```

```
table_references, table_ref
```

```
table_references [CROSS] JOIN table_ref
```

```
table_references INNER JOIN table_ref join_condition
```

```
table_references STRAIGHT_JOIN table_ref
```

```
table_references LEFT [OUTER] JOIN table_ref join_condition
    { oj table_ref LEFT OUTER JOIN table_ref ON cond_expr }
```

```
table_references NATURAL [LEFT [OUTER]] JOIN table_ref
```

```
table_references RIGHT [OUTER] JOIN table_ref join_condition
```

```
table_references NATURAL [RIGHT [OUTER]] JOIN table_ref
```

where *table_ref* is defined as:

```
table_name [[AS] alias] [USE INDEX (key_list)]
    [IGNORE INDEX (key_list)]
```

and *join_condition* is defined as one of the following:

```
ON cond_expr
```

```
USING (column_list)
```

Don't be disheartened by the sheer variety of join types; I'll explain how each of them works below.

The most basic type of join, an **inner join**, produces rows made up of all possible pairings of the rows from the first table with the second. You can perform an inner join in MySQL either by separating the table names with a comma (,) or with the words JOIN, CROSS JOIN, or INNER JOIN (these are all equivalent).

It's common—especially in older PHP code—to use the comma (,) form to create an inner join, and then to use the WHERE clause of the SELECT query to specify a condition to narrow down which of the combined rows are actually returned (for example, to match up a primary key in the first table with a column in the second); however, this is generally considered untidy and bad practice today.

Instead the INNER JOIN syntax followed by a *join_condition* should be used. The ON form of the *join_condition* puts the condition(s) required to join two tables right next to the names of those tables, keeping the WHERE clause for conditions unrelated to the join operations.

As a final alternative, the USING (column_list) form of *join_condition* lets you specify columns that must match between the two tables. For example:

```
SELECT * FROM t1 INNER JOIN t2 USING (tid)
```

The above is equivalent to:

```
SELECT * FROM t1 INNER JOIN t2 ON t1.tid = t2.tid
```

STRAIGHT_JOIN works in the same way as an inner join, except that the tables are processed in the order listed (left first, then right). Normally, MySQL selects the order that will produce the shortest processing time, but if you think you know better, you can use a STRAIGHT_JOIN.

The second type of join is an **outer join**, which is accomplished in MySQL with LEFT/RIGHT [OUTER] JOIN (OUTER is completely optional, and has no effect). In a LEFT outer join, any row in the left-hand table that has no matching rows in the right-hand table (as defined by the *join_condition*), will be listed as a single row in the result set. NULL values will appear in all the columns that come from the right-hand table.

The { oj … } syntax is equivalent to a standard left outer join; it's included for compatibility with other ODBC databases.

RIGHT outer joins work in the same way as LEFT outer joins, except in this case, it's the table on the right whose entries are always included, even if they lack a matching entry in the left-hand table. Since RIGHT outer joins are nonstandard, it's usually best to stick to LEFT outer joins for cross-database compatibility.

For some practical examples of outer joins and their uses, see Chapter 11.

Natural joins are "automatic" in that they automatically will match up rows based on column names that are found to match between the two tables. Thus, if a table called joke has an authorid column that refers to entries in an author table whose primary key is another authorid column, you can perform a join of these two tables on that column very simply (assuming there are no other columns with identical names in the two tables):

```
SELECT * FROM joke NATURAL JOIN author
```

Unions

A union combines the results from a number of SELECT queries to produce a single result set. Each of the queries must produce the same number of columns, and these columns must be of the same types. The column names produced by the first query are used for the union's result set:

```
SELECT …
    UNION [ALL | DISTINCT]
    SELECT …
      [UNION [ALL | DISTINCT]
        SELECT …] …
```

By default, duplicate result rows in the union will be eliminated so that each row in the result set is unique. The DISTINCT option can be used to make this clear, but it has no actual effect. The ALL option, on the other hand, allows duplicate results through to the final result set.

SET

```
SET option = value, …
```

The SET query allows you to set a number of options both on your client and on the server.

There are two common uses of the SET *option* query; the first is to change your password:

```
SET PASSWORD = PASSWORD('new_password')
```

The second is to change another user's password (if you have appropriate access privileges):

```
SET PASSWORD FOR user = PASSWORD('new_password')
```

For a complete list of the options that may be SET, refer to the MySQL Reference Manual.[11]

---

[11] http://dev.mysql.com/doc/mysql/en/set-option.html

SHOW

The SHOW query may be used in a number of forms to obtain information about the MySQL server, the databases, and the tables it contains. Many of these forms have an optional LIKE *wild* component, where *wild* is a string that may contain wildcard characters (% for multiple characters, _ for just one) to filter the list of results. Each of the forms of the SHOW query are described below:

SHOW DATABASES [LIKE *wild*]

This query lists the databases that are available on the MySQL server.

SHOW [OPEN] TABLES [FROM *db_name*] [LIKE *wild*]

This query lists the tables (or, optionally, the currently OPEN tables) in the default or specified database.

SHOW [FULL] COLUMNS FROM *tbl_name* [FROM *db_name*] [LIKE *wild*]

When FULL is not used, this query provides the same information as a DESCRIBE query (see the section called "DESCRIBE/DESC"). The FULL option adds to this information a listing of the privileges you have on each column. SHOW FIELDS is equivalent to SHOW COLUMNS.

SHOW INDEX FROM *tbl_name* [FROM *db_name*]

This query provides detailed information about the indexes that are defined on the specified table. See the MySQL Reference manual[12] for a guide to the results produced by this query. SHOW KEYS is equivalent to SHOW INDEX.

SHOW TABLE STATUS [FROM *db_name*] [LIKE *wild*]

This query displays detailed information about the tables in the specified or default database.

SHOW STATUS [LIKE *wild*]

This query displays detailed statistics for the server. See the MySQL Reference Manual[13] for details on the meaning of each of the figures.

---

[12] http://dev.mysql.com/doc/en/show-index.html
[13] http://dev.mysql.com/doc/en/show-status.html

SHOW VARIABLES [LIKE *wild*]

This query lists the MySQL configuration variables and their settings. See the MySQL Reference Manual[14] for a complete description of these options.

SHOW [FULL] PROCESSLIST

This query displays all threads running on the MySQL server and the queries being executed by each. If you don't have the `process` privilege, you'll only see threads executing your own queries. The `FULL` option causes the complete queries to be displayed, rather than only the first 100 characters of each (the default).

SHOW GRANTS FOR *user*

This query lists the `GRANT` queries that would be required to recreate the privileges of the specified user.

SHOW CREATE TABLE *table_name*

This query displays the `CREATE TABLE` query that would be required to reproduce the specified table.

TRUNCATE

```
TRUNCATE [TABLE] tbl_name
```

A `TRUNCATE` command deletes all of the rows in a table, just like a `DELETE` command with no `WHERE` clause. `TRUNCATE`, however, takes a number of shortcuts to make the process go much faster, especially with large tables. In effect, `TRUNCATE` performs a `DROP TABLE` query, followed by a `CREATE TABLE` query to re-create an empty table.

UNLOCK TABLES

See the section called "LOCK/UNLOCK TABLES".

---

[14] http://dev.mysql.com/doc/en/show-variables.html

UPDATE

```
UPDATE [LOW_PRIORITY] [IGNORE] tbl_name
      SET col_name = expr[, …]
      [WHERE where_definition]
      [ORDER BY …]
      [LIMIT #]
```

The UPDATE query updates existing table entries by assigning new values to the specified columns. Columns that are not listed are left alone, with the exception of columns with the TIMESTAMP type (see Appendix C). The WHERE clause lets you specify a condition (*where_definition*) that rows must satisfy if they're to be updated, while the LIMIT clause lets you specify a maximum number of rows to be updated.

Avoid Omitting WHERE or LIMIT

If WHERE and LIMIT are unspecified, then every row in the table will be updated!

The ORDER BY clause lets you specify the order in which entries are updated. This is most useful in combination with the LIMIT clause—together they let you create queries like "update the ten most recent rows."

An UPDATE operation will fail with an error if the new value assigned to a row clashes with an existing value in a PRIMARY KEY or UNIQUE column, unless the IGNORE option is specified, in which case the query will simply have no effect on that particular row.

The LOW_PRIORITY option instructs MySQL to wait until there are no other clients reading the table before it performs the update.

Like the DELETE query (see the section called "DELETE"), UPDATE has an alternate form that can affect multiple tables in a single operation:

```
UPDATE [LOW_PRIORITY] [IGNORE] tbl_name[, tbl_name …]
      SET col_name = expr[, …]
      [WHERE where_definition]
```

USE

```
USE db_name
```

This simple query sets the default database for MySQL queries in the current session. Tables in other databases may still be accessed as *db_name*.*tbl_name*.

Appendix B: MySQL Functions

MySQL provides a sizeable library of functions to format and combine data within SQL queries in order to produce the desired results in the preferred format. This appendix provides a reference to the most useful of these functions, as implemented in MySQL as of version 5.1.34 (current this writing).

For a complete, up-to-date reference to supported SQL functions, see the MySQL Reference Manual.[1]

Control Flow Functions

IFNULL(*expr1*, *expr2*)
>   This function returns *expr1* unless it's NULL, in which case it returns *expr2*.

NULLIF(*expr1*, *expr2*)
>   This function returns *expr1* unless it equals *expr2*, in which case it returns NULL.

IF(*expr1*, *expr2*, *expr3*)
>   If *expr1* is TRUE (that is, not NULL or 0), this function returns *expr2*; otherwise, it returns *expr3*.

CASE *value* WHEN [*compare-value1*] THEN *result1* [WHEN …] [ELSE *else-result*] END
>   This function returns *result1* when *value=compare-value1* (note that several compare-value/result pairs can be defined); otherwise, it returns *else-result*, or NULL if none is defined.

CASE WHEN [*condition1*] THEN *result1* [WHEN …] [ELSE *else-result*] END
>   This function returns *result1* when *condition1* is TRUE (note that several condition/result pairs can be defined); otherwise, it returns *else-result*, or NULL if none is defined.

---

[1] http://dev.mysql.com/doc/mysql/en/functions.html

Mathematical Functions

ABS(*expr*)

This function returns the absolute (positive) value of *expr*.

SIGN(*expr*)

This function returns -1, 0, or 1 depending on whether *expr* is negative, zero, or positive, respectively.

MOD(*expr1*, *expr2*)

expr1* % *expr2

This function returns the remainder of dividing *expr1* by *expr2*.

FLOOR(*expr*)

This function rounds down *expr* (that is, it returns the largest integer value that is less than or equal to *expr*).

CEILING(*expr*)

CEIL(*expr*)

This function rounds up *expr* (that is, it returns the smallest integer value that's greater than or equal to *expr*).

ROUND(*expr*)

This function returns *expr* rounded to the nearest integer. Note that this function's behavior when the value is exactly an integer plus 0.5 is system-dependent. Thus, you should not rely on any particular outcome when migrating to a new system.

ROUND(*expr*, *num*)

This function rounds *expr* to a number with *num* decimal places, leaving trailing zeroes in place. Use a *num* of 2, for example, to format a number as dollars and cents. Note that the same uncertainty about the rounding of 0.5 applies as discussed for ROUND above.

EXP(*expr*)

This function returns e^{expr}, the base of natural logarithms raised to the power of *expr*.

LOG(*expr*)

This function returns ln(*expr*), or log$_e$(*expr*), the natural logarithm of *expr*.

LOG(*B*, *expr*)

This function returns the logarithm of *expr* with the arbitrary base *B*.

> LOG(*B*, *expr*) = LOG(*expr*) / LOG(*B*)

LOG10(*expr*)

This function returns the base-10 logarithm of *expr*.

POW(*expr1*, *expr2*)
POWER(*expr1*, *expr2*)

This function returns *expr1* raised to the power of *expr2*.

SQRT(*expr*)

This function returns the square root of *expr*.

PI()

This function returns the value of π (pi).

COS(*expr*)

This function returns the cosine of *expr* in radians (for example, COS(PI()) = -1).

SIN(*expr*)

This function returns the sine of *expr* in radians (for example, SIN(PI()) = 0).

TAN(*expr*)

This function returns the tangent of *expr* in radians (for example, TAN(PI()) = 0).

ACOS(*expr*)

This function returns the arc cosine (cos^{-1} or inverse cosine) of *expr* (for example, ACOS(-1) = PI()).

ASIN(*expr*)

This function returns the arc sine (sin^{-1} or inverse sine) of *expr* (for example, ASIN(0) = PI()).

ATAN(*expr*)

This function returns the arc tangent (tan^{-1} or inverse tangent) of *expr* (for example, ATAN(0) = PI()).

ATAN(*y*, *x*)
ATAN2(*y*, *x*)

This function returns the angle (in radians) made at the origin between the positive x axis and the point (*x*,*y*) (for example, ATAN(1, 0) = PI() / 2).

COT(*expr*)

This function returns the cotangent of *expr* (for example, COT(PI() / 2) = 0).

RAND()
RAND(*expr*)

This function returns a random, floating point number between 0.0 and 1.0. If *expr* is specified, a random number will be generated based on that value, which will always be the same.

LEAST(*expr1*, *expr2*, …)

This function returns the smallest of the values specified.

GREATEST(*expr1*, *expr2*, …)

This function returns the largest of the values specified.

DEGREES(*expr*)

This function returns the value of *expr* (in radians) in degrees.

RADIANS(*expr*)

This function returns the value of *expr* (in degrees) in radians.

TRUNCATE(*expr*, *num*)

This function returns the value of floating point number *expr* truncated to *num* decimal places (that is, rounded down).

BIN(*expr*)

    This function converts decimal *expr* to binary, equivalent to CONV(*expr*, 10, 2).

OCT(*expr*)

    This function converts decimal *expr* to octal, equivalent to CONV(*expr*, 10, 8).

HEX(*expr*)

    This function converts decimal *expr* to hexadecimal, equivalent to CONV(*expr*, 10, 16).

CONV(*expr*, *from_base*, *to_base*)

    This function converts a number (*expr*) in base *from_base* to a number in base *to_base*. Returns NULL if any of the arguments are NULL.

String Functions

ASCII(*str*)

    This function returns the ASCII code value of the left-most character in *str*, 0 if *str* is an empty string, or NULL if *str* is NULL.

ORD(*str*)

    This function returns the ASCII code of the left-most character in *str*, taking into account the possibility that it might be a multi-byte character.

CHAR(*expr*, …)

    This function creates a string composed of characters, the ASCII code values of which are given by the expressions passed as arguments.

CONCAT(*str1*, *str2*, …)

    This function returns a string made up of the strings passed as arguments joined end-to-end. If any of the arguments are NULL, NULL is returned instead.

CONCAT_WS(*separator*, *str1*, *str2*, …)

    CONCAT "with separator" (WS). This function is the same as CONCAT, except that the first argument is placed between each of the additional arguments when they're combined.

LENGTH(*str*)

OCTET_LENGTH(*str*)

CHAR_LENGTH(*str*)

CHARACTER_LENGTH(*str*)

All of these return the length in characters of *str*. CHAR_LENGTH and CHARACTER_LENGTH, however, take multi-byte characters into consideration when performing the count.

BIT_LENGTH(*str*)

This function returns the length (in bits) of *str* (that is, BIT_LENGTH(*str*) = 8 * LENGTH(*str*)).

LOCATE(*substr*, *str*)

POSITION(*substr* IN *str*)

This function returns the position of the first occurrence of *substr* in *str* (1 if it occurs at the beginning, 2 if it starts after one character, and so on). It returns 0 if *substr* does not occur in *str*.

LOCATE(*substr*, *str*, *pos*)

Same as LOCATE(*substr*, *str*), but begins searching from character number *pos*.

INSTR(*str*, *substr*)

This function is the same as LOCATE(*substr*, *str*), but with argument order swapped.

LPAD(*str*, *len*, *padstr*)

This function shortens or lengthens *str* so that it's of length *len*. Lengthening is accomplished by inserting *padstr* to the left of the characters of *str* (for example, LPAD('!', '5', '.') = '....!').

RPAD(*str*, *len*, *padstr*)

This function shortens or lengthens *str* so that it's of length *len*. Lengthening is accomplished by inserting *padstr* to the right of the characters of *str* (for example, RPAD('!','5','.') = '!....').

LEFT(*str*, *len*)

This function returns the left-most *len* characters of *str*. If *str* is shorter than *len* characters, *str* is returned with no extra padding.

RIGHT(*str*, *len*)

> This function returns the right-most *len* characters of *str*. If *str* is shorter than *len* characters, *str* is returned with no extra padding.

SUBSTRING(*str*, *pos*, *len*)
SUBSTRING(*str* FROM *pos* FOR *len*)
MID(*str*, *pos*, *len*)

> This function returns a string up to *len* characters long taken from *str* beginning at position *pos* (where 1 is the first character). The second form of SUBSTRING is the ANSI standard.

SUBSTRING(*str*, *pos*)
SUBSTRING(*str* FROM *pos*)

> This function returns the string beginning from position *pos* in *str* (where 1 is the first character) and going to the end of *str*.

SUBSTRING_INDEX(*str*, *delim*, *count*)

> MySQL counts *count* occurrences of *delim* in *str*, then takes the substring from that point. If *count* is positive, MySQL counts to the right from the start of the string, then takes the substring up to but not including that delimiter. If *count* is negative, MySQL counts to the left from the end of the string, then takes the substring that starts right after that delimiter, and runs to the end of *str*.

LTRIM(*str*)

> This function returns *str* with any leading white space trimmed off.

RTRIM(*str*)

> This function returns *str* with any trailing white space trimmed off.

TRIM([[BOTH | LEADING | TRAILING] [*remstr*] FROM] *str*)

> This function returns *str* with either white space (by default) or occurrences of the string *remstr* removed from the start of the string (LEADING), end of the string (TRAILING), or both (BOTH, the default).

SOUNDEX(*str*)

> This function produces a string that represents how *str* sounds when read aloud. Words that sound similar should have the same "soundex string."
>
> For example:

```
SOUNDEX("tire") = "T600"
SOUNDEX("tyre") = "T600"
SOUNDEX("terror") = "T600"
SOUNDEX("tyrannosaur") = "T6526"
```

SPACE(*num*)

This function returns a string of *num* space characters.

REPLACE(*str*, *from_str*, *to_str*)

This function returns *str* after replacing all occurrences of *from_str* to *to_str*.

REPEAT(*str*, *count*)

This function returns a string made up of *str* repeated *count* times, an empty string if *count* <= 0, or NULL if either argument is NULL.

REVERSE(*str*)

This function returns *str* spelled backwards.

INSERT(*str*, *pos*, *len*, *newstr*)

This function takes *str*, and removes the substring beginning at *pos* (where 1 is the first character in the string) with length *len*, then inserts *newstr* at that position. If *len* = 0, the function simply inserts *newstr* at position *pos*.

ELT(*N*, *str1*, *str2*, *str3*, …)

This function returns the Nth string argument (*str1* if $N = 1$, *str2* if $N = 2$, and so on), or NULL if there's no argument for the given *N*.

FIELD(*str*, *str1*, *str2*, *str3*, …)

This function returns the position of *str* in the subsequent list of arguments (1 if *str* = *str1*, 2 if *str* = *str2*, and so on).

FIND_IN_SET(*str*, *strlist*)

When *strlist* is a list of strings of the form '*string1*,*string2*,*string3*,…' this function returns the index of *str* in that list, or 0 if *str* is not in the list. This function is ideally suited (and optimized) for determining if *str* is selected in a column of type SET (see Appendix C).

MAKE_SET(*bits*, *str1*, *str2*, …)

This function returns a list of strings of the form '*string1*,*string2*,*string3*,…' using the string parameters (*str1*, *str2*, and so on) that correspond to the bits that are set in the number *bits*. For example, if *bits* = 10 (binary 1010) then bits 2 and 4 are set, so the output of MAKE_SET will be 'str2,str4'.

EXPORT_SET(*bits*, *on_str*, *off_str*[, *separator*[, *number_of_bits*]])

This function returns a string representation of which bits are, and are not set in *bits*. Set bits are represented by the *on_str* string, while unset bits are represented by the *off_str* string. By default, these bit representations are comma-separated, but the optional *separator* string lets you define your own. By default, up to 64 bits of bits are read; however, *number_of_bits* lets you specify that a smaller number be read.

For example:

```
EXPORT_SET(10, 'Y', 'N', ',', 6) = 'N,Y,N,Y,N,N'
```

LCASE(*str*)

LOWER(*str*)

This function returns *str* with all letters in lowercase.

UCASE(*str*)

UPPER(*str*)

This function returns *str* with all letters in uppercase.

LOAD_FILE(*filename*)

This function returns the contents of the file specified by *filename* (an absolute path to a file readable by MySQL). Your MySQL user should also have file privileges.

QUOTE(*str*)

This function returns *str* surrounded by single quotes, and with any special characters escaped with backslashes. If *str* is NULL, the function returns the string NULL (without surrounding quotes).

Date and Time Functions

DAYOFWEEK(*date*)

This function returns the weekday of *date* in the form of an integer, according to the ODBC standard (1 = Sunday, 2 = Monday, 3 = Tuesday … 7 = Saturday).

WEEKDAY(*date*)

This function returns the weekday of *date* in the form of an integer (0 = Monday, 1 = Tuesday, 2 = Wednesday … 6 = Sunday).

DAYOFMONTH(*date*)

This function returns the day of the month for *date* (from 1 to 31).

DAYOFYEAR(*date*)

This function returns the day of the year for *date* (from 1 to 366—remember leap years!).

MONTH(*date*)

This function returns the month for *date* (from 1, January, to 12, December).

DAYNAME(*date*)

Returns the name of the day of the week for *date* (for example, 'Tuesday').

MONTHNAME(*date*)

This function returns the name of the month for *date* (for example, 'April').

QUARTER(*date*)

This function returns the quarter of the year for *date* (for example, QUARTER('2005-04-12') = 2).

WEEK(*date*[, *mode*])

This function returns the week of the year for *date* by default in the range 0-53 (where week 1 is the first week that starts in this year), assuming that the first day of the week is Sunday.

By specifying one of the *mode* values in Table B.1, you can alter the way this value is calculated.

Table B.1. Modes for week calculations

mode	Week starts on	Return Value Range	Week 1
0	Sunday	0 to 53	first week that starts in this year
1	Monday	0 to 53	first week that has more than 3 days in this year
2	Sunday	1 to 53	first week that starts in this year
3	Monday	1 to 53	first week that has more than 3 days in this year
4	Sunday	0 to 53	first week that has more than 3 days in this year
5	Monday	0 to 53	first week that starts in this year
6	Sunday	1 to 53	first week that has more than 3 days in this year
7	Monday	1 to 53	first week that starts in this year

YEAR(*date*)

This function returns the year for *date* (from 1000 to 9999).

YEARWEEK(*date*)
YEARWEEK(*date, first*)

This function returns the year and week for *date* in the form '*YYYYWW*'. Note that the first or last day or two of the year may often belong to a week of the preceding or following year, respectively.

For example:

```
YEARWEEK("2006-12-31") = 200701
```

HOUR(*time*)

This function returns the hour for *time* (from 0 to 23).

MINUTE(*time*)

This function returns the minute for *time* (from 0 to 59).

SECOND(*time*)

This function returns the second for *time* (from 0 to 59).

PERIOD_ADD(*period*, *num_months*)

This function adds *num_months* months to period (specified as '*YYMM*' or '*YYYYMM*') and returns the value in the form '*YYYYMM*'.

PERIOD_DIFF(*period1*, *period2*)

This function returns the number of months between *period1* and *period2* (each of which should be specified as '*YYMM*' or '*YYYYMM*').

DATE_ADD(*date*, INTERVAL *expr type*)
DATE_SUB(*date*, INTERVAL *expr type*)
ADDDATE(*date*, INTERVAL *expr type*)
SUBDATE(*date*, INTERVAL *expr type*)

This function returns the result of either adding or subtracting the specified interval of time to or from *date* (a DATE or DATETIME value). DATE_ADD and ADDDATE are identical, as are DATE_SUB and SUBDATE. *expr* specifies the interval to be added or subtracted and may be negative if you wish to specify a negative interval, and *type* specifies the format of *expr*, as shown in Table B.2.

If *date* and *expr* involve only date values, the result will be a DATE value; otherwise, this function will return a DATETIME value.

Here are a few examples to help you see how this family of functions works.

The following both return the date six months from now:

```
ADDDATE(CURDATE(), INTERVAL 6 MONTH)
```

```
DATE_ADD(CURDATE(), INTERVAL '0-6' YEAR_MONTH)
```

The following all return this time tomorrow:

```
ADDDATE(NOW(), INTERVAL 1 DAY)
```

```
SUBDATE(NOW(), INTERVAL -1 DAY)
```

```
DATE_ADD(NOW(), INTERVAL '24:0:0' HOUR_SECOND)
```

```
DATE_ADD(NOW(), INTERVAL '1 0:0' DAY_MINUTE)
```

Table B.2. Interval types for date addition/subtraction functions

type	**Format for** *expr*
SECOND	number of seconds
MINUTE	number of minutes
HOUR	number of hours
DAY	number of days
MONTH	number of months
YEAR	number of years
MINUTE_SECOND	*'minutes:seconds'*
HOUR_MINUTE	*'hours:minutes'*
DAY_HOUR	*'days hours'*
YEAR_MONTH	*'years-months'*
HOUR_SECOND	*'hours:minutes:seconds'*
DAY_MINUTE	*'days hours:minutes'*
DAY_SECOND	*'days hours:minutes:seconds'*

TO_DAYS(*date*)

This function converts date to a number of days since year 0. Allows you to calculate differences in dates (that is, TO_DAYS(*date1*)   TO_DAYS(*date2*) = days between *date1* and *date2*).

FROM_DAYS(*days*)

Given the number of *days* since year 0 (as produced by TO_DAYS), this function returns a date.

DATE_FORMAT(*date, format*)

This function takes the date or time value *date* and returns it formatted according to the formatting string *format*, which may contain as placeholders any of the symbols shown in Table B.3.

Table B.3. DATE_FORMAT symbols (2004–01–01 01:00:00)

Symbol	Displays	Example
%M	Month name	January
%W	Weekday name	Thursday
%D	Day of the month with English suffix	1st
%Y	Year, numeric, 4 digits	2004
%y	Year, numeric, 2 digits	03
%a	Abbreviated weekday name	Thu
%d	Day of the month	01
%e	Day of the month	1
%m	Month of the year, numeric	01
%c	Month of the year, numeric	1
%b	Abbreviated month name	Jan
%j	Day of the year	001
%H	Hour of the day (24 hour format, 00-23)	01
%k	Hour of the day (24 hour format, 0-23)	1
%h	Hour of the day (12 hour format, 01-12)	01
%I	Hour of the day (12 hour format, 01-12)	01
%l	Hour of the day (12 hour format, 1-12)	1
%i	Minutes	00
%r	Time, 12 hour (hh:mm:ss AM/PM)	01:00:00 AM
%T	Time, 24 hour (hh:mm:ss)	01:00:00
%S	Seconds	00
%s	Seconds	00
%p	AM or PM	AM
%w	Day of the week, numeric (0=Sunday)	4
%U	Week (00-53), Sunday first day of the week	00
%u	Week (00-53), Monday first day of the week	01
%X	Year of the week where Sunday is the first day of the week, 4 digits (use with %V)	2003

Symbol	Displays	Example
%V	Week (01-53), Sunday first day of week (%X)	53
%X	Like %X, Monday first day of week (use with %v)	2004
%v	Week (01-53), Monday first day of week (%x)	01
%%	An actual percent sign	%

TIME_FORMAT(*time*, *format*)

This function is the same as DATE_FORMAT, except the *format* string may only contain symbols referring to hours, minutes, and seconds.

CURDATE()

CURRENT_DATE

This function returns the current system date in the SQL date format *'YYYY-MM-DD'* (if used as a date) or as *YYYYMMDD* (if used as a number).

CURTIME()

CURRENT_TIME

CURRENT_TIME()

This function returns the current system time in the SQL time format *'HH:MM:SS'* (if used as a time) or as *HHMMSS* (if used as a number).

NOW()

SYSDATE()

CURRENT_TIMESTAMP

CURRENT_TIMESTAMP()

LOCALTIME

LOCALTIME()

LOCALTIMESTAMP

LOCALTIMESTAMP()

This function returns the current system date and time in SQL date/time format *'YYYY-MM-DD HH:MM:SS'* (if used as a date/time) or as *YYYYMMDDHHMMSS* (if used as a number).

UNIX_TIMESTAMP()

UNIX_TIMESTAMP(*date*)

This function returns either the current system date and time, or the specified date/time as the number of seconds since 1970-01-01 00:00:00 GMT.

FROM_UNIXTIME(*unix_timestamp*)

The opposite of UNIX_TIMESTAMP, this function converts a number of seconds from 1970-01-01 00:00:00 GMT to '*YYYY-MM-DD HH:MM:SS*' (if used as a date/time) or *YYYYMMDDHHMMSS* (if used as a number), local time.

FROM_UNIXTIME(*unix_timestamp*, *format*)

This function formats a UNIX timestamp according to the *format* string, which may contain any of the symbols listed in Table B.3.

SEC_TO_TIME(*seconds*)

This function converts some number of *seconds* to the format '*HH:MM:SS*' (if used as a time) or *HHMMSS* (if used as a number).

TIME_TO_SEC(*time*)

This function converts a *time* in the format '*HH:MM:SS*' to a number of seconds.

Miscellaneous Functions

DATABASE()

This function returns the currently selected database name, or an empty string if no database is currently selected.

USER()
SYSTEM_USER()
SESSION_USER()

This function returns the current MySQL username, including the client host name (for example, 'kevin@localhost'). The SUBSTRING_INDEX function may be used to obtain the username alone:

```
SUBSTRING_INDEX(USER(), "@", 1) = 'kevin'
```

CURRENT_USER()

This function returns the user entry in the MySQL access control system that was used to authenticate the current connection, and which controls its privileges, in the form '*user@host*'. In many cases, this will be the same as the value returned by USER, but when entries in the access control system contain wild cards, this value may be less specific (for example, '@%.mycompany.com').

PASSWORD(*str*)

This is a one-way password encryption function, which converts any string (typically a plain text password) into an encrypted format precisely 16 characters in length. A particular plain text string always will yield the same encrypted string of 16 characters; thus, values encoded in this way can be used to verify the correctness of a password without actually storing the password in the database.

This function uses a different encryption mechanism to UNIX passwords; use ENCRYPT for that type of encryption.

ENCRYPT(*str*[, *salt*])

This function uses standard UNIX encryption (via the crypt() system call) to encrypt *str*. The *salt* argument is optional, and lets you control the seed that's used for generating the password. If you want the encryption to match a UNIX password file entry, the salt should be the two first characters of the encrypted value you're trying to match. Depending on the implementation of crypt() on your system, the encrypted value may only depend on the first eight characters of the plain text value.

On systems where crypt() is unavailable, this function returns NULL.

ENCODE(*str*, *pass_str*)

This function encrypts *str* using a two-way password-based encryption algorithm, with password *pass_str*. To subsequently decrypt the value, use DECODE.

DECODE(*crypt_str*, *pass_str*)

This function decrypts the encrypted *crypt_str* using two-way password-based encryption, with password *pass_str*. If the same password is given that was provided to ENCODE, the original string will be restored.

MD5(*string*)

This function calculates an MD5 hash based on string. The resulting value is a 32-digit hexadecimal number. A particular string will always produce the same MD5 hash; however, MD5(NOW()) may be used, for instance, to obtain a semi-random string when one is needed (as a default password, for instance).

LAST_INSERT_ID()

This function returns the last number that was automatically generated for an AUTO_INSERT column in the current connection.

FOUND_ROWS()

When you execute a SELECT query with a LIMIT clause, you may sometimes want to know how many rows would've been returned if you omitted a LIMIT clause. To do this, use the SQL_CALC_FOUND_ROWS option for the SELECT query (see Appendix A), then call this function in a second SELECT query.

Calling this function is considerably quicker than repeating the query without a LIMIT clause, since the full result set does not need to be sent to the client.

FORMAT(*expr*, *num*)

This function formats a number *expr* with commas as "thousands separators" and *num* decimal places (rounded to the nearest value, and padded with zeroes).

VERSION()

This function returns the MySQL server version (for example, '5.1.34').

CONNECTION_ID()

This function returns the thread ID for the current connection.

GET_LOCK(*str*, *timeout*)

If two or more clients must synchronize tasks beyond what table locking can offer, named locks may be used instead. GET_LOCK attempts to obtain a lock with a given name (*str*). If the named lock is already in use by another client, this client will wait up to *timeout* seconds before giving up waiting for the lock to become free.

Once a client has obtained a lock, it can be released either using RELEASE_LOCK or by using GET_LOCK again to obtain a new lock.

GET_LOCK returns 1 if the lock was successfully retrieved, 0 if the time specified by *timeout* elapsed, or NULL if some error occurred.

GET_LOCK is not a MySQL command in and of itself—it must appear as part of another query.

For example:

```
SELECT GET_LOCK("mylock", 10)
```

RELEASE_LOCK(*str*)

This function releases the named lock that was obtained by GET_LOCK. It returns 1 if the lock was released, 0 if the lock wasn't locked by this thread, or NULL if the lock doesn't exist.

IS_FREE_LOCK(*str*)

This function checks if the named lock is free to be locked. It returns 1 if the lock was free, 0 if the lock was in use, or NULL if an error occurred.

BENCHMARK(*count, expr*)

This function repeatedly evaluates *expr count* times, for the purposes of speed testing. The MySQL command line client allows the operation to be timed.

INET_NTOA(*expr*)

This function returns the IP address represented by the integer *expr*. See INET_ATON to create such integers.

INET_ATON(*expr*)

This function converts an IP address *expr* to a single integer representation.

For example:

```
INET_ATON('64.39.28.1') = 64 * 2553 + 39 * 2552 + 28 * 255 + 1
                        = 1063751116
```

Functions for Use with **GROUP BY** Clauses

Also known as **summary functions**, the following are intended for use with GROUP BY clauses, where they'll produce values based on the set of records making up each row of the final result set.

If used without a GROUP BY clause, these functions will cause the result set to be displayed as a single row, with a value calculated based on all of the rows of the complete result set. Without a GROUP BY clause, mixing these functions with columns where there are no summary functions will cause an error, because you're unable to collapse those columns into a single row and gain a sensible value.

COUNT(*expr*)

This function returns a count of the number of times in the ungrouped result set that *expr* had a non-NULL value. If COUNT(*) is used, it will simply provide a count of the number of rows in the group, irrespective of NULL values.

COUNT(DISTINCT *expr*[, *expr* …])

This function returns a count of the number of different non-NULL values (or sets of values, if multiple expressions are provided).

AVG(*expr*)

This function calculates the arithmetic mean (average) of the values appearing in the rows of the group.

MIN(*expr*)
MAX(*expr*)

This function returns the smallest or largest value of *expr* in the rows of the group.

SUM(*expr*)

This function returns the sum of the values for *expr* in the rows of the group.

STD(*expr*)
STDDEV(*expr*)

This function returns the standard deviation of the values for *expr* in the rows of the group (either of the two function names may be used).

BIT_OR(*expr*)
BIT_AND(*expr*)

This function calculates the bit-wise OR and the bit-wise AND of the values for *expr* in the rows of the group, respectively.

Appendix C: MySQL Column Types

When you create a table in MySQL, you must specify the data type for each column. This appendix documents all of the column types that MySQL provides as of version 5.1.34 (current this writing).

In this reference, many column types can accept **optional parameters** to further customize how data for the column is stored or displayed. First, there are the M and D paramotors, which arc indicated (in square brackets when optional) immediately following the column type name.

The parameter M is used to specify the display size (that is, maximum number of characters) to be used by values in the column. In most cases, this will limit the range of values that may be specified in the column. M may be any integer between 1 and 255. Note that for numerical types (for example, INT), this parameter does not actually restrict the range of values that may be stored. Instead, it causes spaces (or zeroes in the case of a ZEROFILL column—see below for details) to be added to the values so that they reach the desired display width when they're displayed. Note also that the storage of values longer than the specified display width can cause problems when the values are used in complex joins, and thus should be avoided whenever possible.

The parameter D lets you specify how many decimal places will be stored for a floating-point value. This parameter may be set to a maximum of 30, but M should always allow for these places (that is, D should always be less than or equal to $M - 2$ to allow room for a zero and a decimal point).

The second type of parameter is an optional **column attribute**. The attributes supported by the different column types are listed for each; to enable them, simply type them after the column type, separated by spaces. Here are the available column attributes and their meanings:

ZEROFILL   Values for the column always occupy their maximum display length, as the actual value is padded with zeroes. The option automatically sets the UNSIGNED option as well.

UNSIGNED   The column may accept only positive numerical values (or zero). This restriction frees up more storage space for positive numbers, effectively doubling the range of positive values that may be stored in the column, and should always be set if you know that there's no need to store negative values.

BINARY   By default, comparisons of character values in MySQL (including sorting) are case-insensitive. However, comparisons for **BINARY** columns are case-sensitive.

For a complete, up-to-date reference to supported SQL column types, see the MySQL Reference Manual.[1]

Numerical Types

TINYINT[(*M*)]

Description:
A tiny integer value

Attributes allowed:
UNSIGNED, ZEROFILL

Range:
-128 to 127 (0 to 255 if UNSIGNED)

Storage space:
1 byte (8 bits)

SMALLINT[(*M*)]

Description:
A small integer value

Attributes allowed:
UNSIGNED, ZEROFILL

Range:
-32768 to 32767 (0 to 65535 if UNSIGNED)

---

[1] http://dev.mysql.com/doc/mysql/en/data-types.html

Storage space:

2 bytes (16 bits)

MEDIUMINT[(*M*)]

Description:

A medium integer value

Attributes allowed:

UNSIGNED, ZEROFILL

Range:

-8588608 to 8388607 (0 to 16777215 if UNSIGNED)

Storage space:

3 bytes (24 bits)

INT[(*M*)]

Description:

A regular integer value

Attributes allowed:

UNSIGNED, ZEROFILL

Range:

-2147483648 to 2147483647 (0 to 4294967295 if UNSIGNED)

Storage space:

4 bytes (32 bits)

Alternative syntax:

INTEGER[(*M*)]

BIGINT[(*M*)]

Description:

A large integer value

Attributes allowed:

UNSIGNED, ZEROFILL

Range:

-9223372036854775808 to 9223372036854775807 (0 to

18446744073709551615 if UNSIGNED)

Storage space:

8 bytes (64 bits)

Notes:

MySQL performs all integer arithmetic functions in signed BIGINT format; thus, BIGINT UNSIGNED values over 9223372036854775807 (63 bits) will only work properly with bit functions (for example, bit-wise AND, OR, and NOT). Attempting integer arithmetic with larger values may produce inaccurate results due to rounding errors.

FLOAT[(M, D)]
FLOAT(precision)

Description:

A floating point number

Attributes allowed:

ZEROFILL

Range:

0 and ±1.175494351E-38 to ±3.402823466E+38

Storage space:

4 bytes (32 bits)

Notes:

precision (in bits), if specified, must be less than or equal to 24, or else a DOUBLE column will be created instead (see below).

DOUBLE[(M, D)]
DOUBLE(precision)

Description:

A high-precision floating point number

Attributes allowed:

ZEROFILL

Range:

0 and ±2.2250738585072014-308 to ±1.7976931348623157E+308

Storage space:

8 bytes (64 bits)

Notes:

precision (in bits), if specified, must be greater than or equal to 25, or else a FLOAT column will be created instead (see above). *precision* may not be greater than 53.

Alternative syntax:

DOUBLE PRECISION[(*M*,*D*)] or REAL[(*M*,*D*)]

DECIMAL[(*M*[, *D*])]

Description:

A floating point number stored as a character string

Attributes allowed:

ZEROFILL

Range:

As for DOUBLE, but constrained by *M* and *D* (see Notes)

Storage space:

Depends on the stored value. For a value with *X* digits before the decimal point and *Y* digits after, the storage space used is approximately (*X*+*Y*)×4÷10 bytes.

Notes:

If *D* is unspecified, it defaults to 0 and numbers in this column will have no decimal point or fractional part. If *M* is unspecified, it defaults to 10.

Alternative syntax:

NUMERIC([*M*[,*D*]])

BIT(*M*)

Description:

An *M*-bit binary value, where *M* can be 1 to 64. In other words, a series of *M* digits, each of which may be 1 or 0.

Range:

As constrained by *M*.

Storage space:

$M + 2$ bytes ($8 \times M + 16$ bits)

Notes:

Intended for storing sets of Boolean (true or false) flags. To write BIT values, use the form b'*ddd…*', where each digit *d* can be 1 (to indicate "true") or 0 (to indicate "false"). For example, an 8-bit binary value where all the flags are true is b'11111111'.

Character Types

CHAR(*M*)

Description:

A fixed-length character string

Attributes allowed:

BINARY

Maximum length:

M characters

Storage space:

M bytes ($8 \times M$ bits)

Notes:

CHAR values are stored as strings of length *M*, even though the assigned value may be shorter. When the string is shorter than the full length of the field, spaces are added to the end of the string to bring it exactly to *M* characters. Trailing spaces are stripped off when the value is retrieved.

CHAR columns are quicker to search than variable-length character column types such as VARCHAR, since their fixed-length nature makes the underlying database file format more regular.

M may take any integer value from 0 to 255, with a CHAR(0) column able to store only two values: NULL and ' ' (the empty string), which occupy a single bit.

Alternative syntax:

CHARACTER(M)

VARCHAR(M)

Description:

A variable-length character string

Attributes allowed:

BINARY

Maximum length:

M characters

Storage space:

Length of stored value, plus 1 byte to store length

Notes:

As VARCHAR values occupy only the space they require, there's usually no point to specifying a maximum field length M of anything less than 255 (the maximum). Values anywhere from 1 to 255 are acceptable, however, and will cause strings longer than the specified limit to be chopped to the maximum length when inserted. Trailing spaces are stripped from values before they're stored.

Alternative syntax:

CHARACTER VARYING(M)

TINYBLOB
TINYTEXT

Description:
A short, variable-length character string

Maximum length:
255 characters

Storage space:
Length of stored value, plus 1 byte to store length

Notes:
These types are basically equivalent to VARCHAR(255) BINARY and
VARCHAR(255), respectively. However, these column types do not trim
trailing spaces from inserted values. The only difference between TINYBLOB
and TINYTEXT is that the former performs case-sensitive comparisons and
sorts, while the latter does not.

BLOB
TEXT

Description:
A variable-length character string

Maximum length:
65535 characters (65KB)

Storage space:
Length of stored value, plus 2 bytes to store length

Notes:
The only difference between BLOB and TEXT is that the former performs case-
sensitive comparisons and sorts, while the latter does not.

MEDIUMBLOB
MEDIUMTEXT

Description:
A medium, variable-length character string

Maximum length:

    16777215 characters (16.8MB)

Storage space:

    Length of stored value, plus 3 bytes to store length

Notes:

    The only difference between MEDIUMBLOB and MEDIUMTEXT is that the former performs case-sensitive comparisons and sorts, while the latter does not.

LONGBLOB
LONGTEXT

Description:

    A long, variable-length character string

Maximum length:

    4294967295 characters (4.3GB)

Storage space:

    Length of stored value, plus 4 bytes to store length

Notes:

    The only difference between LONGBLOB and LONGTEXT is that the former performs case-sensitive comparisons and sorts, while the latter does not.

ENUM(*value1*, *value2*, ...)

Description:

    A set of values from which a single value must be chosen for each row

Maximum Length:

    One value chosen from up to 65535 possibilities

Storage space:

- 1 to 255 values: 1 byte (8 bits)

- 256 to 65535 values: 2 bytes (16 bits)

Notes:

Values in this type of field are stored as integers that represent the element selected. 1 represents the first element, 2 the second, and so on. The special value 0 represents the empty string ' ', which is stored if a value that does not appear in a column declaration is assigned.

NOT NULL columns of this type default to the first value in the column declaration if no particular default is assigned.

SET(*value1, value2, ...*)

Description:

A set of values, each of which may be set or not set

Maximum length:

Up to 64 values in a given SET column

Storage space:

- 1 to 8 values: 1 byte (8 bits)

- 9 to 16 values: 2 bytes (16 bits)

- 17 to 24 values: 3 bytes (24 bits)

- 25 to 32 values: 4 bytes (32 bits)

- 33 to 64 values: 8 bytes (64 bits)

Notes:

Values in this type of field are stored as integers representing the pattern of bits for set and unset values. For example, if a set contains eight values, and in a particular row the odd values are set, then the binary representation 01010101 becomes the decimal value 85. Values may therefore be assigned either as integers, or as a string of set values, separated by commas (for example, 'value1,value3,value5,value7' = 85). Searches should be performed either with the LIKE operator, or the FIND_IN_SET function.

Date/Time Types

DATE

Description:
A date

Range:
'1000-01-01' to '9999-12-31', and '0000-00-00'

Storage space:
3 bytes (24 bits)

TIME

Description:
A time

Range:
'-838:59:59' to '838:59:59'

Storage space:
3 bytes (24 bits)

DATETIME

Description:
A date and time

Range:
'1000-01-01 00:00:00' to '9999-12-31 23:59:59'

Storage space:
8 bytes (64 bits)

YEAR

Description:
A year

Range:

1901 to 2155, and 0000

Storage space:

1 byte (8 bits)

Notes:

You can specify a year value with a four-digit number (1901 to 2155, or 0000), a four-digit string ('1901' to '2155', or '0000'), a two-digit number (70 to 99 for 1970 to 1999, 1 to 69 for 2001 to 2069, or 0 for 0), or a two-digit string ('70' to '99' for 1970 to 1999, '00' to '69' for 2000 to 2069). Note that you cannot specify the year 2000 with a two-digit number, and you can't specify the year 0 with a two-digit string. Invalid year values are always converted to 0.

TIMESTAMP[(*M*)]

Description:

A timestamp (date/time), in *YYYYMMDDHHMMSS* format

Range:

19700101000000 to some time in 2037 on current systems

Storage space:

4 bytes (32 bits)

Note:

An INSERT or UPDATE operation on a row that contains one or more TIMESTAMP columns automatically will update the first TIMESTAMP column in the row with the current date/time. This lets you use such a column as the "last modified date/time" for the row. Assigning a value of NULL to the column will have the same effect, thereby providing a means of "touching" the date/time. You can also assign actual values as you would for any other column.

Allowable values for *M* are 14, 12, 10, 8, 6, 4, and 2, and correspond to the display formats *YYYYMMDDHHMMSS*, *YYMMDDHHMMSS*, *YYMMDDHHMM*, *YYYYMMDD*, *YYMMDD*, *YYMM*, and *YY* respectively. Odd values from 1 to 13 automatically will be bumped up to the next even number, while values of 0 or greater than 14 are changed to 14.

Appendix D: PHP Functions for Working with MySQL

PHP provides a vast library of built-in functions that let you perform all sorts of tasks without having to look to third-party software vendors for a solution. The online reference[1] to these functions provided by the PHP web site is second to none. Obtaining detailed information about a function is as simple as opening your browser and typing:

```
http://www.php.net/functionname
```

As a result of the convenience of this facility, I decided that a complete PHP function reference is beyond the scope of this book. All the same, this appendix contains a reference to the most commonly used PHP functions specifically designed to interact with MySQL databases, so that if you use this book as your primary reference while building a database driven web site, there'll be no need for you to look elsewhere for further information.

Common PHP `mysqli_*` Functions

This list of functions and their definitions are current as of PHP 5.2.9.

`mysqli_affected_rows`

```
mysqli_affected_rows(link)
```

This function returns the number of affected rows in the previous MySQL INSERT, UPDATE, DELETE, or REPLACE operation performed with the specified *link*. If the previous operation was a SELECT, this function returns the same value as mysqli_num_rows. It returns -1 if the previous operation failed.

`mysqli_character_set_name`

```
mysql_client_encoding(link)
```

---

[1] http://www.php.net/mysqli

This function returns the name of the default character set in use by the specified connection (for example, latin1 or utf8).

mysqli_close

```
mysqli_close(link)
```

This function closes the specified MySQL connection (*link*). If *link* refers to a persistent connection (see mysqli_connect below), this function call is ignored. As non-persistent connections automatically are closed by PHP at the end of a script, this function is usually unnecessary.

This function returns TRUE on success, FALSE on failure.

mysqli_connect

```
mysqli_connect(
      [host[, username[, password[, database[, port[, socket]]]]]])
```

This function opens a connection to a MySQL server and returns a link reference that may be used in other MySQL-related functions. This function takes up to six arguments, all of them optional:[2]

host   The address of the computer where the MySQL server is running, as a hostname or IP address string. The special values 'localhost' or NULL can be used to connect to the same computer that's running your web server.

Add p: to the start of this value to tell PHP to reuse an existing connection to the server if one has previously been established by your web server.

username The MySQL username to be used for the connection.

password The password for the MySQL user to be used for the connection, or NULL to connect without a password.

---

[2] PHP obtains the default values for these arguments from your web server's **php.ini** file.

database   The default database for queries using this connection.

port   The port number to connect to on the specified host. MySQL servers usually run on port 3306.

socket   The named socket to use for a local server connection. When connecting to a MySQL server running on the same computer, PHP can use a named socket instead of the TCP/IP protocol to create a more efficient connection.

If the connection attempt is unsuccessful, an error message will be displayed and the function will return FALSE.

mysqli_connect_errno

```
mysqli_connect_errno()
```

If the last call to mysqli_connect failed, this function will return a number that indicates the type of error that occurred. If the last call to mysqli_connect was successful, this function will return 0.

mysqli_connect_error

```
mysqli_connect_error()
```

If the last call to mysqli_connect failed, this function will return a string that describes the error that occurred. If the last call to mysqli_connect was successful, this function will return '' (an empty string).

mysqli_data_seek

```
mysqli_data_seek(result, row_number)
```

This function moves the internal result pointer of the result set identified by *result* to row number *row_number*, so that the next call to a mysqli_fetch_… function will retrieve the specified row. It returns TRUE on success, and FALSE on failure. The first row in a result set is number 0.

mysqli_errno

```
mysqli_errno(link)
```

This function returns a number that indicates the type of error that occurred as a result of the last MySQL operation on specified MySQL connection (*link*). If no error occurred, this function returns 0.

mysqli_error

```
mysqli_error(link)
```

This function returns the text of the error message from the last MySQL operation on the specified MySQL connection (link). If no error occurred, this function returns '' (an empty string).

mysqli_fetch_all

```
mysqli_fetch_all(result[, type])
```

This function fetches the complete contents of the MySQL result set *result* in the form of an array. Each item within that array corresponds to a row of the result set, and is itself represented by an array.

The optional *type* argument can be used to specify the type of arrays that are used to represent the rows of the result set. If specified, this argument must be set to one of these constants:

MYSQLI_ASSOC

   The rows are represented by associative arrays (that is, $results[*rowNumber*][*columnName*]).

MYSQLI_NUM

   The rows are represented by numbered arrays (that is, $results[*rowNumber*][*columnNumber*]).

MYSQLI_BOTH (default)
> The rows are represented by arrays that provided both numbered and associative indexes.

mysqli_fetch_array

```
mysqli_fetch_array(result[, type])
```

This function fetches the next row of the MySQL result set *result*, then advances the internal row pointer of the result set to the next row. If there are no rows left in the result set, it returns NULL instead.

By default, the returned array provides both numbered and associative indexes; however, you can use the optional *type* argument to specify the type of array to be returned. See the section called "mysqli_fetch_all" for more details.

mysqli_fetch_assoc

```
mysqli_fetch_assoc(result)
```

This function fetches a result row as an associative array. It's identical to mysqli_fetch_array called with the *type* argument set to MYSQLI_ASSOC.

mysqli_fetch_field

```
mysqli_fetch_field(result)
```

This function returns a PHP object that contains information about a column in the supplied result set (*result*), beginning with the first column. Call this function repeatedly to retrieve information about each of the columns of the result set in turn. When all of the columns have been described, this function returns FALSE.

Assuming the result of this function is stored in $field, then the properties of the retrieved field are accessible as shown in Table D.1.

Table D.1. Object fields for `mysqli_fetch_field_direct`

Object Property	Information Contained
`$field->name`	Column name or alias
`$field->orgname`	The original (non-alias) column name
`$field->table`	Name or alias of the table to which the column belongs
`$field->orgtable`	The original (non-alias) table name
`$field->def`	The default value for this field, as a string
`$field->max_length`	Maximum length of the column in this result set
`$field->length`	Maximum length of the column in the table definition
`$field->charsetnr`	The number identifying the character set for this field
`$field->flags`	An integer whose bits describe attributes of the field
`$field->type`	An integer that indicates the data type of the field
`$field->decimals`	The number of decimal places in the field (for numbers)

`mysqli_fetch_field_direct`

`mysqli_fetch_field_direct(result, field_pos)`

This function returns a PHP object that contains information about a particular column in the supplied result set (*result*). The *field_pos* argument specifies the position of the column to describe (0 indicates the first column).

The object returned by this function is as described in the section called "mysqli_fetch_field".

`mysqli_fetch_fields`

`mysqli_fetch_fields(result)`

This function returns an array of PHP objects that contain information about each of the columns in the supplied result set (*result*). Each of these objects is as described in the section called "mysqli_fetch_field".

mysqli_fetch_lengths

```
mysqli_fetch_lengths(result)
```

This function returns an array containing the lengths of each of the fields in the last-fetched row of the specified result set.

mysqli_fetch_object

```
mysqli_fetch_object(result[, className[, params]])
```

This function returns the next result row from *result* in the form of an object, and advances the internal row pointer of the result set to the next row. Column values for the row become accessible as named properties of the object (for example, $row->user for the value of the user field in the $row object). If there are no rows left in the result set, it returns NULL instead.

The optional *className* argument specifies the name of a PHP class to use for the object. The *params* argument can be used to provide an array of parameters to be passed to the constructor.

mysqli_fetch_row

```
mysqli_fetch_row(result)
```

This function fetches a result row as a numerical array. It's identical to mysqli_fetch_array called with the *type* argument set to MYSQL_NUM.

mysqli_field_count

```
mysqli_field_count(link)
```

This function returns the number of columns present in the result set of the last query performed with the specified MySQL connection (*link*). This function will return 0 if the last query was an INSERT, UPDATE, DELETE, or other query that does not return a result set.

mysqli_field_seek

```
mysqli_field_seek(result, field_position)
```

This function sets the field position for the next call to `mysqli_fetch_field`.

mysqli_field_tell

```
mysqli_field_tell(result)
```

This function returns the position of the next column of the result set *result* whose description would be returned by a call to `mysqli_fetch_field` (0 indicates the first column).

mysqli_free_result

```
mysqli_free_result(result)
```

This function destroys the specified result set (*result*), freeing all memory associated with it. As all memory is freed automatically at the end of a PHP script, this function is only really useful when a large result set is no longer needed and your script still has a lot of work to do.

mysqli_get_client_info

```
mysqli_get_client_info()
```

This function returns a string indicating the version of the MySQL client library that PHP is using (for example, `'5.1.34'`).

mysqli_get_client_version

```
mysqli_get_client_version()
```

This function returns an integer indicating the version of the MySQL client library that PHP is using (for example, `50134`).

mysqli_get_host_info

```
mysqli_get_host_info(link)
```

This function returns a string describing the type of connection and server host name for the specified (link) MySQL connection (for example, 'Localhost via UNIX socket').

mysqli_get_proto_info

```
mysqli_get_proto_info(link)
```

This function returns an integer indicating the MySQL protocol version in use for the specified (link) MySQL connection (for example, 10).

mysqli_get_server_info

```
mysqli_get_server_info(link)
```

This function returns a string indicating the version of MySQL server in use on the specified (link) MySQL connection (for example, '5.1.34').

mysqli_get_server_version

```
mysqli_get_server_version(link)
```

This function returns an integer indicating the version of the MySQL server to which the specified connection (*link*) is connected (for example, 50134).

mysqli_info

```
mysqli_info(link)
```

This function returns a string that contains information about the effects of the last query executed on the specified connection (*link*), if it was a query that inserted new data into the database (such as an INSERT, UPDATE, or LOAD DATA INFILE query).

mysqli_insert_id

```
mysqli_insert_id(link)
```

This function returns the value that was assigned to an AUTO_INCREMENT column automatically in the previous INSERT query for the specified MySQL connection (*link*). If no AUTO_INCREMENT value was assigned in the previous query, 0 is returned instead.

mysqli_num_fields

```
mysqli_num_fields(result)
```

This function returns the number of columns in a MySQL result set (*result*).

mysqli_num_rows

```
mysqli_num_rows(result)
```

This function returns the number of rows in a MySQL result set (*result*). This method is incompatible with unbuffered result sets created by calling mysqli_real_query followed by mysqli_use_result, or by calling mysqli_query with the *resultmode* parameter set to MYSQLI_USE_RESULT.

mysqli_ping

```
mysqli_ping(link)
```

When a PHP script runs for a long time, it's possible that an open MySQL connection (*link*) may be closed or disconnected at the server end. If you suspect this possibility, call this function before using the suspect connection to confirm that it's active, and to reconnect if the connection did indeed go down.

mysqli_query

```
mysqli_query(link, query[, mode])
```

This function executes the specified MySQL query (*query*) using the specified database connection (*link*), and returns a MySQL result set.

The optional *mode* parameter can be set to `MYSQLI_USE_RESULT` to instruct PHP to download the results from the MySQL server on demand, instead of all at once. This can reduce the amount of memory used by your PHP script when processing large result sets. If you choose to do this, you must make sure to call `mysqli_free_result` before attempting to perform another query using the same database connection.

If the query fails, an error message to that effect will be displayed, and the function will return `FALSE` instead of a result set (which evaluates to `TRUE`). If the error occurs, the error number and message can be obtained using `mysqli_errno` and `mysqli_error` respectively.

mysqli_real_escape_string

```
mysqli_real_escape_string(link, string)
```

This function returns an escaped version of a *string* (with backslashes before special characters such as quotes) for use in a MySQL query. This function is more thorough than `addslashes` or PHP's Magic Quotes feature.

This function takes into account the character set of the specified MySQL connection (*link*) when determining which characters need to be escaped.

mysqli_real_query

```
mysqli_real_query(link, query)
```

A less convenient alternative to `mysqli_query`, this function executes the specified MySQL query (*query*) using the specified database connection (*link*), but ignores the result set returned by the server (if any). If you wish to retrieve the results of a query performed using this function, you must call `mysqli_store_result` or `mysqli_use_result`. You can determine if a result set is available to be retrieved using `mysqli_field_count`.

This function returns `TRUE` if the query was successful, or `FALSE` if an error occurred.

mysqli_select_db

```
mysqli_select_db(link, database)
```

This function selects the default database (*database*) for the MySQL connection specified (*link*).

mysqli_set_charset

```
mysqli_set_charset(link, charset)
```

This function sets the default character set (*charset*) to be used for text values in the SQL queries sent to and result sets received from the specified MySQL connection (*link*). In web applications, it's most common to set the character set to `'utf8'` to submit and retrieve UTF-8 encoded text.

mysqli_stat

```
mysqli_stat(link)
```

This function returns a string describing the current status of the MySQL server. The string is identical in format to that produced by the **mysqladmin** utility:

```
Uptime: 28298  Threads: 1  Questions: 56894  Slow queries: 0
  Opens: 16 Flush tables: 1  Open tables: 8 Queries per second avg:
  36.846
```

mysqli_store_result

```
mysqli_store_result(link)
```

Retrieves and returns the entire result set for an SQL query just performed using `mysqli_real_query` on the specified MySQL connection (*link*). It's much more common (and convenient) to simply use `mysqli_query` to perform the query and then immediately retrieve the results.

This function returns FALSE if there's an error retrieving the result set, or if there's no result set available to retrieve.

mysqli_thread_id

```
mysqli_thread_id(link)
```

This function returns the ID of the server thread responsible for handling the specified connection (*link*).

mysqli_use_result

```
mysqli_use_result(link)
```

Begins to retrieve the result set for an SQL query just performed using `mysqli_real_query` on the specified MySQL connection (*link*). The results will be retrieved from the MySQL server a row at a time, on demand, which can reduce the amount of memory required by your PHP script when working with a large result set. It's much more common (and convenient) to simply use `mysqli_query` to perform the query and then immediately begin to retrieve the results.

This function returns `FALSE` if there's an error retrieving the result set, or if there's no result set available to retrieve.

You must make sure to call `mysqli_free_result` before trying to perform another query using the same database connection.

Index

466

N

O

P

What's Next?

Web designers: Prepare to master the ways of the jQuery ninja!

JQUERY: NOVICE TO NINJA

By Earle Castledine & Craig Sharkie

jQuery has quickly become the JavaScript library of choice, and it's easy to see why.

In this easy-to-follow guide, you'll master all the major tricks and techniques that jQuery offers—within hours.

Save 10% with this link:

www.sitepoint.com/launch/customers-only-jquery1

Use this link to save 10% off the cover price of *jQuery: Novice to Ninja,* compliments of the SitePoint publishing team.

This book has saved my life! I especially love the "excerpt" indications, to avoid getting lost. JQuery is easy to understand thanks to this book. It's a must-have for your development library, and you truly go from Novice to Ninja!

Amanda Rodriguez, USA

Teach yourself SQL—the easy way

SIMPLY SQL

By Rudy Limeback

SQL is a simple, but high-level, language of tremendous power and elegance.

Believe it or not, a few lines of SQL can perform tasks that would take pages and pages of intricate PHP, ASP.NET, or Rails. This is true coder gold, as you can bring it with you, regardless of language or platform.

Save 10% with this link:

www.sitepoint.com/launch/customers-only-sql1

Use this link to save 10% off the cover price of *Simply SQL*, compliments of the SitePoint publishing team.

> *I had no clue SQL had t his much power! I love this book, (as) it's broken down very well and teaches you to fully understand what you're doing with every type of clause.*

Jesse Boyer, USA

How About ...

Use your design skills to earn passive income with WordPress themes

BUILD YOUR OWN WICKED WORDPRESS THEMES

By Allan Cole, Raena Jackson Armitage, Brandon R. Jones & Jeffrey Way

Top WordPress theme designers earn a passive income of $10–25K per month! Read our new book and you, too, can grab a slice of that cake.

Save 10% with this link:

🌐 www.sitepoint.com/launch/customers-only-wordpress1

Use this link to save 10% off the cover price of *Build Your Own Wicked Wordpress Themes,* compliments of the SitePoint publishing team.

> *It's refreshing to come across a book that shows how to build WordPress themes in a step by step, easy to understand format.*

Liza Carey, Graphic Designer, Australia

Create mind–blowingly beautiful and functional forms with ease

FANCY FORM DESIGN

By Jina Bolton, Tim Connell & Derek Featherstone

No longer do you need to worry at the thought of integrating a stylish form on your site.

Fancy Form Design is a complete guide to creating beautiful web forms that are aesthetically pleasing, highly functional, and compatible across all major browsers.

Save 10% with this link:

www.sitepoint.com/launch/customers-only-forms1

Use this link to save 10% off the cover price of *Fancy Form Design,* compliments of the SitePoint publishing team.

Overall it's a good book, entertaining, well-written, not overly long, (and) full of immediately practical examples that anyone familiar with form design and development can use.

Gary Barber, 17 Jan 2010

How About ...

The first guide to tapping into the endless capacity of the cloud

HOST YOUR WEB SITE IN THE CLOUD: AMAZON WEB SERVICES MADE EASY

By Jeff Barr

Stop wasting time, money, and resources on servers that can't grow with you. Cloud computing gives you ultimate freedom and speed, all at an affordable price.

Save 10% with this link:

 www.sitepoint.com/launch/customers-only-cloud1

Use this link to save 10% off the cover price of *Host Your Web Site in the Cloud,* compliments of the SitePoint publishing team.

About Jeff Barr

In his role as the Amazon Web Services Senior Evangelist, Jeff speaks to developers at conferences, as well as user groups all over the world.

Ship To:

Chris Hassen / Polyvinyl
206 N. Randolph St.
Suite M100
Champaign, IL 618203980 USA

Ship From:

TXTBOOKSNOW.COM-HALF
8950 W PALMER ST
RIVER GROVE, IL 60171

Date: 11/14/2011

SKU	Qty	Condition	Title
5418127U	1	Used	Build Your Own Database Driven Website etc
			4 978098057 6818 Refund Eligible Through= 12/16/2011

Page 1 of 1
